The Ilse

The Center for Korean Studies was established in 1972 to coordinate and develop the resources for the study of Korea at the University of Hawaiʻi. Reflecting the diversity of the academic disciplines represented by affiliated members of the University faculty, the Center seeks especially to promote interdisciplinary and intercultural studies. Hawaiʻi Studies on Korea, published jointly by the Center for Korean Studies and the University of Hawaiʻi Press, offers a forum for research in the social sciences and humanities pertaining to Korea and its people.

HAWAI'I STUDIES ON KOREA

The Ilse

FIRST-GENERATION KOREAN IMMIGRANTS IN HAWAI'I 1903–1973

Wayne Patterson

University of Hawai'i Press, Honolulu
and
Center for Korean Studies, University of Hawai'i

05 04 03 02 01 00   5 4 3 2 1

Library of Congress Cataloging-in-Publication Data

Patterson, Wayne, 1946–
The Ilse : first-generation Korean immigrants in Hawai'i,
1903–1973 / Wayne Patterson.
   p.   cm. (Hawai'i Studies on Korea)
Includes bibliographical references (p. 257) and index.
ISBN 0–8248–2093–2 (cloth : alk. paper). —
ISBN 0–8248–2241–2 (pbk. : alk. paper)
1. Koreans—Hawaii—History. 2. Hawaii—Ethnic relations.
3. Immigrants—Hawaii—History. 4. Hawaii—Emigration and immigration.
5. United States—Emigration and immigration—Government policy.
6. Immigrants—Government policy—United States
7. United States—Foreign relations—Korea.
8. Korea—Foreign relations—United States. I. Title. II. Series
DU624.7.K67P36 2000
996.9'00495—dc21   99–37153
                                         CIP

University of Hawai'i Press books are printed on acid-free paper
and meet the guidelines for permanence and durability of
the Council on Library Resources.

Designed by Kenneth Miyamoto

Printed by The Maple-Vail Book Manufacturing Group

To Poe, Cromwell, Nabi and Maxwell,
who always liked to help their daddy

CONTENTS

department, the library of the Center for Korean Studies, and the Archives of the University of Hawai'i; the Hawaiian Mission Children's Society Library; the Hawai'i State Archives; the Bernice P. Bishop Museum; the Hawaiian Sugar Planters' Association Plantation Archives; the Gaimushō Gaikō Shiryōkan (Diplomatic Records Office) in Tokyo; the Presbyterian Historical Society in Philadelphia; the University of Oregon Library Special Collections; the Library of Congress; and the National Archives. Translations of Japanese and Korean language materials are mine unless otherwise noted.

This manuscript has taken shape over the past dozen years, and during that time its development has benefited from the assistance of many institutions and people. I am grateful to the Faculty Personnel Committee at St. Norbert College, which granted me sabbatical leave; to Dean Tom Trebon, whose funding helped subsidize very capable assistants: Nicole Cosgrove, Nora Rosichan, Beth Mazzia, James Bott, and Andrew Kauth; to the universities that invited me to be a visiting professor and that allowed me to make use of their libraries and facilities: the University of Chicago, Vanderbilt University, the University of Wisconsin-Madison, Korea University, Yonsei University, the University of Kansas, the University of Hawai'i at Manoa, the University of Pennsylvania, and the University of South Carolina; to Michael Macmillan, who allowed me to quote extensively from his research on Koreans during World War II; to Ned Shultz and one anonymous reader for their thorough and meticulous reading of the manuscript and their suggestions for improvement; and finally, to my editor, Sharon Yamamoto, for her stewardship of this project from its inception to its final form.

Although I have been assisted by these and other individuals too numerous to mention, I alone am responsible for any errors or shortcomings.

W. P.

PREFACE

Much has been written about immigration to the United States from many parts of the world, including East Asia. Japanese and Chinese immigration have received quite a bit of attention, but the same has not been true for Korean immigration. In an earlier work, *The Korean Frontier in America: Immigration to Hawaii, 1896–1910* (Honolulu: University of Hawai'i Press, 1988 [cloth] and 1994 [paper]), I examined the process by which the first Koreans arrived in the United States. A gap in the literature still existed, however, because there was no study that looked systematically at what happened to these Korean immigrants after they arrived.

The Ilse: First-Generation Korean Immigrants in Hawai'i, 1903–1973 is thus a sequel. It picks up the story where the earlier book ends, covers a longer period of time, and employs not only political and diplomatic history but also a great deal of social history. I hope this study will help correct the imbalance that exists in the study of East Asian immigration to the United States and fill a gap in the literature of the peopling of America. And because during that seventy-year period the vast majority of the Koreans in the United States lived in Hawai'i, this volume comes close to approximating a history of the first-generation Koreans in the United States before the next major wave of immigration in the late 1960s.

One cannot begin to approach this topic without confronting the overriding issue of Korean nationalism and the movement for independence against Japanese colonial rule. Koreans in Hawai'i played a significant role in this movement, and there exists a great deal of documentation about it. Indeed, because the nationalist movement looms so large, it poses the danger of overwhelming the other aspects of the history. Consequently, I made the decision early on not to attempt a complete history of the nationalist movement in Hawai'i here, but rather to look at selected aspects of the movement as they related to other issues concerning the first-generation Koreans. The full story of the Korean nationalist movement in Hawai'i deserves full treatment in a separate volume

Research for this study was carried out at the following libraries and research collections: The New York Public Library; the Hamilton Library, the sociolog

A NOTE ON CONVENTIONS

I have followed the modified Hepburn system of romanization for Japanese names, terms, and places, with the exception of Tokyo, and the McCune-Reischauer system of romanization for Korean terms and places, with the exception of Seoul. For Japanese and Korean names, I have attempted to give the family name first, followed by the given name, as is the customary practice in Asia, and to use the McCune-Reischauer system to romanize Korean names. However, there are many instances among first-generation Koreans where the documents, the individuals themselves, or both employ an alternate spelling or name order, such as Syngman Rhee. Moreover, it is sometimes impossible to determine the correct McCune-Reischauer spelling based on the available documents. And some individuals have more than one spelling of their name. In these instances, some Korean names will not conform to the McCune-Reischauer system and may appear in the Western order of given name followed by family name. Readers should consult the index for more information.

For the sake of parsimony, notes appear in the text in omnibus form. That is, sources used for one or two paragraphs within the text are bundled together at or near the end of that paragraph or those paragraphs rather than scattered throughout the paragraphs themselves and are separated by semicolons. Moreover, when citations within the notes have been abbreviated, readers can find the complete citation in the bibliography.

Regarding specific abbreviations, readers should note that HSPA refers to the Hawaiian Sugar Planters' Association; HSPAPA stands for Hawaiian Sugar Planters' Association Plantation Archives in Aiea, Hawai'i; UHSPJ refers to University of Hawai'i Student Papers and Journals, which I found in the 1970s in a file cabinet in the former building housing the sociology and history departments; Intelligence Files refers to materials in a folder found among the aforementioned papers, which belonged to Andrew Lind, a professor of sociology at the University of Hawai'i who advised the military government on Koreans during the war years.

1

Prologue—The Arrival of the First Immigrants

The Korean community in Hawai'i began to take shape when the first organized group of immigrants, numbering 102, arrived aboard the *Gaelic* at the
port of Honolulu on the morning of January 13, 1903. These 56 men, 21
women, and 25 children constituted the first wave of what would become an
influx of nearly 7,500 persons in sixty-five ships over the next two and a half
years. Since the history of this immigration can be found in my earlier book,
The Korean Frontier in America: Immigration to Hawaii, 1896–1910,[1] it will
suffice to paint in broad strokes some of its major themes as they relate to the
formation of the Korean community in Hawai'i.

Although Koreans had been emigrating since the 1860s to the maritime
provinces of Russia and to Manchuria in China as a result of worsening conditions in the late Chosŏn (Yi) dynasty (1392–1910), the idea of emigration to
Hawai'i originated with the Hawaiian Sugar Planters' Association (hereafter
referred to as the HSPA or the planters) in 1896. As the forces propelling
Hawai'i toward annexation by the United States gained momentum, the planters were faced with the problem of how to maintain their policy of guarantee-
ing a racial mix to prevent any one race from dominating plantation labor. This
long-established policy of mixing the races was threatened by the impending
annexation because it would deprive the planters of Chinese laborers to offset
the Japanese who comprised nearly two-thirds of the plantation labor force.
That is, since the 1882 Chinese Exclusion Act would soon be applied to Hawai'i,
there would be no way to prevent the Japanese from establishing a monopoly
over plantation labor.

Annexation would also mean an end to the stability of the contract labor system, which the sugar planters used to control their largely Japanese labor force,
adding another uncertainty to the labor question. Workers would no longer be
legally bound to fulfill their three-year contracts and would be free to sell their
labor to the highest bidder. And since Hawai'i would now become part of the
United States, plantation workers could (and would) move to California, where
wages were higher. The planters were also troubled by the Japanese laborers'
lack of docility. Their tendency to engage in strikes and work stoppages even

when these were illegal augured ill for the post-annexation period, when such actions would enjoy legal protection. Finally, the prospect of successful and legal strikes, an exodus of workers, and the potential monopoly of labor by the Japanese raised the specter of a wage increase, which the planters were loathe to entertain.[2]

These considerations of the supply, quality, composition, and price of labor are what initially led the planters to think about using Koreans to replace the Chinese as an offset to the Japanese. For the next six years, from 1896 to 1902, these considerations grew, particularly after annexation in 1898, making the perceived need for Koreans even more urgent. Thus when the American minister to Korea, Horace Allen, stopped in Honolulu on his way to Korea after home leave in the spring of 1902, the planters took advantage of this to discuss the feasibility of bringing Koreans to Hawai'i. Allen promised the planters that he would help them get Korean workers.

The initiative now shifted to Horace Allen in Seoul, who, in spite of orders to remain neutral in Korean domestic affairs, convinced Emperor Kojong (r. 1864–1907) of the benefits of allowing emigration to Hawai'i, selected a recruiter (David Deshler), brought over a copy of Japan's emigration regulations as a model, established a Department of Emigration (Yuminwŏn) within the Korean governmental structure to issue passports, and tried, without success, to convince the Korean government to send out consuls to look after Koreans living abroad. Why was Allen so helpful to the planters in their attempts to get Koreans to work in the sugarcane fields of Hawaii? Allen was in profound disagreement with his government's policy of neutrality and nonintervention in Korea because such a policy would make it easier for Japan to take over Korea. By increasing American commercial interests in Korea, such as emigration to Hawai'i, Allen hoped for a resulting increase in the State Department's political interest in Korea.[3]

While the mechanisms were now in place to send Koreans to Hawai'i, there remained the problems of passage money and the laws concerning immigration and contract labor. Few Koreans at the turn of the century could afford passage to Hawai'i and still have enough money to convince immigration officials at Honolulu that they would not become public charges. The solution that Allen devised was to have the recruiter, Deshler, set up a "bank" that would use planter money to "loan" immigrants the necessary funds—about one hundred dollars each—even though such money laundering illegally assisted immigration. Thus Allen had almost singlehandedly solved the problems of convincing the Korean government to allow emigration, had found a way to fund (illegally) the immigrants, and had managed to keep this information from the U.S. immigration authorities. Moreover, Allen, who was knee deep in this enterprise, managed to conceal his involvement from his superiors in Washington, who continually enjoined him not to become involved in Korea's domestic affairs.

During the nearly three years of the immigration, the process survived several close calls. One involved a lawsuit and subsequent investigation by the U.S. government because the planters had illegally promised Koreans jobs on the plantations. Another came from American missionaries who wanted Christian Koreans to stay in Korea to help with mission work. Yet another came from officials within the Korean government motivated either by corruption, Confucian propriety, or anti-Americanism. None of these efforts stopped Koreans. What *did* keep the Koreans from going to Hawai'i was the Japanese, and neither Horace Allen nor the planters could counter them.

From the beginning of Korean immigration to Hawai'i, Japanese emigration agents and the Japanese minister to Korea had registered their opposition. The emigration agents were worried that Korean immigration would cut into their business; the Japanese minister opposed it as harmful to Japanese interests in Hawai'i. Their protests were to no avail, however, as the foreign minister, Komura Jutarō, initially ignored their appeals. But in the spring of 1905, Komura, too, came to oppose Korean immigration to Hawaii.[4]

What caused Foreign Minister Komura's change of heart? In the spring of 1905, the California legislature passed a resolution recommending passage of a Japanese Exclusion Act to pressure Washington into excluding Japanese as it had excluded Chinese in 1882. Passage of the act would place Japan in the same lowly position occupied by China internationally, and psychologically, at least, it would negate all the gains won by a modernizing Japan, which saw itself as equal to the United States and other major Western countries. After all, Japan had the third largest navy in the world, had defeated both the Chinese and the Russians in recent wars, had a Western-style constitutional government, and boasted a rapidly industrializing economy. It was, therefore, in Japan's best interest to prevent the enactment of such an act for reasons of national prestige.

Foreign Minister Komura linked the threat of a Japanese Exclusion Act to Korean immigration to Hawai'i. He had learned that Korean immigrants in Hawai'i were used as strikebreakers to keep the wages of Japanese laborers low. As a result, Japanese workers in Hawai'i were attracted to California where the wages were double those in Hawai'i. The resulting influx of nearly one thousand Japanese workers per month led Californians to advocate Japanese exclusion. If Koreans could be kept out of Hawai'i, Komura reasoned, then the wages would rise to the point where Japanese would be satisfied to remain on Hawaiian sugar plantations rather than move to California. As a result, the threat of a Japanese Exclusion Act would be eliminated.

Thus Japan came to realize that in order to avoid a Japanese Exclusion Act and maintain its international prestige, Koreans would have to be excluded from Hawai'i. And to be sure, doing so would have other benefits as well: it would limit the size of a community that was already showing signs of anti-Japanese activity; it would mollify Japanese emigration agents; it would ensure

Japanese could continue to emigrate to the United States; and it would raise the standard of living of Japanese in Hawai'i. But the primary reason Komura and the Japanese foreign ministry decided to prevent Koreans from entering Hawai'i was that the Japanese, above all else, wanted to avoid the loss of face that would result if the United States excluded Japanese. Ironically, doing so meant that the Japanese had to exclude Koreans from Hawai'i to prevent their own exclusion from the United States.

However, it was one thing for Japan to decide to prevent Koreans from emigrating to Hawai'i, and quite another for it to implement such an action. On the surface, it seemed relatively simple for Japan to prevent Koreans from entering Hawai'i. After all, in the spring of 1905, the Korean peninsula was filled with Japanese troops concluding the war with Russia, Japan had signed a "treaty" of alliance with Korea, and Japanese-appointed advisers were located in the key positions of finance and foreign affairs within the Korean government. Japan simply had to order the Korean government not to allow Koreans to leave. But if Japan *were* to stop Korean emigration in such a high-handed manner, it would call into question—especially with the United States—Japan's claim that it wanted only what was best for Korea and its people, and expose Japan's essentially self-serving motives.

Fortunately for Japan, Komura and his foreign office in Tokyo were aware of significant weaknesses in the Korean government that could be used to Japan's advantage. In fact, one of the weakest links in Korea's government was the emigration process itself. In April 1905, the government had inadvertently permitted one thousand Koreans without passports to depart for Mexico, where they worked on hemp plantations in the Yucatan peninsula in slave-like conditions. The Department of Emigration, which Horace Allen had so carefully helped establish, had been legislated out of existence in 1903, along with its emigration rules and regulations. There was no Korean consul in Merida to look after these new arrivals, and in fact, Korea did not even enjoy diplomatic relations with Mexico! Similarly, Korea did not have a consul in Hawai'i, where over seven thousand Koreans now resided. Korea had played right into Japan's hands.

At this point, it became a relatively simple matter for Japan to halt Korean emigration by appearing to be concerned about the fate of overseas Koreans. The Japanese minister to Korea simply "suggested" to the Korean government that emigration be prohibited temporarily, until the government got its emigration system in order. Until then, Japanese representatives in Hawai'i and Mexico would care for the unfortunate Koreans who had been victimized by their own inept government. Korea was hardly in a position to refuse. Because the government realized it was relinquishing its sovereign right to send its people anywhere they would be accepted, in the summer of 1905, the Korean foreign office decided to send its vice-minister, Yun Ch'i-ho, to Hawai'i and then to Mexico to investigate the condition of Korean immigrants. Upon his return, Yun would draw up appropriate regulations governing emigration that would conform to accepted international norms. Japan now faced the possibility that it would be forced to resort to heavy-handedness and thus expose its selfish motives toward Korea to an international audience, primarily the United States. But Japan still had some cards to play in this game.

In September 1905, Yun departed for Hawai'i and spent about one month visiting all the plantations where Koreans worked. At the end of the month he concluded that Koreans in Hawai'i were generally well treated. He was then supposed to continue on to Mexico, where the real problems lay. But when he contacted Seoul requesting money for boat passage to Mexico, the Japanese adviser to the Korean finance office vetoed the expenditure, leaving Yun with no choice but to return to Korea, his mission unsuccessful.

Japan had prevailed. Yun was in no position to draw up appropriate regulations governing emigration, meaning that the temporary ban would become permanent, especially after Japan established a protectorate over Korea in November 1905. By exploiting weaknesses within the Korean government and wrapping itself in the idealistic cloak of "humanitarian concern" for the welfare of Korean immigrants, Japan had been able to stop Koreans from going to Hawai'i without revealing their true motive to the United States—preventing a Japanese Exclusion Act. Since the United States never discovered Japan's underlying motive, it continued to believe that the Japanese had honorable intentions toward Korea and did nothing to prevent the establishment of a Japanese protectorate in 1905 or, later, the annexation of Korea in 1910.

Thus what Horace Allen and the planters started in 1902 was stopped short by the Japanese just three years later. During that period about 7,500 Koreans had arrived in Hawai'i, sharing three demographic characteristics with their East Asian immigrant counterparts: age, gender, and marital status. That is, like the Chinese and Japanese immigrants to Hawai'i, most of the Koreans were young unmarried males in their twenties. Specifically, there were around six thousand men, about one-tenth of whom were accompanied by wives and children, bringing the total number of women to around six hundred, with about five hundred children. For the next fifty years, the size of the Korean population in Hawai'i would remain around this size.

Several additional attributes of this first group of Korean immigrants are important because they often differentiated the immigrants not only from the average Korean but also from the immigrants from China and Japan. These distinguishing attributes are discussed not just to highlight differences, but because they will be important in explaining why the Korean community in Hawai'i developed as it did.[5]

First, as a group, Korean immigrants were far fewer in number than the 50,000 Chinese who arrived between 1853 and 1900 and the 180,000 Japanese who arrived between 1885 and 1907. This small number is important because it hastened the adaptation of the Koreans to American society, whereas the larger number of Chinese and Japanese immigrants insulated, to a certain extent, the influences of the Western world in Hawai'i and resulted in a slower rate of adaptation.

Second, the great majority of Korean immigrants had lived in the cities rather than the countryside before coming to Hawai'i. This would be expected because David Deshler's recruiting offices (the Tong-Sŏ Kaebal Hoesa, or East-West Development Company) were located exclusively in Korea's ports and larger cities, and because many of the immigrants were connected in some way with Christianity, most of whose missionaries and their converts were located in the cities. Their urban origins distinguish them not only from their fellow countrymen—late Chosŏn Korea was an overwhelmingly rural society —but also from the immigrants from Japan and China. Japanese immigrants tended to originate from the rural areas of western Japan, specifically Hiroshima, Wakayama, Yamaguchi, and Okayama Prefectures, while those from China tended to come from the rural areas of Guangdong Province. This urban orientation of the Korean immigrants will be of importance when we analyze the subsequent development of the Korean community in Hawai'i, particularly their preference for urban residences.

Third, Korean immigrants toiled in mostly nonagricultural occupations prior to their emigration, as would be expected, given their largely urban residence. Many of the immigrants had worked as common laborers or coolies, while others had served as soldiers, minor government clerks, policemen, miners, fishermen, boat builders, railroad workers, woodcutters, household servants, students, political refugees, and Buddhist monks. Fewer than one-seventh had been farmers; many were simply unemployed city dwellers. Thus at the turn of the century urban employment—or perhaps, unemployment—rather than farming, predominated among the Korean immigrants, making them different from most of their farming countrymen, as well as from most of the Chinese and Japanese immigrants to Hawai'i who had also been farmers. As we look at employment patterns in Hawai'i after immigration, it will be important to remember this urban occupational profile.

Fourth, while the case can be made that most Korean immigrants were urban residents working at urban-type occupations prior to coming to Hawai'i, there is evidence suggesting that the city was not necessarily their birthplace or hometown. According to this evidence, a significant proportion originally had been from the countryside but had moved or fled to the cities. Between 1893 and 1905, no less than three armed conflicts—the Tonghak Rebellion, the Sino-Japanese War, and the Russo-Japanese War—took place on Korean soil, causing many Korean peasants to flee to the cities. In addition, famine and oppressive taxes drove farmers from their homes. That a sizable number of immigrants had migrated to cities within Korea prior to leaving for Hawai'i is important, as first-generation Korean immigrants would make a similar rural-to-urban movement in Hawai'i.

Fifth, these pioneer Korean immigrants were widely dispersed geographically within Korea. This is not surprising, since Deshler's eleven recruiting offices were located throughout the entire peninsula, from Sŏngjin and Ŭiju in the north, through cities such as P'yŏngyang, Seoul, Wŏnsan, and Inch'ŏn in the center, to cities such as Mokp'o and Pusan on the southern coast. While perhaps slightly more northerners than southerners emigrated, the fact remains that Korean immigrants came from all over the peninsula, unlike immigrants from China and Japan, who tended to come from one region. This fact would have important ramifications for the development of the first-generation Korean community in Hawai'i because their scattered origins, like their differing urban occupations, made the Koreans as a group much more heterogeneous than the Chinese and Japanese.

Sixth, the Korean immigrant group had what might be termed a bimodal class background. Many, if not most, were from the lower classes, with little or no education. At the same time, a small but significant number were literate, educated, and from the upper classes (i.e., *yangban*). Thus the immigrants came from all levels of Korean society, adding to the first generation's heterogeneous nature. No such heterogeneity existed among the Japanese immigrant farmers, and certainly very few from the Chinese gentry class emigrated to Hawai'i.

Finally, the Korean immigrants had a strong Christian connection. The reason was that the very people most susceptible to the message of Christianity were those city-dwelling Koreans from the lower classes who had been uprooted from their more conservative roots in the countryside—in other words, the type of person who opted to emigrate to Hawai'i. This Christian connection distinguishes the Korean immigrants from their countrymen, who were overwhelmingly non-Christian (there were only about one hundred thousand Christians out of a total population of eight million at the time), as well as from the Chinese and Japanese immigrants. This is not to say that the bulk of the Korean immigrants were baptized Christians when they arrived in Hawai'i, but the evidence strongly suggests that many of the immigrants had some contact with American missionaries in Korea's cities prior to their departure. In the cities they might have gained some literacy in either Korean, English, or both in mission schools; become familiar with Western people, houses, medicine, clothes, foods, and customs; and, of course, become acquainted with Christianity. This characteristic helps to explain why the Korean immigrants overwhelmingly affiliated themselves with Christian institutions after arriving in Hawai'i. Moreover, their attraction to Christianity while still in Korea indicates that they were more "liberal" than most Koreans, having rejected to a certain extent many of the conservative tenets of Confucian Korean society in the late Chosŏn period. This liberal nature helped them adapt more quickly to Western values.

Just as the immigrants from Korea were a diverse group, so also were their reasons for leaving their country and coming to Hawai'i. In explaining the flow of these immigrants to Hawai'i at the turn of the century, some writers have emphasized that it occurred within a world capitalist system that caused cheap labor to move from the periphery to the core. However true that may be, ultimately nobody forced Koreans to go to Hawai'i. Rather, they were rational actors who made up their own minds after weighing factors of push and pull.

Clearly, the most important "push" factor that made people want to leave Korea was the terrible conditions characterizing late Chosŏn dynasty Korea, which made life difficult for the average Korean. One example was famine and the resulting threat of starvation. Even for those Koreans not directly threatened by this, problems such as banditry, inflation, rebellion, war, cholera epidemics, counterfeit coins, oppressive taxes, corruption, maladministration, and grinding poverty provided ample reason to flee the country. And some—mostly demobilized soldiers—left in the fear of an impending Japanese takeover. However, since the majority of the emigrants originated from the urban poor and working class, we must conclude that deteriorating living standards in Korea, rather than Japanese imperialism, was the primary factor in causing people to leave. Whether the emigrants left Korea because of economic hardship, fear of a Japanese takeover, or a combination of both, it is more than likely that such reasons would tend to make these emigrants adopt a settler, rather than a sojourner, mentality in their adopted country, since most would not consider returning to Korea until conditions there improved or until it was liberated from Japanese rule.

But why go to Hawai'i? Koreans had the option of going to China or Russia, and indeed, most did go to those places in the late Chosŏn period. To determine why Hawai'i held promise as a destination, we must look at the "pull" factors that drew emigrants there by first examining an intervening variable—the role of Christianity. Because the percentage of Christians in Korea at the turn of the century was minuscule and because a large proportion of the immigrants to Hawai'i had had some connection with Christianity, it follows that by examining Korean Christians at the turn of the century, we will arrive at some conclusions concerning their motivations.

Most Koreans at the turn of the century were rural peasant farmers whose tradition-bound and Confucian-oriented value system led them to be suspicious of Western ideas such as Christianity and leery of the prospect of immigration to America. But those who fled to the cities at the end of the nineteenth century came into contact with urban-based American Protestant missionaries and became primary targets for conversion. Most were attracted to the new religion by the prospect of a better life. Young, rootless, newly urbanized, unable to perform the required Confucian rituals at the ancestral graveyard, dispossessed of farms and perhaps relatives, and now, perhaps adherents of Christianity, they were confronted with the opportunity to emigrate to

Hawaiʻi. For this Christian minority, the prospect of such a move was not so difficult to contemplate. For one, some of them had already migrated within Korea, and having moved once, it was not difficult to consider moving again. And naturally, as Christians, they were no longer suspicious of, or unfamiliar with, Americans and American customs and were less concerned about fulfilling the dictates of Confucian tradition. Turning to the missionaries for advice, the new converts found that most of the missionaries approved of emigration to Hawaiʻi. In essence, American missionaries seeking converts and David Deshler seeking emigrants recruited from the same pool: urban dwellers of the working class, perhaps uprooted from their homes in the countryside, accustomed to Westerners and Western ideas, dress, food, housing, religion, people, and even language. If these were people being pushed out of Korea primarily by poverty, and who were prepared psychologically by the influence of American missionaries to relocate in the West, then what was it about Hawaiʻi that "pulled" them?

For some, it was religious freedom; for others, it was the chance for an education for themselves or their children. For still others, it was the opportunity to agitate against Japanese imperialism. Finally, for some it was a combination of factors. But for the majority of the immigrants, the prospect of a better life was the primary "pull" factor. It was a sufficiently attractive force not only to those who were being pushed out of Korea because of extreme poverty (and who thus were inclined to be settlers in Hawaiʻi), but also to those who were merely adventurous young men (and who thus were initially inclined to be sojourners).

In fact, there is evidence that initially a significant sojourner mentality existed among the Korean immigrants. This mentality operated as follows: one (usually a single young man) went abroad for a short period of time with the (sometimes unrealistic) hope of amassing a fortune and then returning to the homeland rich and respected. Such thinking was clearly evident among many Chinese and Japanese immigrants. In the latter case, a *dekasegi* tradition of leaving one's home village to work elsewhere temporarily was well established. Like their Chinese and Japanese counterparts, Korean immigrants also sometimes had unrealistic expectations about what awaited them, which initially contributed to their sojourner mentality.

Nearly every source of information available to Koreans painted a rosy picture of Hawaiʻi and the United States. Such information naturally caused some Koreans to think they would get rich quickly in Hawaiʻi, but it is probably fair to say that most simply were optimistic that, with hard work, life would be better in Hawaiʻi. As the immigrants would soon discover, life in Hawaiʻi was no picnic. Nonetheless, it is clear that most Korean immigrants, even those initially inclined toward sojourning, eventually decided that Hawaiʻi was a better place to live and began gravitating toward a settler mentality. Only a small portion—one out of six—motivated primarily by the prospect of getting rich quickly, remained sojourners, and when they realized they would be paid only seventy cents for ten hours of daily work on the plantations, they began making plans to return to Korea.

In sum, the majority of Korean immigrants to Hawai'i left Korea because they were "pushed" out by poverty and deteriorating conditions in late Chosŏn Korea and "pulled" by favorable reports of Hawai'i. And the circumstances under which they left caused most to consider themselves settlers who would remain in Hawai'i, thereby distinguishing them from the Chinese and Japanese immigrants, a much higher percentage of whom were sojourners. Indeed, more than half of the immigrants from China and Japan returned to their native lands. Now that Koreans were in Hawai'i, they, too, faced the prospect of life and work on the sugar plantations.

2

Laboring on the Plantations

Despite the diversity of the first-generation immigrants when they departed Korea, the one thing they all had in common after their arrival in Hawai'i was work on the sugar plantations. The final year of immigration, 1905, marked the high point of Korean presence on the plantations, with five thousand workers making up 11 percent of the labor force, ranking second behind the Japanese at 66 percent and ahead of the Chinese, who comprised 9 percent.[1]

In some respects, the Koreans were more fortunate than most of the other thirty-three ethnic groups who came to Hawai'i to work in the sugarcane fields. Because they arrived *after* annexation to the United States, they entered as free labor rather than as contract labor. Those who had arrived as contract laborers (including all of the Chinese and about half of the Japanese) faced a difficult time. Contracts (usually of three years' duration) were legally enforceable, strikes were illegal, and there was little reason for planters to treat their workers well. After annexation, contracts were illegal, strikes were permitted, and conditions on the plantations improved somewhat, although many of the more odious features of preannexation years remained.

One of the most important aspects of the Korean experience on the plantations was their living arrangements. In general, Korean housing was similar to that given to the Chinese and Japanese. If there were enough Koreans on any given plantation, they were given their own separate camp, usually known as the Korean Camp. Such an arrangement served the interests of both the planters and the Koreans—the manager could pit one race against another and discourage worker solidarity, and the Koreans felt more comfortable living among other Koreans. For example, at Olaa Plantation, the Koreans "were segregated from the other groups and they stayed close together liking it . . . for they could not speak any other language but Korean."[2]

But since there were about sixty-five plantations and only about five thousand Korean workers and their families, separate Korean camps were the exception rather than the rule. Most Koreans found themselves living in mixed camps with workers of other nationalities. One Korean immigrant recalled that "[o]urs was the smallest camp, so far as our own population was concerned.

11

There were six by six rows of cabins in the whole camp, and we occupied only three rows on the east end. The rest was partly occupied by some Portuguese and Puerto Ricans."³ Even with their limited contact with Western missionary culture, these mixed living arrangements marked the beginning of what might be called "culture shock," as Koreans came into sustained contact for the first time with the seemingly strange customs of other ethnic groups in Hawai'i. Because of their small numbers, Koreans were frequently forced to commingle with other ethnic groups in a way that larger immigrant groups, such as the Japanese, were not. This forced commingling, first on the plantations and later off, was an important factor, along with a settler mentality, in hastening the adaptation of first-generation Koreans to Hawaiian society.

For example, the Koreans had come from a tradition where the role of women was severely restricted. But many of their initial cultural encounters suggested new roles for women. According to the immigrant quoted above, "Those Puerto Ricans were the happiest people I had ever seen. (They were of the Negro origin.) They were directly opposite from my cabin, and I could not help watching them sing and dance day and night all the time when they were not working. And that was the first time I had ever seen men and women swinging around in each other's arms. That looked awfully strange to me, of course, as my folks back home had never done such things . . . not even husband and wife together." Traditionally, "respectable women would never dance or sing because in Korea only the *geisangs* (dancing girls) and *mudangs* (sorceresses) who are beyond the pale of respectability were versed in those particular arts."⁴

Moreover, the employment of women in cooking for groups of Korean men further weakened traditional practices. In late nineteenth century Korea, women were secluded and rarely ventured outside the family compound. But as men and women had already been crowded together in steerage during the voyage across the Pacific, when women began cooking and doing laundry for the single Korean men, it merely represented yet another concession to Western customs. The experience that many Korean women gained in cooking and laundering for large numbers of single men was transferred to urban occupations later, when they would operate boarding houses or laundries.⁵

Interaction with native Hawaiians also had an impact on Korean women that often resulted in "culture shock." Because Koreans came from a society where women refrained from direct eye contact with men other than their husbands, "Hawaiians, at first sight, struck fear into the hearts of the Koreans. Their dark skin, large rolling eyes, and general appearance were absolutely strange to them. Moreover, without any restraint they came to the camps to satisfy their curiosity about Koreans and stared at them openly, a circumstance especially distressing to the hitherto secluded Korean women." Not every Korean encounter with Hawaiians was so traumatic, however, since "the natives were so hospitable and generous." One Korean woman remembered her first encounter: "The Kanakas (native Hawaiians) nearby were friendly to us and asked us to attend their church. We didn't know the language, but since we were 'novelties' they loved us an awful lot. We didn't speak their language or anything, but we must have been the first Oriental young folks they had ever seen. They were so happy to see us! And we were so afraid of them—they simply frightened us!"[6]

Within the Korean camp were two types of housing: family and single quarters. For a Korean couple, with or without children, there might be a cottage with a small garden. But since most of the Koreans were single men, they were housed either three or four to a cottage or in a "long house" dormitory. There were usually three or four of these long houses in a camp, built of rough lumber with a tin roof and evenly partitioned into twelve-by-twelve foot rooms with a raised section on the side for eating and sleeping. Other long houses were not partitioned, making them one large room. There might be a lanai outside with steps leading to the ground. On those plantations with only dormitories, married couples and bachelors occupied separate long houses.

Koreans were given straw mats (totjari), or they could purchase blankets from the plantation store to sleep on the wooden floor. Unaccustomed to sleeping on straw mats and unable at first to purchase the mattresses on which they were accustomed to sleeping, they often purchased thick cotton cloth and stuffed it with dried grass. For the wooden pillows (mokjim) to which they were accustomed, they carved out blocks of wood, although they also made pillows stuffed with dried grass, like their mattresses. As they earned money, they were able to afford more comfortable mattresses and pillows padded with cotton.[7]

The plantations varied not only in the type of accommodations, but also in their quality. Some plantations constructed new housing for the recent Korean arrivals or otherwise provided clean and adequate lodgings. When Yun Ch'i-ho made his inspection tour in 1905, he remarked in his diary that the Korean housing he visited was "very neatly kept" and the "best he had seen," a sentiment echoed by the visiting missionary George Heber Jones. Another missionary from Korea, S. F. Moore, noted that the houses in the Korean camp at Kahuku Plantation were "nicely located on high ground. They are kept white with whitewash and were clean." In fact, sanitary laws in Hawai'i mandated a certain amount of cubic feet per person. Some plantations, however, did not provide adequate housing or a pleasant environment for the newly arrived immigrants from Korea. One who endured such conditions remembered his dormitory as a "big barracks which had one big square sleeping room where there was no privacy . . . like animals . . . similar to barns." As for the bathrooms, "[t]here was only one toilet . . . in each camp. No separate facilities were provided for male and female workers. The inside of the camp was dirty and was full of bad odors."[8]

Working and living in Hawai'i necessitated a change from the traditional clothing of Korea. In the subtropical climate, the women wore traditional summer clothing only, made of coarse white cotton from the plantation store. Although formal and holiday clothes quickly were abandoned, since many of the women either worked in the fields or cooked and/or did laundry for the men, most women did not soon adopt Western-style clothing. Korean men, however, adopted Western clothing sooner, and the change was more pronounced, as most had already abandoned traditional clothing before departing Korea. A few men, however, initially continued to wear Korean clothing either for the sake of tradition or to save money. And while most men had already adopted Western hairstyles, a few (one estimate is 2 percent) continued to wear the topknot *(sangt'u)* covered by the traditional Korean horsehair hat *(kat)*. One Korean remembered an incident that caused even these few to change their hairstyles: "There was one man who had a topknot. While he was riding the train, the hat blew off revealing his hair. He felt embarrassed and tried to catch his hat, causing the train to derail. Everybody on the train was scared and the driver threatened to sue him. After an investigation he was arrested and he realized that his hair had caused the trouble, so he cut his hair, even though he had earlier said that he would kill anyone if they tried to cut his hair."[9]

In addition to housing, clothing, and hairstyles, Koreans also had to adjust to higher prices and different types of food. The new Korean customers experienced what would be termed today "sticker shock" when they saw the prices at the plantation store. As one HSPA official informed a plantation manager: "The only trouble thus far experienced with the Koreans is the matter of high cost of food, which rather staggers them as the cost of food in their own country is exceedingly little, but this will adjust itself as time goes on. . . . I hope you will instruct your store people to give them every possible advantage as they are absolutely ignorant as to cost of things they must buy when they first come here." A similar refrain came from another direction: "A gentleman who lives in Honolulu . . . told me that the Koreans had had difficulty on some of the plantations about their food. Rice costs more than they have been accustomed to pay and the same is true of meat so that in some places they had tried to live on flour, but not knowing how to make bread they had a hard time until the company sent a Chinese cook to teach them how to make their bread."

One way to compensate for the high price of food was to grow one's own: "At Waialua and Kahuku this matter [of high food prices] is already in better shape as the [Korean] people now have their own garden truck to help out on the food question." As a result, the HSPA informed the various plantation managers that Koreans "will expect to be provided with a patch of ground in the neighborhood of their quarters where they can plant their garden truck, and as this is an important matter to them I ask that you give your special attention to it." Still, wages of sixteen dollars a month did not go very far. One man remembered that his monthly expenses totaled $12.55, and as a result, "We lost hope because of the expenses. If we wanted to study in school, we could not pay the food charges. Even if we wanted to return to Korea, we did not have boat fare."

And one immigrant's daughter recorded: "When I asked Father years later if we had eaten bananas in Hawaii, he replied that although a big bunch of bananas sold for five cents, he could not afford to buy any. Since we had arrived with only the clothes on our backs and our bedding, we never had enough money left over to buy bananas. We lived in a grass hut, slept on the ground, and had to start from scratch to get every household item."[10]

In addition to the higher prices, the Koreans had to adjust to the different and puzzling foods. One Korean, confronted for the first time with a Western meal, was briefed by his sister, who had lived in Hawaii for several years: "'What's this?' I asked, pointing at a large round piece of meat. 'That's called hamburger.' . . . Strange to eat a large piece of meat all by itself. . . . The dish that shocked me was called 'salad.' I took a mouthful and almost spat it out. It was raw vegetables! So, the Americans ate raw vegetables like cows and goats . . . and glasses of milk for everyone. 'Milk!' I was mystified. 'Yes, milk,' sister Alice explained. 'In America, not only babies but grownups too drink milk every day.'"[11]

Rather than embrace these new foods all at once, the newly arrived immigrants usually arranged Korean-style meals, which were served in a large community kitchen (usually one per camp) at one long dining table made of unpainted lumber with long benches. The meals consisted of some combination of rice, soup, kimchi, dried fish, cooked vegetables, beef, and tinned and fresh fruit. One contemporary observer noted: "The writer visited a Korean camp at mealtime. The men were boarding in a mess which they conducted themselves, ranges and cooking utensils, as well as house and fuel, being supplied by the plantations. Their mess expenses were said by the cook to be six dollars a month. The men were plentifully supplied with boiled rice, a salad of fresh vegetables, and beef stew. The manager of the plantation said that they would buy the cheaper parts of animals, including the head and the refuse meats, and that occasionally they bought fowls, which they stew heads and all. The vegetables were purchased from Japanese market gardeners. Upon another plantation, which also conducts a large cattle ranch, the Koreans buy beef on the hoof, slaughtering it themselves."[12]

Most of the cooking was done by the wives of Koreans who provided breakfast, dinner and a box lunch, which was known by the Japanese term *bentō*. The simple act of eating *bentō*s in the fields with other ethnic groups caused culture shock. Koreans, like the Chinese and Japanese, used chopsticks, never touching food with their fingers. Consequently, the Koreans were astonished to see Portuguese, Puerto Rican, and Spanish workers eating with their fingers. Similarly, they were taken aback by the Hawaiian custom of eating poi and fish with the fingers.

Because the Koreans were few in number, they usually dealt with other nationalities when purchasing food. Along with the Japanese vegetable vendors mentioned above, Chinese grocers counted Koreans among their customers, sometimes with unfortunate results: "Among them [the Chinese], there was a grocer. Many Koreans traded there on credit, but unable to pay back their debts because they didn't earn enough in the first place, the grocer was unable to collect about $800, and was forced to close his business." Sometimes, humorous episodes occurred due to the language barrier: "He and his [Korean] friends wanted to buy eggs from the neighborhood grocery store, but none of them knew the word 'eggs.' One of his friends volunteered to try to buy the eggs by using gestures. He took his white handkerchief out of his pocket and put it around his left fist so that it looked like a very large egg. He moved the fist behind his buttocks, and made the sound of a hen that had laid an egg. The grocery clerk understood the gesture and the sound and brought out a dozen eggs." [13]

Koreans interacted mostly with Chinese and Japanese, since they, especially the Japanese, made up the bulk of the workforce on the plantations. There is little evidence of friction between Koreans and Chinese, even though some Koreans thought the Chinese a bit strange "because of their fondness of keeping their living quarters in darkness and living on what appeared to the Koreans as a lower standard than theirs." There was, however, occasional discord between Koreans and Japanese. Some of it was due to the Korean willingness to help break Japanese-led strikes. At other times, the source was more mundane, such as the act of bathing. After a day of work in the canefields, workers were usually covered with red dust. Sometimes it was so bad that "on the way back from work it was difficult to know who was who." So Koreans bathed daily in a single large tub for a monthly charge of twenty-five cents, one report noting that "on some plantations the Koreans have adopted Japanese customs in this respect." However, the Koreans did not adopt the Japanese practice (which continued through the 1920s) of both sexes bathing together. But since the vast majority of plantation workers were Japanese, the men often passed through Korean camps to the bathhouse wearing nothing but towel loincloths. This offended the Koreans, who "not infrequently got into riots with the Japanese because of this seeming lack of decorum." [14]

Yet despite their differences, Koreans and Japanese had a great deal in common. One Korean remembered that "[e]ven in those early days there were more Japanese in Honolulu and in all the islands than any other race or nationality, and they were operating hotels and all sorts of small businesses. There I discovered that the Orientals go with other Orientals, whether or not they like each other, their appearance, their tastes, their backgrounds, and their living standards being very much alike." Moreover, Koreans were admonished by Yun Ch'i-ho in 1905 "[t]hat the most cordial relations be kept up with the Japanese and other fellow Orientals." [15] In fact, Koreans interacted with Japanese on a daily basis, and these interactions were for the most part cordial and uneventful. While political problems between Japan and Korea would soon spill over into Hawai'i and sour relations between the two groups, the primary concern the Koreans had was with plantation work and the haoles (Caucasians) who acted in supervisory capacities as managers, doctors, and *lunas*.

The plantation work schedule was organized around twenty-six working days per month, ten hours per day, with Sundays off. Every workday began with the piercing sound of the mill whistle at 4:30 A.M. After breakfast, the Korean workers went to the fields to begin working by six o'clock, most taking the flatbed plantation railroad, which traveled on both permanent and temporary tracks. A few owned their own horses or bicycles and rode them to and from work. "Without break" they worked until lunch, when "[t]hey gave us only a half hour lunch. Then we started again until four-thirty."[16]

At the end of the month, the Koreans workers would be paid in cash by presenting their *bango,* or brass disc stamped with their number, which they wore around their neck. Since the payroll records were kept by number rather than name, workers needed the *bango* to be recorded present for work and to receive their pay. Up to 1905 the salary for adult male Korean workers was sixteen dollars per month, the same wages paid to other Asians: "The wages of the [Korean] men are to be on the same basis as fixed for monthly Japanese. If the women desire to work they are to be employed in wahine [female] gangs at prevailing rates, the same with boys." A Korean boy, earning fifty cents per day, remembered his first payday: "So I worked every day, and before I realized, I had come to the end of the first month and my first payday. At the pay master's window I proudly presented my 'bango' or Japanese term for number, stamped on a small brass disc. I received a tiny brown pay envelope containing eight ($8.00) dollars in coin . . . one five-dollar gold piece and three silver dollars . . . for the sixteen days I worked."[17]

In the spring of 1905 the HSPA proposed that the wages of white Portuguese workers, who already received higher wages than Asians for the same work, be increased by two dollars per month. This proposal generated opposition from plantation managers, who argued that the raise should be across the board: "I think this action [the proposed two-dollar raise] has something to do with the exodus of our Japanese to the coast and if the Portuguese should receive an increase of wages the Japanese and Koreans are liable to leave us in large numbers and bring us to a standstill. An increase of wages to one particular nationality naturally means dissatisfaction to others." As a result of this opposition, a raise of two dollars per month went into effect for all workers in May 1905, bringing the wages of Korean adult males to eighteen dollars per month.[18]

As a benefit, Korean workers were provided with free medical care. In fact, when the Koreans first began to arrive in Hawai'i, one plantation manager checked with the HSPA: "Exactly what is the status of the plantations to these people? . . . I assume the usual conditions of house, fuel, and water are borne by the plantation, as is also, I presume, in the interests of humanity, medical service and hospital expense." Yet despite this service, Koreans sometimes did not go to the plantation doctor. One reason was the language barrier—most did not know enough English to explain their problem adequately, or the Korean interpreters made mistakes due to their own linguistic limitations. Another reason was their unfamiliarity with Western medical practices. Koreans who distrusted the plantation doctors could go to the nearest town to buy Oriental herbs from the local Chinese pharmacy. In addition to stewing and drinking these herbs, the Koreans employed acupuncture and cauterizing, and there was usually someone skilled in these techniques at every camp. As a preventive measure, those who could afford it purchased *insam* (ginseng), first from Chinese druggists and then, after a few years, directly from Korea. Even into the 1920s some Koreans continued to refuse Western medicine and instead relied upon traditional Korean medicinal practices.[19]

Sometimes the planters saw the Korean preference for Oriental medicine as a ploy to avoid work. For example, "Mr. Bishop [from the HSPA] has just called and told us that two Koreans had arrived from Hilo, one from Olaa and one from Waiakea, and that the Olaa Korean claimed that he had been told to stop applying for same [easier work on the island of Oahu]. Mr. Bishop, of course, does not take much stock in what he says, as we assured him you had taken special care of the Koreans during the sickness which they have had there; but he thought it best to let us know what this man had to say. He had not seen him, therefore could not give any name or number by which he could be identified. Mr. Bishop will send the man back tomorrow." The manager's reply? "In further connection with the Korean question would say that the Olaa Korean referred to by Mr. Bishop is undoubtedly number 1136 (Plantation number). This fellow has been treated for Eczema of the Scrotum, and according to the report in the surgery was treated several times. Upon being furnished the last treatment which was Zinc-Oxide Ointment, he threw it on the table with the remark that he wanted water medicine. The doctor told him that he was furnishing the proper treatment, whereupon he refused to take the ointment and left." The manager suspected that his refusal to be treated with Western medicine was related to a desire to avoid work: "This fellow with our number 1118 has been of considerable annoyance as they will not work and are constantly pestering me with applications for easier work."[20]

But the main reason some Koreans disliked the plantation doctors was neither language problems nor a preference for Oriental medicine, but rather because the doctors worked for the plantation and therefore could not be completely trusted. Indeed, plantation doctors were in a difficult position in attempting to distinguish malingering from genuine illness. Some evidence suggests that plantations were capable of acting in a humane manner when confronted with illness: "[T]here is one Korean in the first batch who is very badly afflicted with heart disease and is unquestionably unable to perform manual labor or any other. He is remaining around the camp and is not even fit to be used for scavenging duties around the quarters. We have been making slight advances to him through the store to which he is in debt, and which debt is naturally increasing from day to day." But other evidence suggests that such humane treatment was exceptional: "The [medical] treatment was bad," recalled one immigrant. "Plantation doctors were unkind. . . . Sometimes a sick man was forced to work." Another immigrant also charged that most of the doctors were not kind and did not really care about their patients, adding, "I saw with my eyes some of my good friends die in the plantation camps. In fact one of them died in my lap with an unknown illness after he got back from his doctor." Finally, workers went on strike in 1904 when a plantation doctor allegedly caused the death of a Korean worker by kicking him in the stomach.[21]

Since one possible way to avoid work was to fake a medical condition, suspicious managers often did not even bother to consult the doctor.

> If Mr. Paxton will remember, when he was here, one of them [Koreans] brought me a letter written by some acquaintance stating that he was feeble and desirous of obtaining light employment. Just before the departure of these two men to Hilo I interviewed them through the Korean interpreter as they had been hanging around my house for two or three days, and inquired of them what was the trouble. They stated that they were not physically able to perform manual labor. I then asked them what they preferred to do upon which they answered with one accord, "remain in the camp." I then asked them whom they expected would feed them when in the camp, and they answered that they thought that the plantation would until they were strong enough to do work, and I then asked them when that would be and they said they did not know. I then asked them if it would be a short or a long time and they answered, "a long time," so I finally told them to keep away from my house and either work or go hungry and that if I caught them loafing in the camp that I should charge them for their room and force them to work out the amount. Upon eliciting this information from me they decided to leave the place.[22]

The treatment Koreans received on any plantation was often a reflection of the policies and personality of the manager. The HSPA suggested to a manager who was about to receive one of the first groups of Koreans that "[t]hese people have had a hard trip of twenty days from their homes and the rough weather prevailing throughout the entire trip has been hard on them. I therefore suggest that you give them three or four days to get on their feet before turning them to." To the same manager, a high-ranking officer proferred advice on how to get the most from his Korean workers: "Permit me, as having some little knowledge of the Korean character, to make a few suggestions. Under foreign overseers in Korea these people do first class work, although they will stand pushing and being kept at their tasks. I am sure that you will find them very amenable to kind treatment and after they have had time to become

accustomed to the work they will do just as well as the Japanese, but some tact
and judgement must be shown by your overseer in breaking them in. . . . It will
not do to coddle or humor the people too much or at all for that matter, yet
kindness and sympathy can be shown them without spoiling them."[23] Thus one
of the high-ranking officers of the HSPA went on record with advice to treat
the Koreans reasonably well.

For some managers such advice was unnecessary, since they treated their
workers kindly as a matter of course. The first group of Korean immigrants
who had gone to Waialua Plantation elicited the following comment about the
manager from one of the HSPA officials: "Mr. Goodale will doubtless treat
them [Koreans] so well that they will want their friends to follow them." Even
thirty years after leaving the plantations, some Koreans praised their bosses:
"The plantation managers, as a whole, were respected and admired by the
Koreans. They were the individuals with comprehension, foresight, and deep
concern for the general welfare. Even today [1937] there are many managers
of plantations that the Koreans recall with fondness and admiration."[24] Nonetheless, since there were nearly six dozen plantations, one would expect that
not all plantation managers were kind. When Yun Ch'i-ho visited Pepeekeo
Plantation, he "[f]ound the manager, Mr. Webster, the most disagreeable host
I have so far met. He had two or three Koreans, but they all had left him: no
wonder." And at Makee Plantation, Yun noted that "Fairchild [the manager]
does not seem to have the tact for managing a Korean crowd. He does not
seem to be a man of heart. Remarkable that a kindly manager has as a rule, an
orderly set [of workers]."[25]

While managers set the overall climate for the treatment of laborers, it was
the *lunas* whom the Koreans saw every day and whose job it was to supervise
the work gangs in the canefields. In the fields they came face to face with the
strictures of plantation supervision. At this level the experience of the Koreans,
like that of most of the other sugar workers, was largely negative. At one plantation that Yun Ch'i-ho visited, he found that "Walker [the manager] and his
head luna seem to be hard men." At another plantation he noted that "[w]hen
I addressed a group of Koreans numbering about 200, I am told that the policemen and the lunas have been rather harsh in compelling Koreans to work."
When missionary S. F. Moore visited the Koreans in Hawai'i he conceded,
"There are no doubt some instances where the overseers may not be as fine
men as the manager at Kahuku and where the conditions may not be as favorable." One woman who recounted her husband's experience in the field said,
"The workers were under the constant supervision of the luna (field supervisor)
who always watched the movement of each. If he spotted any irregularity, such
as standing straight to ease the pain, he would shout at or whip the deviant
one." And thirty years after their experiences, "exacting and unsympathetic"
was how some Koreans remembered the *lunas*.[26]

Those Koreans who endured the discipline of the *lunas* give voice to the bitterness of their experience. In an interview, one Korean woman who had worked in the fields said, "I'll never forget the foreman. He was French. The reason I'll never forget him is that he was the most ignorant of all ignoramuses, but he knew all the cuss words in the world. . . . He said we worked like 'lazy.' He wanted us to work faster. . . . [H]e would gallop around on horseback and crack and snap his whip. . . . [H]e was so mean and so ignorant!" One Korean worker remembered that "my foreman, who was either a native or Portuguese, urged me along hollering 'biki,' or 'hurry, hurry'"; another recalled: "In the cane field men were driven by the luna (foreman) shouting constantly, "Go ahead, go ahead.'" Still another recalled that "[we] were treated like animals by the lunas or foremen during work, even not allowing us to talk or smoke with each other." Finally, one Korean worker recalled that "[d]uring working hours, nobody was allowed to talk, smoke, or even stretch his back. A foreman kept his eyes on his workers at all times. When he found anyone violating working regulations, he whipped the violator without mercy. If the worker showed any signs of resistance, he would be fired at once."[27]

The role of the Korean interpreters on the plantations was as an intermediary between management and Korean workers. A typical arrangement for the interpreters can be found in the following directive from the HSPA to one plantation: "A party of Koreans is due to arrive per 'China' today and will be sent to your Plantation after passing quarantine and immigration inspection. The exact number will be advised later. They will be accompanied by the Association's Recruiting Agent, C. S. [Chŏng-su] An, also an interpreter who will stay with the party permanently. The permanent interpreter if married is to be paid $30.00 per month and $25.00 per month if single."

With a salary of nearly twice that of a laborer, it was clear that the planters expected the interpreters to help keep the Koreans in line: "You will find that the interpreter above referred to will develop to act also as a luna over the people." And the planters did not hesitate to use them in this way, one interpreter remembering that "I was ordered by the manager to stay in camp and check up on the [Korean] absences and bring the sick persons down to the medical office." As a result, many of the Korean workers tended to view the interpreters with the same suspicion as plantation doctors, managers, and lunas, and this could sometimes lead to trouble. Yun Ch'i-ho's diary notes that "[i]n the morning drove over to the Kilauea plantation, Manager Moore. About 25 Koreans—Mr. M. had a deal of trouble with Koreans on account of a bad interpreter whom he favored against the protest of the laborers." In light of this account, it is difficult to believe the following interpreter's words: "I encouraged them [Koreans] and said that we came out of an honorable country and came to the 'Paradise of the Pacific,' let us be happy and work hard on the fields. . . . I acted as interpreter for the Luna, or Overseer. Thus, we were all happy to work doing the following: row making, digging ditches for irrigation, weeding, stripping, cutting canes and so forth."

Still, interpreters were useful in ironing out misunderstandings on the plantations. Regarding the earlier allegation that a plantation doctor had kicked a Korean worker in the stomach, killing him and triggering a riot, the HSPA wrote to the manager of that plantation: "In re Koreans, we understand Mr. Mead has sent out the interpreter, Mr. An, and hope he will be able to straighten matters out. . . . . We regret to learn that the Koreans are still belligerent but hope that after they learn the details of the coroner's inquest [from the interpreter] they can be induced to return to work peaceably."[28]

If the Korean workers sometimes viewed the interpreters with suspicion so, too, did the planters: "Replying to yours of the 22nd., am sorry to hear that the Korean interpreter does not impress you as being of much use. One of the great difficulties in connection with the Korean immigration is the matter of interpreters. It seems indispensable that we have interpreters; on the other hand the 'students' who are the only available class are apt to be very unfit in a practical way, and do not develop as leaders. In view of the embryo status of the Korean question please be as tolerant as possible as it will be awkward if these interpreters are back on my hands here in Honolulu."[29]

Ever since 1896 the planters had sought Koreans as replacements for the banned Chinese to offset the more numerous and troublesome Japanese worker, who, according to the planters, "is quick to take offense, ready with his fists and altogether a difficult and unreliable employee. Under no pecuniary bind to his employer and attached to the plantation by no sense of loyalty or self-interest, he requires constant oversight."[30] The planters were looking for three characteristics in the Koreans: good agricultural work habits, docility in the face of a harsh working environment, and stability. If they met these three criteria, the Koreans would serve as a satisfactory counteragent to the Japanese as the planters continued to mix the races in an attempt to control labor.

Initially, the planters were pleased with the working ability of the Koreans, who appeared to show promise as plantation hands. A Maui newspaper was quoted as saying that "Korean labor on the plantation is proving satisfactory so far." The manager of Hutchinson Plantation liked Korean workers so much that he wrote the parent HSPA four times in late 1903 and early 1904 asking them to send him more, while another manager stated that "the Koreans have proven to be exceptionally good laborers." Asked about the possibility of obtaining Filipinos, an HSPA executive responded, "If we can get any Koreans we know what they are, and they are undoubtedly superior." And the president of the HSPA, in his annual address, cited the "small number of Koreans, who so far, have given satisfaction."[31]

The newly arrived Korean immigrants also initially pleased the planters with their docility. Koreans tended not to go on strike and demonstrated an eagerness to help break Japanese strikes, spurred by the twin inducements of temporarily higher wages and, increasingly, the chance to retaliate indirectly for what Japan was doing to Korea. In December 1904, when half of the 2,500 Japanese workers on Waialua Plantation on Oahu went on strike, the planters gathered 250 Koreans from various plantations to take their places. Six months later, fifty Koreans filled in when Japanese workers at Wailuku (Maui) struck. In the fall of 1905, 1,500 Japanese went on strike for higher wages in Lahaina (Maui), but the strike failed when Koreans refused to join. In retaliation, the Japanese threatened the Koreans, and the manager had to post guards around the Korean camp. When the Japanese consul-general in Honolulu, Saitō Miki, examining the relationship between Korean and Japanese workers in 1905, interviewed the managers of Ewa, Waialua, and Kahuku plantations on the island of Oahu, they praised the obedience and greater stability of the Koreans and applauded their role as strikebreakers against the Japanese. Saitō therefore concluded that the Koreans were favorably accepted by the planters.[32]

Finally, the planters were also initially pleased with the Korean workers' stability. One reason the planters had originally sought Korean immigrants was because Japanese workers tended to depart for the West Coast, usually California, because of the higher wages there. In 1904, about six thousand Japanese left, and in 1905 the number increased to ten thousand. The planters hoped the Koreans would not follow the same pattern, and indeed, only about one hundred Koreans left for the continental United States during 1903 and 1904. Thus on all three counts—ability, docility, and stability—the Koreans, at least initially, proved the perfect offset to the Japanese.

After this initial burst of enthusiasm, however, the planters quickly became less enamored of the Koreans. One reason was that the Koreans were, in fact, proving to be mediocre plantation workers, despite earlier optimistic reports. When the two-dollar per month raise was broached in 1905, the plantation manager who had earlier written four letters pleading for more Koreans now, in a remarkable turnaround, wrote, "In the opinion of the writer the wages for Koreans should not be raised." A month later, he still complained, "We wonder if this [raise] applies to Koreans as well as Japanese, since the former class is not worth it." Consul-General Saitō's investigation, which concluded that the planters liked the strikebreaking potential of the Koreans against the Japanese, also uncovered that the planters were not impressed with the Koreans as plantation hands. The managers of three plantations on Oahu acknowledged to Saitō that the Japanese workers were more efficient, while the manager of a plantation on Kauai complained that, on average, only half of his 170 Koreans worked, while the rest tended to idle away their time. The collection of reports submitted by every plantation manager in late 1905 to the parent body (the HSPA), which included an assessment of every ethnic group working there, tends to confirm the judgment that Koreans were at best mediocre plantation workers. Because these reports were meant for internal use only, they are candid and objective assessments of plantation labor. They contained scant praise for Koreans.[33]

Why were the Koreans judged mediocre plantation workers, especially compared to the Japanese? One explanation can be found in the racism and discrimination characterizing the sugar industry in Hawai'i. White workers received wages one-third higher than those for Asians for the same work, and upper-level positions remained effectively closed to Asians. Why should one work diligently if there were few material incentives or opportunities for upward mobility within the industry? Perhaps their poor work record reflects early Koreans' recognition of the true nature of plantation life.

But a more powerful explanation can be found by comparing the backgrounds of the Japanese and Korean immigrants. Having been farmers in Japan before coming to Hawai'i, many Japanese were accustomed to agricultural labor and, as a result, were relatively good plantation workers. The planters had high expectations that the Koreans would also turn out to be excellent workers, because when one of the planters visited Korea in 1902, he wrote back: "I feel as confident as I can without positively knowing that the Koreans will prove good laborers if we can get them to the Islands. . . . They are lusty strong fellows and physically much the superior of the Jap. In rice culture and mining work they excel any other nationality and I can't for the life of me see how it is possible for them to prove other than good laborers for us."[34] Yet clearly he was wrong. Why?

In fact, he was not wrong in his glowing report of the average Korean farmer. But the urban background of most of the Koreans who came to Hawai'i made them unfamiliar with agricultural work. One woman, in what would be typical for most Koreans, remembered that "[s]ince [my father] had not had any farming experience, he could not do specialized work such as picking." This distinction between urban dwellers and the few rural farmers among the Korean immigrants was clear at the plantation level. Olaa Sugar Company's manager was unhappy with the first group of Koreans sent to him: "The first lot were more mixed, many of them being from the towns, in addition to their [sic] being some very poor men among them." By contrast, he was pleased with the second group: "I am not desirous of being loaded up with a lot of green men, but as this lot appears to be a very good one, being I understand, all of them from the farming districts, I can stand another lot as I shall replace the Japanese day laborers with them."[35]

If the plantation managers were unhappy with the Korean workers, it is also true that the majority of Koreans were unhappy with plantation life and work. Some were upset because they discovered they could not make the fortunes they expected. One woman wrote of her father: "He came to Hawaii in 1903 purely out of curiosity of this fortune making rumor. To his sad case, there were no such things as money growing out of trees but just fields." Some were disappointed because they found it difficult to save money. A son wrote of his first-generation parents: "Their intention was to return to their land as soon as they had saved some money. In this hope they were disappointed, for they soon found out that it was not so easy to save money as they thought it would be." Others were unhappy because they were forced to live at subsistence levels. In one family, the wife recalled that "[i]f all of us worked hard and pooled together our total earnings, it came to about $50.00 a month, barely enough to feed and clothe the five of us." Still others were put off by the culture shock: "We were sent to a plantation in Maui. We didn't know how we were going to survive. There were not many Koreans there. We shed many tears." Many were unhappy about working conditions they considered inhumane. "We worked like draft animals, cows and horses, in the plantation fields," said one Korean, while another recalled that "the plantation owners treated Korean workers no better than cows or horses, as animals rather than as human beings. Every worker was called by number, never by name."[36]

For most, however, plantation work was simply too difficult. As the newest arrivals, Koreans were placed in the most menial and arduous cultivation jobs on the plantation. Whereas the small percentage who had been farmers in Korea were prepared for the rigors of plantation work, the urban majority simply were not. Bernice Kim observed that "[m]any of them could not stand the strain of ten hours of work in semi-tropical sunshine . . . [since] in Korea many of them had not worked steadily at hard labor, especially the youthful soldiers and minor governmental clerks. . . . Stories are told of how some boys and even men, with fair hands blistered, faces and arms torn and scratched by the cane leaf stickers, would sit between the rows of cane and weep like children." An interpreter remembered, "Almost all of my fellow Koreans were discouraged to live in such a terrible camp and work so hard in the sugar cane field." And one man recounted to his new bride some years later: "After I landed in Honolulu, many of the men who had come on the *Siberia* with me were shipped to Koloa, which is on the island of Kauai. We worked hard. . . . [I stayed on the plantation] four long years. We didn't like the work. The hours were long and the work was hard."[37]

Those who had been students or who had come from *yangban* families found life extremely difficult, both physically and psychologically. "We hid our brother in the house so the plantation owners wouldn't get after him," wrote one woman. "He had the brains of an Edison but was not fit to be a laborer." Another woman wrote: "My father found out that labor in the fields was not what he had thought it would be and his literary soul rebelled to physical labor." And finally, one man recalled his own student experience: "[M]y hands were never used to any rough 'stuff' like that. The only things that I was accustomed to were pen and paper, and nothing else. Although my father was a farmer, I had never done any farm work back in the old country. My father had intended me to be a scholar, and a scholar's hands should be as soft as silk and fingers as pointed as a brush pen. Athletics were never known until the missionaries came with the modern idea of physical training. All forms of physical exertion were not dignified, nor befitting a scholarly person to indulge in, according to the old Korean conception."[38] Consequently, most Koreans were not content on the plantations, and their reactions, when added to their demonstrated inability or unwillingness to handle plantation work, made the planters even less pleased with the Koreans. For the Korean workers, the most drastic response was to leave Hawai'i, going either to the mainland or back to Korea.

Initially, the Koreans did not follow the Japanese to the mainland, but the planters feared "it won't be long before they [the Koreans] will want to go to the Coast, as soon as they get a little ahead in finances." These fears were confirmed when the number of Koreans leaving Hawai'i for California skyrocketed to four hundred in 1905. In February of that year, two recruiters for the Great Northern and the Northern Pacific railroads established headquarters at a Korean-run hotel, the Hansŏng (Seoul), in Honolulu, and offered Koreans daily wages of $1.10 in February, $1.20 in March, $1.30 in April, and $1.50 in May, June, and July—well in excess of the 70 cents per day plantation wage. Additionally, recruiters for orchards in California, spurred by commissions of $10 for every recruit, visited plantations and offered daily wages of $1.50 during the fruit season. Such inducements led one planter to lament that "some 800 to 900 Japs and Koreans left on the *Manchuria* Saturday."[39] Indeed, the only hurdle Koreans faced was the $28 boat passage between Honolulu and California.

Not all Koreans who went to the mainland for higher wages were recruited by companies. For example, "My second brother, Paik Daw Sun, was born on October 6, 1905, in Hawaii. Father was desperate, always writing to friends in other places, trying to find a better place to live. Finally, he heard from friends in Riverside, California, who urged him to join them; they said the prospects for the future were better in America; that a man's wages were ten to fifteen cents an hour for ten hours of work a day. After his year in Hawaii was up, Father borrowed enough money from friends to pay for our passage to America on board the S. S. *China*. We landed in San Francisco on December 3, 1906. . . . Many old friends came with us from Hawaii."[40]

Some Koreans left to fulfill educational objectives or simply out of curiosity. "I came to Hawaii to learn American civilization, and learn something beneficial. When I met Yun Ch'i-ho who was then the Assistant Foreign Minister of Korea, he encouraged me to study in the mainland. So I decided to come over here with my cousin." Another remembered that "I didn't come to Hawaii to make money, and above all it was not a fit place for a human being to live. So I decided to come here [the mainland] to learn, as well as to see what America was like." Others tried to leave but were unsuccessful: "Kim worked in the cane fields as the other men did. He hated it but worked extra hard because there was now another mouth to be fed. They called her Miriam. From the meager salary, wage rather, Kim and his wife (my mother) managed to save a little each month. They had hopes of leaving Hilo for the mainland. However, after staying a little over a year my mother's first husband developed a bronchial infection and died shortly after."[41]

The planters, in short, were being outbid for their labor, which had been difficult enough to get in the first place. Losing that labor to California only made the work situation more difficult. Ideas were floated on how to keep Koreans in Hawai'i. Planters who assumed that immigration from Korea would resume shortly wanted an end to the recruitment of single men, noting that "it is more difficult for them to leave and they prefer to remain at the plantation where they have families." Others in the HSPA complained about the exodus to Horace Allen in Seoul and asked him to pressure the Korean government to appoint "a good Korean consul here who would and could advise these people against going on to California. It is not for their advantage. True, there are a few months in the year when they get wages in excess of those to be earned here, but year in and year out they can do better here than in California."

Unfortunately for the planters, immigration did not resume, a consul was never appointed (providing Japan with an excuse to halt Korean emigration to Hawai'i), and Koreans continued to depart for California, with more than 450 departing in 1906. In 1907, the number dropped sharply to 150 only because President Theodore Roosevelt issued Executive Order 589 in March of that year prohibiting Japanese and Koreans in Hawai'i from moving to the mainland. With only a trickle moving thereafter, it is fair to say that the U.S. government did what the planters had not been able to do—stop the flow to the mainland. Between 1903, when the Koreans first arrived in Hawai'i, and 1907, when Roosevelt issued the Executive Order, about 1,100 Koreans left Hawai'i for the West Coast.[42] For the planters, what appeared to be the solution to their loss was dashed the following year, 1908, when Japan and the United States negotiated the Gentlemen's Agreement, effectively depriving the planters of immigrant labor from Japan (and Korea) and forcing them to turn to the Philippines in what would be the final major wave of labor immigration to Hawai'i, lasting until 1931.

Those who did not leave for California opted to return to Korea, in numbers slightly higher than the 1,100 who went to the West Coast. During 1903 and 1904, only 62 returned to their homeland; in 1905, 219 did so; in 1906, it was 336; and in 1907, 349—the highest number of returnees recorded. After 1907, the numbers began to decline; 105 in 1908, 134 in 1909, and only 55 in 1910, the year Japan annexed Korea. From 1911 through 1915, only 136 returned.[43] In all, around 1,300, or one-sixth of the total number of immigrants, returned to Korea.

Some returned to Korea because, having come as sojourners, they found life and work in Hawai'i too difficult and the promised riches only a dream. The son of one of those returnees said that his father, Chŏng Wŏn-jae, was a wanderer and a loafer who had come to Hawai'i in 1903 after reading a poster in Inch'ŏn. While in Hawai'i, he converted to Christianity, "but after eight years of hardship, decided it was too much for him." Others who returned to Korea did so simply because they were homesick. In 1906, a Korean newspaper ascribed such a motive to returning immigrants. And one writer estimated that about 60 percent of those who returned did so because of homesickness.[44]

Since only a small number returned to Korea, it is appropriate to ask if most Koreans saw themselves as better off in Hawai'i. Those who viewed immigration positively naturally spoke favorably on the issue. Such people included the planters; missionaries like Reverend George Heber Jones, Reverend S. F. Moore, and Homer Hulbert; and diplomats like Horace Allen and Yun Ch'i-ho. But their judgments must be viewed with caution and supplemented by the opinions of the immigrants themselves.

To support the hypothesis that most Koreans saw themselves better off in Hawai'i, despite their aversion to plantation work, one must look at quantitative measures of relative salary and cost of living indicators. These indicators, as cited by those who observed Koreans firsthand, tend to support the proposition that Koreans were better off, despite the fact that food and other essentials were more expensive in Hawai'i. For example, only nine months after the Koreans had begun arriving, and when the salary for an adult male was still only sixteen dollars a month, a plantation manager was amazed that one Korean had in such a short time earned enough for return passage to Korea and went on to comment on the financial rewards accruing to Koreans: "I learn from [the interpreter] Mr. An [Chŏng-su] that one of our Koreans is returning home to his parents, they desiring his return. He has, I understand, saved enough money to pay his passage. These men, I have ascertained, support themselves at a cost of from Four Dollars to Four Dollars and a half to the individual. This allows a considerable saving to them under the present wage rate, which must be to them munificent."

When Yun Ch'i-ho went on his inspection tour in the fall of 1905, he, too, found evidence of financial well-being: "Those who do work earn more than he could in Korea. A girl of fourteen in Wailua earned $14 a month. The laborers on the Ewa Plantation have more than a dozen of [bicycle] wheels. It made me mad to hear a big strong fellow whine that he could not make enough to pay his passage back." Even the Japanese government, which began to observe Koreans about fifteen years later, when food expenses in Hawai'i had reached thirteen or fourteen dollars a month, noted that the only Koreans suffering financially were those who had many family members unable to work, those who indulged in wasteful habits, or those who made excessive contributions to political causes.[45]

Another indicator of financial well-being was the accumulation of savings. Koreans began to make bank deposits almost immediately after arriving. Consider the letter from one plantation manager to a Honolulu bank: "Enclosed please find draft #687 drawn to your favor for one hundred and seventy five ($175.–) dollars, which kindly place to the credit of the following Koreans, under such terms as will give them the benefit of your highest interest: Chong Pil Ho $65, Yee Chin Pak $60 and Kim Chee Choon $50, and kindly forwarding to me deposit books." Yun Ch'i-ho also related a similar experience: "An elderly man has saved over $500—$400 in bank. Two other men are carrying about $300 in their pockets. I did my best to persuade the men to keep their savings in the bank or in the office."[46]

Remittances to immigrants' families in Korea was yet another indicator of financial comfort. S. F. Moore, the missionary in Korea who had supported immigration to Hawai'i, visited Koreans in Hawai'i in 1903. Moore noted that "[w]ages are $16 gold per month and although these men had been there but a few months they had money to send home. One man sent $25 (gold) to his wife, and a number sent smaller sums." Reverend George Heber Jones, the earliest supporter of Korean immigration to Hawai'i, made his own inspection in the winter of 1905–1906 and also commented on remittances: "Koreans are financially well-off. . . . Koreans sent a lot of money back to Korea." In Korea, former missionary Homer Hulbert, the editor of the *Korea Review* and another supporter of Korean immigration, wrote, "We learn recently the Koreans sent Yen 500 ($250) of their earnings home to Korea in a single draft." In fact, according to one estimate, by 1916 Koreans in Hawai'i had sent $50,000 back to Korea in the form of remittances.[47]

Koreans themselves painted a picture of financial security. A Korean interpreter observed as early as 1905: "My countrymen working here . . . spend $7 or $8 a month for board and are well satisfied. Their total expenses are not more than $10 a month. In Korea they never earn over $4 or $5 a month, and spend $2 or $3 for living. They spend more in Hawaii, but still are able to save more than at home." One Korean woman, who was paid less than a man on the plantation, analyzed her situation favorably in economic terms. When asked if she regretted coming to Hawai'i, she answered "No, it was better than Korea because in a month we could get rice, soy sauce, and if you needed anything, it eventually could be bought. . . . [I]n those days, we were paid 54 cents for ten hours of labor, but it was still better than Korea. There was no way to earn money there."[48]

If the evidence suggests that Koreans on the plantations were able to establish themselves financially, why, then, are there indications that poverty was one of the reasons Koreans were unhappy on the plantations? While it is true that plantation wages were meager, it was nonetheless possible for most Koreans to get by. Moreover, indications are that Koreans' unhappiness with the plantations was not so much because of wages, but because of the work and the working conditions. For those who had been farmers, there was little question that, even on the plantations, life in Hawai'i was better. In 1905, Reverend George Heber Jones asked one Korean if life in Hawai'i was more difficult; he received the following answer: "No, it is much easier than life on the farms in Korea. When at home we had to work from the first faint streaks of dawn until dark at night and yet the returns are pitifully small. Here everything is according to system. We have our daily assignments to work. They are accomplished long before sundown and we are then free to do as we like. Our work is planned out for us and working by system it becomes comparatively easy while the returns are astonishingly large."[49]

The small number of returnees to Korea and the evidence that most Koreans saw themselves as better off in Hawai'i suggest that most Korean immigrants were—or would soon become—settlers not sojourners who intended to remain in Hawai'i (although not necessarily on the plantations). If we compare the return rates of Koreans with the Chinese and Japanese, we find that half of the Chinese (23,000 out of 46,000) returned to China and more than half of the Japanese (98,000 out of 180,000) returned to Japan.[50] In sharp contrast, as already noted, only one-sixth of the Koreans returned to Korea. These statistics suggest that the Korean immigrant experience was significantly different from that of the Chinese and Japanese in that Koreans were more prone to be settlers.

There were two reasons for this. First, the Koreans were refugees from the chaotic conditions characterizing the final years of the Chosŏn dynasty. The Japanese, by contrast, had left a proud, nationalistic, and modernizing society, to which, if they were disappointed in the life Hawai'i offered, they could (and did) return in large numbers. The Koreans would have to think twice about doing the same. And even though they discovered that the streets of Hawai'i were not "paved with gold," most Koreans concluded that, despite the odious plantation system, conditions were superior to those they had left, a sentiment accurately captured by one planter who visited Korea: "I feel furthermore that as compared with the Japs they will be more permanent as they should have no home ties or at least should have none considering the way they are ground down at home, and the advantages they would enjoy in the Islands as compared with what they have at home should tend to make them a fixture."[51]

The second reason most Koreans became settlers rather than sojourners can be found in events in Korea. In 1905, Japan made Korea a protectorate; in 1910, it annexed Korea. As a result, many of the Korean immigrants felt stateless, stranded in Hawai'i and unwilling to return to a homeland controlled by Japan. Only a drastic change in the East Asian political situation—a Korea independent of Japan—could cause the Koreans even to consider returning. And since independence would take four decades, an early return to Korea was out of the question.

Because the Chinese and Japanese had the realistic option of returning to their homelands, they did not feel driven to succeed in Hawai'i. The Koreans, by contrast, were virtually forced to succeed in Hawai'i, since there was no going back. Unlike sojourners, who saw their future in their birthplace, the Koreans, as settlers, saw their future in Hawai'i. This settler mentality suggests that the Koreans were psychologically able to adapt more quickly than their sojourning counterparts from Japan and China. In short, the Koreans had no choice but to "make it" in Hawai'i.[52]

If the above analysis is correct, we should find evidence of the Koreans' rapid acculturation in Hawai'i at a relatively early stage. And indeed, such evidence is found in abundance, ranging from the mundane to the metaphysical. When Reverend George Heber Jones arrived in Hawai'i in 1905, he noted the change at once: "Koreans in Hawaii learned quickly. They had to learn what to wear and where to get it, what to eat and where to buy it and how to cook it." He concluded that "Koreans live well. They wear American clothing, eat American food, and act as much like Americans as they can." Another visitor from Korea in 1905, Homer Hulbert, came to a similar conclusion: "They do not sleep on the floor but have beds like Americans. . . . I saw no Koreans in native dress and coiffure, but all were clothed and groomed in good shape." Another observer noted: "It was a general opinion among plantation people that the Koreans spent more money the longer they remained in Hawaii, increasing their standard of living with longer residence. They buy American clothing and adopt American habits to some extent."

Korean attempts to learn American ways were also noted early on. One planter recalled: "Differing from other workers, hardly a day passed but one or another [Korean], dressed in his best, 'called' at my bachelor quarters after supper, just to talk. Their questions often stumped me, covering as they did current world events and the 'mores and manners' of Hawaii-nei. Being as I subscribed to Mainland and home papers, they toted the discards and undoubtedly read the lot." Koreans in Hawai'i even impressed observers with their growing facility in English. Horace Allen, speaking from his medical practice in Toledo, refuted the notion that Koreans were not intelligent: "As for being stupid, they learn English faster than either the Chinese or Japanese and are most faithful patrons of any school to which they may obtain entrance." Several decades later, one researcher concluded that first-generation Koreans generally spoke better English than either the Chinese or the Japanese, despite the fact that the latter two had been in Hawai'i longer.[53]

At a higher level, some observers, many of whom were familiar with turn-of-the-century Korea, found what they considered to be even more significant transformations occurring among the Koreans in Hawai'i, specifically regarding the basic issues of Korean character. At this time, from the Russo-Japanese War of 1904–1905 to Japan's annexation of Korea in 1910, the popular press and political leaders in the United States tended to characterize Korea and its people negatively. Not only did these reports persuade President Theodore Roosevelt that the Japanese takeover would benefit Korea, but they also propagated the notion that there were fundamental flaws in the Korean character. Perhaps the most influential of these writers was George Kennan, who briefly visited Korea and wrote two articles in *Outlook* in 1905 titled "Korea: A Degenerate State" and "The Korean People: The Product of a Decayed Civilization." In these articles Kennan depicted Koreans as stupid, dirty, lazy, disorganized, and dependent on others, and the Korean government as inept, oppressive, and corrupt. By contrast, Japan and the Japanese were shown in a much more positive light.

Were there, in fact, fundamental weaknesses in the Korean character? It is no exaggeration to say that at the turn of the century, Korea was ill-governed and that consequently Koreans were subject to calamity and oppression. Indeed, this was the primary reason Koreans left for Hawaiʻi in the first place. Faced with such a situation, it was perhaps a rational response for Koreans to appear lazy because, as Kennan observed, the Korean government "takes from the people, directly and indirectly, everything that they earn over and above a bare subsistence, and gives them in return practically nothing."[54] Thus it is not difficult to imagine how outsiders such as Kennan could form a negative opinion of Koreans and their character given their response to a corrupt government.

At the same time, however (albeit less well publicized), there existed evidence showing that Koreans were the equal of any other race. The key factor in this evidence appears to have been the environment, specifically residence outside Korea. Reports by the missionary Isabella Bird Bishop on Koreans who had emigrated to the Vladivostok region in Russia found them living clean, orderly, and prosperous lives and at the same time adapting quickly to the Russian Orthodox religion and becoming fluent in the Russian language. Similar reports surfaced about Koreans who had migrated to Manchuria in China.[55] Based on the reports, it is clear that Koreans simply required an environment in which they could fully utilize their abilities. Those who were familiar with Korea and its people quickly recognized that Hawaiʻi provided such an environment, and their words of praise for the Koreans there can be seen, in part, as a response to the negative views of the Korean character that predominated at the time.

One of these people, Reverend George Heber Jones, was quick to fix the blame on Korea for the Koreans' negative reputation: "It is the environment. In Korea was the oppressive weight of past tradition, language, association which anchors the Korean to the past." By contrast, he exulted, "The Korean in Hawaii seems like a different man. He is self-reliant and independent in character, better able to take care of himself and meet responsibility. . . . Upon arrival, he is lifted from this weight [of tradition]. In the new environment he is compelled to move, unlike in Korea. Ideals of industry, honesty, liberty, even-handed justice, generosity, and intellectual improvement abound. He is shaken away from old native ideals and philosophy. He also understands Western civilization better than the native Korean." Homer Hulbert wrote that "[t]hese Koreans [in Hawaii] are learning to be energetic, self-reliant, steady and thorough going. It can do them no harm and must do them good. In a few cases the results are harmful but they are so few that they do not count for much." Horace Allen said: "We have a few thousand of these people within our own gates—at Hawaii. They are liked much better than the Chinese or Japanese. They are sober, patient, hard working and industrious, and so frugal that in order to have money in [the] bank they are inclined to go without sufficient food."[56]

Koreans in Hawai'i also came to embrace Western concepts of time, order, and equality. According to their defenders, "In Korea, there is disorder, houses are built haphazardly." In the United States, by contrast, "there is order, where the hours of work are regulated, . . . everything is done according to plan, and the worker is paid on a fixed scale on a fixed day." And whereas in Korea one finds "the slow and easy life," in the United States, "[t]ime shortens. There are more things to do in less time, it seems. So the Korean in Hawaii learns that 'time is money.'" Moreover, in Confucian Korea, a hierarchical society was reinforced by levels of speech. But in Hawai'i, as Jones observed, there was a "change in language" in that Koreans "[n]ever use low language to each other" because "[t]hey know that in the sight of the law all are equal and a man who in Korea might be entitled to the highest consideration meeting in Hawaii a man of the lower class will address him in the highest forms of Korean speech. It would be risky for him to do otherwise."[57]

The above observations must be viewed with some caution, however, proferred as they were by those who were convinced of the rightness of immigration to Hawai'i, the innate worth of the Koreans as a race, and the superiority of American culture. To be sure, while there was obviously some measure of truth in their views, they are, to a certain degree, exaggerated and should not blind us to the fact that by no means did Koreans abandon all vestiges of traditional customs. In fact, evidence seems to suggest that acculturation was selective and that rapid adjustment to Western ways did not preclude the abandonment of traditional patterns of thought and behavior. The persistence of such traditional ideas would generate some friction several decades later, when the second generation arrived. At this juncture, as we look ahead to the future of the Korean community, it is not inappropriate to sketch out in a preliminary fashion some other attributes that point to sustained acculturation, adjustment, and, indeed, upward mobility in American society:

Koreans left plantation work faster than any of the other thirty-three ethnic groups in the history of Hawai'i.

After leaving the plantation, Koreans recorded one of the highest rates of urbanization of any ethnic group.

Second-generation Korean children stayed in school longer than any other ethnic group, including Chinese, Japanese, and Caucasian.

Second-generation Koreans recorded one of the highest rates of professionalization.

Both first- and second-generation Koreans exhibited more liberal and egalitarian attitudes toward social issues than Chinese or Japanese.

By the time the second-generation Koreans reached maturity in the 1960s and 1970s, they had achieved the highest per capita income and the lowest unemployment rate of any ethnic group in Hawai'i, including Caucasians.[58]

To explain how the Koreans came to exhibit these attributes, we need to go beyond the first point that the Koreans were psychologically prepared for rapid acculturation. To do so, we make use of two additional analytical tools—one supplied by sociologists who have studied the Korean community in Hawai'i, the other supplied by the characteristics and backgrounds of the immigrants themselves. Only by combining all three can we come up with a satisfactory explanation of Korean acculturation.

Sociologists at the University of Hawai'i who began looking at the Korean community in the 1930s provide the first tool. These social scientists tended to emphasize the small size of the Korean population in Hawai'i. They argue that, because the small Korean group necessarily interacted more frequently with other ethnic groups, they were under more pressure to conform to the prevailing modes of behavior, speech, and customs than would a larger group. The Japanese, on the other hand, could pass an entire day of activities using only the Japanese language, wearing Japanese clothes, buying Japanese goods, and meeting only Japanese people. Unlike the more numerous Japanese, the Koreans were unable to maintain a separate existence either on the plantations or, later, in the cities. As a result, they were forced to mingle frequently with other ethnic groups, resulting in more rapid acculturation. The small numbers of Koreans also helps explain why they would later have one of the highest rates of what the social scientists called "social disorganization." This disorganization included outmarriage, mental illness, suicide, divorce, juvenile delinquency, and criminal convictions.[59]

The "small size" theory contributes to the analysis of why Koreans adjusted so rapidly, but this theory is based exclusively on new-country (Hawai'i) conditions. Used by itself, the limitations of this model become apparent when viewing other small groups who immigrated to Hawai'i at about the same time, such as the Puerto Ricans, about a thousand of whom arrived in 1901. The Puerto Ricans exhibited rates of social disorganization similar to Koreans, but they did not exhibit marked rates of adjustment and upward mobility. To help explain the rapid adjustment of Koreans, we must also consider the background and characteristics of the immigrants, which, as shown above, differed from the Chinese and Japanese, as well as from the majority of Koreans in Korea.[60]

The background and characteristics of the Korea immigrants can help explain why Korean children continued in school longer than Chinese, Japanese, and Caucasian children and why they subsequently recorded one of the highest rates of professionalization. While all three East Asian nations traditionally had a high regard for education, we may speculate that the reason the second-generation Koreans had a superior record in school and higher rates in the professional ranks was the presence of many former students and lower-level clerks among the first generation. Their influence may have given added impetus to the generational transfer of aspirations and ability.

Koreans in Hawai'i also exhibited rapid changes in diet, dress, hairstyle, home furnishings, habits, and speech—in marked contrast to the Chinese and Japanese, who clung to their native dress, diet, habits, and language long after immigrating. While it is true that the small size of the Korean group put them under more pressure to conform to prevailing modes than a larger group like the Japanese, more needs to be said. Most Korean immigrants were from cities with considerable foreign influence, most notably from American missionaries; hence Western customs were not completely alien to them. On the other hand, most of the Japanese immigrants came from rural southwestern Japan, where foreign influence was minimal. In language acquisition, probably very few of the Chinese or Japanese immigrants could speak English when they arrived in Hawai'i. Among the Koreans, however, were a small but significant number who knew a little English, through either their training at mission schools or their association with Americans in urban Korea, giving them a distinct advantage in acquiring English skills.

I have already noted that the Koreans left the plantations faster than any other ethnic group in the history of Hawai'i and subsequently recorded one of the highest rates of urbanization there. The small size of the Korean population does not help us understand why this should be so, but the fact that most Korean immigrants were from the cities does indeed help explain why Koreans were anxious to live in the cities. Simply put, they were uncomfortable in a rural agricultural setting. This movement from the plantations to the cities (primarily Honolulu and Hilo) is another indicator of rapid adjustment, as Hawai'i, like much of the rest of the United States, was urbanizing at a rapid rate. Cities were seen as places where future opportunities lay. As Koreans realized that plantations sat on the lowest rung of the socioeconomic ladder in Hawai'i, they quickly left for a more urban setting, thereby effectively taking the first step toward upward mobility.

First- and second-generation Koreans also exhibited values and attitudes toward social issues that were markedly more liberal and egalitarian than those of the first- and second-generation Chinese and Japanese. One would not expect this, considering that Korea was perhaps the most traditional and conservative of the three East Asian countries. To be sure, this liberal attitude can be explained to some degree by the "small size" theory discussed above. A better explanation, however, lies in those attributes of the Korean immigrants themselves. First, unlike their countrymen and the immigrants from China and Japan, the urbanized Koreans, before their departure, had exhibited nontraditional, even iconoclastic, values by their adherence to Christianity, which preached equality before God, and their rejection of Confucian propriety. Second, and perhaps more important, was the diversity—in social, economic, geographical, and employment terms—of the Korean immigrants. Unlike the Japanese, who were a relatively homogeneous lot from southwestern Japan, or the Chinese, who came primarily from one region in Guangdong Province, the Koreans came from all over the Korean peninsula and from all walks of life. With differing accents, customs, and habits reflecting their diverse occupations and origins, their hallmark was their heterogeneity. This diversity made it difficult for an orthodox standard to be erected or maintained in Hawai'i, and promoted tolerance and liberal values, which were subsequently transferred to the second generation.

In sum, the Koreans quickly became aware that they were better off in Hawai'i than Korea due to economic considerations and because of the tragic political situation in their homeland; hence only a small fraction returned to Korea. Adopting a settler mentality, they began to adapt quickly to American society, aided by their small numbers and their characteristics, which distinguished them from other East Asian immigrants. Their record of rapid adjustment and mobility was unprecedented. To continue this journey, however, they had to leave the plantations and move into the cities.

3

Organization and Disorganization

Whereas 2,400 Koreans left Hawai'i either for California or to return to Korea, about 5,000 remained in Hawai'i. For them, the options were to stay on the plantations or leave them. For those who opted, at least initially, to stay, even though they were unhappy with the conditions, there were three choices: strike to force better treatment, move from plantation to plantation looking for better conditions, or simply not exert themselves.

The Koreans tended to be relatively more docile and less strike-prone than the Japanese, but there were exceptions. For example, in late 1903, a group of Koreans from the two plantations of Waiakea and Wainaku on the island of Hawai'i came to Honolulu to complain of ill treatment. The planters told them that there were no openings on Oahu and that they should return to Hawai'i, their fare being paid by the planters. In another incident in 1903, sixty-two Koreans "suddenly quit work" on Kilauea Plantation on the island of Kauai with the intention of going to Honolulu. In the spring of 1904, a "temporary disturbance" among Koreans was noted at the Laupahoehoe Plantation on Hawai'i in connection with the discharge of a Korean interpreter. Later that summer, two hundred Koreans on Waipahu Plantation on Oahu mobbed the plantation doctor because, they claimed, in an incident recorded earlier, he had killed an ailing Korean worker by kicking him in the stomach. At about the same time, in August 1904, Koreans struck twice on the Olaa Plantation on Hawai'i, complaining about a bad *luna,* although the manager dismissed their claims as "imaginary." In June 1905, 160 Koreans went on strike to protest the firing of 80 Koreans for beating a *luna* at Maui's Paia Plantation, resulting in the arrest of four of the leaders and a near riot. While troublesome, the planters did not view such activities with undue alarm, concluding that the Korean disturbances "have not had industrial import and are to be classed as riots rather than strikes."[1]

Why were the Koreans more docile and less likely to strike than the Japanese? One reason offered by an immigrant was their newly arrived status: "[W]e Korean immigrants did not protest against the inhumane treatment by the plantation owners because first, we did not know enough language to express our hardships to the superior, and second, we were always in fear of losing our jobs in case we complained against their treatment. Third, the interpreters and foremen had a tendency of taking sides with the plantation owners because they were paid well. Under these given circumstances, we thought that we were just helpless human beings in the white man's society."[2]

But the main reason the Koreans were more docile was that, having come from urban settings, they did not envision themselves on plantations in the long run and saw the low wages, poor working conditions, and limited opportunity for advancement as temporary inconveniences to be endured before moving on to the city, where they would be on more familiar ground. By contrast, the rural origins of the Japanese immigrants meant that most had few other job skills and thus saw plantation work as a long-term proposition—a perspective borne out by their relatively slow departure rate from the plantations. Naturally, they would be keenly interested in improving plantation working conditions, wages, and opportunities for advancement, for which strikes were the primary means of accomplishing these objectives.

Because the HSPA was still concerned that two-thirds of its labor force consisted of strike-prone Japanese, and because the Koreans were more docile and willing to be strikebreakers, the planters were able to overlook the fact that Koreans as a group were not particularly good field workers. As such, the planters endeavored to make Koreans better workers and to keep them on the plantations as a continued offset to the Japanese, particularly since it was not clear how Filipino immigration, which started in 1907, would turn out. At the same time, the Koreans were responding to their dissatisfaction with plantations in their own way: by moving from one plantation to another or, simply, idling away their time.

Koreans began to move from plantation to plantation seeking better conditions and more humane treatment. Many moved more than once. In fact, nearly one-third of the respondents to a survey indicated that they had moved to five or more plantations. One that seemed to attract Koreans was Ewa Plantation on the island of Oahu, which boasted a kindly manager, the first Korean Christian church, and proximity to Honolulu. It also had enough Koreans (five hundred by the fall of 1905) that it began to resemble a "normal" Korean community, with a sizable number of women and families. One immigrant recalled his own journey to Ewa Plantation: "Now, we who had just arrived from Pyongyang were still wearing our long traditional clothes. So, thus dressed and wearing woven shoes of dried grass, we went out to the fields to haul huge sacks. We labored there about four months. Then we heard about Ewa plantation which could be reached by boat, not far from Honolulu—they say about a thirty minute ride by train from Honolulu. We escaped and got to Ewa." But this is not to say that Koreans did not also leave Ewa, despite its advantages. As early as June 1904, Manager Renton of Ewa wrote to John Bull, the manager of Waipahu Plantation, asking, "Will you kindly let me know if any of our Koreans have left Ewa and obtained work at Waipahu, and, if so, how many?"[3] Clearly, such movement from plantation to plantation annoyed the managers, who never knew from one day to the next how many workers would be available.

Planters were also upset that many Koreans did not appear to work very hard. One told a Korean interpreter that "Koreans are lazy people; you have to whip them."[4] To be sure, we would expect a certain percentage of malingerers, given the urban profile of many of the immigrants who had come from Korea. Others were simply waiting until they felt secure enough to try their luck in the city. But since the Koreans were still seen as a necessary offset to the Japanese, the planters seized every opportunity to make them work harder, keep them from moving from plantation to plantation, and keep them from striking. The first opportunity came in September 1905, just two months after the last of the Koreans had arrived in Hawai'i, when Yun Ch'i-ho, the vice minister for foreign affairs of Korea, came on an inspection tour.

As soon as Yun arrived, he was inundated with manager complaints. On Makee Plantation, which had two Korean camps with about two hundred Koreans, "Fairchild [the manager] said the Koreans are the worst laborers he has." At Pacific Sugar Mill, which had 150 Koreans, Yun was informed by the manager that "[t]here is a Korean, No. 702, who is a habitual lay-offer, but Mr. Forbes dares not fire him, because he might cause a general exodus of his men." On Kekaha Plantation, Yun found "about ninety Koreans. Nearly thirty lay off every day. . . . [Manager] suggested the pass-book system to make the idlers among Koreans to work or to quit the country." Even other Koreans complained about this behavior: "Wherever I went, the complaint [by the Koreans] was not so much against the plantation managers as against the loafers among the Koreans." Another Korean remembered that "the plantation work was very hard work but some of the Koreans did not know how to work," adding wryly that "[s]ome of the Koreans were lazy and wanted to live without hard work."[5]

While Yun recognized that many Koreans were unhappy on the plantations and thus did not work very hard, he did not blame the planters. In fact, Yun saw much that he liked about the HSPA, "that solid and able body," and the plantation system during his month-long tour. He approved of the strict regimen: "While the Koreans complain that they have been too roughly treated, their compulsory work helped them to earn money," and he also recommended a passbook system "to compel the loafers to work or quit." Yun even quoted the scriptures in expressing his disdain for loafers: "[Koreans] have found written over the islands the eternal truth uttered by St. Paul, 'If any would not work, let him not eat.' Between the broad Pacific on one hand and starvation on the other, even a Korean has to work." Clearly, Yun was squarely on the side of the planters in their dealings with Koreans, as evidenced by his final report to the planters on the day he departed for Korea: "Mr. Yun stated that he had visited all the Plantations where there are Koreans and that he found that the Koreans were well treated by the managers; that complaints among the Koreans are not against the plantations or the managers, but that they had complained to him of a bad class among their own people."[6]

During his tour, Yun concluded that the poor work habits of the Koreans were the result of defects in their character. "It interests and pains me to learn that some of the characteristics of the Kanaka (native Hawaiian) are those of Koreans (1) Good nature (2) Hospitality—I am told a Kanaka lives upon his more fortunate friend or relative until the latter goes broke. They then move into another fellow's hut and sponge on him until he gets bankrupt, and so on. (3) Laziness. A Kanaka would not work unless he is compelled by hunger. Then he works for a few dollars and as long as that lasts he is happy and lazy again."[7] Given his attitude, Yun's solution lay not so much in changing the plantation work system, but by transforming the character of the Koreans themselves.

Yun's attempts to make the Koreans contented, hard-working plantation hands took the form of lectures on the Protestant work ethic and good old-fashioned values. At Ewa Plantation, Yun advised the Koreans to be "industrious, clean, steady, faithful." On a plantation on Maui, Yun found "[a]bout 200 Koreans in two camps, Kaanapali and Lahaina [and] [g]ave them necessary exhortations." On another plantation, Yun told one hundred Koreans at the Christian Chapel "[t]hat they should teach the more ignorant brethren in the plantations the habit of industriousness, of thriftiness, of cleanliness, and of steadiness." On the island of Hawai'i, Yun "admonished the Koreans not to wander around from one plantation to another." He also "advised the Koreans not to strike as their inefficiency as workmen and the smallness of their number would cause the managers no inconvenience if they all struck."[8]

Naturally, Yun's message had the enthusiastic support of the planters. At the Makaweli Plantation on the island of Kauai, one eyewitness recalled that Yun arrived "in the plantation manager's wagon. When he arrived, the plantation company received him as a[n] honor[ed] guest. All the Koreans were called in from cane fields to honor and hear him in the Korean church there. More than 300 Koreans stood in line to pay him respects. When Baron Yun came to the church, he sat in the pulpit and spoke to the audience about half an hour. The essence of his speech was three-fold: 1. Act kindly to the plantation managers and win their hearts; 2. Stay on one plantation calmly and do your best for your work by studying how to grow the sugar; 3. Save all you can and come back to your fatherland." While the planters may have enjoyed hearing Yun wax eloquent on the virtues of hard work, it is not at all clear that the Korean workers in the audience reacted the same way. One researcher who interviewed some who had listened to Yun concluded, somewhat hopefully, that "they came to be serious minded about their work and their country's fate." But another dismissed Yun's lectures as "haranguing and admonishing the Koreans in the manner of the officials of old Korea," and even Yun himself noticed that his Korean audiences were sometimes "not very attractive or attentive."[9]

Despite all the efforts of Yun and the planters, most Koreans remained dissatisfied with plantation life and work. Moreover, as a largely bachelor community, their lackadaisical attitude toward the work was often accompanied by activities suggesting a lack of cohesion in the Korean community. Leading the list was excessive drinking, but gambling, fighting, sexual assault, and embezzling were also included. Although the planters usually did not concern themselves with what went on after working hours, others, including some Koreans, Christian clergy, and Yun, did, either because of the moral dilemmas these activities posed or because they disrupted normal life on the plantations.

Numerous reports surfaced about such problems. One report on Koreans stated, "No complaint was made of their using opium, but they are fond of intoxicating liquor, and occasionally have a lively time after payday." Sundays also presented a problem. While Christians (and others) went to church, often because there was nothing else to do, others spent their Sundays drinking (to "drown their sorrows") and gambling, one immigrant recalling that "[n]on-Christians just sang 'Arirang,' played the 'Canggu' (Korean Drum), or drank wine bought from Japanese wine shops." One worker, a Mr. Kim, remembered that "the general spirit of a Korean community during the first few years was much like that of a mining camp—boisterous, happy-go-lucky, high feeling of fellowship, drinking, gambling and careless generosity." A Korean interpreter who witnessed this behavior offered reasons for, and consequences of, such behavior: "The ignorant lower people who had been restrained by a tyrannical [Korean] regime became self-indulgent and did not respect their elders when they came to a free world. Many of them were often disorderly under the influence of alcohol and fights occurred continuously on every plantation where Koreans worked. This led to mistreatment by the managers and led other people to despise them. It also made it difficult to earn money through steady work." [10]

Sometimes conditions degenerated to a point that the plantation managers had to act. "When he [Yun] reached the Kekaha plantation company, [he] was appealed to by the managers to admonish the Koreans there. They complained that the Koreans there had been habitual drunkards and damaged the plantation company properties very often. Baron Yun, after giving a long lecture to the Koreans, told them to behave themselves as if they were the representatives of Korea in Hawaii. If any Korean be found again drunken, drown him in the name of Korea." One incident, somewhat embellished, tells of another frustrated manager: "Concerning the unruly and disorderly manners of some of the Korean immigrants, . . . the rumor was not groundless. Many of the Korean immigrants were recruited from among an uneducated, poor class of Koreans. Most of them lived in Korea as wandering vagabonds. They did not like to work at one place, and yet they came to Hawaii out of curiosity and adventure. Most of them could not stand the unbearable hot weather in the cane fields. Many of them made attempts to escape. On one occasion, some fifty Korean immigrants on the Kilauea Plantation, Kauai, were taken by order of the company to the uninhabited mountains by night on the charge that they were vagrants and drunkards. They were taken by rail and left there to die. However, they all reached Kealia, Kauai, on foot next day, some thirty miles away from Kilauea."[11]

Moreover, because Korean plantation society was largely made up of bachelors, the few married women and their teenaged daughters inevitably faced the risks of sexual assault. One interviewer noted, "Most of the 6,000 single and unmarried Koreans were young and unfamiliar with cultured life. There was need of protecting the 600 families. Drunkenness and unruly manners among these unmarried Koreans had to be defended against. Peace and order in the Korean camps or villages on each plantation were of primary concern for them." One immigrant put it bluntly: "Koreans were ignorant and made many problems for women." And a nineteen-year-old woman remembered her parents warning her that "[i]nasmuch as I was a teenager, I was told to stay away from the 'bad' plantation workers."[12]

Problems among the Korean community seemed particularly acute on the island of Hawai'i, where, according to Yun, the Christian presence was weaker than on the other islands. His diary is replete with disparaging references to the Koreans he met there. "After dinner [on Kohala Plantation, I] went to the church where nearly 200 Koreans were gathered. . . . The crowd struck me as rather rowdy." At another camp on that plantation he wrote: "This being the Kohala district, the centre of disaffection and of anti-Christian agitations, I had to take special pains to advise, to reprove and to warn the people." On Makee Plantation, Kapaa Camp, Yun "addressed a very disorderly, discontented and dirty looking crowd, at 8 p.m. I am told Kapaa is a regular rendezvous for loafers, gamblers and roughs of every description."[13]

The Korean community on Hawai'i (and to a lesser extent on the other islands) also had its share of card sharks, ripoff artists, and embezzlers—harbingers of what would later be termed "white-collar crime." One Korean recalled, "Moral conditions were bad. A group gambled beside a sick man's pillow." Yun railed against "[t]hese parasites [who] go from one camp to another, carrying a pack of cards and with it disorganization and demoralization," and concluded that this behavior "would be injurious to the Koreans who are already in the islands and disgraceful to Korea." In another instance, Yun noted in his diary that "Horner [Kukaiau's manager] told me there used to be a bad egg who organized a society among the Koreans for the purpose of finishing $2 from every man who worked more than the laziest. The rascal was expelled from the camp and the trouble ceased." Another entry notes that "Kim Kyu Sup, who is now in jail for having embezzled some money belonging to a society now defunct, is another [bad egg]." Finally, Yun wrote: "There are three Korean young men located in the town of Hilo. [One of them is] Kim Moon Sung, who acts as interpreter in the court. . . . Kim Moon Sung is a regular scamp. He tells lies by the years without the least efforts. He served his terms three times in the Hilo jail. He pretends to speak Japanese, Russian and English. He cheated an old man out of over a hundred dollars. The old man, Moon Suk Yong, begged me to get back the money for him. I asked the young fellow about it, but he denied that he had ever touched a cent of the old man's money. As I am just passing through here without any power of law in my hand I had to quietly drop the whole subject, hoping to see the sheriff of the town about it." The next day, Yun found the opportunity to report the case: "Before leaving the town at 9 a.m. for the S.S. Kinau I saw the Deputy Sheriff, Mr. Fetter, and asked him to help the old man to get the money back from the scamp, Kim Moon Sung."[14]

Reverend John W. Wadman, the superintendent of the Hawaiian Mission of the Methodist Episcopal Church, accompanied Yun and confirmed his observations. "I made an extensive tour of this large Island [Hawaiʻi] some weeks ago with Hon. T. H. Yoon, Vice-Minister of Foreign Affairs, and had a fine opportunity of inspecting the conditions of the 3,500 Koreans scattered over more than a dozen plantations, stretching over the entire eastern coast, a distance of over one hundred miles. The Koreans on Hawaii are in a very needy condition and fearfully immoral influences prevail among them. Gambling and drinking are common practices. The camps are infested with ring-leaders in all bad things, so that as laborers they have lost caste among the managers and their reputation is very bad indeed."[15] Partly as a result of his tour with Yun, Wadman would soon play a leading role in spreading Christianity among the Koreans.

Yun and Wadman saw Christianity as the solution to this moral breakdown —a logical conclusion given Yun's own Christian views and his training at Vanderbilt University's seminary. By Yun's reckoning, those Koreans who were Christians or who worked on plantations where there was a strong Christian presence were more content, better behaved, and law-abiding. Many of Yun's speeches to Koreans were held, appropriately, in Christian chapels on the plantations. Yun wrote approvingly in his diary that on Kahuku Plantation, "Hyon Soon, the son of Hyon Jei Chang, is their preacher." On Makawili Plantation on the island of Maui, where he addressed 390 Koreans, Yun noted: "Christian element strong hence more orderly. The people seemed contented." And he was pleased to observe at Union Mill Plantation that "[t]he people—about thirty—seemed contented and said that the [anti-Christian] agitators had not been tolerated in their camp."[16]

Homer Hulbert, the missionary publisher from Korea who came to Hawaiʻi on the heels of Yun's 1905 visit, tended to be more optimistic about Korean character than Yun. Hulbert thought the problem was limited to a handful of ne'er-do-wells who took advantage of the naïveté of the average Korean: "With very few exceptions the Koreans are quiet and well behaved people. There is a small gang of ten or twelve in Honolulu who are exerting a bad influence. They draw in the unsophisticated Korean from the Plantation and get him to drinking and gambling." Naturally, he approved of Yun's efforts: "Hon. T. H. Yun, who was sent from Korea to look after the interests of the Koreans here, has just finished his investigations and has returned to Korea. He spent several weeks travelling about visiting every group of Koreans and making excellent speeches which did much to encourage and strengthen the Koreans in their fight against fortune. In every place he consulted with the managers of the companies as to the needs of the Korean and there can be no doubt at all that his visit will result in great good."[17]

Although Yun did what he could during his month-long tour, his moralizing was no match for the widespread disorder that plagued the Korean community. Plantation managers generally took a hands-off approach, and the long arm of the law seldom extended deep into the plantation camps. And while the Christian element, already substantial, would continue to grow, that approach was at best a long-term solution. In the short run, creating order among the Koreans on the plantations fell mainly to the Koreans themselves, as they could best recognize and deal with the threat to peace and tranquility in their daily lives. Their solution was an attempt to recreate some of the self-governing organizational structures with which they were familiar in Korea. As they experimented with these organizations, various permutations and offshoots developed. The organizations ran the gamut from law-and-order and mutual-aid types to nascent political ones. Those who led these organizations were Christians, those with families, and those who had been farmers in Korea. Farmers in particular were involved because they had lived in villages and thus were familiar with the village-style organizations that would become the prototype, and because they were most likely to remain on the plantations for a longer period of time. Consequently, they had a vested interest in organizing a stable community.

Because the farmers among the Korean immigrants were accustomed to the rigors of agricultural work, they tended to be among the few hard working and relatively contented individuals on the plantations. One immigrant recalled, "It was hard work, but some Korean farmers thought that plantation work was easier than working in the native Korean farm fields, because the plantation owners supplied all necessary tools to do the job." Bernice Kim, in doing research in the 1930s, concluded that "[t]he Korean farmers who came to Hawaii worked well and steadily in the fields. Others were not particularly fit for plantation type of work." And while previous farming experience helps to explain success on the plantation, it was still possible for those without a farming background to succeed: "After leaving Korea, Mr. Kim came to Honolulu in the year 1903. From here, he was sent to [the island of] Hawaii as a laborer. At first the plantation work was too much for him for he had never worked in the fields, but through sheer determination, he soon became a skilled worker and for his personality and his name, he was respected by all."[18]

These relatively few former farmers received accolades from the plantation managers and *lunas*. At Union Mill Plantation, Yun recorded: "Head *luna*

pleased with his Koreans. He said 'Oh, the Koreans are awful good workmen.'"
Speaking with the manager of Hakalau Plantation, Yun noted that "Mr. Ross is
well pleased with the Koreans. He said they excel in cutting and loading." Manager Horner of Kukaiau Plantation told Yun that "in 25 years of his experience
he has not seen better workmen than the Koreans. Of the 60, from 40 to 55 go
to work every day." On Niulii Plantation, "Mr. Hall [the manager] has about
thirty Koreans with whom he is well pleased. The people seem to be contented." The manager (McLain) of Koloa Plantation told Yun that "the Koreans are better workmen than Japanese when the latter first came; that the
Koreans learn quicker to handle teams and machines than the Japanese; and
that he has had no trouble with Koreans so far, nor does he expect any." On
Koloa, Yun "[a]ddressed an orderly and contented crowd of Koreans, who
spoke kindly of the manager." [19] The ex-farmers were the ones to take the lead
in organizing Korean community life on the plantations.

Any Korean camp with enough people organized a *tonghoe,* or village council. At one such camp, members were assessed an initiation fee of one dollar
plus membership fees of fifteen cents each month. The *tonghoe* elected a *tongjang,* or headman, by a vote of all qualified adult males—qualifications being
based on such things as age, education, upright conduct, honesty, and sincerity. On some plantations, there was no fixed term for the *tongjang,* who could
be removed by popular vote if he proved to be unsatisfactory; on other plantations, the *tongjang* was elected once a year. The *tongjang,* who received no
salary, acted as judge in all disputes, saw that the rules and regulations were
observed, and meted out fines and punishment to offenders. Visitors to the
camp first had to call on the *tongjang.* And the *tongjang* also endorsed newcomers from other plantations for work to the manager of their plantation.
What made the *tonghoe* a particularly Korean-style organization was its emphasis on age and its exclusion of women from active participation. Below the
tongjang was the *sachal,* or sergeant-at-arms, who acted as chief of police and
who was chosen for his physical attributes. Assisting the *sachal* were the
kyŏngchal, or police. The *sachal* and *kyŏngchal* kept order at meetings and
brought rule breakers in front of the *tongjang* and *tonghoe.* The *sachal* would
also go to neighboring camps after 9 P.M. in search of Koreans who should have
already returned to their plantation.

Regulations and penalties were determined at mass meetings. At Kahuku
Plantation, for example, the *tonghoe* came up with the following: "For the welfare of fellow Koreans, we organized a self-ruling association. The rules were
as follows: (1) Strengthen love of fellowship. (2) Respect and protection of
ladies. (3) Prohibition of gambling, drinking liquor, and no allowance to the
camp by any suspicious women." Other camps included prohibitions against
drunkenness, fighting, gambling, and illicit sexual relations. Penalties included
warnings, fines, floggings, being placed in stocks, and, as a last resort, banishment for repeat offenders. Koreans were fined one dollar for drunkenness,

whereas drunken brawling and gambling in Japanese or Chinese camps drew a five-dollar fine. One eyewitness reported that an unfortunate Mr. Ch'oe was put in the stocks and flogged for his "habitual drunkenness and disorderly conduct." If a man were the instigator of an "affair," and if it was his first offense, he would be fined three dollars. A subsequent similar offense would result in flogging and banishment from the camp. If a woman were guilty of having an affair, she and her husband were asked to leave the camp. If offenders thrown out of the camp had no money, they were given traveling expenses.[20]

The efforts of the *tonghoe* met with success, and soon nearly all plantations with Koreans had them. Interpreter Hyŏn Sun noted that "the morale of Korean villages became better gradually. As these types of self-regulations proliferated everywhere, Korean wanderers decreased." The *tonghoe* also made certain plantations more attractive to Christian Koreans with families. "The news about our self-ruling Kahuku Korean camp was spread all over Hawaii. Many married Koreans came to the Kahuku Camp. The outstanding persons I still remember are mostly Christian families from Pyung Yang." As further evidence of the *tonghoe*'s success in maintaining law and order, "the local authorities tacitly recognized the self-government of the Koreans in each camp, for they generally accepted what the Koreans had done among themselves whenever any lawbreakers were dealt with."[21]

After a few years, as the troublemakers left the plantations and the need for maintaining law and order diminished, some *tonghoe* began to take on mutual-aid responsibilities where "[t]he purpose was to help each other in case of difficulties and to share happiness or misery." In some camps, all the money from dues and fines was pooled monthly and allocated for educating children, food for the sick, celebrating traditional Korean holidays (when the rules against drinking were suspended), and passage for invalids back to Korea.[22] The addition of mutual-aid functions represented growing organizational sophistication for the *tonghoe*, but they were by no means the only organizations that provided a form of mutual aid.

Another organization that was created during the early stages of the Korean plantation experience and that coexisted with the *tonghoe* was the sworn brotherhood. Sworn brotherhoods began as mutual-aid organizations and, like the *tonghoe,* evolved as circumstances changed. Sworn brotherhoods originally promoted such things as group unity and working for mutual benefit. Its origins stemmed from the natural feelings of group solidarity that developed in new and often difficult surroundings. "Each looked upon another Korean as a brother or a sister and the esprit de corps was admirable; it was one for all and all for one." This feeling was translated into rendering assistance, both morally and financially, to ailing fellow Koreans. It also guaranteed that Koreans who moved from plantation to plantation seeking better conditions were welcomed: "From whatever place or plantation a Korean may have come, he was always welcomed and warmly received in any other Korean camp."[23]

Sworn brotherhoods also provided protection from other races on the plantations. This might occur "[a]ny time a Korean was embroiled in trouble with someone of another nationality, [or] if he had been unjustly treated or beaten." Thus "[i]f any of the sworn brothers had quarrels with any foreigners, all the brothers became one in unity to help him." One former member of a sworn brotherhood "had fifty sworn brothers, and all the brothers came to help in time of need." However, sometimes this "help" led to brawls: "men of the entire camp would get together and demand satisfaction which usually took the form of a mob fight. These fights could be stopped only by the plantation police force." Even when there was a possibility that the Korean was wrong, "should there be a shadow of a doubt, all would go out to fight, regardless, because a Korean was in trouble."[24]

More often than not, the Japanese were the targets of these group attacks. Incidents such as the following, headlined in the newspaper as "A Wily Jap Got the Koreans' Cash," could mobilize a sworn brotherhood into action:

Twenty-four Koreans working at Waipahu have about come to the conclusion that a crowd of Koreans can make a good deal of trouble when their money is taken. The Koreans the other day each intrusted $12 to the care of a Japanese *luna* who, it is said, bore an excellent reputation. Notwithstanding his good name the Japanese disappeared from the plantation Sunday evening with the $288 and was supposed to have come to Honolulu. When the luna did not appear for work on Monday morning the Koreans held a council of war and a man was sent to inform the police of the affair. Officers were sent to the various coastwise steamers as it was thought that the man would probably try and get away to the other islands. A special officer was also sent down the railway. At one of the stations yesterday afternoon he came across part of the crowd of Koreans who were setting upon a Jap and fast doing him up. The officer interfered and the Koreans claimed that the Japanese they were beating was the man who robbed them of their money. The fellow was therefore brought to Honolulu last evening and lodged in jail pending the investigation which the police are making.[25]

Sworn brotherhoods sometimes also specifically targeted Japanese after the establishment of the protectorate in 1905, when some Japanese began to assume an air of superiority over the Koreans. According to one Korean, "They [the Japanese] always looked down on us. It usually irritated our pride. Besides, we Koreans had short tempers." Another Korean recalled that "Koreans hated working with the Japanese on the same plantations, but occasionally the foremen ordered everybody to work together in order to get the work done at one time. Often fist fights took place between Japanese and Koreans. Most of the time Koreans won the fight, because many Koreans were ex-soldiers who knew how to subdue the enemy." And many sworn brotherhood members began to think politically: "Some ex-soldiers [in the sworn brotherhood] wanted to return to Korea in order to clean up the pro-Japanese Korean leaders in Seoul." As Japan's hold over Korea tightened, the Japanese consul-general in Honolulu advised his countrymen to avoid Koreans.[26]

While the sworn brotherhood possessed certain admirable traits such as group solidarity, mutual aid and protection, and protonationalism, it had negative qualities as well. For one, it certainly did not promote interethnic harmony. And it ironically became a vehicle for factionalism and division within the Korean community. For example, the sworn brotherhood sometimes undermined the *tonghoe* in its efforts to maintain law and order. In the case of a mob fight between sworn brothers and foreigners in which the Korean was obviously wrong, the *tongjang* levied a heavy fine upon the offender, who "resented punishment inflicted by an outsider."[27] That the *tongjang* was considered an "outsider" by members of the sworn brotherhood indicates that at times the two organizations competed for influence.

Another negative trait of the sworn brotherhood was the appearance of regionalism. One writer concluded that Koreans "later forgot their primary objectives of protecting the mutual interests of their fellow countrymen, because they could not transcend the narrow scope of localism. Those from the same localities in Korea cliqued together and became a source of weakness for Korean societies." Another early observer acknowledged that "[a] North and South sectionalism was still evident among Koreans from those parts." This regionalism sometimes caused sworn brotherhoods to degenerate into warring gangs whose enemies were no longer foreigners, but other Koreans instead. "The scope of these sworn brotherhoods included merely mutual protection from foreigners at first, but later on the scope was further extended to resistance to all those not belonging to their own brotherhood." Even the planters observed that, concerning riots, "[i]n the case of Koreans, these troubles have been in nearly all cases entirely among themselves."[28]

Besides the *tonghoe* and sworn brotherhood, a third organization appeared that would dominate the Korean community for the next four decades: political societies that focused primarily on Korea and its fate. The establishment of nationalist societies represented a certain degree of organizational sophistication and maturity as the concerns of the Korean community began to spread beyond the more mundane problems of law and order, mutual aid, and protection to issues touching on international relations. As further evidence of increasing organizational sophistication, these political societies attempted to centralize control and overcome the fragmented *tonghoe* and sworn brotherhoods, which were dispersed among the dozens of plantations on four islands. Like the other organizations, however, these nascent political organizations also suffered from factionalism.

Factionalism was not new to the Korean political experience, as it was one of the key reasons for the decline of the Chosŏn dynasty. In describing Korean political culture, many scholars of Korea—as well as Koreans themselves—

have commented on factionalism. It is not surprising, then, that Koreans identified factionalism as an obstacle to the unity of political organizations in
Hawai'i. The interpreter Hyŏn Sun commented, "The causes of we Koreans'
downfall may be many. But the one which is chronic that cannot be cured even
with mysterious doctor and medicine is the 'difficult-to-gather and easy-to-
disperse' syndrome." Yun Ch'i-ho noted that "[t]rue to their national characteristic, the Koreans in Hawaii . . . are divided among themselves."[29] A look at
the first openly political organization among the Koreans in Hawai'i, the Sinminhoe, illustrates these factional struggles and serves as an introduction to
subsequent organizational efforts.

The Sinminhoe was founded on August 7, 1903. One of the founders, Hyŏn
Sun, recalled the circumstances: "All the outstanding young Koreans from all
the islands were gathered in Honolulu under the leadership of Hong Sung Ha
[Hong Sŏng-ha]." While its purpose was "to educate Koreans in Hawaii and to
seek common interests through commercial activities," it is clear from Hyŏn's
description of the first meeting that concerns about the decline of Korea were
paramount: "After discussing the dangerous situation in Korea, we organized
the Shin Min Hoi, or the new people's society." By the time the first branch of
this organization was established on Kauai in December 1903, the purpose had
become clearly political: "to rebuild Korea with regenerated people at home
and abroad." Another source states, "Its purposes were to promote . . . reform
of the home government." Almost immediately, however, factional problems
arose to render the Sinminhoe ineffective. Hyŏn obliquely hints at that when
he complained that the organization was begun only "after great difficulties."[30]

First, factionalism within the Sinminhoe was driven in part by denominational disputes between Methodists and non-Methodists. Most of the Koreans
who had been Christians before coming to Hawai'i were converted by American Presbyterian missionaries. But since the Presbyterian Church did not have
a presence in Hawai'i, the majority of the Korean Christians chose the Methodist Church, while a smaller number affiliated themselves with the Episcopal
Church. And still other Koreans considered themselves Buddhists. Several of
the founders of the Sinminhoe, including Hyŏn Sun and Hong Sung-ha, were
closely associated with the Methodist Church. Hong, for instance, had, since
March 1903, collaborated with the Methodist minister George L. Pearson to
publish the first Korean newspaper in Hawaii, the *P'owa Hanin kyobo*
(Hawaiian-Korean news), which was sold at churches on Sundays.[31]

A minority faction consisting of Buddhist and Episcopal members arose
against the mostly Methodist leadership of the Sinminhoe. This anti-Methodist
opposition faction launched their own newspaper, the *Sinjo sinmun* (New tide),
published twice a month from March 1904 until April 1905, "spreading slan-
der" and "reporting always the quarrels between this and that man or between
this and that denomination," according to Yun Ch'i-ho. Yun felt that, instead,
"the little paper *Sinjo sinmun* . . . should devote its columns to instructing the

people in matters useful to them, such as the history of the Islands, the use of banks, etc." He was well aware of the denominational dispute that spawned the rival group and its newspaper. As his diary records, "When I got through [talking], the [Episcopal] Bishop [Restarick] had the very bad taste to ask me to interpret for him. As my refusal would give a cue to the crowd to start an anti-Episcopal feeling I quietly consented." Supportive of Christian unity, Yun "told the Koreans among other things . . . [t]hat Christians should not quarrel over denominational questions."[32]

A second issue that split the Sinminhoe was a dispute over repayment of Korean immigrants' boat fare to Hawai'i. The planters had paid their passage in violation of American immigration laws, but it is unclear whether the Koreans were responsible for repaying it. In 1904, A. W. Taylor, an employee of the recruiter David Deshler, arrived in Hawai'i demanding that Koreans repay him for the passage money. The opposition faction supported repayment, but the Sinminhoe leadership instructed Koreans not to give Taylor any money in view of the difficult life they endured on the plantations. When Taylor went to plantations trying to collect, he was threatened by the Koreans; at Ewa Plantation he was beaten, and eight Koreans were charged with assault. The case was later brought to trial, but since Taylor disappeared, the case was dropped. Nonetheless, "the wrangling among the Korean community continued as before."[33]

Third, the Sinminhoe suffered from what one of its founders termed "corruption of executives." Yun Ch'i-ho noted in his diary that one leader, Kim Kyu-sup, "is now in jail for having embezzled some money belonging to a society [the Sinminhoe] now defunct." Kim, according to Yun, was one of "a nasty viperous gang of bad eggs at the head of which stand Yu Han Yung, Kim Ik Sung, and Choi Yung Man." Yun's diary indirectly gives some indication of how Kim embezzled the money from the Sinminhoe when he warned Koreans "[t]hat collections should not be levied on the people for this and that and other undertakings without being able to carry any one single project in to satisfactory effect."[34]

The fourth and most salient reason for the Sinminhoe's troubles came when it proclaimed its political agenda. Since it had been formed, at least in part, as a result of the "dangerous situation in Korea," and since it espoused reform of the home government, questions of loyalty to that government were raised and became the source of factional disputes. The opposition faction seized upon the fact that the Sinminhoe leadership used the more modern democratic word "citizens" (simin) rather than the traditional term "subjects" (sinmin) in referring to themselves. It also noted that Hong Sung-ha, in his desire to promote the reform of the Korean government, had gone so far as to draw up a shadow government with Sŏ Chae-p'il (Philip Jaisohn) as prime minister and Yun Ch'i-ho as foreign minister, creating the impression that the Sinminhoe wanted to overthrow the current government and replace it with this "provisional government."[35]

Yun castigated Hong as a "fool" for having put together this list "in fun" and noted that the opposition faction, led by Kim Kyu-sup, used this issue to fan the fires of factionalism. "Kim Kyu Sup and his gang saw their chance in this and denounced Hong and his friends as conspirators or yŏkjŏk [traitors]." The opposition faction used the occasion to form the Ch'ungŭihoe (Loyalists Society) and dubbed the Sinminhoe the Yŏkjŏkhoe (Traitors Society). Another opposition leader, Kim Ik-sŏng, then attempted to take a contingent of supporters from the island of Hawai'i to Honolulu to "punish the conspirators." Yun commented that "[t]hese wretches are worthy imitators of the Peddlers and other rascals who got money and office by informing His Majesty [Emperor Kojong] against imaginary traitors."[36]

This brouhaha over the alleged "provisional government" gave rise to a rumor that Yun's 1905 visit to Hawai'i was not, in fact, to inspect the living and working conditions of Koreans on the plantations, but rather to ascertain whether these Koreans were planning to overthrow the Chosŏn dynasty. The rumor was started because, for one, the opposition faction within the Sinminhoe supposedly reported these "traitorous activities" to the Korean government. Moreover, because many Koreans, including those in the Sinminhoe, were dissatisfied with Korea's corrupt politicians, they condemned the government, using their newly gained freedom of speech. As a result, rumors circulated in Korea that the Koreans in Hawai'i had indeed established a provisional government and were attempting to overthrow the current government. The Korean government thus supposedly became concerned enough to send Yun to investigate under the pretext of inspecting the plantations, while actually trying to flush out traitors.[37]

In fact, Yun was worried not about traitors, but that the linking of "traitorous" behavior with Christianity would serve to discredit Christianity. "As most of Hong's associates were or are professing Christians, Kim [Kyu-sup] and Yu [Han Yung] have been actively stirring up bad feelings among the Koreans that the Christians are plotting to overthrow the Korean government." Earlier, Yun had characterized Kim and Yu as "a brood of vipers . . . living on meanness and treachery," and continued: "As the word 'traitor' or yokjok has the most hateful and dreadful associations in the mind of the Korean, and as the youthful vipers have been circulating the report or lie that all those who return to Korea from the Islands are imprisoned or decapitated, a sort of panic has seized the ignorant people. Kim and Yu have associated [with] Cho Dal-gu, etc. professional gamblers, going about among the Koreans in the Kohala district, stirring up the people against Christians and other comparatively more decent fellows."[38]

Yun did his best to stifle this factional dispute, telling a Korean audience that "the word 'traitor,' or 'Yuk-Juk,' has been used by wicked men during the last ten years to kill patriotic men and to purchase the imperial favor for selfish ends; that these so called loyal men, but real traitors, have brought Korea

to the present state of degradation and desolation; that whoever calls another
Korean a traitor or conspirator against the government is himself worse than
any traitor can be; that those who try to injure their fellow countrymen by digging this damnable pitfall are vipers, and that whoever carries about in his person a list of ministerial candidates in order to accuse someone of [a] treason-
able plot are themselves the most dastardly cowards and traitors and liars."[39]

As a result of this infighting, the Sinminhoe disintegrated in the spring of
1904, and the personalities associated with it went their separate ways. The
president, Hong Sŏng-ha, returned to Korea, his religious and publishing activities being taken over by Reverend Yun Pyŏng-gu. Yun started publication of
Sisa sinbo (The Times), also known as the *Hanin sisa* (Korean Times), twice a
month, beginning in June 1905. Its purpose was "to open Koreans' eyes and
ears," and it was supported financially by both Koreans and the Methodist
Church. In December 1904, the Methodist minister George L. Pearson, who
had acted as Hong's patron, resigned as head of the Methodist Mission in
Hawai'i and was succeeded by Reverend John Wadman.[40] As for Hyŏn Sun,
another founding member of the Sinminhoe who had been working as an interpreter on Kahuku Plantation, he was approached by Wadman and asked to join
in Methodist Church work. In January 1905, Hyŏn went to Honolulu, where he
and several other Koreans rented a house for twelve dollars a month and did
church work. In addition, he worked as an interpreter for the immigration station and the local and circuit courts. Later that year, Wadman sent him to
Lihue, Kauai, on church business. That winter, Hyŏn ran into his old friend
from Korea, Reverend George Heber Jones, who was returning to Korea after
a furlough. Jones asked Hyŏn to return to Korea where he would be provided
with an important church position. Hyŏn accepted the offer and returned to
Korea in May 1907 with his wife and three children aboard the *Nippon Maru*.[41]
The Sinminhoe itself was resurrected in Korea in 1907 under the sponsorship
of An Ch'ang-ho, who had been living in California since 1902 and who was
well aware of Korean political activities in Hawai'i. It is no coincidence that
An's efforts were made shortly after Hong Sŏng-ha, the former president of
Hawai'i's Sinminhoe, and Hyŏn Sun, one of its founders, returned to Korea.

And what of the opposition faction of the Sinminhoe? This group, numbering about fifty (mostly Episcopalians), established the Ch'inmokhoe (Friendly
Society) at Ewa Plantation in May 1905. In 1907 it was renamed the Ch'ŏnhŭng
Hyŏphoe (Lightning Flourishing Society). It began publishing the *Ch'inmok
Hoebo* (The Friend) monthly for about a year, from May 1906 to April 1907,
and later published the monthly *Ch'ŏnhŭng Po* (Lightning Flourishing News)
from May 1908 to March 1909, both containing "beneficial scientific knowledge to lead Koreans into civilization." The president of the society was Kim
Ik-sŏng, the same man who had earlier attempted to "punish" the "traitors" in
the Sinminhoe. Not surprisingly, when the Korean community attempted to

unify politically in 1907 and again in 1909, the Ch'ŏnhŭng Hyŏphoe remained outside the fold until it finally agreed to unite in the spring of 1910.[42]

As the end of the first decade of the twentieth century approached, many organizations proliferated in the Korean community, joining or supplanting the earlier *tonghoe* and sworn brotherhoods. The following partial list illustrates the number and variety of these organizations:

Silchihoe (Practical Society)
Chaganghoe (Self-Strengthening Society)
Puhŭnghoe (Restoration Society)
Kungmin Kongdonghoe (National Cooperative Society)
Sin'ganhoe (New Korea Society)
Waipahu Kongdonghoe (Waipahu Cooperative Society)
Ŭisŏnghoe (Righteousness Fulfilling Society)
Kongjinhoe (Mutual Progress Society)

In all, there were approximately two dozen such organizations with agendas of mutual benefit and political activism. They all had grandiose names, published newspapers, and boasted, at least on paper, of a sophisticated hierarchy, with officers having titles such as chairman or president, vice chairman, secretary, and supervisor. The societies were not only dispersed geographically, since most Koreans were still on the plantations, but they were also fragmented politically because of the continuing factionalism in the Korean community. "Increasing rivalry and bickering" characterized the relations among these various groups, resulting in, as one observer noted, "many organizations like the Kongjinhoe, Ilsimhoe, and Ch'inmokhoe [being] organized only to be crushed because of the ignorance of their founders and inexperience of their proceedings." And all of the newspapers published by these organizations were "extinguished."[43]

While it was perhaps true that "at that time [the first decade of the twentieth century] the political consciousness of the Koreans was very weak," efforts were made toward unity, particularly in the face of the increasingly ominous events taking place in Korea, where the Japanese had forced Emperor Kojong to abdicate the throne to his more pliant son, Sunjong, in 1907. Beginning in early 1907, for six months, most of the societies took part in negotiations aimed at creating a unified organization. Finally, on September 2, 1907, thirty representatives assembled in Honolulu to declare the formation of the Hanin Hapsŏng Hyŏphoe, or United Korean Federation. The federation absorbed most of the earlier societies and *tonghoe;* in their places were created forty-seven branches with a total membership of over one thousand members paying annual dues of $2.25. The federation's central office and meeting place was located in downtown Honolulu, and it purchased printing machines and Korean type to publish a newspaper known variously as the *Hapsŏng Hoebo,* the *Hap-*

sŏng Sinmun, or the *Hapsŏng Sinbo.* The newspaper was printed from October 22, 1907, until January 25, 1909, and according to one observer, it "has power in Korean society." Remaining outside this federation was the Ch'ŏnhŭng Hyŏphoe (as noted earlier), the remnants of the opposition faction of the Sinminhoe, but "both organizations are well consolidated, have the spirit to lead Korean society, have many members, and are in good financial condition."[44]

For nearly two years the Hanin Hapsŏng Hyŏphoe remained the most ambitious attempt at unification by the Korean community in Hawai'i. On February 1, 1909, it merged with the Kungminhoe, known variously in Hawai'i as the Kookminhur or, in English, the Korean National Association (KNA). The KNA was founded in San Francisco by An Ch'ang-ho, who had returned from Korea after he had established the Sinminhoe there, and its members were mostly those Koreans who had earlier left Hawai'i. On that day in February about one thousand Koreans took time off from work and gathered in Honolulu. All the plantations and government offices recognized this as a day of celebration for the Koreans, and the deputy governor and various other officials attended the festivities. From 1909 until 1913 the KNA remained the preeminent Korean political organization. As noted earlier, even the fractious Ch'ŏnhŭng Hyŏphoe joined in the spring of 1910. The KNA established its own newspaper, the *Sin Han'guk Po,* translated as the *United Korean Weekly,* on February 15, 1909, and continued until the end of July 1913. On August 1, 1913, the paper was changed in format and renamed the *Kungmin po,* or *Kook Min Bo* (translated as the *Korean National Herald*), and would appear continuously for the next fifty-five years.[45]

From 1903 to 1913, there were a large number of Korean organizations in Hawai'i. In fact, there were so many, with so many permutations, that *dis*organization rather than organization could be said to characterize that first decade. Clearly, however, the assertion that "for over ten years (1903–1913) there was no dissension or feeling of partisanship among the Koreans in Hawaii" cannot be sustained.[46] Yet that decade ended on a hopeful note: the Korean community was for the first time united behind the KNA, whose attention was focused by the events of 1910, when Korea was annexed by Japan and turned into a colony. As Japan tightened its grip on Korea, and as the Koreans in Hawai'i gained more experience, political consciousness would grow. But not far behind was the ever-present factionalism that had plagued earlier efforts at unity.

4

Methodist Mission Work

At the beginning of 1906, there were 4,700 Koreans on the plantations, representing 10 percent of the workers—down from the 11 percent of the previous year, but still slightly ahead of the Chinese (9 percent) and behind the Japanese (66 percent). Of the Koreans, 4,400 were engaged in cultivation, with the remaining 300 engaged in transportation and other jobs.[1] Koreans still had a poor reputation as workers. A 1909 labor report for one plantation on the island of Hawai'i is typical. There, only Puerto Ricans worked less than Koreans, and the Koreans were ranked in last place of the ethnic groups, with the manager saying, "The Koreans are the least desirable."[2] Moreover, most Koreans, as shown earlier, were not happy on the plantations, finding life and work there distasteful. While some responded by striking, malingering, or moving from plantation to plantation, the vast majority, at some point, decided to leave the plantations altogether and move to the city. Since they increasingly saw themselves as settlers rather than sojourners, Koreans were acutely aware that employment opportunities and economic benefits were much greater in the city; hence they were naturally drawn to it. The planters, on the other hand, attempted to stem this Korean exodus, make them better workers, and discourage them from moving from plantation to plantation, because they were still useful as strikebreakers—and this would soon be demonstrated in the major strikes of 1909 and 1920. In their efforts, the planters enlisted the aid of the Methodist Mission in Hawai'i, which seized the opportunity to proselytize among these newly arrived immigrants.

In addition to leaving for the cities, Koreans also continued to migrate frequently from plantation to plantation. For example, from 1912 to 1922, Makee Plantation's monthly labor statement shows that the number of Koreans working in its canefields varied from a low of nineteen to a high of fifty-nine. One reason for this variation was that sometimes plantations short of labor would "raid" other plantations, promising higher wages or better conditions. To end this practice, plantation managers entered into agreements with each other not to do so. Consider the following letter from the manager of one plantation on the island of Hawai'i to another on the island: "A large number of our Filipinos, Japs and Koreans have gone to your place, Sixteen Miles Section, where, as we are told, they are guaranteed more money than our agreement with them called for. Since we paid for their transportation from Honolulu but had hardly more than a couple of days use of their labor, we think it would be only fair that your Company should reimburse us for at least their transportation." The other manager responded: "Some days ago about twenty Koreans arrived [here. . . . Because of] the understanding which we have with each other, these people were refused work, and were still at the village at Sixteen Miles yesterday afternoon. They will not work here. . . . Where these Koreans are going I do not know, but I can assure you that they will get no work here."[3] Despite such understandings, however, Koreans continued to "plantation hop."

The biggest problem the planters faced with the Koreans was their rapid departure from the plantations to the city—so rapid, in fact, that it would eventually set a record for departure rates. By the end of 1906, the Korean plantation population had dropped to 3,615, matching the Chinese population at about 9 percent of the labor force. In 1907, another 1,000 Koreans left the plantations, leaving only 2,638, or 6 percent of the labor force. By 1908, only 2,125 Koreans—4.5 percent of the labor force—were left on the plantations. In other words, roughly one-quarter of the Koreans left the plantations every year.[4] If a major strike had not occurred in 1909, there would have been only about 1,700 Koreans remaining on the plantations.

To prevent the problems they faced with the Koreans, the planters sponsored Christian mission work on the plantations. They were convinced, as Yun Ch'i-ho had been, that Christian Koreans made better, more reliable, and more law-abiding plantation workers, and that a strong Christian presence on the plantations would make Koreans more stable, thereby cutting down on "plantation hopping" and moves to the city. Since many of the immigrants had been associated with Christianity in some way before leaving Korea, the planters' approach held a certain degree of logic. And since the plantation managers were themselves Christians, they would hardly oppose mission work among the "heathen" on their plantations.

However, perhaps unbeknownst to the planters, Koreans had already begun to organize Christian religious activities on the plantations, without any external prompting. According to one account, the first worship service was held as early as July 4, 1903, in Mokuleia, Oahu, less than six months after the arrival of the first Koreans. At Kahuku, Hyŏn Sun remembered that "[w]e organized a Christian church and about fifty persons worshiped God led by Yun Chi Pong on every Sunday morning." Since there were no Korean churches yet built, services on the plantations were held in the boardinghouse kitchens. The pastors were plantation workers who had had some missionary training in Korea.[5]

The first plantation to sponsor Christian mission work was the Ewa Plantation, which had a large number of Koreans. The Koreans there collected three hundred dollars and requested that a church be built. The manager, Renton, "was greatly pleased and said that they were better than he because they believed in God firmly even though they were laborers." As a result, in October 1904 Renton donated $750 to build a church and used the $300 collected by the Koreans to furnish it. Perhaps not coincidentally, only four months earlier Renton had complained that his Koreans were leaving for Waipahu Plantation. The Ewa church was dedicated on April 30, 1905, with 110 people in attendance.[6] While Renton was under no outside pressure to build the Korean church, other plantation managers soon would feel pressured by the superintendent of the Methodist Mission.

Beginning in 1903, under the auspices of Reverend George L. Pearson, the first superintendent of the Hawai'i Methodist Mission to work with Koreans, the Methodists began to organize among the Koreans by taking these newly formed congregations and bringing them under their authority. Hyŏn Sun describes the takeover process at the plantation where he worked: "Under the leadership of Lim Chung Soo, the Sunday worship group was reorganized under the discipline of the [Methodist] church. In the month of August [1903], Reverend Pearson came down to Kahuku and preached at the Korean Methodist Church and baptised our girl child (born May 8, 1903), Alice."[7]

After more than a year of such work, Pearson was replaced in 1904 by Reverend John W. Wadman, who for sixteen years had been a missionary in Japan. For the next nine years, Wadman would be the prime mover in organizing Methodist mission work among the Koreans and in convincing the planters to support such work. According to his own testimony, Wadman "at once entered upon the work of the Mission with great zeal and energy." By the time Homer Hulbert arrived in Hawai'i in 1905, he (Hulbert) was able to write that "Rev. J. W. Wadman makes frequent trips throughout the islands visiting the Koreans and looking after their religious and educational interests. He has enrolled over 1,600 men and women on the records of the church, as members or probationers, and seven chapels have been erected."[8]

In replacing Pearson, Wadman took over the Korean Methodist Church in Honolulu, where Koreans were now starting to live. Hyŏn describes the church's founding as follows: "During the winter season of the same year [1903], a couple of young men came to Honolulu. . . . Under the leadership of Reverend Pearson, the Korean Methodist Church was established in Honolulu and Hong Sung Ha [the leader of the Sinminhoe] was appointed as a local preacher." When the church was fully incorporated into the Methodist Mission in 1905, Min Chan-ho became the first official pastor. Initially members met in a private home, but in 1906 a church building was erected in downtown Honolulu in what would later become known as the Korean Compound. The first Korean Methodist Church in Honolulu had twenty-three parishioners by 1906 and a Sunday School with thirty-five pupils and six teachers. The *Korean Christian Advocate* was published (in Korean) from this building and distributed to all plantations where Koreans worked.[9]

On the plantations, one of the first things Wadman did was organize a cohort of Korean Methodist ministers to attend to the religious needs of their countrymen. Some ministers were attached to particular plantations; the itinerant pastors ministered to several plantations. One such itinerant minister was Paek Sin-ku, whose son related that "[b]ecause my father had training in the missionary field, they wanted him to be a traveling missionary among the Korean camps in the Islands. For about a year he was paid by the church board." Hyŏn Sun recalled how he was drafted for similar work: "Reverend Wadman and Yun Pyung Koo came down to Kahuku and asked me to join the church work. As I had the same idea for a long time I said 'yes' and resigned from the Kahuku Plantation. On the 5th of January, 1905, I went out to Honolulu with my wife and baby girl, Alice. We settled down in a rented house for $12 a month. . . . While Yun Pyung Koo remained in Honolulu as interpreter for Reverend Wadman, I was ordered to take care of the Christians at Mokuleia and Kahuku. Finally two chapels were built at Mokuleia and Kahuku." [10]

Hyŏn Sun's account of his own experiences provides a glimpse into the early days of mission work on the plantation. Hyŏn was not happy being an itinerant pastor on the island of Oahu: "On March 19 [1905] our second girl baby was born in Honolulu. The first agreement was that Yun Pyung Koo would go to the mainland for higher education and I would take his position [as translator for Reverend Wadman] with the salary of $40 a month, but Yun remained in Honolulu while I was a traveling preacher. My wife complained that we had been living on only $25 a month and spent the couple of hundred dollars we saved while in Kahuku. She urged me to resign." [11]

At this time, the Episcopalians, who were also trying to initiate mission work among the Koreans, tried to lure Hyŏn away from the Methodists. "At that time we had good and kind friends—Dr. Camp and his wife. They were Episcopalian. They advised us to join the Episcopal Church. Dr. Camp took me around inside of his church and he said he would give us a house and my salary would be $40 a month. But I did not accept right away. However, I sent a letter of resignation to Dr. Wadman." Wadman reacted swiftly. "In the morning of the next day, Dr. Wadman came to my house and asked me to go to his office with him. I did as he asked me. Dr. Wadman wept and told me as follows: 'There are over 8,000 Koreans, but there is no consul, nor very few competent teachers. Would you remain with us for your people?' I was also moved and said, 'Yes, I will remain with you for my people.'" [12]

Just as the Episcopal Church in Hawai'i was unsuccessful in enticing Hyŏn to join, it was also not very successful in attracting large numbers of Koreans. There were, however, a few Koreans who had been members of the Church of England (Anglican or Episcopalian) before leaving Korea and who wanted to retain that affiliation in Hawai'i. In 1903, about fifty Episcopalians, led by Pak Sang-ha, organized themselves in Honolulu into the Ch'ŏnhŭng Hyŏphoe (Lightning Flourishing Society) (see Chapter 3) and met in a rented room where some American Episcopalians taught them English. They soon came to the attention of the head of the Episcopal Church in Hawai'i, Bishop Henry Restarick, who noticed that "one of the applicants, Choy Chin Tai (John Choi), had been trained in a mission school, and I found on enquiry that he was of good character and sincere in his religion, so I appointed him catechist."[13]

Other Koreans, including conservative non-Christians, soon joined this Episcopalian organization—but for political rather than religious reasons, as they were upset with the seemingly radical Sinminhoe and its domination by Hong Sŏng-ha and the Methodists. Restarick had noticed that "a number of them [Koreans], mostly non-Christian, came to me in the summer of 1905 and asked me to minister to them." Restarick may have had an inkling of the political controversy surrounding the Sinminhoe, because he did observe that Koreans "are not an easy people to deal with, as they are divided into factions which quarrel and sometimes come to blows." The early career of Kim Ik-sŏng, a leader in the anti-Sinminhoe faction, is instructive in looking at the linkage between religion and factionalism. An Episcopalian active in the Ch'ŏnhŭng Hyŏphoe, Kim took the name Isaiah and in 1907 became the first lay reader of the separate congregation for Koreans, called St. Luke's.[14] Thus the Episcopal Church and the Ch'ŏnhŭng Hyŏphoe became vehicles for both religious expression and factional struggle.

Lacking a church building, Korean Episcopalians held Sunday worship at St. Elizabeth's Episcopal Church, the Chinese worshipping first, and the Koreans after. The first confirmations were held in 1908, and a Korean language school was established that continued to operate until the beginning of World War II. In 1908, there were approximately one hundred baptized Koreans, and in 1909 they petitioned for a Korean-speaking priest. Restarick responded by selecting the original founder of the Ch'ŏnhŭng Hyŏphoe, Pak Sang-ha, later known as John S. Pahk, to attend divinity school in San Francisco. Pahk had previously served as Restarick's interpreter and as a teacher at the Korean language school operated by the church. When he returned to Honolulu in 1916, he became the first ordained Korean priest in the Episcopal Church.[15]

Though the locus of Episcopal Church work was in Honolulu, it did attempt to organize plantation workers. One worker named Cho recruited in Kahuku, Oahu, and in Kona, Hawai'i. In Lahaina, Maui, Episcopal ministers were able to recruit thirteen Koreans. There were also Episcopal missions at Olowalu, Kohala, and Makapala on Hawai'i, where a night school operated. But for the most part, these missions were unsuccessful. As Restarick noted, "These were all given up because the Koreans went away. For years after they came to Hawaii these people frequently changed their place of residence, which led to the closing of several of our missions among them." Thus the mainstay of the Episcopal presence in the Korean community remained St. Luke's Church in Honolulu, which by the early 1920s numbered 110 members.[16]

Consequently, it was the Methodists who dominated religious life in the Korean community in Hawai'i, and efforts by Episcopalians and others to win converts and attract workers such as Hyŏn Sun remained largely unsuccessful. After his refusal to change affiliations, Hyŏn was rewarded with a raise of five dollars per month and sent "by the order of Dr. Wadman" to minister to the plantations on the east side of Kauai. Thus, after touring Oahu's plantations with Yun Ch'i-ho in the fall of 1905, "I [Hyŏn] took my family, with $30 a month from the Methodist Mission Board, to Lihue, Kauai. We settled down in the Korean camp. I began to preach the gospel to all Koreans in Lihue, Hanamaulu, Kapaa, Kialia, and Kilauea. There were about 2,000 Koreans on the island of Kauai." By the end of 1905, Hyŏn was one of thirteen evangelists on the Methodist Mission Board's payroll, all of whom were "doing earnest and successful work." [17]

The efforts of Hyŏn and other Korean Methodist ministers demonstrated to the planters and Wadman that their presence on the plantations was beneficial. "Besides preaching, I [Hyŏn] used to help the welfare of the Koreans and straighten [out] misunderstanding[s] between the Korean workers and the plantation officers." And it helped that Hyŏn made a good impression on the planters on Kauai: "There I met with rich people such as the Rice family, Mr. George Wilcox and Mr. Hans Isenberg. Mr. Isenberg asked me, 'What is your business?' I said, 'I am a preacher.'" When Isenberg said that Korean workers needed to be whipped, Hyŏn responded, "The end of a whip is hatred, but the end of God's word is Love." Isenberg's response? "Alright, you better stay with us," and he promised Hyŏn a house, a church, and traveling expenses. "For traveling expenses, Mr. Isenberg used to give me $10 a month. Mr. Wilcox gave me also $10 a month. I bought a horse and Father Rice supplied a sulky when I took a long-way trip. I was led to convert several hundred Koreans to Christianity and finally a beautiful chapel was built by the help of Mr. Isenberg." [18]

Besides conducting worship services and serving as mediators between the planters and their Korean workers, preachers like Hyŏn also offered language classes. Korean language was offered to the children, and if the pastors spoke English (and several did because of their contact with American missionaries in Korea), they would teach English to the adults. Hyŏn, who spoke English, "started the English language class at night and we had about thirty young men in the class." Other plantations also had English-language night schools for Koreans, some of which had been started by Reverend Pearson before he was replaced by Wadman. Often these language schools would be housed in the Korean church itself, as described by one eyewitness on the island of Hawai'i: "At the back of the Korean camp at Kamei on Hakalau plantation is a little wooden building set apart from the rest of the houses. It is the Korean language school during week days and the Korean Methodist church on Sundays. Once a month the Korean minister of the Hilo Methodist church goes to Kamei to preach. On other Sundays informal services are conducted by a lay preacher of the camp. This school house is a humble structure like the rest of the camp buildings but built so that it can well be combined as school and church. In front in the single room of the building is a small platform, the pulpit on Sunday and seats for the students on week days and members of the congregation on the Sabbath."[19]

Despite his raise, Hyŏn, now in Kauai, still wanted to serve as Wadman's interpreter in Honolulu, as he had originally been led to expect. In this hope, however, he was disappointed. "In the month of November [1905], after Yun Pyung Koo left Honolulu and went to the Mainland for further education [and, with Syngman Rhee, to plead for American support for Korean independence with President Roosevelt], Min Chan Ho and his wife came [from Korea] to Honolulu as interpreter for Dr. Wadman, and his duty was to take care of the Korean Methodist Church in Honolulu." Thus rebuffed, Hyŏn busied himself with other activities that would prepare him for a career move. "I attended two Methodist annual conferences in 1906 and 1907 under Bishop Hamilton. I passed the ministerial course, namely theology, homiletics, and church history. . . . I acted as interpreter for the immigration station and for local and circuit court. So I learned naturally some American law."[20]

The opportunity Hyŏn had been waiting for was not long in coming. "During the winter season [1906–1907], I happened to meet [missionary] Dr. George H. Jones in Lihue who was going back to Korea from his furlough. He advised me to come back to Korea and he promised to give me a very important position. So I agreed with him. . . . In the spring of the same year [1907] I wrote to Dr. Jones in Seoul about my returning to Korea. I got his answer right away. I would be welcomed and he would give me a position. I was glad to get some financial help from Mr. Hans Isenberg and Mr. George Wilcox and some money from Kim Pyung Koo and Hong Tuck Soo. The amount of money was about $1,000. My wife and I and three children, two girls and one baby boy, Peter, who was born in Lihue, left Honolulu in the month of May 1907 on a Japanese ship by the name of *Nippon Maru*."[21] Hyŏn was destined to play a major role in the Korean nationalist movement and would return to Hawaii in 1923, after spending sixteen years in Asia.

The example set by Hyŏn and the other pastors on the plantations in preaching, converting, teaching, and mediating was not lost on the planters or on Wadman—particularly the fact that the planters on Kauai were willing to contribute financially to Hyŏn's activities. If these planters were willing to support such mission activities, Wadman reasoned, then would not other planters be willing to do the same among the Koreans? If Wadman could convince the planters that his Korean pastors could make the Koreans work harder and remain on the plantations, then surely the planters would back them financially. Wadman's approach proceeded on two levels. At the upper level, he targeted the parent organization, the HSPA, for the "big-ticket" donations. Below that, he sought more modest levels of financial support from the managers of the individual plantations.

Wadman's first contact with the HSPA came indirectly in the summer of

1905, when the Japanese consul in Honolulu, Saitō Miki, wrote the HSPA a letter identifying himself as the diplomat in charge of Koreans in Hawai'i and asking them for financial assistance in setting up a Korean relief society. In the letter, Saitō suggested that Wadman head this society (for reasons that will soon become apparent). The HSPA favored the idea of such a society with Wadman in charge, calling him a "desirable man to act as custodian and distributor of any charitable fund." Consequently, the HSPA decided to contribute $250 "after [E. Faxon Bishop] conferred with Mr. Wadman on the subject." With the planters' money, Wadman launched the Korean Benevolent Association "[a]t a largely attended meeting of all the Koreans residing in Honolulu, together with representatives from several plantations." Wanting to show the planters that the Koreans were also contributing to their own welfare, Wadman charged all Koreans wishing to become members an initiation fee of one dollar and quarterly dues of fifty cents. And in a bid to ingratiate himself with the planters, Wadman stipulated in Article 11 of the association's constitution that its treasurer "shall . . . deposit [all monies] for safe keeping in the Savings Department of Bishop and Company, Bankers."[22] This was significant because the Bishop Bank was controlled by the planters.

Once the HSPA had contributed such a munificent sum of money, Wadman felt free to request additional donations at regular intervals. For example, in the summer of 1908, the planters received a letter from Wadman "requesting a contribution from the Association for the purpose of Korean charities." As before, the HSPA authorized a contribution of $250. Two years later, in 1910, Wadman again was "showing urgent need . . . of financial assistance." The HSPA responded this time by donating $100. In 1912, after receiving "a letter from Rev. J. W. Wadman . . . outlining the work and needs of the Korean Benevolent Association . . . [i]t was voted that the Treasurer be authorized to pay to Mr. Wadman the sum of $200 for the benefit of the organization."[23] Clearly, Wadman was a successful fund-raiser.

Wadman was also successful in persuading the individual plantation managers to contribute to his work. At the lower level of the plantation hierarchy, his aim was to get managerial support for the institutional trappings of his mission work—building churches and paying the salaries of the Korean pastors. To obtain this support, he knew he had to offer the plantation managers something in return—for example, assistance in making the Koreans more steady and efficient plantation workers. In a 1904 letter to John Bull, the manager of the Waipahu Plantation on Oahu, Wadman wrote: "After speaking to you for a moment a day or so ago, I visited the Korean Camp and got the men together for a little talk in which I endeavored to [illegible] them up and ask them to try and do better—all of which they promised to do—including the [illegible]. I am [illegible] arranging for the bearer of this [illegible], Rev. Mr. Kim, pastor of the Ewa plantation, to visit your plantation once or twice a week so as to try and get these men to do better and help all he can to bring about a better state of things." Having made these assurances, Wadman not so subtly pressed Bull to build a church for the Koreans: "I will call after two or three weeks and have a chat with you about the building."[24] As evidence of his powers of persuasion, he received the following response: "I . . . note what you say in regard to the building of a Korean meeting house. I think your idea is a good one and I will do the best I can to have a building erected at the Nine and One-half Mile Camp." Wadman wrote back to thank the manager, telling him that for the Koreans, "it will be good news to them and cheer them up wonderfully."[25] Having met with success, the confident Wadman pushed for more chapels the following year.

Besides creating a better worker, Wadman was quick to point out that his churches also were more likely to keep the Koreans from leaving the plantation: "These little chapels which we are building like the ones we have put up at Ewa, Kahuku, Waialua, Eleele, etc, etc, *help greatly to keep the Koreans in one place* and so in the end it pays the plantations for any [illegible] they may feel disposed to make in this direction."[26]

Wadman also wanted the plantation managers to subsidize the salaries of the pastors who he assigned to serve there. Excerpts from letters to two plantation managers are typical of his appeal and reveal a great deal about the inner workings of mission work among the Koreans. At first, Wadman pleaded poverty, lamenting to one manager, "I am in financial distress over my mission work among the Koreans, i.e. the needs are so great on the different plantations among these poor helpless people." To another manager, he wrote, "My great difficulty is the matter of finances. The Mission pays Hong $25 per month and $3 towards his traveling expenses around the plantation. Our appropriation from the Mission Board in Philadelphia for the Korean Work in Hawaii is $2000 per annum. We have now established about 22 Korean Mission Churches here and there with twice as many out-stations. This $2000 does not begin to go half-round and so I am obliged to beg or borrow. . . . Hence, if I do not succeed in receiving a few more donations, I shall soon come to grief and be driven to the necessity of closing up some of the work. . . . It would mean a sort of set-back to the whole Korean Church and disturbs them (Koreans)."

Wadman then turned to peer pressure. To one manager he wrote, "In all cases the managers are exceedingly kind and help us considerably with donations to the work. Ewa, Waialua and Kahuku on this island and others in Kauai and Maui, Mr. Borkhauser, Mr. Baldwin, etc. all kindly assist." To another, he specifically outlined the generosity of other managers: "Papaaloa plantation needs a man and they are willing to pay half his salary." And, he added, "Many plantations kindly donate, some $10 monthly, others $15, others give $20 or $25. Ewa gives us $25, Waialua $30, McBryde $10, Honokaa $10, and so on. Were it not for these monthly donations, I could not begin to carry on the work as I do."

Wadman also made sure to praise the character and accomplishments of the pastors he wanted the planters to subsidize. To a manager on Oahu, he wrote:

"I have sent for two or three more good first class well trained teacher-evan-
gelists and they will soon be here from Korea. There are a half dozen plantations which need such men to work among its people and in several cases the
managers have already promised to assist in paying the bills. Mr. Kim was here
this morning from Waipahu and reports very favorably on his work. Among the
300 or near Korean planters there, he has about 75 enrolled as Christians and
he is opening a little school for the children, some 10 or 12 [illegible] taught.
. . . Kim is a good, sincere, reliable man and I want very much to have him
there."

Wadman went on to remind the managers that subsidizing pastors was good
for plantations because a Christian presence attracts family men and transforms the character of the workers. Quoting one of the Korean pastors, Wadman wrote: "He says the men are all well satisfied and like the managers
exceedingly well. . . . [H]e feels sure that others will be attracted to Waipahu—
especially family men. The little school will help out." To another manager he
wrote: "Wherever our little Church is established and a faithful pastor resides
with his [illegible] school and night classes, besides his Sunday services, a better class of people is raised up and more healthy moral atmosphere prevails. It
really pays."[27]

After a decade of Methodist mission work on the plantations, however, the
situation changed. Plantation managers became increasingly unwilling to contribute to pastors' salaries and church construction. First, the dwindling number of Koreans on the plantations meant that they could not help defray
expenses, despite Wadman's assurances that "he would endeavor to collect
from the Koreans further contributions." Second, although Wadman undoubtedly did much good, he was largely unable to fulfill his promise to make Koreans better workers, much less keep them on the plantations. As one planter
noted, "Mr. Wadman made promises . . . which he has not lived up to and in
the writer's opinion the monthly donation should be . . . afterwards considered
on its merits if it should be continued or not." Finally, the Korean Methodist
Church found itself on the brink of a factional split. It appeared that Wadman
had lost his influence, and in 1914, he resigned and was succeeded by Reverend William Henry Fry.[28]

Like his predecessor, Fry also approached the HSPA for assistance in Korean
mission work, but he had to use a different approach, because Methodist welfare work was now concentrated in the Honolulu area, where many Koreans
now lived. Unlike Wadman, Fry appealed to the HSPA's sense of civic duty.
His "requests . . . for contributions by this Association toward the Korean . . .
welfare work in Honolulu" resulted in a grant of $250, because the HSPA felt
"the work has its value in tending to lessen crime and give these races a better
standing in the community, they being people that have been brought here by
the Association." And it continued to donate thereafter: in 1917, it gave
another $250; in 1918, because of the shortfall of other support due to World

War I, it donated $500; in 1919 and again in 1920, it donated $250.[29] Thus by the beginning of the 1920s, Fry had succeeded in gaining some degree of regular charitable support for Korean welfare work from the HSPA.

Fry also continued to appeal to the individual plantation managers for assistance with Korean work, particularly for the salaries of the Korean pastors. His tactics were similar to Wadman's, but, aware that Koreans were leaving the plantations in droves, Fry felt obliged to add, "Assistance of this nature is given only so long as returns are forthcoming. For example, if the Koreans should leave your plantation, Mr. Cho would of necessity have to go with them to minister to them. In that case your grant would cease; I would not wish it otherwise."

Fry's main argument, however, like Wadman's, was that mission work would eliminate the shortcomings attributed to Korean workers. "It is purely a business proposition, since the men who don[']t drink, gamble, and roam about the country are a better asset to the church and school for keeping men settled and contented. We have tested it out on this island [Hawai'i] greatly to the satisfaction of all concerned." Fry even promised a reverse migration of Koreans back to the plantations: "I have just made a tour of all the islands and have arranged to work in connection with the plantation companies with the object of centering all the Koreans on the plantations. I find that many of them have drifted into other pursuits for which the[y] are not adapted. After several conferences with some of their leaders we have decided to urge them back to the Sugar Plantations where they can have steady employment and fair treatment." Fry then explained why he felt Koreans were better off on the plantations: "Twenty five Korean workmen left Kona [Plantation] a few days ago. They went to Kona and engaged in the Coffee Raising Business; they had no experience and failed; they became so embarrassed with debts that they had to leave. Our slogan this year then is 'Back to the Plantations.' I am pressing this for two general reasons. (1) We cannot follow them with church and school privileges if the[y] scatter themselves about. (2) We must depend upon the Sugar Plantations for financial assistance if we are to maintain our mission work."[30]

While the fund-raising techniques of Wadman and Fry were similar, Fry was less successful than Wadman. For example, Fry received the following response to one of his appeals: "I am in receipt of your letter of the 18th instant with reference to placing your Korean Pastor, Rev. Y. T. Cho on our pay roll at $18 per month. Your letter has had my careful attention, but I regret to have to inform you that I do not see my way to grant your request in this connection. At the present time we only have one Korean on our pay rolls, though there are a few independent planters of that nationality living in this district. I am very sorry to disappoint you in this connection, but feel under the circumstances that I cannot do otherwise."[31] And unfortunately for Fry, such rejections were not uncommon.

As Koreans continued to leave the plantations, other managers lost interest in subsidizing Korean churches and pastors' salaries. For example, in 1915, Fry apparently heard that Honokaa Plantation was thinking of dropping its monthly subsidy for the Korean pastor because too many Koreans were leaving the plantation. Fry went to the Koreans there and "made it plain to them that they could not expect help from [the] company unless they could make themselves worthwhile to [the] company. I made it plain that those at Honokaa must not leave to work elsewhere and that they must encourage others to come. I explained that the Mission Board could not be responsible for the entire support of the Honokaa pastor and that they must make their presence a valuable asset to the manager. To this they agreed, and stated that they would encourage the most desirable members of their class to come to Honokaa." Nonetheless, the manager discontinued the monthly subsidy, despite Fry's plea that "[i]t will work a great hardship on our Mission Work in Honokaa if your company feels compelled to withdraw its support" [32]

The reduction in financial support led, quite naturally, to problems. Some Korean pastors found themselves entirely dependent financially on the dwindling number of Koreans on their plantations, while other pastors abandoned the plantations entirely, despite Fry's efforts to keep them on the job. "Mr. K. H. Park wanted to be relieved from the work at Pahala. . . . I refused to let him go at first but found that he was bent on going anyhow. . . . He received no remuneration from the mission any more but is paid wholly by the Koreans for teaching their language school." [33]

In the midst of these troubles, in 1923 Fry decided to recall Hyŏn Sun, then in China, to help the Methodist mission among the Koreans in Hawai'i. Hyŏn recalled his experience: "After three years of service as pastor for the Korean Methodist Church in Honolulu I was transferred to Lihue, Kauai in 1926 with the whole family. The church I built in 1906 was still on the hill-top. . . . First of all I called on old friends. One was Mr. George Wilcox who was very glad to see me. He gave me $500 for a Ford car and he promised to give me $25 per month for my traveling expenses. Then I called on Mrs. Dora Isenberg who also promised to help me with $30 per month. . . . Alternatively I used to travel to the east side for one week and the other week to the west, holding meetings for children and adults, teaching the Bible to the children and preaching the gospel to the adults. Thus for fourteen years [1926–1940] I worked for the Korean people on the island of Kauai." [34]

Other Korean ministers, like Hyŏn, remained on the plantations on the other islands—even after most Koreans had gone to Oahu—fulfilling, at least in part, the promises made to the plantation managers. For example, on Maui in the late 1930s: "My father is the only residential preacher in the camp from outside towns and villages. The parsonage is placed in the camp and it is significant in that such an arrangement is most beneficial and convenient for the people. The minister performs a two-fold function. Besides being the 'church-boss' as the laborers call him, he also caters to their economic and social needs.

Certain individuals and families constantly go to him for advice and aid. He is the medium through which these individuals keep in touch with the plantation manager."[35]

But in the end, most pastors, including Hyŏn, could not resist the allure of the city and its greater financial rewards. As Hyŏn himself wrote, "Our children all went to Honolulu. With the help of Mrs. Dora Isenberg, we purchased a big house at Anapuni Street in Honolulu. In February, 1940, I resigned from the ministry. My wife and I left Kauai and settled down in Honolulu with all our children. In the spring of 1940, we leased a five-acre parcel of land on Kokohead outside of Honolulu. We raised mostly carnation flowers and some cucumbers. We did very well summer and winter throughout both years, 1940 and 1941."[36] Within two decades, the locus of Korean religious activities had shifted mainly to Honolulu.

Nonetheless, the work carried out by Pearson, Wadman, and Fry on the plantations left some important legacies. First, the Koreans in Hawai'i had become overwhelmingly Christian (primarily Protestant) and were avid in their support. Certainly, many of the Korean immigrants had been associated with Christianity even before leaving Korea, but the mission efforts on the plantations served to solidify and expand upon this base. By World War II, there were approximately 1,000 Methodists, 1,000 Korean Christian Church members (an offshoot of the Methodist Church, associated with Syngman Rhee), 200 Episcopalians, 200 Seventh Day Adventists, and from 100–300 Catholics. Only 30 Koreans were identified as Buddhists, and 20 were affiliated with the Chŏndogyo or Tonghak. By contrast, most first-generation Chinese and Japanese immigrants practiced the religions of the old country—primarily Buddhism.[37]

Second, mission work on the plantations gradually fostered greater equality between the sexes. As one observer noted, "At first it was very difficult to have the few women folk in camp attend service. The main drawback was the Korean custom of not associating with the opposite sex. Even in daily life men did not speak or pay attention to women unless absolutely necessary. Gradually, the strict separation became more modified and women began to go to church services. . . . This modified association of the sexes was still full of restraint and modesty. In church the women sat close to the front, or in the extreme back or all on one side of the congregation."[38] Mixed church attendance, combined with the concept of equality before God, led first-generation Koreans closer to the American ideal of gender equality.

Finally, the schools that were set up on the plantations under church sponsorship not only helped adults learn English to prepare them for commercial activities in the city, but they also played a role in the early education of the second generation of Koreans. The entrepreneurial skills of the first generation and the educational success of the second generation, are clear evidence that the churches laid a solid educational foundation.

5

Exodus to the City

No race worth bringing to the islands will be content to remain permanently with its only prospect a life lived at the end of a plantation hoe

COMMISSIONER OF LABOR STATISTICS IN HAWAI'I, 1915

Despite the best efforts of the Methodist Mission and the sugar planters, it was
impossible to keep Koreans on the plantations. The city (primarily Honolulu,
but also Wahiawa, Oahu) held greater allure for most Koreans. After peaking
at 5000 in 1905, about one-quarter of the Koreans left the plantations every
year thereafter. One would thus expect that for the year 1909 only about 1,700
Koreans would remain. Yet in that year, the number of Koreans on the plantations actually increased to 2,229, or 5.3 percent of the plantation labor force.

Why the increase in 1909? When the Japanese plantation workers went on
strike that year, the Koreans, joined by Chinese, Hawaiians, and Portuguese,
flocked to the plantations to act as strikebreakers. While some Koreans were
motivated by anti-Japanese nationalism, the primary incentive was financial
gain, as strikebreakers were paid $1.50 per day, or twice their normal wages.
Two years later, when about seventy Japanese longshoremen went on strike at
the Oahu Railway Company, which served the plantations, the strikers were
again replaced with Koreans.[1] In both cases, by using Koreans as strikebreakers, the planters were able to defeat the strikes; hence they naturally wanted to
keep Koreans on the plantations.

Unfortunately for the planters, the Koreans did not remain. First of all, once
the strike was over, wages returned to prestrike levels, so there was no longer
a financial incentive to stay. Second, because the planters now began aggres-
sively to import Filipino labor (small numbers of Filipinos had been arriving
since 1907, and over the next two decades the total would swell to 120,000),
wages remained depressed, further keeping Koreans away from the plantations.
Third, after the 1909 strike, Koreans and other Asian workers still received only
eighteen dollars per month compared to the twenty-two to twenty-four dollars

per month non-Asians (Portuguese, Spanish, Hawaiian, Puerto Ricans and Russians) received for the same work. Fourth, rigid discipline and harsh working and living conditions remained a reality on the plantations. Moreover, by 1910, Japanese comprised nearly one-quarter of the overseers on the plantations, and most Koreans found the prospect of working under Japanese supervision distasteful. Finally, since the strike was generally confined to the plantations on Oahu, many of the Korean strikebreakers who came from the other islands opted not to return once the strike was over, and instead remained in or around Honolulu.[2]

Consequently, despite the temporary increase in the Korean population on the plantations in 1909, the exodus continued. In 1910, there were only 1,753 Korean laborers, representing about 4 percent of the plantation labor force. By 1915, Koreans represented only 3 percent of the plantation workforce (1,449 workers). In 1916, despite a salary increase in 1915 from eighteen dollars to twenty dollars per month, their numbers dropped to 1,300, and there appeared to be no end to the Koreans' flight.

In 1920, however, the plantations experienced another temporary upsurge in the Korean population, with their numbers climbing to about two thousand. The reason? The Strike of 1920. As in 1909, anti-Japanese nationalism and the lucrative strikebreaker's wages lured some Koreans back to the plantations, at least temporarily.[3]

The strike, confined to the island of Oahu, began in January 1920 and was cosponsored by Japanese and Filipino plantation workers. When it began, fifty Koreans on Waipahu Plantation were the only ones to continue working; another thirty-seven Koreans who had initially gone on strike were soon back on the job. In 1919, Japan had brutally suppressed the Korean independence movement; as a result, many Koreans in Hawai'i retaliated against the Japanese. On the evening of January 29 the Korean National Association (KNA) held a meeting in which the association's leadership supported the strike, while the rank and file members did not. The meeting became stormy and ended with the replacement of the officers and the issuing of the following statement: "We do not wish to be looked upon as strike breakers, but we shall continue to work in the plantations and we are opposed to the Japanese in everything." Twelve days after the meeting, a group of more than one hundred Korean men and women established what they called a Strikebreaker's Association and sent a committee to offer its services to HSPA secretary Royal D. Mead.[4] In a struggle between class and racial solidarity versus national feeling, the latter won out.

Of course, while anti-Japanese sentiment was strong, the financial benefits of strikebreaking were not lost on the Koreans. In 1909, Korean strikebreakers received double their normal wage; in 1920, they were paid three dollars a day, or *triple* the normal plantation wage. When the HSPA decided to send 250 strikebreakers to Waialua Plantation, Manager Goodale specifically requested Koreans. On that plantation, the fifty-four Korean strikebreakers represented more than twice the number of any other strikebreaking ethnic group, and at first, they worked jointly with the one hundred Koreans already working there as regulars. Of course, once the long-time employees discovered that their wages did not match those of the strikebreakers, they quit.[5]

Since many Koreans had already moved to Oahu, it was relatively easy for them to act as strikebreakers there. And many of those who came to Oahu in 1920 as strikebreakers chose not to return to the outer islands. As a result, the Korean community in and around Honolulu became a reservoir of anti-Japanese strikebreakers. This location also gave the Koreans a certain degree of freedom in that they could choose to work on the plantations or not as they saw fit. They often expressed this freedom by moving from plantation to plantation, much to the planters' dismay. At the Oahu Sugar Company's Waipahu Plantation during the 1920 strike, the number of Koreans varied from a low of 80 to a high of 140, with a great deal of volatility from day to day. For example, 140 Koreans worked on March 13, but only 116 Koreans worked there the following day.[6]

After the 1920 strike (the planters once again ending it with the help of Korean strikebreakers), Koreans resumed their rapid exodus from the plantations for the same reasons the Korean strikebreakers had departed the plantations after the 1909 strike. Wages returned to their normal low rate, and the 1921 decline in agricultural prices meant they would not soon be increased. And plantation discipline was still harsh. Thus the number of Koreans on the plantations dropped from a high of 2,000 in 1920 to only 1,200 the following year. By 1924, there were fewer than one thousand Koreans on the plantations. And by the beginning of the 1930s, the number had dropped to a little under five hundred, where it remained until those workers retired. For those few Koreans who remained on the plantations after 1930, life remained difficult, not only because of the harsh work and low wages, but also because of what one sociologist termed "biological instability." In other words, most of the remaining Korean men on the plantations were now over forty-five years old, and they had to "compete" with Filipino workers in their twenties.[7] Thus within twenty-five years, or one generation, over 90 percent of the Koreans had left the plantations—a rate unmatched by any of the other thirty-two ethnic groups that at one time or another had worked on the sugar plantations in Hawai'i. In fact, the majority of the Koreans had left the plantations within the first decade.

At the end of their first decade in Hawai'i, many of the Koreans who remained on the plantations opted to be contract workers rather than day workers. In fact, by 1915, the proportion of Korean contract workers was larger than that of any other nationality. For example, in 1916, one-third of the Olaa Sugar Company's twenty-four independent contractors were Koreans who were responsible for areas between five and fifteen acres in size. Contracting was like farm tenantry or sharecropping, where title to the sugarcane fields remained vested in the plantation, but individuals or groups of laborers could enter into a contract for a specified area on the plantation to weed, irrigate, cut, and load, or take on the more extensive task of bringing a crop to maturity, with compensation given at the completion of the task. The contracting laborer lived as a tenant on the plantation and received a minimum wage and turnout bonus from the plantation pending the harvesting of his crop; the plantation also provided the finances for irrigation, fertilizers, and tools. Under this arrangement, the tenant was responsible for any loss caused by his own neglect or carelessness.[8]

The main advantage to contracting was that one could earn more money. In 1915, Korean contractors averaged twenty-four dollars per month, while day laborers averaged twenty dollars per month. Contracting also was an intermediate step between plantation work and owning one's own business. In addition, those who left the plantations for the city but were unable to find jobs there often used contracting on the plantations as a financial "safety net." Consider the following letter written by the leader of a group of Koreans in Honolulu to the manager of Honokaa Plantation: "I am going to tell you all about the my best plan for our Korean hardworking laborers. . . . I hope and willing to have a permission from you to . . . bring the Korean hardworking plantation men about twenty three or more already in my hand in the Korean Hotel on King St. Honolulu at present. Please Mr. Morrison if want any working men any time of this year what is you did told me some weeks ago in your house. Therefore I was working hard for got the men from so many places in town those who are looking for working sugar cane plantations [sic]." The writer wanted Morrison to provide boat passage for him and his men to the plantation, on the island of Hawai'i: "One thing I just want to tell you all about the plan, if you have a favor for me the permission allow our men on your ship which is landing in your Co. every week. We shall be glad to have that and must thank you too. After we got out on your plantation to start working every day ending of month pay the steamer fare little by little in two months time, so I am waiting for your kind letter from you very soon [sic]." The man had been urged to write by Wadman, who had been trying to get Koreans back on the plantations, as discussed in the previous chapter: "When I came back to town saw Dr. W. Wadman spoken about you, he said to me you were very kindness and truth and justice manager in Hawaiian island. Thank you very much all these. My men and myself only standing at the wharf in Honolulu simply waiting for your kindness letter from your plantation [sic]." Despite this apparent willingness to work hard, however, other Koreans who had contracted with that plantation were not so diligent, leading Morrison to comment about one group of twenty Korean contractors: "[I am] heartily sick of Young Si Moon and his stiffs. . . . During their contract we had to go to their camp every day and stir them out. . . . [We should] have fired him out long ago."[9]

Of course, contracting on the plantations was not the only option the Koreans had. Another option—especially for Koreans working on plantations on the island of Hawai'i—was to move to Kona either to grow coffee, harvest tobacco, or work on the macadamia nut farms. But the results were mixed. As mentioned earlier, in 1915, the twenty-five Korean men who had gone to Kona to raise coffee failed. On the other hand, twenty other Koreans who had grown tobacco in Korea were successful in that business in south Kona. And by the mid-1930s, about one hundred men were working in Kona's macadamia nut farms.[10]

Yet another option was to start a farm or work for other Korean farmers raising vegetables, rice, gourds, melons, cucumbers, pigs, or chickens. To be sure, those who opted to remain in agriculture did so because city work required capital. One such Korean said: "After the plantation we went to so many places! We went wherever we were told there was good work. Mostly farms. [We did not go to the city because] you need capital to start a business in the city." For those who attempted to go into independent farming, however, the evidence suggests that most were unsuccessful. A Japanese report in the mid-1920s stated that "many of them failed because of a lack of money and management experience so that now there are only two houses which grow melons and only one which raises cucumbers, chickens and pigs."[11]

The most popular option for Koreans who wanted to leave the sugar plantations but remain in agriculture was the pineapple industry on the island of Oahu. In the socioeconomic environment of Hawai'i, where any occupation outside the plantations represented a step up, entry into the pineapple industry, by its very nature, represented the first step up for hundreds of Koreans leaving the plantations. The pineapple fields presented distinct advantages over the sugar plantations, the first of which was better wages. In 1915, Korean men who worked in the pineapple fields received ninety-five cents a day, compared to seventy-five cents a day on the plantations. Another advantage was that the much newer pineapple industry, begun in 1901 by James D. Dole, was less bound by obsolete tradition and rigid discipline. A third advantage was the proximity to urban areas, midway both physically and psychologically between the plantation and the city since the pineapple fields in central Oahu were only about twenty miles from Honolulu. Korean workers first appeared in the pineapple fields in 1908, and by 1915 there were 123 Koreans working there.[12]

Whereas many Koreans viewed their work in the pineapple fields as a way station on their journey to the city, others chose to remain in the pineapple fields, where they were later joined by Korean women. As late as 1938, the 141 Korean men in the pineapple industry comprised about 3 percent of the workforce; the 235 women represented about 5 percent. By that time, men were earning nearly nineteen dollars a week and women nearly thirteen dollars a week. And some Koreans had moved upward, becoming foremen or section chiefs.[13] The relatively large number of Koreans in the pineapple fields was reflected in the sizable Korean community in the central Oahu city of Wahiawa, which enjoyed significant growth because of the pineapple industry and, later, the establishment of army and air force installations.

Aside from those Koreans who worked in the pineapple fields of central Oahu, even more were attracted to the cannery in Honolulu, where the wages were higher than in the pineapple fields. By 1915, 297 Korean men worked there, earning $1.11 per day, along with 106 Korean women, who earned 59 cents per day. By the 1920s, Koreans were earning nearly two dollars a day there. And by 1938, 101 Korean men, representing 3.4 percent of the workforce, and 217 women, representing 4.8 percent, worked in the cannery.[14]

Thus by the end of the 1930s, more Koreans (about seven hundred) worked in the pineapple industry (the fields and the cannery) than on the sugar plantations. And the influx of these Korean cannery workers led to the first real community of Koreans in the Liliha and Palama districts of Honolulu. While not truly a "Koreatown," this area was popular with Koreans because of its proximity to the cannery and the low rent. And since the area was also near the waterfront, men who had worked as dockhands in Korea could find jobs in their original line of work. Finally, other Koreans settled in these districts simply because a number of fellow Koreans were already established there.[15]

Most Koreans, however, moved to the city simply to start their own businesses. Koreans truly made their mark in the realm of independent small business—a trend that began almost immediately after their arrival in Hawai'i. As early as 1907, before he returned to Korea, Hyŏn Sun observed that "there are many peddlers, restaurateurs, cart-sellers, barbers, hot-tub keepers, grocery keepers and medicine sellers. The Koreans who can speak English work as shopkeepers in small American shops or translators in Plantations or courts to earn 30–70$ per month."[16] In starting independent businesses, Koreans copied the earlier pattern of the Chinese and Japanese, giving them something in common with their East Asian counterparts.

Since the more numerous Japanese and Chinese were already well established in independent small businesses in the city, why would the Koreans want to compete? One reason is clear: as most Koreans had been urbanites originally, it was natural for them to return to the city. Second, since the number of Korean small businesses was never very significant, they did not engender the resentment of the white economic establishment, as the large numbers of Chinese and Japanese businesses had earlier. Third, Koreans were willing to risk the competition because only in the cities could they establish a large enough population to maintain social, political, and religious organizations of their own. Fourth, Koreans were by nature more individualistic and resentful of regimentation, hence their desire to leave the plantations. In recent years, anthropological studies have concluded, as did Bernice Kim during her fieldwork in Hawai'i in the 1930s, that Korean aversion to regimentation is more intense than that of most ethnicities and that this led them into small business. One man who employed Koreans remarked that they "were as individualistic as New Englanders, each for himself but loyal to the job and the boss." Finally, a longtime resident of Honolulu suggested that Koreans had little choice but to go into inde-

pendent business because "insurance companies would not bond Koreans; no
other group was similarly discriminated against."[17]

While the above reasons for starting a business in the city were unique to
Koreans, there were additional reasons that Koreans shared with their Chinese
and Japanese counterparts. The first was racism, which limited the employment
opportunities for Asian immigrants. Put simply, early twentieth century Honolulu was not a place of equal employment opportunities. As Andrew Lind flatly
stated, "opportunity for Orientals is limited to informal 'understandings' within
certain fields." A second reason was the common desire to make more money
and attain a higher social status. Lind noted, "[T]he plantation is associated in
the minds of both immigrants and their children with inferior status, and to
accept permanently such a position would be to admit personal and family failure." He went on to say that "certainly the remarkable infiltration of Japanese,
Chinese and Korean immigrants into the field of small store-keepers has been
attended by a most decided rise in self-esteem and status in their respective
communities. Even the humble peddler of cakes and vegetables enjoys considerable status in the eyes of his countrymen since this occupation marks an
advance from and an independence of the humiliating plantation control."[18]

Koreans sometimes opened businesses based on some experience on the
plantation. Operating small shops selling groceries, drugs, or general mer-
chandise, for example, "has provided most immigrants with a stepping stone to
economic and social achievement. In Hawaii, the Chinese, Japanese and Koreans have been noticeably inclined toward this particular channel of advancement." One Korean woman recalled that on the plantation her husband "at one
time . . . sold cold drinks from his room. He did well and business picked up,
so he then set up a general store selling things to wear, to eat, and tools to use
on the farm. He carried on this business from a home." Other examples
included a Mr. Kim, "who accumulated $10,000 operating a grocery store on
Ewa plantation and was called the most successful Korean businessman [before
he] became bankrupt as the result of a momentary failure. Another prosperous
grocery store started by Song Wŏn-gyu in Waipahu plantation moved to Honolulu." A mid-1920s survey of 546 Korean families found that more than half
(293) were engaged in miscellaneous shop-keeping. Another report indicated
that "the Japanese and Koreans have made the greatest inroads upon the retail
trade, showing indexes of occupancy in 1920 of 1.21 and .77 respectively. These
indices have undoubtedly increased considerably since that time."[19]

Some Koreans, having learned how to repair items such as shoes, clothing,
and furniture on the plantation, decided to take up similar work in the city.
Bernice Kim concluded that occupations requiring manual dexterity were well
suited to the Korean, who was generally "deft and quick in learning to use his
hands." An observer noted that "the Koreans appear to have succeeded unusually well as competitors to the Chinese in the shoe-making and tailoring trades,
these being among the few non-plantation pursuits in which the Koreans have

thus far effectively established themselves." Perhaps not atypical is the experience of Kim Tai-yoon (Kim T'ae-yun), who had come to Hawai'i in 1905 at the age of eighteen with her husband and who moved from plantation to plantation along the Hamakua Coast of Hawai'i repairing shoes and secondhand furniture before moving to the city. But while some no doubt gained experience in the furniture business on the plantations or in Korea, others learned on the job. For example, in 1915, Lee Nai Soo (Yi Nae-su) was hired by the Coyne Furniture Company as a cabinetmaker. His skills were such that he was able to get four other Koreans into his department by the end of the year. As new hands they received eighteen dollars a week; later, as they learned the trade, their salary increased to twenty-one dollars a week. These men had had no special training, instead learning the business after getting into it. Later, some of them were even able to open their own establishments.[20]

Other Koreans, having out of necessity learned to sew their own clothes on the plantations, became tailors in the city, fashioning both men's and women's clothes. One of the first was a man who came to Hawai'i as a boy: "[I was in Honolulu] about five years. When I was fifteen years old, I worked at a tailor shop. A man's tailor shop. I was working learning how to make clothes. Man's tailor . . . make pants for six months; then six months on coats. Then you work for the master at $1.00–$2.00 a month. Later, you learn to make overcoats and vests, then become a regular tailor. [The owner was] Ahn Won-ku. [Our customers were] regular people—civilians. Army had nothing to do. [At that time] only one man had a tailor shop." A sociologist writing at the time stated that "dressmaking has become the particular domain of the Japanese and the Koreans." The same writer also noted that "the tailoring trade is gravitating increasingly into the hands of the Orientals, the Chinese, Koreans, Japanese and Filipinos ranking in the order named."[21]

Still others started laundries, sometimes combining them with sewing and tailoring. One woman remembered that "[our family] had no jobs in Honolulu, so . . . [w]e took in laundry at home. [We did the wash] all by hand, scrubbed on a board. After a full day's wash our hands and knuckles would sorely bleed." Another recalled, "I bought a sewing machine and took in sewing. My mother and sister-in-law took in laundry. They scrubbed and starched and ironed and mended for five cents a shirt. For twenty-five cents I made shirts with hand-bound buttonholes. That's how we made a living. If we all worked hard, we earned $50.00 per month to feed the five of us . . . so three of us worked; one took in sewing and the other two took in hand laundry."[22]

Koreans also soon took advantage of the growing military presence, particularly in the central Oahu town of Wahiawa, where there were already several hundred Koreans working in the pineapple fields. Not long after Schofield Army Barracks and Wheeler Air Force Base were established in Wahiawa after 1912, Koreans came to monopolize the laundry and tailoring businesses that catered to the servicemen. And when Pearl Harbor Naval Base was established, the Koreans soon dominated the laundry and tailoring trade in that area as well. One sociologist wrote at that time, "[I]n Honolulu the Koreans have within recent years achieved a particularly strong position in the tailoring business and now virtually monopolize the tailoring for the military population."[23]

Finally, Koreans who had operated boardinghouses on the plantations transferred their skills to the city, where they opened hotels or lodging houses that catered to the Koreans arriving from the plantations. As early as 1907, one observer wrote, "There are four Korean hotels in Honolulu, two of which are Haedong and Jinbo; [these] hotels have good service and are clean."[24]

Of course, many of these callings required a significant amount of capital to get started—an amount sometimes beyond the means of an individual or family. It was difficult for Koreans to get a regular bank loan, so to obtain financing, they relied on a traditional system of rotating credit known as *kye,* similar to *tanomoshi* among Japanese or *hui* among Chinese. The *kye* worked as follows: each member of a *kye* contributed, for example, twenty dollars. Thus among ten members, the total would be two hundred dollars. Whoever needs the money bids for it by offering a certain rate of interest to be paid back to the contributors; the highest bidder takes the sum. This system depended a great deal upon the honesty and integrity of the members, although usually members were already bound together based on clan ties, provincial origins, or, simply, the face-to-face relationship among friends. Many Korean businesses were started with the assistance of the *kye.* For example, Kim Pyung Sup borrowed two hundred dollars from a *kye* to buy tools and supplies to open a furniture repair shop in Wahiawa. Through his experience in repairing furniture, he later learned to make new furniture.[25]

Although some Koreans came to Honolulu with a definite plan, many arrived without any job prospects or particular skills and simply took the first opportunity to present itself. After working on the plantation for four years, one man recalled: "We didn't like the work. The hours were long and the work was hard. We heard there were better-paying jobs in Honolulu. We imagined Honolulu was a big, glamorous metropolis. When we first came to Hawaii as *yi-min* [immigrants], we all dreamed of wealth. We could see no way of getting rich if we remained on Kauai. So we took the boat to the big city. Honolulu was a busy city. There was much to see. But we had to find work. Somehow I heard about a job as a yardboy. I grabbed it. My boss was Mr. Hackfeld. I was twenty-one then. My friends got other kinds of jobs, as houseboys or as laundry shop helpers. We all earned so little. I began farming vegetables on the side after my work on my boss' yard."[26]

Some Koreans arrived in the city and simply drifted from job to job: "At first, I worked on the sugar plantation. After a while, I worked at the Immigration Office. . . . I also worked as an interpreter at the sugar refinery [for] about three years. [Then] I assisted Rev. Min Chan-ho from Korea and assisted the newly arrived Koreans. . . . I moved over to work with youth clubs, then moved again to work in the sugar company-owned stores. . . . I also taught at the Korean language school for four years. I wandered about, known as a teacher." Another recalled: "I weeded in the sugar plantations and when that was done, I cooked rice for the Koreans. I served as cook . . . for 40 to 50 people, but they got away without paying. . . . Later I came out to Honolulu and tried selling clothing and yardage, but this wasn't very successful. So I wandered a bit."[27]

Life in this new urban environment was often difficult, especially in the early years after leaving the plantation, and initially many were unable to find success. In the 1920s Japanese survey of 546 Koreans mentioned earlier, a total of one hundred, or nearly 20 percent, reported being jobless. One reason given was the stiff competition of the Chinese and Japanese, although the survey— not surprisingly, given its Japanese origin—cited "wasteful habits" and "forced contributions to political causes." Nevertheless, the Koreans did not give up easily. As one sociologist remarked, "[D]espite repeated failures, the ex-plantation [Korean] is willing to hazard another attempt in a new line of business or another location."[28]

Generally speaking, Koreans met with economic success when they moved into the city. By the mid-1920s, some tailoring and laundering establishments in Honolulu took in about one hundred dollars a month. In Wahiawa during the same period, there were already a dozen laundry establishments with property worth about fifty thousand dollars. A number of grocery stores took in several hundred dollars a month. Those Koreans working as day laborers in the city earned about three dollars a day. And even in the pineapple fields of Wahiawa, several hundred Koreans earned over two dollars a day. The Japanese survey also acknowledged the potential for earning substantial sums of money, even though food expenses hovered around fourteen dollars a month per person. The survey concluded the following: few Koreans were suffering financially, those who lived in the cities were doing rather well, and as a group, their economic power was increasing. Sociologists came to a similar conclusion: "It is significant that of the two smaller immigrant groups which arrived at about the same time, the Puerto Ricans and the Koreans, the latter had by 1930 graduated out of the laboring class to a far greater degree than had the former, and insofar as comparable data are available at a later date, they indicate an increasing differential between the two groups."[29]

In sum, except for those who worked in the cannery, most of the Koreans who went to the cities worked in a hodgepodge of independent business pursuits. Besides those already mentioned, some of the more common occupations involved carpentry, musical instrument repair, flower gardening, and dockwork. By 1930, statistically speaking, excluding those who worked on plantations or pineapple fields or on independent farms, Korean men were employed in the following occupations: other labor, 11 percent; craftsmen, 10 percent; operatives, 8 percent; clerical workers, 8 percent; managers and officials, 4 percent; sales workers, 4 percent; other service workers, 3 percent; domestic workers, 2 percent; and professional workers, 2 percent.[30]

The rapid movement of Koreans to the city, particularly Honolulu, is reflected in the statistics. By 1910, only five years after immigration from Korea had ended, 10 percent of the Korean population in Hawai'i resided in Honolulu. A decade later, more than one out of four Koreans (27 percent) lived there, surpassing the Japanese at 22 percent. And by 1930, two out of five Koreans lived in Honolulu, whereas only one-third of all Japanese lived there. If Honolulu County is included, by 1930, almost two-thirds of the Koreans lived in or around Honolulu; 10 percent were concentrated in Wahiawa. Thus the Koreans were similar to the Chinese, who had arrived much earlier and were much more urban-oriented than the Japanese, who remained in rural agricultural occupations for a much longer period. And when compared with the Puerto Ricans, who arrived on the plantations at the same time as the Koreans, we find that only 15 percent of the Puerto Ricans had established themselves in Honolulu by 1920, as opposed to 27 percent of the Koreans.[31]

Like other ethnic groups, in the early years, Koreans sought each other's company for comfort and mutual support in Honolulu, leading to small Korean settlements in the Liliha and Palama districts, as noted earlier, and, to a lesser extent, on the slopes of Punchbowl Crater among the Portuguese. However, they were never able to establish a separate community or a single integrated center for their cultural life. This was true not only because of their small numbers—the 6,461 Koreans in 1930 represented only about 2 percent of Hawai'i's population—but, as we shall see, also because of divisions within the Korean community. Moreover, unlike the mainland United States, there was no strong disposition toward racial segregation in Honolulu. Thus Korean urban residential patterns, shaped by their lack of numbers, factional divisions, and an ethos of integration, tended to promote more rapid acculturation than those of a larger population like the Japanese, because of forced interaction with non-Korean neighbors. The same pattern of forced interaction was also found in Korean business activities. Since Korean businesses had too few Korean customers, they had to serve a non-Korean clientele in order to survive. Japanese businesses, on the other hand, usually could rely solely on Japanese customers.[32]

So rapid and complete was the Korean exodus from the plantation to the city that rural Koreans soon became a rarity. "Of the ten or more [Korean] families who used to be in Kekaha, I believe only one or two families are now left. Those who have left have all come out to Honolulu. Perhaps only a few of the remaining Korean children even know Korean today. They tend to fraternize with Portuguese and Hawaiians and part-Hawaiians. They are not even a minority; they just don't count, so far as numbers go. Eventually, I think even the few remaining ones will leave for Honolulu. One of the rare Korean girls left in Kekaha is married to a Part-Hawaiian. She and another sister are about the only young [Korean] females left."[33]

Taken together, the rapid Korean movement into the city and their residential and occupational patterns there suggest that Koreans adjusted more quickly than the Japanese to an urbanizing culture and had successfully figured out how to find success in a frontier capitalist setting. Their concentration in small independent shops and commercial ventures resulted, in many cases, in financial rewards in excess of anything that could be earned on the plantations. Koreans were also aware that in this new society, status depended on income gained through hard work rather than on the traditional determinants in Korea such as birth and family connections. Sociologists argue that entry into commerce and trade constituted not only the major vehicle for advancement in American society for East Asian immigrants, including Koreans, but that it also represented an indicator of Americanization. As Lind put it: "[T]he plantation frontier transforms the plodding peasant into the money-seeking climber."[34] Using this as a measure of acculturation and given the rapid influx of Koreans into this line of work leads to the inescapable conclusion that the acculturation of Koreans was indeed swift. Absent from this discussion of the exodus from the plantations, the start of commercial ventures in the city, and acculturation is the important role of picture brides in the process. It is to this subject that we now turn.

6

The Picture-Bride System

Only about one in ten of the adult immigrants between 1903 and 1905 were women, nearly all of them accompanying their husbands. As a result, there were virtually no single Korean women for the bachelors to marry. It also means that much of what has been told thus far has been a male-oriented story. In the period between 1910 and 1924, an influx of picture brides (estimates range from between six hundred and one thousand) came to Hawai'i to equalize somewhat the ratio of men to women.[1]

The origins of the picture-bride phenomenon can be traced to the 1908 Gentlemen's Agreement between the United States and Japan. While that agreement prohibited the issuance of visas to Japanese workers, it did permit entry to family members. When Japanese picture brides began arriving in Honolulu, it was clear that Koreans could use the same system. The term "picture bride" or "picture marriage" *(sajin kyŏlhon)* refers to the exchange of photographs between the prospective bride and groom through an intermediary. After both sides agree and the groom pays the appropriate fees, the bride travels to Hawai'i and is married at the immigration station to the man she has only seen in a photograph. Of course, it was always possible for Koreans in Hawai'i to return to Korea to obtain a wife, and a few men did so, but such a venture was costly and time-consuming. The picture-bride system was a much more convenient alternative. Since both Korean and Japanese families traditionally practiced arranged marriages, the picture-bride system was simply a long-distance adaptation of an age-old tradition.

It is not clear exactly how the Korean system began or who the first picture bride was, because there are several varying accounts. According to one, it was the Methodist minister Min Ch'an-ho who first began to arrange the importation of picture brides in 1909. Another, more detailed, account suggests that the first picture bride arrived in Hawai'i through the efforts of a woman named Paek Yesoo from the northern Korean city of Wiju. She reportedly sent the first woman, Sara Choi, as a bride for thirty-eight-year-old furniture maker Yi Nae-su. Choi arrived on November 28, 1910, and was married to Yi four days later by Reverend Min Ch'an-ho. The second picture bride, also sent from Wiju by

Paek Yesoo, was a twenty-three-year-old named Myong-son who had previously been betrothed to a nine-year-old boy when she was thirteen. She arrived on December 24, 1910, aboard the *Mongolia,* having been promised to Paek's relative in Hawai'i, Paek Man-kuk, a thirty-nine-year-old minister. Yet another account suggests that the first picture brides from Seoul and central Korea were sent by Cha Kongsam, who had gone to Hawai'i in 1904 but returned to Korea five years later. Cha sent some photographs to Pak Laisun in Hawai'i, and Pak sent pictures of prospective grooms back to Cha.[2]

While the precise origins of the picture-bride system are unclear, we do know that most of the brides came from Kyŏngsang Province in southeastern Korea, which includes Pusan, Korea's largest port and second largest city, as well as Taegu and the port city of Masan. The first brides from this area were sent by relatives of men in Hawai'i. While it is not entirely clear why most of the picture brides came from Kyŏngsang Province, it did suffer the most severe dislocations after 1910, when the imposition of Japanese colonial rule resulted in many Koreans being dispossessed of their land. And since Korea had not yet been industrialized, those who did lose their land often had no choice but to leave their country. Thus while many of the unemployed men went to Japan, where an economic boom associated with World War I had created a demand for workers, women, by contrast, seized the opportunity to go to Hawai'i.[3]

Four groups potentially stood to benefit from the picture-bride system: the men who would gain wives; the women who would gain husbands; the intermediaries, who would realize a profit; and the planters. Several writers have erroneously asserted that the picture-bride system was started by plantation managers who were grappling with the unruly behavior of the Korean bachelor community. That is, the plantation owners supposedly encouraged the importation of picture brides as a means of "settling down" the men and making them better, more stable, sugarcane workers. However, unlike their sponsorship of Christian mission work on the plantations, there is no evidence that planters encouraged picture brides as official policy. They probably did welcome such a development, assuming that family men would make better workers. But if the planters had hopes that picture brides would stem the exodus of Koreans from their plantations, they were mistaken. Instead, the arrival of picture brides tended to accelerate the already rapid departure of Koreans for the city.[4]

We know that planters did not officially sponsor picture brides because the one time they were given an opportunity to do so, they declined. According to the minutes of the HSPA trustees, the opportunity appeared early in 1912: "Mr. Smith stated that he had been approached by Mr. J. Lightfoot, a local attorney, who has asked if the Association will make a loan of $500 to C. H. Young (Yong), a Korean employment agent here, for the purpose of defraying his expenses in making a trip to Korea to bring back the wives of a considerable number of Korean men now here; it also being proposed that for each Korean woman brought here by him a credit of $5 be made on account of the amount of the loan." The planters refused to go along: "Mr. Smith stated further that having made some inquiry as to the character and responsibility of the man C. H. Young (Yong), he has found that he is not such a person as should be entrusted with any such mission, even if the mission itself were favored, and he could not recommend the loan." As a result, "[i]t was considered by the Trustees that while the bringing in of Korean women was desirable, they could not see their way clear to make such a loan to C. H. Young (Yong) and that Mr. Lightfoot should be so advised."[5]

For the men involved, of course, the picture-bride system offered them a modicum of normal family life in Hawai'i now that it was apparent they would not soon return to a Korea torn by domestic chaos and Japanese domination. Moreover, the initiation of the picture-bride system just five years after immigration ended in 1905 is another indicator that Koreans were quickly making the transition from sojourner to settler, realizing that their futures lay in Hawai'i rather than Korea. This conclusion is supported by the fact that after 1910, the year Japan ended Korean independence and the picture-bride system began, the rate of return to Korea was negligible.

The motivations and characteristics of the women who became picture brides were not very different from those of the men in Hawai'i who would become their husbands. Like many of the men, the women were fleeing poverty and were attracted to the supposed riches of Hawai'i. And many of the women were also in some way connected to Christianity. Both men and women were also quite young, the majority being seventeen to twenty-four years old, although some were as young as fifteen or as old as forty.[6]

On the other hand, these men and women differed in certain ways. One significant difference was that while the men had been primarily urban residents from all over the peninsula, the picture brides largely came from rural southeastern Korea. Also, with few exceptions, the picture brides were apparently relatively uneducated, a result of traditional Confucian beliefs that women did not require a formal education. According to one source, some had never gone to grade school and could barely write their names in Korean, and of those who had started grade school, most had not finished. Further, only about 5 percent had attended high school. A survey of forty-nine picture brides confirmed this, showing that fourteen had no education whatsoever, twenty-two had only one to three years, eight had four to six years, four had seven to nine years, and only one had ten to twelve years of education. In some cases, leaving for Hawai'i interrupted their education. On the other hand, those few who had received a higher education were "liberated women" and had worked as teachers, nurses, or church workers.[7]

The portrait of picture brides fleeing rural poverty is borne out by personal accounts. One account stated: "Young Oak's family had always been struggling. Her father's silk merchant business was failing [and] the family had no other source of income. . . . Her family used to live in a small house in the backyard of her maternal grandmother. Occasionally her mother collected grain and vegetables in exchange for dress-making services. Sometimes the family skipped meals." One woman recalled her own background: "I was born in 1904. There were seven of us, three brothers, three sisters, and myself. My parents were very poor. . . . My place was a very small country village, only about one hundred houses."[8]

Like their future husbands who preceded them, most of the picture brides were attracted by the wealth they believed awaited them in Hawai'i. More often as not, however, these hopes were wildly unrealistic: "I came to Hawaii as a picture bride . . . because I had heard so many times about an uncle on my mother's side who was doing quite well for himself in Hawaii. It just sounded like a dreamland to me. . . . I had heard in Korea that Hawaii was a paradise. People spoke of clothing that grew on trees, free to be picked, and the abundance of fruits and all kinds of foods. Money, they said, was not necessary for survival and could be saved for future use. I heard only of prosperity and wealth in the islands."[9]

Such unrealistic expectations of wealth were encouraged by the intermediaries, just like the recruiters who had lured their husbands-to-be a decade or so earlier. One matchmaker told some prospective picture brides: "You girls know the respectful Mr. Koo, who is a teacher at the Ham An Normal School. His sister went to Hawaii not long ago and married a Korean man. Lately the family has been receiving money and expensive clothes. If I were you, I would definitely go to Hawaii. There no one worries about their next meal and firewood. . . . [I]f you girls marry these men, it will bring you and your family a great fortune." One picture bride recalled the pitch delivered to her by the intermediary: "This man told me to expect to see money growing on every tree. My eyes were dreamy. I believed him because he said everybody in Hawaii was rich." Another picture bride recalled, "The go-between said there would be so much food we'd never be hungry. That stuck in my mind. On the farm there was never enough to eat."[10]

While economic improvement was the most salient factor in explaining the influx of picture brides into Hawai'i, some had other motives. For several it was their association with Christianity. After one woman met some missionaries, "since then her wish to go to the fairyland of America was always on her mind. Every time she heard the magic word America she got excited. . . . [S]he was just overwhelmed with the idea of America." For adventurous educated women, becoming a picture bride represented a chance for independent travel: "I . . . met one of these matchmakers with my friends and . . . in those days it seemed the only route by which a girl could possibly go to America alone."[11]

Other women wanted to escape Japanese domination. One recalled, "People can't talk, can't walk around. Under the Japanese, no freedom. Not even free talking. A very hard time . . . Hawaii's a free place, everybody living well. Hawaii had freedom, so if you like talk, you can talk; you like work, you can work." Another picture bride reminisced to her grandson: "Japanese I no want.

They take over Korea. They take all metal bowls and chopsticks, so everybody get wooden kine bowl and wooden chopstick. . . . [I]n Korea everybody no get money." One second-generation Korean recalled that "my mother was ready to be imprisoned as a political activist in Seoul. . . . She was eighteen years old at that time."[12]

The few who possessed some education and the heightened expectations of liberated women sought to escape the traditional limitations placed on Korean women and explore new horizons: "I was a nurse in Masan. I was nineteen years old. I had a good ear for picking up languages. I worked as a nurse in a Japanese hospital and had reached a certain degree of proficiency in Japanese. On holidays I would often go to the theater to see a movie. Spontaneously, in my mind arose a yearning for the magnificent cultural activities which appeared in American movies." Another, who had attended a church-run night school for four years and a Japanese-run normal school for two, "had never wanted to marry a peasant boy from the other side of the hill nor tread the same path as other women she had seen. She thought she had been cut out for a better lot than that of a village peasant wife."[13]

Some women, often from prosperous backgrounds, were motivated by the opportunity to pursue higher education, a route not usually open to early twentieth century Korean women. "Is there a college I can attend if I should go to Hawaii?" asked one eighteen-year-old potential picture bride of the intermediary. Another "had a burning desire to travel and study. . . . She was seventeen and the youngest of three children when she decided to leave home and go to Japan to see for herself 'that other world' that the girls in the dormitory dared only to whisper about. . . . [S]he left her family and home forever in 1917. While in Japan, she learned that she could get to America only as a picture bride. . . . [I]n her heart, she was only going to 'borrow' someone's name to gain legitimate entry to America, and then pursue her own goal to study."[14]

Others wanted to escape the oppression women experienced in a society still largely governed by Confucian precepts. These precepts included the strict segregation of the sexes, arranged marriages, concubinage, wife beating, and domination by mothers-in-law. As one woman recalled, "That time girls in my village can't walk even ten miles outside. Can't go any place, only to Sunday School. . . . It was very unusual, because girls always only were home their whole life before they marry. Never went out, only stayed home—working, sewing, working. That time a girl very seldom went out to a foreign country." Another woman who had endured a marriage arranged by her parents said, "I was already married to a man younger than myself. We were not poor. But my husband had a concubine and he spent every night out drinking. So I decided to run away." One matchmaker who recognized that escape from in-laws could be a selling point told prospective picture brides: "If you marry here, you become a slave to your husband and his parents until you die. In Hawaii, no one bothers you."[15]

Whatever these women's reasons were for wanting to become picture brides, there were hurdles to overcome, not the least of which was securing parental permission, especially that of the father, who headed the household and who decided when and whom his daughters would marry. Of course, those who were teenagers were clearly still under their parents' authority. One went so far as to steal her father's *tojang* (seal) to forge exit documents. One fifteen-year-old recalled her parents' anger when she broke the news to them. Another "boarded a ship at the Pusan port with five other girls, despite my family's disapproval of my departure." Three young women who were considering becoming picture brides told the matchmaker they were nervous because they had not yet talked it over with their parents. Another recalled, "About two weeks before I have to leave [for Hawai'i], I tell my father and mother. My father was very angry. My mother was very sad, and my father only blame my mother, fighting, you know. . . . I was so scared, afraid of father and mother. I only cry by myself. On the day I leave . . . only my mother bring me to the train station. I was very sad because of my parents. Father was still mad."16

Potential picture brides feared their fathers' reactions, but mothers also opposed their journeys to Hawai'i. One picture bride recalled her mother's tearful reaction when she told her parents she was leaving to marry a Korean man in Hawai'i: "What kind of joke is this by a sixteen year old girl? Do you know how far away America is?" Another recalled, "In 1915, I decided to go to Hawaii and asked my mother whether I could be a picture bride. . . . My mother thought I was crazy and tried to persuade me to abandon such a notion, but in vain." Another appealed to her skeptical mother: "If I marry someone here in Ham An, what is my chance to find a man with wealth and a good reputation. As you know, being a daughter of a poor family with little education, I will repeat the same hardship you have gone through. So try to see my marriage in a positive light."17

Another hurdle the brides faced was Confucian tradition. In a Confucian society, adult children are obligated to care for elderly parents and perform the traditional rituals at their deaths. Shirking such duties was considered unfilial. However, since many of the picture brides were Christian, such considerations weighed less heavily on their minds. Some picture brides were chastised by an elderly Korean woman: "I don't understand why you nice-looking girls want to go to Hawaii. Haven't you heard all sorts of miserable stories about picture marriage? Can't you find a decent man in your village? It is never too late to change your mind. Remember, it is an unpardonable sin to cause heartache to your old parents and have them miss you until they are buried. Not having seen their loved ones so long, they will never close their eyes when they die." The brides-to-be, however, "did not seem to pay attention to the typical scoldings they had heard so many times."18

The picture-bride system was also perceived as unseemly, as the reputation of the entire family was involved. One local Japanese newspaper in Korea, upon learning that a woman in that district had become a picture bride, ran a story titled, "Lee Young Oak Sold to Hawaii for Money." As a result, one woman made her arrangements in secret: "Nobody know I was going to Hawaii. If they know, everybody have a big surprise. Only my auntie and I know. My auntie living in Pusan. I went to my auntie's house. My cousin was getting married and I was going to sew clothes. I was telling a lie. So, I came there and I secretly make my passport ready. I make it secretly because that time me going to Hawaii alone is just like girl selling." Another picture bride endured the following: "There were tears and loud wailing at the shocking news. In-Sook was accused of selling herself for prostitution, of having disgraced the family. It was tearfully impressed upon her that no member of their clan would ever be able to face the community or hold up their heads as long as they lived. In-Sook expected this reaction and waited for the day when she would be released from this turmoil and be established in the world paved with gold and live in the security of her chosen husband. That dream sustained her through the months of daily mounting mental and physical revilement and condemnation."[19]

The mechanics of how the system operated in Korea centered mainly upon the role of the go-between, or *chungsin,* as the person was known in Korea. Some go-betweens actively searched for picture brides, while others simply waited for prospective brides to come to them. Go-betweens were both male and female, and all were well dressed. Some were relatives of Koreans already in Hawai'i, others had gone to Hawai'i and returned to Korea, and some were not relatives at all.

Sometimes the young women initiated the process by seeking out the go-between. "There was a man at Chunju from Hawaii. A number of us . . . decided to visit him. It was rumored that he knew how young girls could go to Hawaii, or even to the United States itself. We met him at the home of Pastor Kim. We hardly dared look directly at him. Our eyes drank in his dapper figure, his smartly pressed Western clothes. He smoked cigars and he studied us carefully. When his eyes met mine, I felt as though he were undressing me. It was that kind of look. My face burned and I wanted to run away. But even more I wanted to learn something about this 'magic route' to America. So I remained and asked questions. He sat perfectly still for a few minutes and then spoke in a voice both soothing and calculating. 'You are all very pretty.' After a few seconds' pause, he resumed. 'You can become picture brides.' This was strange talk. What could a picture bride be?"[20]

Other times, the go-between sought out young women. According to one account, in 1916, a "well-dressed old lady" was wandering around a village near Chinju and spied a young woman. The following dialogue ensued:

Woman: "What is your name, and how old are you?"

Girl: "My name is Lee Young Oak and I am fifteen years old."

"Young Oak, would you be interested in going to America?"

"Are you Jinjoo Grandma?"

"Yes."

"Grandma, I am only fifteen. Can I still marry?"

"Why not? Although you are fifteen years old, you look at least eighteen. Moreover, you are pretty. Whoever takes you is a lucky man."

Since this woman had already arranged for a few girls from the village to go to Hawai'i, she was well-known in the village. She told Young Oak that many Korean girls were going to Hawai'i to marry Korean men who were making a good living.[21]

Sometimes the go-betweens went to the families first, understanding the powerful role of the parents, and used the familiar promise of riches to persuade the family. One man went to the Lee family in Taegu in 1912 and "informed them that he knew of an unparalleled opportunity for their daughters to become rich if they married bachelors living in Hawaii. He painted glowing pictures of how prosperous these men were and how they move in circles with other wealthy men of position and prestige."[22]

The entire transaction, of course, centered around the exchange of photographs. For the young women, typically the go-between brought along a Japanese photographer to take pictures of them dressed in their traditional silk dress, the *chima chogori*. After the pictures were taken, and in a few instances doctored to disguise disfigurement, as one go-between told a group of prospective brides, "I will send your pictures to my boss in Hawaii with your names and ages written on the back of the pictures." In this particular instance, the young women begged the go-between to keep the photography session a secret in case it all fell through. They did not want to risk the loss of face that accompanied a broken engagement or lose the chance to marry someone in their village—for what young man would want to marry someone who had been rejected by another?

As for the photographs of the prospective grooms, deception was the norm. First of all, the men were usually at least twice as old as the brides. Second, the rigors of plantation work often exacted a toll on them physically, making them look even older. Third, long hours in the subtropical sun gave the men a deep tan, which would hardly prove attractive to women whose idea of genteelness was a pale complexion. Finally, few of the men were wealthy; certainly their poverty was unlikely to attract a fetching young lady.

To combat these problems, then, the men somehow had to conceal their "defects." For example, they would often rent or borrow a suit to give the impression of wealth. Some would also have their picture taken in front of the plantation manager's house or their employer's house, giving the impression that it was their own. Or, perhaps the picture was taken with the prospective groom's foot resting casually on the running board of an automobile to give the impression that he was the car's owner. Others would apply talc to their dark faces to give themselves the pale skin of an upper-class professional. Still others had the photographer touch up the pictures to make the subject appear younger and/or less tanned. And some simply sent photographs taken years earlier. One man recounted: "Then we heard of men who were getting wives from Korea. We were excited. We thought we should wait till we save enough money. When we heard that it might take months or years before we could get a wife we started our application. First, we wore our Sunday suits and went to a photo studio. I trembled when I handed my picture to an agent. Some of the men were so nervous they laughed, as if the whole thing was a joke." And one man told his daughter that it was her mother who had tricked *him:* "My father arrived from Korea . . . at about age 12 and lived on Maui with his dad and brother. . . . The arrangements for the picture bride marriage were made by the minister. My father said there were ten pictures of women to choose from. After his choice was made, and his bride arrived at the pier, my father said she looked no older than fourteen. He explained that when she had sent her picture to him she had written that she was sixteen on the back of the picture. After she arrived, he didn't have money to send her back to Korea. They began life in one bedroom with one sewing machine in Maui."[24]

Nonetheless, the women in Korea suspected subterfuge on the part of the prospective grooms. Stories such as the following were sure to raise suspicions: "[My aunt] came to Hawaii as a 'picture-bride' at the age of sixteen to be married to a man who, to her horror, she later found out, was 72. It appears that the qualifications of the potential husband, because of the distance or for other reasons not clearly known, was not investigated by the family of the bride." In one instance, a woman was concerned because her prospective groom had had his picture taken in the sitting position, raising the fear that he was in some way incapacitated.[25]

In theory, both parties were given a choice, as each was able to examine photographs of the other. Yet in practice, the one who chose first had the advantage, since the one chosen could then only accept or reject. Sometimes the men chose first. One go-between in Korea told the prospective picture brides that when she returned she would bring photographs of the grooms as well as money. Two months later she produced three pictures and gave each girl a specific picture, according to the writing on the back of each one. Nineteen-year-old Sunhee was matched with a thirty-seven-year-old, twenty-one-year-old Subi was matched with a thirty-eight-year-old, and fifteen-year-old Young Oak was matched with the oldest of the three. On the back of this picture was written, "My name is Chung Bong Woon and I am 42 years old. I picked Lee Young Oak."[26]

Understandably, Young Oak was shocked by the age of her prospective husband: "Jinjoo Grandma, how come I was matched with the 42 year old man? Didn't you know I am the youngest of the three? I am sure the marriage broker or the man in Hawaii mistook my picture for someone else's. Otherwise such a match could not happen." The matchmaker replied: "According to the letter of my broker in Honolulu, Mr. Chung is the best of the three men. The broker felt that Mr. Chung deserved the best picture bride. So he gave Mr. Chung the first choice, and he picked you from the three pictures. Not only is he a good man but also he has quite a bit of money. He is a gentleman from the Choong-Chung Province. Therefore, don't feel so bad about his age." Young Oak thus accepted because "the fact that he was living in America and had a lot of money made other conditions almost insignificant as far as she was concerned." The other two women had also complained that their grooms were too old, to which the matchmaker replied: "I know the men are old, but old husbands know how to treat their wives right." [27]

In other cases, the women got first choice. In one instance, the male go-between, asking the woman to choose, "brought a large packet of pictures. Each picture was three inches by two and a half inches, showing only the man's head and shoulders. On the back of the picture was the man's name and his place of residence." In another instance, one woman recalled, "As we turned the word [picture bride] over, perplexedly, on our tongues, he [the matchmaker] rummaged through his pockets and pulled out pictures of men. They ranged from very young to very old, from handsome to ugly, from thin to fat. I could not comprehend what this had to do with us. 'If you will pick from these photographs the man you would like to marry, I will take your picture to him, and if all is agreeable to the man and a suitable dowry and transportation funds are provided, I will make arrangements for you to go to America to marry him.' Being the chosen rather than the chooser was naturally just as disconcerting to the men as it was to the women. "One man asked, 'If my wife is fat and ugly can I send her back?' The agent glared at him. He scolded, 'Our work is very serious.' We didn't know whether he meant no fat girls would be sent." [28]

Once both sides reached an agreement, family registers were exchanged, and the men had to come up with *chunbi*, or preparation money. At a minimum, this expense totaled slightly over one hundred dollars and included traveling expenses for the bride (about seventy dollars), the commission for the marriage broker (about thirty dollars), and photography expenses (about twenty dollars). Yet many accounts suggest that the actual amount was usually much higher—in the neighborhood of three or four hundred dollars, which was quite a sum at that time. To raise such a large amount, the men sometimes had to resort to the *kye*, just like those who needed capital to start business ventures in the city. [29]

There were three reasons that such large sums were paid out. First, some of the marriage brokers were crooked and swindled the men by charging them for nonexistent expenses. Second, the men wanted to convince their prospective brides that they were indeed wealthy so the women would not change their minds and refuse to come to Hawai'i. For example, one man, Mr. Chung, sent a total of 1,700 yen ($850) to his prospective bride. Of course, occasionally the woman accepted money from her prospective husband and then did not go. When this occurred, it led some local Japanese officials, who considered such behavior dishonorable to the Japanese, to require that picture brides deposit any money received from Hawai'i with them until departure to ensure the women would keep the marriage promise. Third, the men often bribed the marriage broker either to ensure they be given first choice or that they be matched with pretty girls. In other words, the more money one paid, the younger and prettier the wife would be—insurance of a sort.[30]

At this point in the process, the bride's name was entered into the Japanese Family Register *(koseki)* of the husband, and she applied for a Japanese passport. Once she received it, she then applied for a visa to the United States, either at the American consulate in Seoul or in Japan.[31]

All that remained now for the picture bride was travel preparations. I have reconstructed this process using the memoirs of one picture bride, who first went to Seoul to obtain a visa and undergo a physical examination at the American consulate. Upon her return home, she began English studies. On the day of her departure, she took a horse-drawn wagon from her village to Masan, and from there she took a boat to Pusan. From Pusan she took another boat to Yokohama, where she stayed at an inn for picture brides run by a Mr. Kim. In Yokohama, she had another physical examination, which consisted of tests for trachoma and parasites. She failed the latter test, but by switching stool samples with another picture bride who was still waiting for passage money, she was later allowed to depart. After nine days at sea, she arrived at the immigration station in Honolulu, where she was served a typical Japanese meal of rice, miso soup, *takuan* (pickled yellow roots), and fish. At the immigration station she had another physical examination and a literacy test.[32]

Now it was time for these newly arrived picture brides to meet their grooms for the first time, armed only with a name and a photograph. A new life in Hawai'i was about to begin, and there were many adjustments to be made.

Here is a typical scene at the immigration station at the wharf: "Then the husband came in. The immigration officer asked, 'Mr. Chung Bong Woon, is this the woman you have invited to marry?' 'Yes' Then, 'Miss Lee Young Oak, is this the man you saw in the picture, and did you come to marry him?' 'Yes. I came to marry Mr. Chung Bong Woon.'" At this point, many of the women felt they had been deceived. Most of the picture brides had come to Hawai'i expecting to marry young and vigorous men of considerable means and to enjoy comfortable lives. These unrealistic expectations were dashed at the immigration station: the men waiting for them were almost invariably poor, older, stooped, wrinkled, and very dark.[33]

Accounts by the picture brides themselves confirm their feelings of betrayal. When twenty-three-year-old Soo Yun met her husband-to-be, she expected to see a rugged, hardy man. Instead, she met a tiny, darkly tanned man with "few exciting features. . . . Frankly, I was disappointed." Another was "so surprised and very disappointed, because my husband sent his 25 year old handsome looking picture. . . . He came to the pier, but I see he's really old, old looking. He was 45 years old, 25 years more old than I am. My heart stuck. I was so disappointed, I don't look at him again." Another recalled, "When I first saw my fiance, I could not believe my eyes. His hair was grey and I could not see any resemblance to the picture I had. He was a lot older than I had imagined." One woman found that her new husband, who had sent her $250 in Korea, worked on a plantation and was thirteen years older than she was: "When I see him, he skinny and black. I no like. No look like picture. But no can go home." Some could see their intended husbands from the deck of the ship and were so shocked that they refused to disembark and begged the crew to take them back to Korea. But the crew knew the brides did not have the money to return, so they were forced off the ship and led into the immigration building, some crying, "Mother, Mother, take me home, take me home."[34]

A few of the couples were married immediately at the immigration station, but most of the weddings were scheduled a few days after the bride's arrival. A typical sequence of events can be reconstructed based upon a composite of several accounts. The groom, who had recently arrived from one of the outer islands, went to the immigration station to claim his bride-to-be. As they exited, his picture bride walked three feet behind him to a borrowed car, which they drove to a Korean inn located less than a mile from the immigration station. At the inn, they checked into a special corner room reserved for just such occasions. After checking in and having a meal of kimchi, hot bean paste, and rice wrapped in lettuce, they went shopping in the city. After two nights at the inn, the groom brought the bride a bouquet and they were married at the Korean Methodist Church in Honolulu, the bride wearing the traditional *chima chogori* and the groom giving her a gold wedding band costing about seven dollars. That evening, a banquet was held at a Korean restaurant. They then honeymooned for ten days on Oahu before boarding the ferry to their outer-island home. On the evening of their arrival, they went to the Korean Methodist Church on the plantation, where they were greeted by the local Korean community.[35]

Often, however, things did not go quite so smoothly. Most of the women were still in a state of shock when they reached the Korean-run inn in Honolulu. The innkeepers were eyewitnesses to the traumatic scenes often played out in front of them: "[There were] many Korean picture brides who did nothing but cry day and night from the moment they checked into the inn. Even after the crying phase some wouldn't speak a word for days; they would emerge only to eat. Only the men's threats to deport the girls back to Korea forced them to marry the men they came for." Another Korean innkeeper recalled: "Usually the disappointed brides would desperately fight back the husbands who try to approach them. Then the women scream as their husbands hit them out of anger and frustration. Sometimes we have to break into the rooms when we think that the couple has become too violent." A sympathetic female inn-keeper agreed with the picture brides that "the men they came to marry looked too old and boorish. The older bachelors who were usually in their 30s and 40s were deeply tanned, wrinkled, and even bent from years of hard labor. Planta-tion life made them look older." One bride-to-be recalled her own experience at the inn: "I don't eat and only cry for eight days. I don't eat nothing, but at midnight when everybody sleeps I sneak out to drink water, so I don't die. I was so angry at my cousin because she arranged the marriage."[36]

In the first of what would be several major adjustments, most of the women went ahead and married their intended husbands, despite their deep disap-pointment, feeling they had no other choice. Not only did they lack money for the return passage, but a return to Korea meant too much loss of face. As one woman remembered: "But what could I do? I had just arrived from Korea—to get married—and I couldn't very well return home." Another thought to herself: "If I don't marry, immigration law send me back to Korea free. Oh, I was thinking, thinking. I came once, better I marry and stay here. That time it was hard to come out so how can I go back? My parents would be very shame, so I can't go back." Another decided to marry her forty-six-year-old groom because she felt sorry for him: "I did not have it in my heart to disappoint or hurt such a middle-aged man like him." Naturally, the men were aware of their new brides' disappointment: "Sensing her coolness towards him, he asked, 'Do you wish to marry me or do you have other ideas?' She answered, 'If you wish marriage, I'll marry you.' He said, 'Yes, I do wish marriage.' So they were mar-ried, but not happily." In fact, only a small number of picture brides refused to marry their picture grooms; these women were taken care of by church-operated charities.[37]

Second, the newly arrived brides had to adjust to the living arrangements and economic circumstances in which they now found themselves—especially those whose husbands worked on the sugar plantations. Many of the brides had been led to believe by the go-betweens and their future husbands that a com-fortable life awaited them in Hawai'i. It was immediately obvious upon arrival, however, that such was not the case. For example, one picture bride was met by a groom wearing the same clothes and shoes he had brought from Korea years before. Another bride noted immediately that her husband's "palm was as hard as a rock, not the soft hands of a scholar or official." Yet another bride discovered that her husband was "poor [because he was] working on the plan-tation . . . [and,] aware of her husband's meager wages, [s]he knew she had to abandon her dream of attending college in Hawaii."[38]

This new, hard life was reflected in the brides' accommodations. "[My] first stove was a tin can with a hole cut out for the pot [and my] home was con-structed of wooden slats which offered no privacy at night when the lights were on," recalled one new bride. Another found that her new home was "worse than the servants' quarters back in Taegu. There was only one room to cook, sleep and entertain. The floor was bare wood. Furnishings were crude and sparse. How had she come to choose this harsh life? For many days she cried alone. Her life was nothing like what she had imagined or what her parents wanted for her."[39]

Even worse, their new husbands expected them to work as well. One woman, who had apparently been well-off in Korea, complained that "I had to work like a servant," while another said, "Look at me now. My husband doesn't earn enough so I have to scrimp and save. I have to take in washing and ironing for unmarried men. And a baby keeps coming every year!" New brides who had to work on the plantations with their husbands fared the worst of all. One woman lamented: "Oh what a destiny! How come I have to work in this strange cane field! I cried many nights but soon I gave up." Another woman who had to live on the plantation recalled, "Almost every night [I] felt like crying." One picture bride "found the situation quite to the contrary [of what I had expected]. . . . I decided to work, since I had heard that my husband had spent one month's worth of his earnings on our wedding. When I told my husband of my intentions to work, he was not surprised at all but seemed to have expected it all along. It was very hard work for me. I arose at four . . . cutting sugarcanes, watering, and pulling out weeds. . . . [M]y back ached. . . . We were meant to work, I believe, rather than to enjoy our life together."[40]

Despite their disappointment, the overwhelming majority of the picture brides stayed in Hawai'i and made the necessary adjustments (although at least one pregnant bride returned to Korea after only six months). Most were too ashamed to inform their families in Korea of the reality of their hard lives in Hawai'i, one woman saying that "I was discouraged and found it useless to write home. Besides, I did not want to have to lie about the rough life I was leading." Since returning to Korea was not a realistic option, most picture brides did whatever was necessary to improve their financial status and working and living conditions. For most, as we have seen, this meant going to work. For some on the plantations this meant moving to other plantations, as the men had been doing already. But for most couples on the plantations, the desire for better working and living conditions led them to leave the plantation entirely and move to the city. Many, prompted by the 1920 strike on Oahu, came there as strikebreakers with their new brides, and when the strike ended, they stayed in or near Honolulu and pursued other lines of work.[41]

For most couples, their new living and working situations led to at least the approximation of equality in marriage. To be sure, a few men took advantage of their new brides, like the following: "The city presented its problems of unemployment, but my mother because of her training at the Bible Institute was able to earn a few dollars a day working in a tailor shop. My father, well, being the scholarly type, was content to be supported thus and made little effort to look for jobs which were not readily available anyway." A more typical experience, however, was this: "Halmunee [Grandmother], not yet twenty, . . . arrived in Hawaii sometime around 1914 [and] married . . . a man some twenty years her senior. Her years of struggle began. . . . Later, Halmunee and her family moved to Honolulu to [work as a tailor]. For Halmunee, these were unrelentingly hard years; by now, she had five babies to care for. She had learned swiftly to do all the most backbreaking and menial tasks, and she had looked squarely into the face of poverty."[42]

Of course, the grooms also had to make adjustments. The imminent arrival of a bride from Korea led many men to leave the plantation for the city, because they knew the women would not be happy on the plantations, and because plantation work did not correspond to their portrayal of themselves as successful men. While waiting for their future wives to arrive, some men found new jobs in or around Honolulu so they would not have to return to the plantation.[43] Thus those planters who had hoped that the arrival of picture brides would contribute to Korean stability were disappointed, as Koreans' desertion of the plantations actually increased rather than decreased.

Many of the men who were already in the city scrambled to improve their living conditions when they learned that their brides were en route. In 1912, one man who worked as a yardboy in the Manoa section of Honolulu and lived in a shack behind his employer's house decided he needed more income since he was going to be joined by a wife, so he asked his employer if he could rent a piece of land adjacent to the property. When asked what he would do with the land, he answered, "I like grow vegetables. I like sell. Make extra money." His employer agreed to rent him the land, and when he had grown enough to fill a cart, he pulled it to downtown Honolulu to sell at the fish and vegetable market. He also rented a one-room apartment only a few days before his bride arrived. While it was "shabby," it was still an improvement over his previous quarters.[44]

Another adjustment the picture brides faced was residing in a Korean community that was intensely anti-Japanese. Since the picture brides had come from Korea after its annexation by Japan in 1910, a number of them could speak Japanese. As a result, there were times when they found it convenient to use Japanese when shopping at Japanese stores. Yet their anti-Japanese husbands objected to their use of the language, one husband informing his new bride not to speak Japanese anywhere, under any circumstances, even to the Japanese, or he would send her back to Korea.[45]

In addition, the newly arrived picture brides had to adjust to the new and often strange American customs and diet. An item as simple as a beverage could illustrate this, as one picture bride recalled: "During the coffee breaks the majority of the workers drank coffee with their snacks, but I could not drink the bitter coffee and could not help but think of our native drinks and foods I used to have back home in Korea." In some cases the husband assumed the role of teacher in matters such as Western table manners, with one telling his new bride: "When you eat soup, you are not supposed to make a noise. It is also the habit of white people not to open the mouth with food in it. Chew your food with lips closed."[46] Later, as the picture brides learned of more abstract values such as equality, independence, and individualism, they found that they conflicted with more traditional expectations still extant in the Korean community in Hawai'i.

One such expectation was the necessity of the picture bride to conform to the role befitting a Korean woman and wife. But complicating this adjustment was the fact that the expectation sometimes contradicted the need to adopt American customs and values. Because most of the picture brides had left Korea at a very young age, many found themselves singularly unprepared to acquit themselves in a manner satisfactory to their husbands. For instance, one picture bride, to her husband's consternation, did not know how to cook rice or wash clothes. Others had left Korea before learning the proper "etiquette" appropriate to their station. Consider the following exchange between a young picture bride and an older Korean man who angrily berated her: "What is your name? What kind of woman are you? Who is your husband? Don't you know how to address an older person in a respectful way?" She answered: "Sir, I am sorry for not knowing the proper way of speaking to an older person. Since I came to Hawaii as a picture bride when I was sixteen, I haven't had the chance to learn proper manners. Please forgive my ignorance and impoliteness. Please teach me the proper way of addressing an old man."[47] Although ignorance of proper forms of address might have caused the picture brides some difficulty within the Korean community, it would, on the other hand, allow them easier access to standard English usage and the egalitarian values associated with it.

Indeed, the arrival of the picture brides into Hawaiian society at an early age *did* result in the transformation of their language along Western lines and a gradual abandonment of traditional status-based usage. Researcher Dong Jae Lee found that picture brides in Hawai'i tended to adopt more egalitarian usage in addressing people, using "Mr." or "Mrs." plus the surname, using the word "you," and addressing others by their first, or given, name. Consequently, they largely abandoned traditional forms of address, including the deferential suffix -*nim* or the use of the surname plus a title. This egalitarianism also resulted in the disappearance of speech-level differences between husband and wife, making them linguistically and socially more equal, as opposed to the gender-based traditional Korean superiority of males over females.[48] The longer the picture brides remained in Hawai'i, faced with the contradictory pressures of adopting American values versus fulfilling traditional expectations, the more the former won out.

Despite the fact almost all of the picture brides married the men who had sent for them, evidence suggests that many of these unions did not conform to the usual parameters of married life. For those brides with older husbands, the relationship was often based more on notions of filial piety than love. One picture bride addressed her husband as *aboji,* or "father." Another recalled: "I found then that he was 46 years old. He was more like a father than my husband and he did treat me more like a daughter. However, his age did not bother me too much. I felt I could trust and lean on him. We settled on the big island of Hawaii where my husband had been working. A month after we were settled, my uncle gave us a visit, wondering how I was doing. I told him that I was fine and did not regret my doings. . . . My husband being thirty years my senior, I definitely looked upon him more as my father than my husband. . . . I do not ever recall using or hearing the word 'love' between us. Life was so dry and routine that any sort of warm feelings were out of the question."[49]

At worst, however, these marriages were often marred by mutual recrimination—the wife feeling that she had been tricked and the husband feeling that she did not appreciate the expense involved in bringing her to Hawai'i. Marriages like this did not begin well, such as the one in which, after the wedding, "we didn't talk to each other for three months, living together in the same house." Even when a move to the city eased somewhat the initial financial hardships, many of the marriages remained on shaky ground. As one field researcher in the 1930s candidly admitted, "[M]any of the picture bride marriages have turned out not too happily," with the brides expressing their resentment through "bickering and shrewishness."[50]

From this, a pattern developed in which some households were dominated by the younger brides. For example, one man whose mother came from Masan in 1916 at the age of seventeen to marry his father, who was eighteen years her senior, remembers that his household was dominated by his mother. Why was this the case? First, because the women, after exposure to the American concepts of personal happiness and freedom, began to question the traditional subservience to the husband and the stigma against divorce—now they saw divorce as a possible avenue of escape from an unhappy marriage. And second, because there still remained many eligible single Korean men in Hawai'i. Thus not only did the women dominate, but they also initiated most (90 percent) of the many divorces and near-divorces.[51]

But unhappy marriages were not the only problems facing these couples. Most of the marriages began in a condition of severe financial constraint. As (bad) luck would have it, just as some of these newly formed families were beginning to prosper financially after a decade or so in Hawai'i, the Depression struck in 1929, throwing them into an economic tailspin. In one case of bad timing, "her husband decided to begin a business of his own. They leased land on the heights above Honolulu, long since choice real estate, and began growing carnations. Flowers have always brought money in Hawaii—being in demand for leis. The peak prosperity of the twenties was passing, however, and their new business floundered." Another picture bride was in Korea for a four-month visit with her parents in 1935 when her husband lost his job as a locomotive maintenance man on the plantation and was forced to move to Honolulu without a job. When she returned, she took control of the family finances by renting a house for use as a grocery store and residence. After five months, the grocery business failed, so she found a job for her husband in the pineapple fields on the island of Lanai.[52]

Another problem these new families faced was the harsh reality that the men, because they had married and started families late in life, would soon be physically unable to provide for their still-young families and look forward to enjoying a normal retirement. While the average man might retire at age sixty, these men did not have that luxury, because their children, still growing and going to school, were not old enough to support them in their old age. Publications in Korea had made such a dire prediction even as the picture brides were leaving for Hawai'i. A decade later, other publications ruefully noted that, for their overseas compatriots, "now the gray hairs are many and they cannot work."[53] Consequently, the picture brides often had to pick up the slack and support the family.

Even worse was the prospect that the picture brides would become widowed at a relatively young age. And since many had borne a large number of children, they would have to support a large family alone. One picture bride recalled her own experience:

> There was a terrible turning point in my life during my seventh year in Hawaii [1922]. My husband had passed away after being ill for two whole years and left me behind with five young children. It was very sad and depressing, but I could not spare the time and energy for crying. I was faced with a dilemma. I had all my children and myself to support. I worked without rest, straight through the week. There were no more Sundays to look forward to. I did any kind of work I could lay my hands on. I drew water from the well, carried sugarcanes, did other people's laundry, and so on. Fortunately, my children were taken care of by some church people during the daytime so that I could work. We moved from our apartment to an abandoned house on the hill in order to save rent. I had a little further to walk to work, but I had to do anything to save money. After a while, my body could not keep up with this sort of hard work and routine. One day when I was drawing water from the well . . . I lost all consciousness. . . . [I] was in a coma for twenty days and I found myself on the island of Oahu. I believe that it was quite a miracle that I was alive.[54]

One mitigating factor for the widowed picture bride was the fact that there were many opportunities for remarriage, as eligible men still outnumbered eligible women. One picture bride discovered upon her arrival that her husband had a severe case of tuberculosis, and he died within a year. She then remarried and had five children. Consider also the following: "One day, three years after my husband's death, my uncle and minister visited me with a proposition to remarry. They introduced me to a Mr. Choi who was ten years older than I was. I took a liking to him since he was not a plantation worker. I thought about it over and over again until finally I decided to remarry after I received an encouraging letter from my mother. After we were married, we moved into town and bought a house. This was only the beginning of a new life for me. . . . I had another son and when he was fifteen years old, I became a widow for the second time."[55]

While the lives of many picture brides were indeed difficult, their arrival between 1910 and 1924 marked an important milestone in the Korean community in Hawai'i. They helped "normalize" the skewed gender ratio of the community so that by the 1920s, it was no longer dominated by bachelors. By 1930, because of the second generation *(ise)*, the number of men and women under age twenty-four was nearly equal, whereas there were substantially more men than women in the over fifty age group. Indeed, by 1930, a majority (54 percent) of the Koreans in Hawai'i were American citizens, having been born in the United States.[56] These developments were important because they hastened the adoption of American values. Had the Koreans in Hawai'i remained largely bachelors, like the Chinese in America who were prevented from importing wives because of the Chinese Exclusion Act of 1882 (1900 in Hawai'i), there would have been no significant second generation, and the community would continue to be dominated by the values of the older, more traditional, generation. As it was, the specific gravity of the Korean community would soon begin to shift to the more Americanized second generation.

Another important legacy of the picture brides was the boost they gave to the Korean nationalist movement in Hawai'i. No less nationalistic than their husbands, they knew from firsthand experience the outrages committed by the Japanese in Korea, unlike their husbands, who had left Korea before the protectorate and annexation. The brides' nationalism was apparent in all aspects of their lives. One man recalled that when he was a boy, his picture-bride mother always reminded him to hate Japanese, telling him that one Korean equaled ten Japanese. A picture bride, who was visiting her parents in Korea, participated in the March First demonstrations of 1919 and was thrown in jail by the Japanese authorities. On her way back to Hawai'i in 1921, she was detained in Yokohama and again jailed for two months.[57]

Picture bride organizations such as the Yŏngnam Puin Hoe (Yŏngnam Wives Society) also organized nationalist activities, inviting visitors from Korea to speak at church or at their meetings. One woman remembered the effect of such a speech by a Korean singer on her picture-bride mother:

> I listened with rapt attention, not so much because I felt sorry for the suf-
> fering in Korea but because this was the first time my mother openly
> revealed her feelings about the plight of her people. Heretofore she was like
> most of the older people I knew, who did not say much to us of the younger
> generation about their frustration and their desire for independence. [She]

seemed . . . apologetic and ashamed of the status of their people, of themselves who were "a people without a country." . . . After the tenor's departure
from the islands, I noticed the parishioners gathered each Sunday with
renewed energy and unabashed vociferation for their country's imperative
need for freedom. They cursed the loathsome, frenzied activities of the Japanese. The perpetrators of suffering were labelled "crazed people." The men
swore at the *weh-num,* the spiteful enemy. The women wept, holding hands,
and decried the state of affairs in their homeland.[58]

In 1924, with the passage of the Immigration Act, the picture-bride phe-
nomenon came to an end. Aimed primarily at the Japanese, the Act affected
Koreans as well, since Korea was part of the Japanese empire. The Koreans in
Hawai'i spared no effort to free Korea from Japanese rule. This effort, and the
Japanese response, is the subject to which we now turn.

7

Futei Senjin:
Japan and "Rebellious Koreans"

The Korean nationalist movement, known variously as the Korean independence movement *(tongnip undong)*, the March First (1919) Movement *(samil
undong)*, or the *Mansei!* (Long Live Korean Independence) Movement, is in
many ways the centerpiece of the experience of the first-generation Koreans in
Hawai'i. People who know very little about modern Korean history nonetheless
are still likely to view Koreans as nationalistic. The roots of this nationalism are
not difficult to understand. Korea had been an independent country for more
than a millennium prior to the twentieth century and had in the course of its
long history developed its own unique culture and civilization. For Japan to rob
Korea of its independence and identity by annexing it in 1910 was to invite a
resistance movement of massive proportions not only among Koreans there,
but also among those living outside the country. The Koreans in Hawai'i were
no exception, and they threw themselves into the nationalist movement with a
fervor unmatched by any other overseas nationalist movement.

While the nationalist movement was of central importance to the Koreans
in Hawai'i, the subject must be approached with caution. For one, there already
exist secondary studies of the Korean nationalist movement in Korean, Japanese, and English that include the activities of the Koreans in Hawai'i. Second,
much of the primary source material is biased in some way. Third, it is easy to
assign so much importance to the nationalist movement that it overshadows
the other aspects of the first-generation Korean experience in Hawai'i. At the
same time, it is a subject that cannot be ignored. As a result, the discussion of
the nationalist movement in this study can focus on only part of the story. For
example, the activities of the Sinminhoe were examined in some detail earlier
(see Chapter 3). And later in this study, the nationalist movement during the
Pacific War will occupy our attention. The focus of this chapter is the relationship between the nationalist movement in Hawai'i and the Japanese government, and it is based largely upon documents held in Japanese archives in
Tokyo. A definitive history of the Korean nationalist movement in Hawai'i
remains to be written and is properly the subject of another book.

At the risk of oversimplification, the Korean nationalist movement in Hawai'i split into two camps in the years after 1913. One group followed the lead of Syngman Rhee (Yi Sŭng-man), who advocated a diplomatic approach to freeing Korea from Japanese control. This group had its own organization, the Dongji-hoe (Comrade Society), its own newspaper, the *T'aep'yŏngyang Chubo (Korean Pacific Weekly)*, and its own church, the Korean Christian Church. The second group originally formed around Park Yong-man (Pak Yong-man), who advocated a military approach against Japan. It, too, had its own organization, the Kungminhoe (Korean National Association), its own newspaper, the *Kung-minbo (Korean National Herald)*, and its own church, the Korean Methodist Church. Other organizations and newspapers that supported these two factions or split from them came and went with dizzying speed. Each side opposed the other even to the point that it affected residential patterns of the Koreans in Hawai'i. Perhaps the only issue the two sides agreed upon was the need to end Japanese control of Korea. But even before this split, the Korean community in Hawai'i had begun to oppose the growing dominance of Japan over Korea.

The anti-Japanese movement among the Koreans in Hawai'i began in 1905, the year Japan established a protectorate over Korea. The first contentious issue arising between Japan and the Korean community in Hawai'i concerned appropriate diplomatic representation. Ever since the establishment of the Department of Emigration [Yuminwŏn] in 1902, the Korean government had been reminded first by the Russians, then by Horace Allen, and finally by the HSPA, to send consuls to areas overseas, like Hawai'i, where Koreans lived. Despite this repeated prodding, two years went by without the appointment of a Korean consul to Honolulu. This egregious oversight on the part of the Korean government did not go unnoticed by the Japanese government, which then began to exploit this weakness in a broader campaign to absorb the functions of the Korean Foreign Office and prevent Korean immigrants from going to Hawai'i. In this way, Japan could avoid being excluded from the United States—a process summarized in chapter 1 of this book.

In June 1904, in the midst of the Russo-Japanese War, the Japanese chargé d'affaires to Korea, Hagiwara Shuichi, recommended that the Korean government appoint Saitō Miki, the Japanese consul general in Honolulu, as honorary Korean consul in Honolulu. Two months later, the Japanese minister to Korea, Hayashi Gonsuke, made a similar recommendation and implied (falsely) that Emperor Kojong approved of the idea. Clearly, Japan was putting pressure on the Korean government. At the same time, and from a different angle, the Koreans in Hawai'i were also pressuring the Korean government for a consul. When it became apparent that they could not expect much from the Korean government, Koreans in Hawai'i began to take the initiative, annoying the Japanese government in the process. In January 1905, they sent a memorial to Emperor Kojong requesting a Korean consul. They argued that "all the other nations have consuls and if it is a question of money the petitioners with other Koreans in Hawai'i will provide the funds for maintaining the consulate." The

Korean government ignored their offer, allowing the Japanese campaign to control Korean foreign relations in general and the Koreans in Hawai'i in particular to continued unimpeded. Finally, in May 1905, after a year of Japanese pressure, Emperor Kojong finally gave in and appointed Saitō as honorary Korean consul in Honolulu. The dismay of the Koreans in Hawai'i was predictable: "Korean immigrants in Hawaii desire a consul of their own nationality instead of a Japanese subject."[1]

So irate were the Koreans in Hawai'i that Saitō had been named Korean consul that in July 1905 they sent Yi Tong-ho to the Korean Foreign Office in Seoul with a petition so moving that people reportedly shed tears. The petition read:

> Although we the Korean emigrants in Hawaii have shallow knowledge of the world, we are well aware of the fact that as there cannot be two suns in the heaven, so there cannot be two kings in a country. We take pride in our loyalty to the king [sic] of Korea, though we are far away from the country. There are some 7,000 of us in Hawaii, but the home government does not take care of us. Are we not Koreans? Some ten ethnic groups in Hawaii have their own consuls for the protection of their lives and property, except us Korean emigrants. We feel as if we were a flock of sheep without a shepherd and a boat without an oar. We have requested on several occasions the home government to send our consul. Should the home government appoint a foreigner [Saitō] as a Korean consul, we will never accept him as our consul. Is it because of financial problems that the government is moving to appoint a foreigner as Korean consul in Hawaii, in spite of the fact that Korea is an independent country? If this is the reason, we are ready to raise the money necessary for establishing and operating a Korean consulate.[2]

While the Korean government still made no reply, the Koreans in Hawai'i had clearly gone on record that they would not accept Saitō as their consul.

Saitō moved quickly to carry out his new consular obligations to the Korean immigrants. In August 1905, he wrote to the HSPA and suggested the formation of a Korean Benevolent Association, then solicited contributions. Knowing that Koreans would not cooperate if they knew of his involvement, Saitō shrewdly kept the contents of his letter to the planters secret until it appeared over a month later in a September issue of the local Japanese newspaper, the *Yamato shinbun*. For the same reason, Saitō suggested that Reverend John W. Wadman head the association. As a result, on August 24, 1905, the Korean Benevolent Association was founded with Saitō's initiative, with planter money, and with Wadman at the helm. While Saitō's actions were arguably humanitarian in nature and something that any effective consul would have done, Japan was at that very moment in Korea citing such "humanitarian concern" to argue that no more Koreans should emigrate without Japanese approval. As for the Koreans in Hawai'i, they had made it clear to Japan that there would be no cooperation with Saitō or the Japanese consulate in Honolulu. Indeed, seven years later, in 1912, when Wadman received a $750 donation from the Japanese consulate to support the school for Koreans that he had established (known as the Korean Compound), Koreans were furious and refused for a time to let their children attend classes there. Wadman asked Syngman Rhee, who had recently arrived in Hawai'i, to intercede and assume the post of principal at the school.[3]

A second stumbling block in the relations between the Japanese government and Koreans in Hawai'i arose when the latter began attempts to get a hearing for their cause with prominent American politicians and at international meetings attended by the United States. Sensitive to the possibility that the American government might support these anti-Japanese Koreans, the Japanese were alarmed when, in the summer of 1905, Reverend Yun Pyŏng-gu left Honolulu to meet with Syngman Rhee, then a student on the mainland, to appeal to President Theodore Roosevelt during the upcoming Portsmouth Peace Conference ending the Russo-Japanese War. Acting Hawai'i governor A. L. C. Atkinson had helped Yun meet with Secretary of War William Howard Taft, who was passing through Hawai'i on his way to Japan to sign the Taft-Katsura Memorandum in which Japan and the United States agreed not to interfere, respectively, in the Philippines and Korea. Taft in turn gave Yun a letter of introduction to Roosevelt, and in August, Yun and Rhee presented to the president "A Petition from the Koreans of Hawaii to President Roosevelt," dated July 12, 1905. Roosevelt deflected their request, telling them to go through the acting minister to the United States, Kim Yun-jong, who in turn told them he could do nothing without instructions from the government. So Yun returned to Hawai'i, empty-handed.

Although Yun and Rhee had failed to get Roosevelt's assistance, primarily because Roosevelt approved of the Japanese takeover of Korea, the Japanese were so embarrassed by Yun's mission that a Japanese newspaper in Hawai'i went to great pains to announce (falsely) that "Korean Going to Mainland Not a Peace Envoy—Goes To Solicit Funds for Korean School and Hospital in Hawaii." Two years later, a Korean representative was sent to the Hague Conference in 1907 seeking a hearing, with similar results. Nonetheless, the Koreans in Hawai'i would continue to seek the assistance of the U.S. government in their quest to free Korea from Japanese control, provoking the anger of the Japanese government.[4]

The Japanese government was also angered by the advocacy or use of terrorist tactics by the Koreans in Hawai'i against Japan. The Koreans were already indirectly involved in such tactics when one of them, Chang In-hwan, moved to California and assassinated the pro-Japan American, Durham White Stevens, in San Francisco on March 23, 1908. By supporting these tactics, the Koreans in Hawai'i became part of a larger phenomenon of overseas Korean terrorism that the Japanese had to face. For example, 1909, Itō Hirobumi, the first resident-general of Korea, was assassinated in Harbin by An Chung-gŭn. From this point, some Koreans in Hawai'i occasionally would advocate militant resistance to Japan, actions that did little to endear them to the Japanese government.

Another strategy the Koreans in Hawai'i used to challenge the Japanese government was to consolidate themselves organizationally in order to focus more directly on Japan. When Japan established the Protectorate in November 1905, most of the Korean organizations on the sugar plantations added anti-Japanese activities to their agenda. As Koreans began to leave the plantations and move to Honolulu, these myriad groups, as recounted in chapter 3, became consolidated first into the Hanin Hapsŏng Hyŏphoe (United Korean Federation) in 1907 and then, in 1909, into what has been known variously as the Kungmin-hoe or the Kook Min Hur (Korean National Association, or KNA). When Korea was annexed by Japan in 1910, anti-Japanese activities became paramount.

Just as many other governments have claimed when confronted with a nationalist movement against them, the Japanese government viewed the Korean independence movement in Hawai'i as the handiwork of a few outside agitators who did not enjoy broad support. It viewed the formation of the KNA as the work of several dozen intellectuals who had left Korea after 1905 because of "political disappointment or discontent," and who had first gone to the mainland United States for an education before arriving in Hawai'i. According to the Japanese, this handful of intellectuals, who "misunderstood the principle of freedom," was able to manipulate these "uneducated laborers" through their "exaggerated" speeches and newspaper articles, so that the average Korean did not know the real story. "Since the majority of the first generation have very little education and cannot even write their names," a Japanese report intoned, "they tend to be easily influenced by the propaganda of Korean independence activists. The activists take full advantage of these people and in their propaganda the activists claim the Japanese government is evil and that it is their duty to expel the Japanese from Korea. Ordinary Koreans, with their rather simple intellectual constructs, take the words of the activists as they are, without even doubting them, and tend to hate the Japanese. Thus it is a commonly shared opinion among Koreans that Koreans should never accept the Japanese annexation from the viewpoint of racial self-determination and patriotism and that Koreans in Hawaii are free from control of the Japanese government."[5]

While satisfying itself that Korean nationalist activities in Hawai'i were the product of this small group of intellectuals, the Japanese government nonetheless kept a close eye on the movement, not so much because it directly threatened Japan's control over Korea, but because it had the potential to generate terrorist incidents and, more seriously, garner the sympathy of the U.S. government, something the Koreans in Hawai'i had been pursuing since 1905. This latter effort was increasingly a potential problem because not only did the United States and Japan have serious differences over immigration policy and racial discrimination, but they were also developing differences over China.

Although the United States and Japan were allies against Germany during

World War I, the United States nonetheless took exception to Japanese actions in China. The United States saw Japan's retention of Shandong Province and its presentation of the Twenty-One Demands to China as potential violations of its Open Door policy. Conversely, the Japanese knew that the anti-Japanese nationalist movement in China, which would be known as the May Fourth Movement, was spurred in part by the idealistic self-determination speeches of President Woodrow Wilson. Moreover, the leader of the Chinese nationalist movement, Sun Yat-sen, had been educated at Iolani High School in Hawai'i, and his organization, the Guomindang, was financially supported by the Chinese there. Japan was aware that American sympathies lay with the Chinese against further Japanese encroachment and were wary that Korean nationalists might likewise turn American leaders against Japan's control of Korea. Indeed, Koreans continued to attempt attracting prominent American politicians and diplomats to their cause at venues such as the Democratic National Convention in 1919 and the Washington Conference in 1922. Koreans, the Japanese said, "believe that Japanese sovereignty over Korea is incompatible with the policy of the United States which supports freedom and equality. Koreans also note the preponderance in size and resources of the United States as compared to Japan. . . . [T]hey try to let the Americans recognize the acute need of Koreans to have an independent country."

The attempts by Korean nationalists to win the moral and diplomatic support of the United States was seen by the Japanese not only as a threat, but also as a continuing manifestation of Korea's weakness, which prompted the Japanese takeover in the first place. Japan viewed such tactics condescendingly as "toadyism" (*jidai shisō;* Korean: *sadae sasang*), marking the Koreans as a people undeserving of independence. Japan thus had to establish a protectorate over Korea's foreign relations in 1905 precisely because of this fundamental weakness in Korean foreign policy decision making. Having relied upon the Chinese for centuries before the bonds had been broken by the Sino-Japanese War in 1895, the Koreans had never developed the ability to be independent. Rather, Korea continued to seek out "big brothers" for protection in international affairs, and when it turned to Russia after 1895, the Japanese had been forced to go to war a second time over the Korean peninsula in the Russo-Japanese War of 1904–1905. Even now, after annexation in 1910, the Koreans continued to exhibit this weakness, hoping that their independence could be won through the aid of an American big brother. This confirmed to the Japanese that Korean thinking had not really advanced and that Japanese control was still necessary.[6]

The Japanese Foreign Ministry (Gaimushō) in Tokyo and the Government-General in Seoul (Chōsen sōtokufu) were thus alarmed when they received reports from the Japanese consulate in Honolulu in 1915 that the American government showed apparent signs of support for the activities of the KNA. While noting that the KNA "ostensibly" had as its primary aim the improve-

ment of the condition of Koreans abroad, the Japanese government fixed its
attention on the second article in the KNA's constitution, which advocated the
overthrow of Japanese rule in Korea and the reestablishment of Korean independence. If these reports of American support were true, then difficult times
lay ahead for Japanese-American relations.

The Japanese reports cited three instances of American support for the
KNA. The first occurred when the KNA dedicated its new headquarters in
December 1914 and invited the governor of Hawai'i, Lucius E. Pinkham, to
attend. Although he did not attend, he sent a letter in which "he expressed the
hope that the Society [KNA] would realize its aims." The second instance was
two months later, at another public meeting to celebrate the anniversary of the
KNA's founding, where the mayor of Honolulu was in attendance. The third
involved the activities of one of the KNA leaders, Park Yong-man, who had
acquired pineapple fields on Windward Oahu to support a military school, "the
aim of the school being to prepare for revolution in Korea." His cadets had
even marched in review at the dedication of the KNA headquarters. How
could such activities proceed without the approval of American officials?

Japan acknowledged that political exiles received asylum in all countries and
that at that time Chinese revolutionaries were receiving such asylum in Japan.
What concerned the Japanese government was "the unfortunate effect resulting from the reports sent back to Japan of American officials giving their
approval to the cause of the Society." Such reports "tended to create in the
minds of the Japanese a belief in the hostility of the United States to Japan."
The Japanese Embassy in Washington brought these concerns to the attention
of the Department of State, which queried the Department of the Interior,
which in turn wrote to Governor Pinkham for information. So little did Pinkham know about the Koreans in Hawai'i that, before replying, he sought and
received information from the Reverends Wadman and Fry of the Methodist
Mission in Hawaii.[7]

Armed with their information, Pinkham responded to Washington that he
had so little knowledge of the KNA that "[y]our communication of July 12th
. . . was the first I ever heard of the political activities of the Korean National
Association." Nor did he know anything about the KNA's newspaper, the
Korean National Herald, since there were in Hawai'i "a variety of ethnic publications that under ordinary circumstances are not screened by the government." He further stated that he had "inferred that the new [KNA] building
was an offshoot from the schools . . . which seemed crowded and [that] more
room [was] required for Korean benevolent and charitable organizations." He
explained that the congratulatory note he had sent to the KNA was a normal
part of his duties as governor in which he "is constantly called upon for certain
official courtesies," and that he "deemed the Koreans entitled to the same
courteous treatment as other nationalities." Given all this, Pinkham expressed

surprise at the Japanese reaction: "I fail to see where he [the Japanese ambassador] can extract sympathy for revolution from a letter strictly referring to local social meeting, local benevolence, and local betterment."

Pinkham also maintained that he was unaware of Park Yong-man's military training activities and downplayed their importance. He had noticed nothing out of the ordinary about Park's calling card when it had been presented to him, "nor had I ever heard of the pineapple enterprise on the windward side of Oahu." Regarding profits to support military training, Pinkham said, "I doubt if there are any at present in raising pineapples." As for weaponry, "we keep close observations on arms in possession in the Territory," and he stated that "none are found in hands of Koreans." In fact, Park's cadets trained with wooden broom handles in place of real rifles and firecrackers instead of explosives. Finally, Pinkham suggested that shady dealings and factional splits in the Korean nationalist movement lessened the significance of these activities: "I am inclined to believe, if investigated, the whole scheme will be found to be a swindle on the poor simple Koreans by a few of their shrewder countrymen." Moreover, "I understand that during my recent absence on the Pacific Coast there occurred some friction among the Koreans, the details of which I have not at hand." The governor concluded as a result that the KNA did not represent a threat to Japan and hoped that this information "will convince the State Department to the correct Korean situation."[8] As there were no further Japanese complaints to the U.S. government about support for Korean nationalist activity in Hawai'i, the Japanese may well have accepted Pinkham's account at face value. In addition, Japan was now well aware that serious splits within the nationalist movement weakened the independence movement in Hawai'i.

One example of this factional split was the *Izumo* Incident of 1917. That year, the Japanese warship *Izumo* paid a visit to Hawai'i. Park Yong-man, lamenting Korea's lack of military power, used the opportunity to editorialize in his group's newspaper that the Koreans in Hawai'i should capture or destroy the *Izumo* and in so doing proclaim Korean resistance to Japan. This suggestion was in keeping with Park's approach to achieving Korean independence through the use of military force. Syngman Rhee, the leader of the opposing faction, ridiculed Park's suggestion by wondering how his group could sabotage the ship with sticks (referring to the broom handles used by Park's cadets) or firecrackers. According to one source, Rhee actually informed the police about Park's plan to scuttle the Japanese ship.[9] At any rate, the ship sailed without incident, and factional disputes within the Korean nationalist movement deepened, to the delight of the Japanese government. Japan was thus unprepared for the events that would cause these two factions to unite two years later.

The 1919 March First Movement (Japanese: *sannichi undō*) in Korea, which saw mass demonstrations against Japanese control and for Korean independence, took Japan by surprise and had a significant impact on Japanese policy toward Koreans both inside and outside Korea. Inside Korea, the movement forced the initiation of a more liberal policy known as *bunka seiji*, or cultural policy, carried out by a new governor-general, Saitō Makoto. Outside of Korea, the most important consequence of this new policy was the increased attention given to overseas Koreans, including the Koreans in Hawai'i, and the commissioning of studies on their welfare. To Japanese eyes, these studies would be a pragmatic response to the March First uprising. But to the Koreans, such increased surveillance was seen as a sinister plot to spy on and defuse independence activities. That these studies were not primarily intended for the welfare of overseas Koreans is suggested by the fact that some of the reports were issued by the *keimukyoku*, or the police bureau of the governor-general's office in Seoul. Moreover, several of the reports refer to Koreans as *Futei Senjin*. The Japanese word *"futei"* can be translated as "insubordinate" or "recalcitrant." *Senjin* is a shortened form of *Chōsenjin*, or "Koreans," and is a derogatory Japanese slang word akin to the English words "Jap," "Chink," or "Gook." Four such studies were conducted between 1921 and 1926, dealing either wholly or in part with the Koreans in Hawai'i. The material was collected by the Japanese consulate in Honolulu using Korean-language newspapers, interviews, and Korean informants.[10]

The studies showed that the Japanese had been aware of the rise of factionalism within the Korean nationalist movement in Hawai'i as early as 1907. Of the two main factions in Hawai'i, the Japanese were more favorably inclined toward Syngman Rhee's faction than the one led by Park Yong-man because Rhee argued that Japan was too strong to defeat militarily and stressed long-term solutions such as education and diplomacy, whereas Park urged terrorism and militant resistance. The Japanese preference for Rhee's nonviolent methods in Hawai'i, despite their potential to garner the support of the United States, mirrored the Japanese preference in Korea of the evolutionary cultural nationalists rather than the revolutionary radical nationalists. It was thus with some satisfaction that they noted the failure of Park's military training activities in 1917. Then came the cataclysmic events of 1919.

In Seoul and Tokyo, the events of 1919 were cause for concern because Woodrow Wilson's call for the national self-determination of colonies led Korean nationalists to believe that the United States backed their cause. The Japanese blamed Wilson not only for the March First Movement in Korea, but also for the May Fourth Incident in China two months later. Although Wilson was not referring to Korea and China but rather to former colonies of Germany, his ideas nonetheless inspired many Koreans, a large number of whom, the Japanese believed, did not previously have anti-Japanese feelings. The Japanese also complained that Wilson had single-handedly unified the previously divided Korean nationalist movement.[11]

The March First Movement indeed strengthened Korean resolve to work for independence from Japan. In Shanghai, a Korean provisional government was formed, led in part by Koreans from Hawai'i like Syngman Rhee and Hyŏn Sun. In Hawai'i itself, a greater degree of coordination with the nationalist movement on the mainland was forged by the arrival in June of two emissaries from the San Francisco branch of the Kungminhoe, Hwang Sa-yong and Kang Yung-so. Their arrival was duly noted by the Japanese. Moreover, the warring factions in Hawai'i called a truce and resolved to unite against the Japanese and support the provisional government in Shanghai. As a gesture, Park Yong-man's group decided to discontinue publication of its newspaper. Financial contributions to nationalist causes in general and the provisional government in Shanghai in particular increased.

But Japan soon noted that the newfound unity within the Korean nationalist camp in Hawai'i was short-lived. By the fall of 1919, the two factions had resumed feuding, and Park's group resumed publication of its newspaper—not once a week as before, but now twice weekly. Indeed, it was the factional twists and turns within the Korean independence movement in Hawai'i to which the Japanese devoted most of their attention in their studies. They knew the names of all the leaders, their myriad organizations, their newspapers and journals, and their most important followers.[12]

The Japanese had also been worried about Hawai'i's financial links with the provisional government in Shanghai, especially since Syngman Rhee's group, the Dongjihoe, claimed that it had raised sixty thousand dollars for it. But when the Japanese investigated, they found that the actual amount was closer to ten thousand dollars, the bulk of which was spent on propaganda and living expenses in Hawai'i, with only a few thousand dollars actually going to Shanghai. And when Park Yong-man, who was in China at the time, came out against the Shanghai provisional government, the flow of money from Hawai'i to Shanghai began to decrease. When Rhee returned to Hawai'i from Shanghai in 1921 and announced a fund-raising drive, the Japanese noted with satisfaction that he was able to raise only one-third of the stated goal. Clearly, factionalism was limiting the amount of money contributed by Koreans in Hawai'i. Japan also uncovered other reasons why Koreans were increasingly reluctant to contribute. Many potential donors were frustrated by continuing evidence of waste, fraud, embezzlement, and corruption—charges that had reverberated throughout the nationalist movement since the beginning. Some donors, the Japanese noted, began to complain when Koreans beset by disease or poverty received nothing from nationalist leaders and had to turn to American benevolent organizations for assistance. Some Koreans also disliked the tactics used to raise money, which often bordered on coercion; the Japanese reported that "[i]n Hawaii, many well-disposed and law-abiding farmers are forced by threats to contribute money to the independence funds."[13]

These Japanese-commissioned studies of Hawai'i's Koreans also analyzed the group's potential to win U.S. support. The Japanese were cheered by the fact that even though Korean nationalists believed they could achieve independence with American help and disseminated this idea to the average Korean, Washington indicated that it did not want to alienate Japan by supporting the Korean nationalist cause. Yet despite this official stance, Japan suspected some weakening from time to time. One report, for example, alleged that Syngman Rhee received unspecified "assistance" when he returned to Hawai'i from Shanghai. Japan also knew that anti-Japanese politicians in Hawai'i and the mainland made liberal use of material provided by Korean nationalists. In Honolulu in particular, Japan suspected that the authorities not only supported Korean independence, but actually favored the more militant Park faction. They reached this conclusion based on their report of a brawl, which was broken up by the police, between the two factions involving between thirty and forty Koreans. At the trial, Rhee's supporters were found guilty, leading the Japanese to believe that it was a case of unequal justice. The Japanese even speculated that the Koreans in Hawai'i might turn to communism and the Soviet Union if the United States spurned them.[14]

As evidence of Japan's concern that prominent Americans in Hawai'i were sympathetic to the cause of Korean independence, a circular was distributed by the Japanese consulate in Honolulu to the planters in 1922. The circular, titled "An Appeal to the People of the United States," was signed not by a Japanese but by a Korean named Hon Jun Pyo (Pyo is apparently the surname), who identified himself as a "Delegate of the Persons Interested in the Welfare of the Thirteen Provinces of Korea." This one-page broadside asked the planters "to use your influence and good offices to clear away the delusion to which our [Korean] brethren now resident in your country are all subjected." It went on to say that Koreans in Hawai'i "are plotting intrigues," "fabricating facts," and "planning to stir up international trouble." Claiming that "the Japanese Government have (sic) made utmost efforts to improve Korea," the writer said that "we [Koreans in Korea] are all feeling satisfaction," but that these gains are refuted by "refugees aspiring for empty reputations and cunning people engrossed in promoting their personal interests." The open letter concluded by noting, "We believe that [you planters] will easily see through their evil designs in trying to utilize other people's sympathy" and will "[d]isapprove the detestable and outrageous acts of the Koreans and guide them in a manner calculated to enlighten their mental blindness." A postscript asked the planters to circulate an enclosed letter to the Koreans in Hawai'i.[15]

That letter was titled "A Few Words to our Brethren, the Koreans, Residing in the United States of America" and was again signed by the same mysterious "Hon Jun Pyo." Pyo regretted that "some of our brethren who reside in foreign countries are secretly planning or devising some means to stir up international trouble." While acknowledging that the Japanese were guilty of "some facts of misgovernment and imperfections," nonetheless, "when we compare it with the government before 'Sotoku Seiji' [Government-General Politics], we must recognize that the present government is far better than what preceded it."

The letter then cited a long list of the ills of the late Chosŏn dynasty followed by a series of economic statistics to demonstrate the benefits of Japanese colonial rule to Korea. The letter also gave voice to a somewhat slanted view of history that stated, "The Japanese and Koreans are originally descended from one stock, but in the middle ages they separated and formed different nations." Now, with annexation, there has been a return to "the original state." Koreans abroad should accept the inevitability of this merger, for to believe otherwise would not only be "against the tendencies of the world" but also "utterly against the dictates of reason and common sense." The concluding message to Korean nationalists in Hawai'i was: "those who disregard these underlying principles and engage in intrigues are sure to end in an utter failure."[16]

In sum, the Japanese found both good news and bad news after they began looking closely at the Koreans in Hawai'i following the March First Movement. The bad news was that the events of 1919 had stiffened the nationalist resolve of many of these Koreans: those in Hawai'i supported the Korean provisional government in Shanghai financially; some American politicians, including several in Hawai'i, were sympathetic to the Koreans; Koreans in Hawai'i believed Woodrow Wilson and the United States supported Korean independence; and Koreans considered the Japanese consulate in Honolulu to be a den of spies. The good news was that Syngman Rhee's nonviolent faction had more followers than Park Yong-man's militant faction; the amount of money coming from Hawai'i to support the independence movement and the provisional government in Shanghai was exaggerated and on the decline; factionalism and corruption weakened the nationalist movement in Hawai'i; the U.S. government officially denied helping the Korean nationalist movement and remained friendly to Japan; and anti-Asian racism in the United States tended to bring Koreans and Japanese closer together.

The Japanese reached these conclusions based on information collected by the Japanese consulate in Honolulu. For their part, the Koreans in Hawai'i were convinced that the consulate was a spy headquarters trying to exert control over them. Early on, Koreans had been ordered to register at the Japanese consulate, but most had refused, arguing that they were Korean nationals who had come to Hawai'i with Korean passports. However, before long, many Koreans had no choice but to fill out what was (later) called a Korean registration card *(Kankoku toroku kaado)* at the consulate if they wanted to visit or conduct business in Korea or Japan. And all the Korean picture brides were in the Japanese register, since they had come to Hawai'i on Japanese passports. The registration process was another way the Japanese government collected information on Koreans in Hawai'i. While registering Koreans was not terribly sinister and could perhaps be justified as a routine procedure on the part of the consulate, most Koreans tended to echo the sentiments of one of their leaders who said, "The Japanese by nature and habit are all spies."[17]

Allegations of Japanese spying were reinforced when incidents like the following took place. In 1921, when the faction supporting Syngman Rhee dedicated a new building for their Korean Christian Church, Koreans and foreigners—except Japanese—were invited to the ceremony. But since a notice appeared in a local Chinese newspaper inviting anyone to attend, Consul-General Yamazaki and Embassy Clerk Kashimura attended the dedication ceremony uninvited to listen to the remarks of the guests. Additional charges of espionage rang out in the spring of 1925, when the Japanese government appointed a Korean, Yang Chae-ha, to the Japanese consulate-general in Honolulu as vice consul for "special duties" among Koreans in Hawai'i. As one newspaper report put it, Yang's appointment "has aroused great indignation in the Korean colony here. Representatives of seven Korean organizations, meeting today, adopted resolutions protesting against what they declared was 'an extension of the Japanese spy system.'"[18]

Outraged at this attempt either to coopt or spy on them, the Koreans in Hawai'i vented their outrage in the pages of the KNA's newspaper, the *Korean National Herald*. Its editorial outlined four points. First, Koreans in Hawai'i were free from Japanese control, since their passports had been issued by the Korean government. Second, Yang was unacceptable because he was under the control of the Japanese. Third, Korean affairs in Hawai'i had always been managed by Korean organizations. Fourth, the Japanese government was spying on Koreans in Hawai'i in a secret attempt to disturb the Korean community. The Japanese government, not surprisingly, analyzed the objection to Yang differently. It felt the Koreans were protesting because they saw the appointment as a Japanese attempt to counter negative reaction to Korea's annexation and to show that the Japanese government did not discriminate against Koreans. Japan thought the Koreans were also protesting because they wanted to demonstrate to the United States their dissatisfaction with Japan's dominion over Korea.[19]

Thus from the point of view of the Koreans in Hawai'i, the Japanese consulate-general in Honolulu served as the symbol of Japan's domination over Korea and the focal point of the espionage effort against them. Any contact, however routine, with the consulate by a Korean was viewed with suspicion by the Korean community. Especially after the March First Movement of 1919, no Korean wanted to be seen entering the consulate. The Japanese noticed that "[i]f a Korean were to go to the Consulate, he is likely to be labeled a traitor and treated harshly by his fellow Koreans. So if Koreans need to visit the Consulate, they will usually ask a Japanese to act as a middleman to go to the Consulate in his stead. So, for a time, no Koreans visited the Japanese Consulate."[20]

But when the Immigration Act of 1924 (often erroneously labeled the Asiatic Exclusion Act) was passed, the Japanese saw it as an opportunity to come together with the Koreans in Hawai'i against racial discrimination in the United States. The Act had been passed primarily to prohibit Japanese picture brides from entering the United States, which they had been doing since the

Gentlemen's Agreement in 1908, and naturally Japan saw this as an affront to its dignity. But since Korea was part of the Japanese empire, the Immigration Act also prohibited Korean picture brides from coming to Hawai'i or the mainland United States. The Japanese consulate in Honolulu felt optimistic that Korean anger against them would be deflected as a result of the United States' anti-Asian policy.

In fact, the consulate claimed that passage of the Act tended to diminish anti-Japanese feelings on the part of the Koreans in Hawai'i and noted with approval that there was an increase in Koreans coming to the consulate to conduct business. As the consulate optimistically reported: "Despite the anti-Japanese movement, there have been some pro-Japanese Koreans who enjoy close relationships with the Japanese. These Koreans acutely sense the crisis resulting from racial discrimination against Asians in the United States and they even predict a possible racial war. When observing the discrimination against Japanese in particular, many of these Koreans fear it might affect their own status. Some Koreans pretend to be anti-Japanese even if they are pro-Japanese at heart, since they are not willing to be labeled as such from other Koreans."[21]

Also, by the mid-1920s, it was readily apparent to the Koreans in Hawai'i that the March First Movement had essentially failed in its objective to win Korean independence from Japan. Some Koreans began to accept what appeared to be the inevitable—that Korea would remain part of the Japanese empire for the long term. This sentiment not only caused the nationalist movement in Hawai'i to lose steam, but it also led in some cases to limited accommodation with the Japanese. One example of such cooperation occurred when Reverend Min Chan-ho asked permission from the Japanese consulate to go to Korea with twenty students from Hawai'i to raise funds for Syngman Rhee's Korean Christian Church and its academy. The Japanese cited this request as a good omen that anti-Japanese feeling among Koreans was decreasing. Even in matters of language, some Koreans in Hawai'i made, consciously or unconsciously, accommodations to the overwhelming Japanese presence both in Hawai'i and in their homeland. Some, for example, referred to *kye* by its Japanese equivalent, *tanomoshi*. Others referred to the *tosirak* box lunch as *bentō*. Some second-generation children were referred to by the Japanese term *"nisei."* Others went so far as to send their children to Japanese language school.[22]

By the end of the Taishō period (1912–1926), the Japanese had concluded that the Korean nationalist movement in Hawai'i was not a threat to its national interests and therefore did not warrant further attention. The fact that the last official report on nationalist activities of Koreans in Hawai'i was issued in 1926 is evidence of this. After that, the Japanese government ignored them, concluding—as would the U.S. government fifteen years later—that factional infighting in Hawai'i rendered the movement impotent.

The nationalist movement in Hawai'i thus failed to contribute to the liberation of Korea. Moreover, if it is to be judged on the criteria of thinking and acting independently and abandoning *sadae,* then one must conclude that it failed. And it also failed in its efforts to garner the support of the United States. Michael Robinson's study of the nationalist movement inside Korea concludes that it failed there not only because of the efficiency of the Japanese police, a point made by Chong-Sik Lee, but also because of factionalism between the radical nationalists and the cultural nationalists, giving equal causal weight to these factors. The experience in Hawai'i tends to support the view that the nationalist movement failed more because of factionalism than because of Japanese repression.[23]

The political animus that the first-generation Koreans in Hawai'i directed against the Japanese government and its local representative, the consulate-general in Honolulu, sometimes spilled over to the Japanese in Hawai'i, especially the first generation, or *issei.* The earlier anti-Japanese actions of sworn brotherhoods and strikebreakers in 1909 and 1920 had been largely plantation phenomena. After 1920, political considerations became paramount in the relationship between Japanese and Koreans in Hawai'i in a largely urban setting.

Anti-Japanese feeling among Koreans can be found in a wide range of situations. Consider the following two social work cases. The first discussed problems in dealing with Korean welfare cases in Honolulu. It stated that because of Korea's political history of "national inadequacy," Koreans are "mistrustful," "aggressive," "have a keen feeling of injustice," and are "oversensitive to slights or discrimination." The report concluded that "[i]t is questionable as to whether a Japanese worker would be wholly acceptable in a Korean home of the immigrant group where the feeling is very strong." The second case involved a Korean social worker in the Honolulu YWCA who, following the association's policy of racial fellowship, regularly attended Japanese and other ethnic functions there. But she was forced to stop attending Japanese functions because of the criticism she received from other Korean women.[24]

While some Koreans went out of their way to avoid Japanese, others did not hesitate to express their nationalistic feelings to *issei.* Such a confrontation occurred one day when a Japanese driver picked up a Korean walking up a hill. Almost immediately, the Korean asked, "Why not Japan give Korea her independence?" When the Japanese driver asked him why Japan should do so, the Korean passenger said that Japan treated Koreans harshly. The driver responded that he thought Koreans were being treated fairly and asked the Korean if he thought Korea could win against Japan. "Surely," replied the Korean, "because it was told that the United States will come and aid us in time of war with Japan." The Japanese man disagreed and told the Korean to look at his arm. "Is not the color of my arm same as yours? Are we not brothers? Are we not very much closer than the Americans are to you? We must be good friends, because we all belong to a large race family—a yellow race."[25]

Other Koreans expressed their dislike of Japanese publicly. In one incident, a Korean bus passenger got into an argument about the fare with the Japanese driver. "If you grumble—no ride bus," said the driver. The Korean man answered, "You damned Japanese! All Japanese no good like you." Even Korean ministers could not suppress their anti-Japanese feelings. At a gathering of Christian ministers of different denominations and racial groups in 1936, a Korean minister stood up and attacked the Japanese, causing the Japanese ministers to walk out. One of them said, "To such unwarranted, narrow minded remarks aimed at us we didn't care to listen. It wasn't the proper time and place for it."[26]

At times the second generation, both Korean and Japanese, were caught up in the animosity between first-generation Koreans and the Japanese. "I remember that about ten years ago there was a tiny Korean school in Kekaha. . . . As I recall it, one of the plantation workers of Korean immigrant stock was the teacher. How well he was qualified to be a teacher, I don't know. . . . I am quite sure that they [the students] heard, if not actually studied, Japanese hatred in this school. Because on the occasions when I had quarrels with Koreans they used to throw into my face epithets and accusations about Japanese imperialism which they themselves couldn't have thought up. Perhaps they heard them at home. I'm likely to think that the parents urged the teacher to teach it in school."[27]

And sometimes—although as we will see in chapter 10, not often—the anti-Japanese feelings of the parents spilled over to their children: "I am a Korean and it is natural for me to be prejudiced against the Japanese. . . . [W]hen I meet my Japanese classmates day by day, I try to be nice to them . . . but still there is the prejudice. . . . They make me unhappy; they make me hate them. I wish this hate would die, but it never will until Japan gives Korea her independence and a square deal. I am not so prejudiced against the other racial groups, for there is no such driving force of hatred against them."[28]

While it is fair to say that most first-generation Koreans disliked Japan and that some took this out on the *issei* in Hawai'i, for other Koreans there was some ambivalence. That is, on one level Koreans disliked what the Japanese were doing to Korea, but at the personal level a distinction could sometimes be made. As one second-generation Korean woman recalled, "[M]y father spoke quite harshly about the Japanese and yet one of his best friends was a Japanese merchant."[29]

It is interesting to examine how the Japanese responded to the overwhelming antipathy of first-generation Koreans. In fact, Japanese were evenly split into three groups: positive, neutral, and negative. One-third of the Japanese were neutral toward Koreans because, given the small number of Koreans, they simply had not had any personal experience with them.[30] As for the one-third who professed negative feelings toward Koreans, there were essentially three reasons: socioeconomic, political, and face-to-face encounters.

First-generation Japanese ranked Koreans eighth out of eleven (only Spanish, Filipinos, and Puerto Ricans were ranked lower) on the socioeconomic scale, and this low ranking contributed to a relatively negative overall impression. Politically, the Japanese regarded Koreans as "people with strong revolting spirit" or "very suspicious people." One expressed his exasperation thus: "Independence! Independence! Oh, how I hate to hear the Koreans shout." Another related how and why he turned against Koreans: "Prior to the Koreans' movement for their independence I had friendly feelings toward the Koreans. I used to talk with the Korean men. My friendly feeling toward the Koreans in Hawaii was like the sort of fellow feelings we have toward our people. See, Korea was part of Japan and it was very natural for me to think the people of Korea as part of us. But since their cry for independence I have had antipathetic feelings toward every Korean." Finally, negative feelings could come from face-to-face encounters that went bad. Consider the following episode in which a Japanese couple bought a house, which was being rented by Koreans, for their elderly mother: there was an "awful mess" in trying to get the Koreans to move out. After four months, the Japanese couple finally told the Koreans that they were going to move the mother into the house. This made the Korean husband "wild with rage," and he swore at the Japanese woman over the telephone. "Enraged," she stated that of all the races, the Koreans were the worst. Moreover, the house reeked of kimchi, cockroaches infested the kitchen, mice nested under the sink, tin cans littered the yard, and dirt lodged everywhere.[31]

Finally, one-third of the Japanese professed friendly feelings toward the Koreans. This group ranked Koreans a relatively high fourth in overall preference, behind other Caucasians, Chinese, and, of course, Japanese. They overlooked the low socioeconomic ranking of Koreans because of their racial and cultural similarity and echoed the official line of the Japanese government: "Koreans are no longer different people from the Japanese. They belong to Japan. I feel that it is the duty of every Japanese to establish closer contacts with the Koreans in Hawaii. We must walk together with our hands united." This group showed favorable attitudes toward Koreans as playmates for their children, as houseguests, and as marriage partners: "I believe that the second generation Japanese should intermarry with Koreans in Hawaii. It is only in this way that we can ever hope for the mutual cooperation and understanding between the Koreans and the Japanese."[32]

In sum, despite the fact that most first-generation Koreans hated Japan, there were a variety of responses to individual Japanese. Similarly, there was an even greater variety of responses by first-generation Japanese toward Koreans, and these were often colored by political ideology, perceived socioeconomic status, or personal experience. As the children of the first-generation Koreans matured, they, too, would be perceived by others based on what might be called a bimodal set of characteristics—to which we now turn.

8

Educational Achievement and Social Disorganization

An important aspect of the experience of the first-generation Koreans in Hawai'i is how and why they educated their children, how the second generation reacted to educational opportunities in Hawai'i, and what the consequences were. We shall find that many second-generation Korean children excelled academically, but that both they and their first-generation parents were simultaneously plagued by high rates of social disorganization.

Several hundred children (mostly infants) had come to Hawai'i with their parents between 1903 and 1905 or were born almost immediately afterward. They were generally referred to as the "middle generation" and were the functional equivalent of the more recent "1.5 generation." A much larger cohort of children comprising the true second generation were born after the arrival of picture brides between 1910 and 1924, and most of them reached school age in the 1930s. This chapter begins with the middle generation, but the bulk of the discussion will concern the much larger second generation.

Perhaps the best known school that catered to the middle generation was the Korean Compound, which offered instruction through the eighth grade. It was established in downtown Honolulu in 1906 by Reverend John W. Wadman and the Methodist Mission to serve the growing number of Korean children who had recently left the plantations with their parents. Wadman's wife became the principal, and faculty consisted of five American teachers and two Korean language instructors. The Korean Compound also served as the residence for the pastor of the Korean Methodist Church and the office of Wadman, the superintendent. Students supported themselves by working in the school's shoemaking shop, working during vacations on the plantations or in the pineapple fields or cannery, or working as household servants before and after school. The aptitude of the Korean students was recognized by Wadman even at this early stage: "They all make good students being quick to learn and eager to advance. Our graduates have mostly done well." By 1915, two of its graduates were already enrolled in the College of Hawai'i, soon to be known as the University of Hawai'i.[1]

But for more of the children in the middle generation, Korean language school on the plantation, usually taught by the Methodist pastor, was the defining part of their educational experience. These language schools were held in the late afternoon or evening, where students were taught not only language, but also Korean history, customs, and ethics. Like most children, the middle generation would have much preferred doing something else, as the following woman, born in 1907, recalled: "We all were taught to speak and write Korean, our native language, and in order to acquire perfection father sent us to the village language school. Then I took no interest and only conceived it merely as a 'bore' and a waste of time. It came to me that English was sufficient and that going out to play was more enjoyable than going to school where we would find a man teacher who never forgot to leave his yardstick on the table in preparation for an emergency if such should arise. . . . That faithful old Confucius scholar eagerly bent to penetrate our stubborn minds to the wonders of the ancient classics."[2]

These Korean language schools, like their Japanese and Chinese counterparts, served several functions, which appealed to the first-generation Korean parents. One function, of course, was to teach Korean children who were growing up in a predominantly English-speaking environment the language of their parents. Another function was to develop attitudes and standards favorable to good social conduct. Yet another was to place one's children with other Korean children to strengthen ethnic solidarity. Moreover, bilingualism gave the children a better chance at good employment. Training in the Korean language would also allow for further education in Korea. Finally, since the younger generation would eventually leave home, language training enabled them to maintain written communication later on.[3] Yet while the desire to establish Korean language schools was there, the obstacles to doing so proved difficult to overcome.

Korean language schools in Hawai'i never really flourished, especially compared to the Japanese language schools. In the first decade or so, when most Koreans were still on the plantations, there simply were not many children to educate because the Korean community was still largely a bachelor society. In 1910, just before picture brides began to arrive, there were only 164 Korean children old enough to be registered in the public schools. Even if every one of those children had attended Korean language school, there still would not be very many schools in existence. In the 1920s, as the newly arrived picture brides began giving birth, the number of Korean children increased, but the number of Korean language schools did not grow commensurately. In 1921, there were 8 Korean language schools with 337 students, compared to 14 Chinese language schools and 175 Japanese language schools. Four years later, in 1925, there were only nine licensed Korean language schools, an increase of only one. By contrast, there were 10 Chinese language schools and 142 Japanese language schools. Language schools served two-thirds of the Japanese children and one quarter of the Chinese children, but only one-fifth of the Korean children.[4]

The 1930s saw a major increase in the number of Korean schoolchildren when a bona fide second generation began to emerge. The 1930 census showed a 30 percent increase in the number of Koreans in Hawai'i, from 4,950 in 1920 to 6,461, representing about 2 percent of the population of Hawai'i. There were now more native-born Koreans (3,477, or 54 percent) than foreign-born (2,984 or 46 percent), and 2,767 or 45 percent, of them were under the age of fifteen. Despite this increase in the number of Korean children, however, in 1931 there were only ten Korean language schools with an enrollment of 520.[5]

Why did the Korean language schools fail to proliferate? One reason was that Koreans were leaving the plantations for the cities,where they were not as concentrated and could not form Korean enclaves, unlike the Japanese. A second reason was the lack of suitable *han'gŭl* type, which hindered work on Korean language textbooks. Further, the time of greatest need—the 1930s— coincided with the Depression, making it economically difficult to support such schools. Another problem centered around Korea's unique status, especially in comparison with Japan and Japanese language schools. While there was a great deal of trade between Hawai'i and Japan, trade between Hawai'i and Korea was minimal; hence there was less reason to learn Korean for business purposes than Japanese. Moreover, few Koreans in Hawai'i sent their children to Korea for further education because of its colonial status. On the other hand, a substantial number of Japanese (usually the eldest male, known as *kibei*) returned to Japan for education.[6]

Contributing to the dearth of Korean language schools was the notion that foreign language schools represented a hindrance to Americanization. Especially after World War I, when "100 percent Americanism" was strong, language schools were seen by some as a threat to social and national unity, despite the observation that "in no way do they undermine American citizenship." Nonetheless, public opprobrium and subsequent legislation resulted in licensing, censorship of textbooks and curriculum, and a decrease in the time spent in class to one hour a day after school or on weekends and holidays. At one point, as one observer noted, "these institutions practically ceased to function." The Koreans, who wanted to be good Americans, sensed this suspicion toward language schools, and the damage was done. A larger percentage of the Korean second generation than their Japanese or Chinese counterparts never attended a language school. Korean children could, of course, speak and understand some of the Korean used in the home, but they clearly were more comfortable with English, in which they excelled.[7]

One reason the second-generation Korean children did well in English was the fact that many of their first-generation parents had a certain degree of facility in that language. Sociologists who observed the first generation agreed that they generally spoke better English than the Japanese, who had arrived earlier. In 1910, of East Asians in Hawai'i over the age of ten, 37 percent of the Chinese, 21 percent of the Japanese, and 18 percent of the Koreans could speak

English, reflecting the order of their arrival in Hawai'i. Ten years later, in 1920, the Koreans had caught up to the Japanese, with nearly half (45 percent each— the Chinese were up to 62 percent) speaking English. And by 1930, 70 percent of the Koreans and the Japanese could speak English, approaching the Chinese at 78 percent. Another source states that 82 percent of all Koreans could speak English by 1930. By contrast, the Puerto Ricans, who had arrived in Hawai'i at the same time as the Koreans, had very low English literacy rates. One observer went so far as to say, "It is probable that in spite of the nationalistic spirit of the Koreans that theirs will be the first Oriental language to succumb before the English tongue in Hawaii."[8]

The sociologists who examined these statistics state that the Koreans acquired English skills more rapidly than the Japanese because the small size of the group and their scattered condition made English more necessary for them than for the more numerous and concentrated Japanese. Koreans who went into business in Honolulu had to cater to non-Korean clientele to survive, unlike most Japanese businesses. Thus while the small size and the geographical scattering of Koreans made it difficult for them to sustain language schools, it also contributed to the first generation's more rapid English acquisition than first-generation Japanese. But there were two additional reasons for this. First, as was shown in chapter 1, many of the immigrants from Korea already knew some English because of their connection with American missionaries in urban Korea. Second, the first-generation Koreans had quickly adopted the mentality of settlers rather than sojourners, and this demanded familiarity with the English language. Thus their rapid acquisition of English is both a result of this settler mentality as well as yet another indicator of their rapid adjustment to the culture of their host country.

Given all of this, we would expect the second generation to do well in English, as was in fact the case. The same sociologists who noted the rapid acquisition of English by the first-generation Koreans also noted "the unusually good mastery of English which the [second-generation] Korean students are often said to have." Even Koreans noticed that they tended to use English when their Japanese schoolmates used Japanese: "The Japanese [high school students] always spoke in Japanese when an outsider came within their immediate group. The Chinese and the Koreans very seldom used their own foreign language even at home."[9]

The second-generation Koreans were not only good at English, they also compiled an outstanding scholastic record in the Hawaiian public school system. Similar to their ability in English, the scholastic excellence of the second generation was in part a result of the generational transfer of values and attitudes brought from Korea and acquired in the United States. Although most of the first-generation Korean immigrants had come to Hawai'i for economic reasons, a strong secondary impulse was a desire for education. Reverend George Heber Jones, the missionary from Korea who was familiar with these first immigrants, noted when he visited them in Hawai'i in 1906 that "Koreans are eager to learn. Half of the Koreans are there in hopes of getting some kind of education. As students they excel."[10]

The first generation had come from a Confucian culture in Korea that had prized education and placed scholars at the top of the occupational and social hierarchy. Moreover, a number of the male immigrants had benefited from some form of schooling in the cities in Korea, and some had held minor positions that required a certain degree of literacy and professional aptitude. When these immigrants came to the plantations of Hawai'i and found that they were unable to pursue an education, their aspirations were transferred to their American-born children. And since the first generation quickly became settlers rather than sojourners, they realized that the road to success in the new society lay primarily in a good education. Thus they urged their children to make the most of their education.[11]

To achieve this, the first generation had to modify some of the traditional values that might hinder their children from taking full advantage of the educational opportunities the new society offered them. First, they discarded the traditional idea of educating only boys. American law mandated that both boys and girls attend school; thus, although there was still a preference shown toward sons, the gender gap was rapidly being eliminated. Second, since the Koreans had been mostly urban residents before coming to Hawai'i, they had already rejected the practice of rural agricultural societies of encouraging their children to take employment as early as possible in order to assist the family economically.[12] Thus armed, the second-generation Korean children were poised to do well in Hawai'i's educational system.

Many indicators demonstrate the academic achievement of the second generation in Hawai'i. Korean students were ranked second behind northern Europeans in intelligence (Japanese were third and Chinese seventh). Korean children started school early (ranking third behind the Chinese and other Caucasians) and tended to stay in school longer (second only to the Chinese). A 1925 study on mental retardation found that Korean children had lower rates of retardation than any other group of children of immigrant parentage. Koreans were among the top four racial groups in eighth grade mathematical achievement, along with Chinese, Japanese, and Caucasians. Of all children aged six through fourteen, Koreans had the second highest representation in the public schools; of children aged fifteen through nineteen, Koreans ranked first. By the twelfth grade, the Koreans ranked second in representation, behind other Caucasians and ahead of Chinese. In 1936 at the University of Hawai'i there were 81 students of Korean parentage, or 189 to each 1,000 aged eighteen to twenty-one years. For all other groups combined, there were only 71 to each 1,000 in the same age group. One of the researchers who compiled these statistics concluded that the Koreans were taking the greatest advantage of school opportunities, followed by Chinese and Japanese.[13]

It is fair to conclude, then, that the second-generation Koreans excelled academically and, like the children of Chinese and Japanese immigrants, ranked at or near the top of nearly every index of scholastic achievement. Since the Koreans were the last of these three groups to arrive in Hawai'i, their achievement ranks very high indeed. It came at a time when the sugar industry, the press, and some segments of the public did not favor higher education for the masses because it would lure them away from the humble position into which they were born. Thus these attendance and academic achievement indicators reflect a strong educational urge among both the first- and second-generation Koreans. There was every reason to expect that such stellar performance would continue in college and the professional world.

Before labeling Hawai'i's Koreans a model minority, with all the stereotypes and assumptions this appellation carries, it is important to note that there was a price to be paid. In contrast to the Japanese, both first- and second-generation Koreans ranked high in areas that sociologists termed "social disorganization," including intermarriage (outmarriage), divorce, dependency, mental illness, suicide, juvenile delinquency, and crime. The causes were threefold: few language schools, the small size of the Korean group, and urban residence.

Since most second-generation Korean children did not attend language schools, most could not read or write Korean. More important, however, since these language schools reinforced the influence of parents and traditional values, and since most Korean children did not attend, some tended to disrespect parental authority or Korean culture. Korean parents often had more difficulty persuading their second-generation children to respect and adhere to Korean norms than Japanese parents had in convincing their children to respect Japanese traditions. After all, most Japanese children attended language school, and Japan was prospering as a nation, in contrast to Korea. Unacquainted with, or having rejected, the values of their parents' homeland, second-generation Koreans more fully embraced the culture and values of their new country, often to the chagrin of their more traditional-minded parents. When the parents attempted to impose their cultural values and control, this often led to conflict with their more Americanized children—which was sometimes played out in the larger society. However, children who had attended language schools were less frequently found in juvenile court.[14]

The small size of the Korean group and their urban location also contributed to social disorganization. Unlike the numerous Japanese, Koreans could not form an all-encompassing homogeneous community embracing only Korean people, Korean institutions, and Korean cultural values. Nor was there a need to, since there was no overt discrimination against Koreans and thus no need to create an insulated ethnic community for protection. And since there was a greater tendency toward social disorganization in the city than in rural areas, the urban Koreans were thus more vulnerable to it. By contrast, the less-urbanized Japanese exhibited much fewer indices of social disorganization.[15] Because of their more rapid rate of acculturation, the Koreans escaped from the old standards before gaining control of the new standards and thus experienced more severe social dislocations. The Japanese, by contrast, acculturated more slowly and therefore maintained a higher level of social stability and control.

Koreans also experienced a high incidence of interracial marriage (or out-marriage). This trend began in the first generation and mushroomed in the second generation. To be sure, most of the first-generation Korean men pre-ferred to marry Korean women, but since there were none available, except for a few who had come over with their parents between 1903 and 1905, the men began to import picture brides in 1910. In that year, there were about 4,000 males but only 600 females of all ages, or 633 men for every 100 women. The picture-bride system, which lasted for fourteen years until 1924, did mitigate this unbalanced sex ratio somewhat. Still, there were about 2,000 more Korean men than women in 1920 (3,498 males versus 1,452 females). Some of these Korean men remained lifelong bachelors, but others who could not or chose not to acquire picture brides from Korea sought brides from females of other ethnic groups.[16]

There were few obstacles to first-generation Korean men selecting brides from among the other ethnic groups because of a vague sense of racial equal-ity and the absence of any sentiment against interracial marriage. In one sense, interracial marriage can be seen as an indicator of acculturation. As a rule, interracial relationships at the first stage are usually entirely economic in nature and relatively impersonal. But at a second stage comes social relations, and here intermarriage occurs. Thus a certain amount of acculturation—par-ticipation in the life of a common community and culture—as well as a lack of immigrant women are needed before intermarriage can take place.[17] One second-generation female recalled how such a match came about on Waialua Plantation: "We were interesting spectacles. My father was Korean and my mother Spanish. The neighbors of our village eagerly waited for any new addi-tion to the family. They wondered what kind of social individuals would be borne from this strange marriage. The village we lived in was called Spanish camp, though the Spaniards had long deserted the camp. . . . Many of the men however had mingled quite freely with the Spaniards and Portuguese."[18]

Thus during the first twenty-five years or so of the Korean community's existence in Hawai'i, outmarriage was undertaken almost exclusively by males of the first generation. For example, during the period 1912–1917, over four hundred Korean men were married and over three hundred Korean women were married. Not a single one of those Korean women (most of them were picture brides) married a non-Korean, but about one-quarter of the Korean men outmarried. As one report noted with astonishment: "It is noteworthy and most extraordinary that all of the women, without exception, married Korean men. The women of *no other race* in Hawaii have a like record for tenacious adherence to racial lines. The women of no other race have married only men of their own race. The Korean men have 'outmarried' to some extent, but not the women." During the picture-bride period (1910–1924), the outmarriage rate for men declined somewhat but then rebounded after passage of the Immigration Act of 1924, as there were still many more Korean men than Korean women. And beginning in the 1920s, Korean women began to out-marry. Between 1920 and 1924, 150 Korean men and 21 Korean women out-married, and between 1924 and 1928, 169 Korean men and 71 Korean women outmarried. The percentages for the decade between 1920 and 1930 show that 18 percent of the grooms and 5 percent of the brides married non-Koreans.[19]

Thus up to 1930, when most of the first-generation Korean marriages took place, it was mostly the men who outmarried because of the disproportionate gender ratio. Korean women did not need to outmarry because there were more than enough Korean men available. As the sex ratio equalized somewhat after 1930 with the births of second-generation Korean females, one would expect a decrease in outmarriage among Koreans, but such was not the case. Outmarriage, now primarily a second-generation phenomenon, actually increased after 1930 for both Korean men and women. By contrast, most Japa-nese, both first and second generation, married other Japanese.[20]

Besides outmarriage, Koreans also ranked high in the area of divorce. I have already noted in chapter 6 some of the causes for divorce, particularly the unhappiness of the picture brides with their elderly grooms. Between 1913 and 1933, three-quarters of Korean divorces were initiated by the wife. And, although the general trend was more toward outmarriages ending in divorce, the divorce rate was actually higher for inmarried Koreans (mostly picture-bride marriages), at twenty-one per one thousand, than outmarried Koreans, at nine per thousand. Because most of the inmarriages involved (younger) picture brides, a study linking age, marriage, and divorce among ethnic groups in Hawai'i concluded the following: "A Korean man, for example, might well pon-der the advisability of wedding a Korean woman twenty years his junior; in both age and race, their marriage would face serious risks." Others blamed the high divorce rate in part on the small size of the Korean community, noting that the small Puerto Rican group also had a high divorce rate. The divorce rate began to rise for Koreans beginning in 1913, during the early years of picture-bride importation, peaked during the years 1925–1927, just after the end of the picture-bride system, and then began to decline. Examining a single year for comparative purposes, in 1927 on Oahu, of 1,080 Korean marriages, 21 ended in divorce, for a rate of 19.4 per 1,000, which was about three times the Chi-nese rate of 7.1 and the Japanese rate of 6.3.[21]

A third index of social disorganization was the rate of dependency, of which the Koreans had the second highest rate in 1934 at 133 per 1,000, behind only the Puerto Ricans at 298 per 1,000, for men aged twenty to fifty-four in Hono-lulu County. The Korean rate was more than twice that of the Chinese, at 57 per 1,000, and almost three times that of the Japanese, at 47 per 1,000. Sociol-ogists have suggested that dependency occurs when isolated individuals crack under the economic pressure of modern competitive life. Researchers have found that the highest rates occurred in those areas with the greatest heterogeneity, while the lowest rates occurred in homogeneous neighborhoods. Once again, the small size of the Korean population was noted: "It is noteworthy that the Puerto Rican, Korean, and Spanish groups, numerically the weakest of all the racial elements in the city and therefore least competent to build up areas of close settlement or to meet the demands of their needy, have the highest rates of public dependency." Again, a lack of numbers and geographical dispersion contributed to social disorganization.[22]

While the above statistics on dependency, compiled in the early 1930s, relate to able-bodied Koreans, by the 1940s, many of these (mostly male) Koreans were approaching sixty years of age, an important milestone in Korean life known as *hwangap*, when a man traditionally retires and is thereafter supported by his children. But not all elderly Korean men in Hawai'i were able to enjoy this. Some, "through force of circumstances or unwisely, spent their earnings and at present have been reduced to a stage of economic dependency." Others were "disabled by age, illness and other physical handicaps [and] are either bachelors or widowers without any children." Moreover, in Korea, "[b]egging is an accepted form of economic subsistence for those who have neither families, relatives nor friends." As a result, "[t]here seems to be a minimum of stigma attached to the receiving of help. The consensus of opinion of the men . . . seems to be . . . that the factors leading to dependency have been of such a nature that the men could not help but seek assistance. The majority of them have no relatives to turn to. They feel that the lessened capacity for work has been an inevitable result of an effort to adjust in a foreign country. They are of the universal opinion that there is no other recourse but to seek assistance from a government which is providing for them. . . . They feel that many other old people are being cared for similarly and therefore the general tendency is more or less a natural acceptance of public assistance."[23]

Another indication of the Koreans' tendency toward social disorganization was their high rate of mental illness and suicide. In fact, Koreans had the highest rate of mental illness of any ethnic group in Hawai'i, at 235 per 100,000. And the Korean suicide rate was also very high at 75 per 100,000, compared to the Chinese at 32, the Japanese at 27, and the average rate of 23 per 100,000. Psychologists blamed the small size of the Korean population for these high rates, noting that another small group, the Puerto Ricans, had the second highest rate of mental illness, while the much larger Japanese population was the least likely to suffer from it. In general, Koreans gave more "neurotic" responses when tested. They preferred intellectual amusements, were careless about loans, left tasks unfinished frequently, and "let go when angry"; and over half believed themselves to be their parents' favorite. One report concluded that Koreans "are a very unhappy group on the whole, although their feelings alternate, for they are easily discouraged, lonely, feel they deserve a better lot, things go wrong for them when it is not their fault, they are often burdened by a sense of remorse, and the majority have had friends who have turned against them. No wonder over half (15 percent more than the next lower group) often 'feel just miserable.'"[24]

Koreans also ranked high in juvenile delinquency among children ages ten through seventeen. With 1,391 cases between 1929–1930, only the Puerto Ricans (2,810), Hawaiians, part-Hawaiians (1,710), and Filipinos (1,664) had more cases than the Koreans. The Korean rate was nearly twice that of the Chinese, who accounted for 812 cases, and more than four times that of the large Japanese population, which, with 314 cases, had the lowest rate. As with other indices of social disorganization, the small size of the Korean population, and the resultant lack of a concentrated population area, was identified as the reason for the high rate of juvenile delinquency. Indeed, unlike the highly segregated Japanese, the Koreans were among the least segregated of the ethnic groups and continued to become even less segregated. Sociologists discovered that the cases of Japanese juvenile delinquency came from those neighborhoods where the Japanese population was not highly concentrated, that is, where the Japanese mixed with the rest of the population. Since the Koreans were so few and thus lived in ethnically mixed neighborhoods, the result was a high delinquency rate. As Andrew Lind observed, "Delinquency and Americanization occur most rapidly in those sections of the city where there is a conflict of a number of distinctly different cultures and values, none of which is taken very seriously by the second generation. Americanization, in the sense of the breakdown of the traditional primary group controls and the individualization of behavior, proceeds at an unusually rapid pace in such areas."[25]

An inside look at juvenile delinquency, written from the perspective of a twenty-year-old Korean female, attributes the high rate to generational differences in values, a subject which is examined more fully in the next chapter.

> The younger folks have been said to be literally running wild, to be morally degenerated. What are the reasons for juvenile delinquency?. . . The answer is that the older generation have lost their moral authority over the young or else it has been weakened. They were reared in a different civilization from their young. They cannot understand the hopes fears and desires of the youngsters. They do not realize that to do justice to the young, they must adjust themselves to new conditions and to new ideas. But the older people have been taught to look upon life differently. They see things with eyes of the past while the young, with democratic ideas instilled into them by schools and societies, always look ahead. . . . The young and old are at swords's points. Neither side would come halfway. The old follows customs, traditions, restrictions while the young follows his own intuitions, his judgments and his ideas. So, the juvenile delinquency can be traced to this weakening of the moral authority of the parents. . . . [P]arents want obedience and when disobeyed are angered, embittered and do not come half way. . . . A Korean

is proud and sensitive and dares not bring shame as long as he is in that home but he commits crimes when he is outside the home influence."[26]

Finally, the Koreans exhibited a high incidence of adult crime—according to the indices, much higher than the Japanese. Although Koreans represented less than 2 percent of the population in Hawai'i, they accounted for 5 percent of all prison inmates in 1929. There were twice as many Japanese prisoners, at 10 percent, but the Japanese represented fully one-third of the population in Hawai'i. Looking at the inmate population of Oahu Prison during the period 1932–1936, Koreans represented between 4 and 5 percent of the inmates, whereas the number of Japanese was only two or three times that of the Koreans. A similar pattern emerges in parole statistics: between 1933 and 1936, Koreans accounted for around 3 percent of the total number of parolees, roughly one-third of the percentage of Japanese parolees. Between 1915 and 1924, over half of all Korean criminal convictions had been for gambling, violation of narcotics and liquor laws, and public drunkenness. In the following decade, most Koreans were arrested for burglary and more sophisticated economic crimes like fraud, embezzlement, and forgery. These latter crimes, which required a certain degree of understanding and familiarity with American society, is, perversely, yet another indicator that Koreans were highly Americanized.[27]

By the 1930s, then, the leading interpreter of the Korean community at the time, Bernice Kim, would conclude that Koreans were known for two things: their political movements and youth and adult delinquency. And while praising the rapid adjustment of Koreans to American society ("The Koreans compare favorably with the two older and more numerous Oriental groups."), she also recognized that such rapid adjustment had taken its toll: "Within a generation, the change from Korean to American ideas and practices has taken place, a change too rapid and unselective, resulting in an appreciable personal and social disintegration."[28]

As we shift our focus to the interaction between the first- and second-generation Koreans, it is well to put the preceding discussion into a context that would occupy observers more than a half century later, at the beginning of the twenty-first century. That is, if we look solely at the educational achievements of the second-generation Koreans as a group, it may be tempting for some to anoint them a "model minority" to be admired and emulated by other ethnic groups. Yet such an appellation would mask the fact that this generation would grow up largely ignorant of their parents' language and culture and that they (and their parents) would suffer from high rates of mental illness, suicide, juvenile delinquency, crime, dependency, and divorce. Moreover, even if we look at the glowing educational statistics of the second generation, it should be remembered that many Koreans (especially males) did not achieve marked success in school. In sum, the picture is a mixed one—one that belies the label "model minority."

9

Intergenerational Conflict

The first-generation Koreans in Hawai'i had been relatively quick to adjust to American values and ideas because of their atypical background in Korea, their status as settlers rather than sojourners, the relatively small size of their community, and the absence of any legal barriers to acculturation except for the denial of citizenship and the right to vote. As a result, many first-generation Koreans distanced themselves somewhat from a set of Confucian values and Korean behavior patterns that had been brought from their homeland and that all three East Asian immigrant groups shared to a certain extent. But while the first-generation Koreans put a greater distance between themselves and these values than the Chinese and Japanese, this did not mean they completely discarded traditional Korean values and behavior. Consequently, there was a certain degree of tension between the more conservative first generation and the more liberal second generation, who often saw their parents as hopelessly old-fashioned over a wide range of issues.

One such issue was residence. To be sure, most first-generation Koreans had already left the rural areas for Honolulu, but those younger Koreans whose parents were still on the plantations felt the need to make a geographical break. As one observed: "The families had depleted; the second generation couldn't wait to leave the plantations. When they finished high school, and some even before graduation, the young ones left the plantations behind for the big city, Honolulu, in search of jobs and a better life."[1]

Clothing preference was another source of conflict between generations, as well as within the first generation. Most first-generation men wore Western clothes, but the "self-conscious" women for the most part continued to wear the Korean *hanbok,* with a long skirt and a short waist. Only a small minority wore American dress. And their children "are conscious that they are different if they wear their own [Korean] costume to school. They all wear the American dress; only on certain occasions when required to, do they wear Korean costume."[2]

Food was another area that led to differences, both between generations and within the first generation. One recent arrival from Korea remembered the contrast between the Korean meals he had been accustomed to and those he experienced in Hawai'i: "I ate . . . no more rice gruel for breakfast. No; instead I drank fresh orange juice, and ham and eggs, and toast with butter and jam. I also ate enormous chunks of meat called steak, and raw vegetables." Sometimes the more Americanized men of the first generation came to prefer Western-style meals: "[Mother's] diet consisted mainly of soups, kim chee, and fresh vegetables. If it weren't for my father who insisted on seeing meat on the table she would not have served it. . . . My mother, however, took only occasional bites of the meat."[3]

More salient, however, was the difference in food preferences between generations, especially since, by one account, nearly two-thirds (63 percent) of the first generation ate Korean food all or most of the time. One food-related generational difference involved the supposedly therapeutic properties of seaweed soup. First-generation mothers took seaweed soup after giving birth, just as they would (and did) in Korea. But the middle- and second-generation mothers took seaweed soup after giving birth only if there was a first-generation woman living in the same household. One woman remembered her own experience with her mother: "[W]hen my babies were born she insisted on keeping me confined in bed for a month while she fed me and my husband seaweed soup and chicken. She cleaned our house and did the laundry, too. I argued I had read in the papers that some women got up and even traveled on cruises with their husbands only two weeks after giving birth. But according to Korean beliefs I was not strong enough to emerge from bed until my baby was a month old."[4]

An even more vexing and divisive food issue involved garlic and kimchi. To be sure, many second-generation Koreans enjoyed kimchi and integrated it with the Western food to which they had become accustomed. Sometimes this made for some rather odd combinations, as when one girl said, "I'd like to have milk and my kim-chee sandwich please." At the same time, the second generation was sometimes embarrassed by the garlic smell pervading their homes. Some felt constrained from bringing their friends to their home, which reeked of "odor (which) is due to the garlic," while others asked their mothers to make kimchi without garlic, since kimchi "is found at each meal, summer or winter, breakfast, dinner, or supper." As one contemporary pointed out, "[T]he young people strongly object to the garlic used in making kimchi because in associating with a cosmopolitan group which does not eat garlic, it renders the users of garlic or onions unpleasant. To the old people kimchi without garlic is simply not kimchi." One second-generation woman remembered that when her mother returned from visiting Korea and brought back winter kimchi, "[m]y brothers . . . could not stand the strong aroma of these foods. Whenever one of the crockery pots was opened, they cried, 'Ooh, stink! stink! We don't want to eat that!' and ran out of the kitchen."[5]

The first generation sometimes compromised with their children by making kimchi less highly seasoned and allowing it to ferment for only a few days rather than the usual two-month period. The first generation also compromised by introducing coffee at meals and having a Western-style breakfast of fruit, cereal, and coffee, then serving Korean-style food for the two remaining meals. The exception was the sandwich lunches the children took to school.[6]

Similar generational differences can be seen regarding eating instruments. The first generation used chopsticks and bowls exclusively because they believed (like the Chinese and Japanese) that food was not to be touched by one's fingers. This was why the first generation was initially shocked by the native Hawaiian practice of eating fish and poi with their fingers. The second generation also used chopsticks, but "fingers are used if the occasion calls for such action."[7]

Generational differences were also found in the observance of various celebrations and commemorative days. The first generation celebrated American holidays like Christmas and the Fourth of July, but they also celebrated traditional holidays such as the emperor's birthday and the lunar (Chinese) New Year. The second generation, on the other hand, generally celebrated only the American holidays. And the first generation, unlike the second generation, carried on the tradition of the one-year-old vocational ceremony, or *toljanji,* where the boy would not only receive presents of cloth and money, but would also "choose" his future vocation. The child, dressed in a scarlet silk skirt with a multicolored sash, was placed in front of a small table upon which had been placed articles symbolic of different vocations. Reflecting the traditional high regard for education, books and pencils were placed in the middle front so that when the child reached out, he would "choose" the symbols representing scholarship.[8]

First-generation celebrations often provided the occasion for a large Korean feast. The women, as already noted, were usually attired in traditional Korean dress, while the men wore American suits. Korean food, prepared by the women, would be served to the men and women separately, in keeping with the dictum of the segregation of the sexes. The only American food served was soda. These celebrations often involved Korean dancing and singing, accompanied by traditional drums and cymbals imported from Korea. The singing and dancing would be performed exclusively by young men because "respectable" women did not dance in public, as that was the realm of déclassé *kisaeng* (dancing girls) and *mudang* (shamans).[9]

However, such attitudes were not held by the second generation, some of whom took an interest in Korean music and dance. In 1922, an association called Nampungsa, composed of first-generation immigrants who had had some formal training in Korea, was established. It imported musical instruments from Korea and taught traditional music and dance to the younger generation. In 1927, it was succeeded by another organization, the Hyŏngjye Club, formed by Whang Ha Soo, who worked at the YWCA and who had come to Hawai'i after attending a women's college in Alabama. Known popularly as the Hyung Jay, or "Elder Sisters," Club, it organized traditional Korean dance activities for second-generation Korean women in Hawaiʻi, enlisting the aid of several traditional musicians among the male Korean population. Whang's influence led the Korean community to accept dance performances by second-generation females, devoid of all social stigma.[10]

Another source of conflict between the first and second generation was language. When polled, nearly three-quarters (71 percent) of one sample of first-generation Koreans reported using Korean all or most of the time at home and expected their children to know enough Korean to function efficiently within the household. Yet English was the native tongue of the second generation, and, combined with the relative lack of Korean language schools, this created a mini-language barrier between the generations. As one contemporary report noted, the first generation spoke Korean with a dash of pidgin English, the middle generation spoke Korean and English with Korean carryovers, and the second generation spoke "tainted" Korean to the first generation and English among themselves and with others. Another contemporary observer noted, "It is very difficult to find a child, even a grown up born in Hawaii, who can fully express his thoughts purely in Korean. Parents born in Hawaii do not converse in Korean, but in English and their children do not know how to speak Korean except a few ordinary words used often at home." One writer implied that friendship patterns were partially responsible for this: "The [Korean] children here . . . have playmates of various nationalities. They talk in all kinds of languages—pidgin English, Japanese, Hawaiian, Korean and what not." This naturally also had an impact on parental control: "Very few families have their children speak Korean more often than English. . . . [So] parents being unable to speak the language very well did not understand their children and did not have great influence on them."[11]

For the second generation, mastery of the English language was crucial to their success. Consider the following, admittedly isolated, instance where a boy was sent back to Korea for schooling, similar to the *kibei* among Japanese Americans: "Yee spent nine years of his life in Korea . . . [and] was an outstanding pupil in his school. When a second world war seemed inevitable, Papa sent for him. . . . Here, his troubles began. When he attended the American schools, Yee was placed in the tenth grade—he was eighteen years of age at the time. . . . [How can anyone] make good grades if he does not understand his teacher? How can anyone understand his teacher who speaks English when he doesn't know that language? Schooling was a hard and long battle for Yee. We tried and could not help him in his difficulties."[12]

Besides the language barrier, even the way of speaking differed between the generations. Remembered one second-generation Korean educated in Korea: "I was amazed. Such a manner of speaking [English] completely violated all the proper speaking manners I had learned in Korea: keep your face expressionless, don't reveal your emotion when you speak, and so on, until one could cultivate the perfectly immobile face of a cultured person. Now I had to forsake all the discipline and training and learn to speak in a different form; with a wide open mouth, bare teeth and flipping tongue—in general, with a contorted face. It was embarrassing even to try."[13]

Using English also made it difficult for the second generation to give proper respect to their elders, which indirectly spawned a sense of equality: "I discovered English also meant learning new attitudes and relations, and learning, above all, a different sense of values. English was not only a language; it was a way of life. My attitude toward the elders and the authority, including the teachers, was no longer born of fear and submission. There were no separate polite forms of speaking to parents and elders or authorities as it is with the Korean language. In the Korean language, every expression and communication varied, depending on the comparative age and status. One spoke one way to a younger or an inferior person; quite another way to a person of equal age and status. And the expression changed totally when addressing an older person. Here in America, I used the same words with them as with my friends. In such insidious and subtle ways, my relations with everyone was placed on equal terms."[14]

The traditional hierarchy within the family was also subjected to reinterpretation by the second generation, often to the consternation of their parents. In Confucianism, the family was more important than the individual, and within the family a hierarchical structure was maintained through certain rules of behavior. Ancestors were superior to living descendants, parents were superior to children, elders were superior to those younger, and males were superior to females. Those below were, in theory, dependent upon those above them for guidance and therefore were required to be deferential.

At the apex of the family hierarchy were the ancestors, who represented the extension of the family system beyond the grave. Many first-generation Koreans in Hawai'i had abandoned ancestor worship because, practically speaking, most of their ancestors were buried in Korea and because their Christianity did not support ancestor worship. Said one second-generation Korean: "My mother never talked to me about ancestors." Still another said simply that there was "no ancestor worship" in his home. Finally, one recalled, "We never talked about [ancestors] with my parents, partly due to the language barrier."[15] For these families, there were no generational differences.

But other first-generation Korean parents did believe in ancestor worship and the spirit world and saw no contradiction in practicing Christianity and venerating family ancestors. This sometimes led to intergenerational tension. For example, some elderly Koreans insisted that they not be cremated because "after one is dead, why torture them by burning?" Others wanted elaborate funerals with flowers and expensive caskets and wanted their jewelry buried with them in preparation for the hereafter. The second generation, by contrast, preferred simple funerals and had no objection to cremation. Other first-generation parents believed that meticulous grooming of the father's grave would please his spirit, which in turn would send good fortune to his descendants.

One second-generation Korean reported, "My mother always said this was so," while another parent lamented that "[w]e are old-fashioned. Our children don't believe it. They seldom accompany us to go to the graveyard." For those in the second generation who did go to the graveyard, "[w]e do give flowers, but don't know [about ancestors]."[16]

In fact, few, if any, second-generation Koreans subscribed to ancestor worship and the belief in the existence and usefulness of ancestral spirits. When asked, a typical second-generation response was: "It is hard to believe; I cannot see and cannot say." Another said: "We are not concerned [with ancestors] much; Koreans are the most 'liberal.'" And a third stated that they were "[n]ot so much indoctrinated [about ancestors]." Nor did the second generation believe that dead ancestors could help the living, one stating that "[y]ou have to fight by yourself; you cannot believe in the spirit." They also rejected the Confucian notion that they should look to the past, and in particular to their ancestors, for models of behavior. As one put it, "All is past; it is now modern time." Another said, "It is more our own assertion among our generation; we do not follow any [ancestral example]."[17] Thus the veneration of ancestors, already partially abandoned by the first generation, was almost completely absent in the second generation.

For those in the first generation who clung to some aspects of ancestor worship, the death of a family elder carried prescriptions for mourning, which the second generation was reluctant to follow. One prescription was the wearing of white—as one would in Korea—as a sign of mourning. By contrast, second-generation Koreans wore black. A second, and perhaps more salient, feature of ancestor worship was the rules governing the mourning period. However, one such mourning ritual went by the boards as a result of the enforced blackout during World War II: "From the moment the body was ready for viewing, it was the custom for family and close friends to gather together day and night before the funeral to observe a prolonged wake around the clock. But after December 1941, the all-night vigil was abandoned. Strangely, no one missed it, and everyone agreed it was a sensible change. Some people mentioned how disrespectful and tasteless it used to be when some of the 'mourners' passed the night sitting in an adjoining room laughing and joking, playing cards, even gambling and drinking; their excuse was they could not sit frozen in grief hour after hour through the night."[18]

Generational differences sometimes arose concerning what was or was not permissible during the one-year mourning period. For example, it was not considered appropriate to get married during that period, and the death itself was said to cast a shadow over the propitiousness of any match. Consider the case in which the mother of the family passed away: "At first the anguished words, weeping, and sighs were all we heard from the callers. But those sounds gradually diminished and I became aware of the guests' whisperings and strange murmurings, which made me feel uneasy. The callers cast glances toward our father every now and then. What were they saying under their breath? The night before the funeral, a few moments before the prayer service was to begin, a woman boldly walked up to my father. 'Mr. Kwon, do you know that in Korea when a death in a family occurs before a wedding, it is taken as a sign, a warning? We think it means the marriage of your son is ill-fated. You should ask him not to marry this girl.'" In this case, the father did not feel bound by this restriction: "The woman stopped when she saw the look of astonishment come over my father's face. His heavy eyes opened wide, then narrowed with anger. 'How can you say that? My son's marriage is not your business.' I trembled with confusion. Could they be right? How superstitious these people are, I thought." [19]

For the first generation, traditional Korean Confucian values dictated that the family was more important than its individual members. One manifestation of this was a heightened concern for maintaining appearances and not dishonoring the family name, which placed a great deal of pressure on the second generation. Many among the first generation, and even the small middle generation, adhered to this idea and attempted to pass it on to their children: "The family name means the world to them. They must bring honor to the family but they must never dishonor the good name. They would rather die than bring dishonor to the name." Consider also the sentiments expressed by a woman of the middle generation who found American families lacking in this respect: "These few homes in which I worked were well-to-do families who were respectful people in the public eye. To my great dismay I found the family conditions corrupt to its very soul with no honor or respect for their names. With this light I have reasoned and have convicted the Americans as people with a lower moral standing. The strict Oriental moral code seems to be a necessity if the American people want to raise their moral standard. When I noticed such degraded actions of the American people I felt proud, oh so proud, for being a Korean." [20]

As time passed, however, adherence to this ideal slipped considerably, and even the first generation sometimes put individual goals before those of the family: "[M]y father began dropping from church attendance. This upset my mother. She knew he favored his workshop over Sunday worship. Before long he stopped going to church altogether. She begged him to keep up the appearance of family unity." But it was the second generation that most emphatically rejected the seemingly overweening concern for appearances. As one woman recounted, "My [first generation] mother is always cautious about our impression to others. For example, about yardwork, when my husband rests, my mother asks him to do yardwork. She said, 'If I am one of your family members, I have to say what I see—it is necessary. You can't be resting leisurely like this in Korea!' Then I talk back, 'We're not in Korea!' My mother also said all the time, 'How dirty it looks in the eyes of others!' I said, 'Don't mind others' feelings.' The way of her life is quite different from ours. Always my mother 'pushes us to do quickly.'" [21]

Many in the first generation felt their children should uphold family appearances by holding a prestigious job or befriending prominent individuals. But the second generation saw things differently. "I don't know about it [glorifying the family]; I do day-to-day work, not for the sake of getting a name." And consider the experience of Mr. Lee, a thirty-two-year-old second-generation Korean who worked as a pipefitter and who had married a woman from Korea: "He . . . often came home in dirty clothes and with dirty hands. His wife repeatedly asked him why he did not look for a white-collar job . . . explaining that in Korea, even if the pay was very little, an individual would have more prestige and be more respected if he accepted a white-collar job than if he accepted an industrial job with higher pay. His wife complained about his friends, but he could see nothing wrong with them. Her objections were not because they were people of different races but because they were ordinary individuals and not persons of prominence."[22]

To be sure, keeping up appearances had its advantages not only for the family name, but also for the individual, in terms of upward mobility. "When my eldest brother [George] had his first job, the family helped in every possible way that we thought was essential in his making a good impression on his employer." Still, the pressure of maintaining the prestige of the family was felt by his sister. "I felt as though I dare not ruin the reputation my family had— Brother George's excellent position in a well-known business firm, Alice's teaching in the public schools, and Esther's ability as a stenographer at the Navy Yard. I had often wondered what I would become in order to contribute to the well-established reputation the family upheld in the community."[23]

Perhaps the most important relationship one had was with his or her parents. Parents were directly below the ancestors in the family hierarchy, occupying a superior position in the family because they were older and more experienced. The children were dependent upon parents and were expected to obey and be loyal to them—a concept known as filial piety. One aspect of filial piety was to repay the debt to one's parents for conceiving and rearing them. In old age, parents expected that the children would commemorate their *hwangap,* or sixtieth birthday, with a big celebration in traditional Korean fashion, then care for them in their (the children's) households, creating an extended family. Some first-generation parents "took it for granted," and often their children responded as expected.[24]

Indeed, many second-generation Koreans were motivated by strong feelings of filial piety to care for their parents in their declining years. A researcher who interviewed some of them analyzed their thinking as follows: "They have a strong feeling of attachment for their elders who have been reduced to a state of dependency and are no longer fully able to support themselves or to carry on their lives without assistance. They regard caring for the aged as part and parcel of normal family life. Whether the aged have made no effort to provide for their old age or whether their present status has been a result of unavoidable circumstances, the younger people still engender this sense of loyalty and responsibility for the care of the aged. Many of them are unwilling to marry until they have maintained an adequate provision for their parents." For example, the family of one invalid father "refused to have him hospitalized, knowing that at the hospital he would lack the more personal attention. Furthermore, he completely revolted [against] the idea of being confined in the hospital even to his dying day. With this feeling in mind, the children made it a point to adhere to his wishes altho they had the doctor visit their father daily. The feelings and wishes of their father was more important to them."[25]

But not all members of the first generation demanded such devotion. For many of them, there existed "a general striving towards self-sustenance and a greater degree of independence in old age." One second-generation Korean remembered that his parents "didn't expect anything from us [children]." When Korean elders (mostly picture brides) were asked about living with their son's family, their most frequent response was "independent households necessary" followed by "independent households if possible." Not a single respondent chose the option of "must live together." Moreover, less than one-fifth of the respondents in fact lived with their children. These independent-minded senior citizens, one report stated, "have made a conscious effort to maintain themselves and are still desirous of continuing to be self-sustaining as long as possible. Some of these people have relatives and families, but they do not conceive of relying on such. These independent aged cannot conceive of having to spend the rest of their lives in idleness and dependency. They feel that their children have responsibilities of their own, that the parents' chief duty is to provide a basis for their offspring only to facilitate the children's own sense of self-independence, rather than to have them become responsible for their parents."[26]

In this area, then, problems between generations would arise only when the first generation demanded, but did not receive, the expected care from their children. And it is clear that the second generation, like the first, was split on the issue. As one Korean observer noted, "A slow, unconscious shift is taking place within the Korean group from a close adherence to the principle of filial piety to a relative laxity in conforming to this principle." One Korean who subscribed to the notion of filial piety and caring for elderly parents complained that their children were "radically different." That is, many had no desire to take their parents in, saying, "Now the government supports the elderly" and "We didn't ask our parents to be born; why should we repay them?" Researchers interviewing these "unfilial" children found some of them to be "prejudiced over some maltreatment experienced as a child. . . . [T]he younger generation feels no gratitude and rebels against the traditional sense of filial piety . . . [because they] had to struggle for themselves. Thus, why should the elders expect any compensation at a time when the younger generation has added responsibilities of their own? This is a situation where the youth are not seriously concerned with the criticism of their relatives and friends, for they feel perfectly justified in feeling the way they do." [27]

Fathers in a traditional Korean family often were distant authority figures responsible for setting a good example and, when necessary, meting out discipline. In Hawai'i, this distance was exacerbated by the fathers' advanced age. Often in such settings the younger mother acted as mediator between father and children. It is clear from the reminiscences of the second generation that they wished their fathers had been less formal. One woman whose father was a minister wrote, "[My father] has not come into daily contact with us as he should have done, but still his personality, his manliness, his thoughtfulness and purity seem to guide us, and though my mother may be thought of as the head of the family, still my father is the real head of the family." Another woman whose father was a grocer wrote, "Papa is the most influential figure in my family. Papa may have his one or two faults, but we children, that is my brothers, sisters, and I, respect him highly. . . . I remember, too, how we children made Papa very angry at times. . . . Papa is a very patient man, but he also is a man who believes in disciplining his children. When Papa stormed into our bedroom, we used to rush for the exit. The belt lashed across some very uncomfortable spots as we shizzed through the room. . . . But Papa is really a good man who loves his children." [28]

Perhaps the most eloquent lament about a distant father figure came from one of the sons of Reverend Hyŏn Sun. "Father and I, as with all brothers and sisters in a Korean family, never had an open personal relationship. We accepted and respected each other's family status; father and son and brothers and sisters, older or younger. I don't remember ever having spoken to my father as a person. . . . It didn't mean there was any animosity among us, nor that there was no feeling for each other. My heart was always filled with pride and admiration for my father. What it did mean, however, . . . [was] that . . . he was still the child of the ancient and feudal social system. . . . Should the necessity ever rise for father to communicate with his son, it was always conveyed through the intermediary of the mother." [29]

Also central to traditional Korean Confucian values was the notion that children should obey one's parents and elders without question, as they were older and wiser. Harmony would result when one acted properly toward those above them in the hierarchy, and the bonds thus created would be reciprocated to one's benefit. It is clear that many Koreans subscribed to this notion and did their best to instill it in their children. One first-generation Korean told his children, "If you ignore your parents, you know nothing." The first generation even felt free to dictate to their grown children, one adult second-generation Korean ruefully noting that "[m]y parents still tell me what to do." Some among the second generation accepted this: "[W]ith the aged and the past generation, I have decided to listen to them to see whether I could take over from them the precious and passing traditions and ideals. . . . I have been able to

venerate and respect the older generation with more sympathy and kindness."
Others rationalized the need for deference to elders by noting that Koreans in
Hawai'i "are mostly extended family." Another put obedience to parents and
elders in Christian terms, saying, "It is also according to the Bible." Finally, one
second-generation Korean said of obedience, "It's a law of nature."[30]

But not all first-generation Koreans demanded absolute obedience. When
one group of aging Koreans was asked about the filial behavior of their own
children, the two least frequent responses were "absolute submission" and
"should defer." In such families, intergenerational conflict would be minimal
over this issue.[31]

In fact, most of the second generation were not prepared to obey blindly the
dictates of their elders or accept that they were dependent upon them. When
polled, second-generation Koreans generally disagreed with the statement, "An
individual's most important duty and responsibility are toward his parents,
which takes precedence over any other interest, including self-interest." As one
Korean wrote about his own second generation, "In Hawaii the children's
respect of parents are different. They respect and obey their parents to a certain degree. In any discussion if their ideas do not agree with their parents they
stand staunchly by their ideas until it is explained fully as to why they are wrong.
Children in Hawaii are not so easily suppressed." One said, "I cannot depend
on parents; we are more individualistic," while another said, "Everything is self-
centered; [success] depends on individual efforts only." The notion that deference would ultimately be reciprocated was rejected by one Korean out-of-hand
as "rather hypocritical." As parents themselves, the second generation recognized their limits: "We could advise [our third-generation children only] when
they are young and unaware of what is what." Another second-generation parent commented, "Regardless of good or bad, we taught our kids to speak out."
Informed by values of equality and individualism, most of the second-generation Koreans (like the second generation Japanese and Chinese) thus tended to
be more "liberal" than their parents.[32]

Thus when a reluctant generation resisted their elders' demands for unques-
tioning obedience, the potential for conflict arose. Note the inherent tension
in the following situation, where a young Korean woman was reluctant to work
for her father: "Then followed a speech on filial piety, the first of many on the
subject I was to hear. . . . 'This is *our* family business, a business for all of us.
We should all work together. Your mother helped build it. Now it is your duty
and your brothers' and sister's.' I had always respected and honored my parents' wishes and expectations in the past. But I thought we should have held a
family discussion before such major decisions were made. . . . Adherence to
the hallowed Old World custom of filial piety drove my father into conflict in
achieving the good life for his children."[33]

Because the family represented the most important social institution in
Korean Confucian values, traditional ideas about the size and composition of

the family were brought to Hawai'i by the first generation—ideas that generally were not shared by the second generation. One value was a preference for large families as economic security in one's declining years. In general, the average number of children in a first-generation Korean household in Hawai'i was large—between six and seven. This fact was not lost on sociologists, who suggested that, on this particular indicator of acculturation to American values, first-generation Koreans ranked low.[34]

A preference for sons was another traditional Korean value. Males were believed to be more important economically to the family than females because men tended to secure better jobs and were therefore better equipped to support their parents in their old age. Second, when a daughter married, tradition had it that she became the property of her husband's family. Third, only males could perpetuate the family line. Indeed, it was the sons' filial duty to marry so they could in turn produce sons to keep the family line going. A second-generation Korean woman recalled, "My parents complained that my brother hesitated about getting married." And as one (first generation) "mother always said [to her son, 'You should] get married and have sons.'" By contrast, giving birth to a girl was akin to what the Chinese referred to as "small happiness." One second-generation Korean woman ruefully recounted the reaction to the birth of her daughter: "Philip bought several boxes of cigars and chocolates to pass out to well-wishers, but the cigars remained almost untouched in the boxes. He heard such jibes as 'You pass out cigars when you have a son!' or 'I'll take one when it's a boy!' I wondered how much Philip wished we had a son as our first-born. And I wondered how disappointed the baby's grandparents were. I knew that in Korea sons were a source of great pride since they carried on the family name."[35]

Since sons were preferred, it could lead in some cases to preferential treatment, in keeping with the traditional Confucian dictum that males are superior to females. But pressure from their children often forced the first generation to retreat from this position. For example, in traditional Korea, only sons were provided with formal education, while daughters were trained to become "good wives and wise mothers." But mandatory public education and prodding by their (female) children often had the desired effect: "My parents up to this time were rather old-fashioned, but thru my fluency in their language, gradually I have succeeded in convincing them that some of their ideas are not in accord with the modern ideas. . . . Now, my parents are quite modernized. . . . They believe in educating all their children, both girls and boys. I was never discouraged by my parents in my work." Pressure from their children also led first-generation parents to relax somewhat their traditional notions of the woman's place: "The womenfolks have been given greater freedom. A few years ago, they were not allowed to carry on conversation with men on the streets, they were deprived of all educational advantages, they were looked upon as inferior to men; but with the opening of their eyes by the aid of the youngsters, women have been treated as equals, they have been allowed greater freedom, they have been allowed to attend night schools, social activities and meet new faces and new living conditions."[36]

Still, there was a persistent belief among the first generation that while girls should be educated and given a modicum of freedom and equality, males remained the primary providers and heads of the households and therefore should get preferential treatment—an opinion not dissimilar to the prevailing opinion in the United States in the first half of the twentieth century. One second-generation female wrote, for example, "I heard many people of my race remark that a girl seldom succeeds in her ambition and that her duty is to stay at home." Another female recalled a remark that indirectly assumed the primacy of the male: "My parents said if the husband gets sick, the woman should be the breadwinner; women need education too." One second-generation Korean woman said, "My mother sent me to school, but she said always, 'it will bring disaster if a woman knows more than a man,'" and yet another reported, "My 91-year old mother still insists that 'boys should never carry dishes [and] prepare separate food in a new dish for boys.'"[37]

The evidence suggests that the second generation was divided on the issue of female equality, as was the general public. Some embraced equality, like the second-generation Korean man who had grown up in Korea and recalled his struggle to accept it: "In this new world, women were not the creatures of home drudgery. Girls competed on equal terms with boys in school, and there were almost as many women as men in colleges and universities. I was amazed to find women lawyers, doctors, and even politicians. My old 'ideas' about women seemed almost feudal, but discarding them was not too easy; the old concepts and attitudes seemed to be ingrained in my veins. But helping with washing dishes in the kitchen (unheard of in Korea), sweeping and mopping the floor on Saturdays (also never seen in Korea), and on occasion even ironing my own clothes (certain disgrace in Korea) helped me to shed some of my old misconceptions of women, slowly but surely."[38]

But other second-generation Koreans held on to the notion of male superiority. One stated, "Still, the husband is the 'bread-winner,' so he should be the head of the family." Similarly, another second-generation Korean, when asked about a hypothetical situation in which only one of their children could be educated, answered that the son would be given the opportunity, "because he has to earn his bread and butter and the additional education can help him to that end, whereas the girl will get married and her husband will support her." Finally, one member of the second generation foresaw grave consequences in the emancipation of Korean women: "But with all this freedom comes the falling down of women. Being free, they began to entertain ideas different from before, they like to take chances, the home drudgery seems to irk them, the caring for the children seems to tire them so they think of destructive ideas like desertion, divorce, breaking up of families."[39]

Another gender issue leading to generational conflict was the traditional belief in the segregation of the sexes. In Korea, boys and girls were strictly segregated at an early age. Indeed, a young woman in Korea typically would not be in the company of a male outside the home until her wedding day, when she would become the wife of someone chosen by her parents. The idea of dating or even dancing with the opposite sex was unheard of. When the first generation came to Hawai'i, some continued to practice such segregation. "Dad never did believe in us girls working outside. The boys worked during the summer, but the girls remained at home. He believed in the old Korean custom where girls were not allowed to be seen too much out in public. I couldn't even go to the show with my friends; it had to be with my father and mother." Segregation of the sexes continued even after marriage, in the Korean churches as well as at social gatherings and formal meals.[40]

In the more open atmosphere of Hawai'i, this segregation appeared anachronistic to the more liberal second generation, many of whom believed in the equality of women and that women should be free to socialize with the opposite sex, dance with, date, and marry whomever they chose. Implicitly, they rejected the traditional Korean attitude of female subordination. "I admire the American respect for women and the American home life; they depict civilization and progress," wrote one second-generation Korean woman. A second-generation young man who was educated in Korea recounted his own changing attitudes regarding segregation of the sexes: "I was also beginning to come in close contact with girls. In Korea, any relationship with girls was governed by the teachings of Confucius: 'Boys and girls should be separated when they reach the age of six.'" And yet, he found that in Hawai'i, "[m]y attitude toward girls and women was also changing. There was no moral dictum. Boys and girls grew up together, went to school together, played together. And when they reached high school age, fifteen or sixteen, they began playing the 'dating' game. . . . If I had played such a 'dating' game in Korea, I would be scandalized, or worse, ostracized, by the family and relatives. And the girl, if there were such a girl in Korea, would be in disgrace for life." And when he first saw people dancing in Hawai'i, it was a scene where "men and women were clinging to each other and whirling around and around with the music. It was so embarrassing, I couldn't look at them directly, but I could see the faces of some men and women almost touched each other. I saw enough and walked away. At home, I told my mother what I had seen. 'Barbarians!' she snorted. And here I was in Hawaii, dating and dancing with no feeling of shame or embarrassment."[41]

Some first-generation Korean households not only treated their sons differently from their daughters, they also treated the boys differently based on age. Traditionally, the oldest son was just below the parents in the family hierarchy and as such received preferential treatment. For example, circumstantial evidence suggests that some eldest sons were afforded more opportunities to pursue higher education, which in turn resulted in better jobs. When the first generation was asked which of their sons was most successful, more than twice as many indicated that the first son, who often had a college education, was more successful than the second son, whose education was more likely to be senior high school.[42]

Another example of preferential treatment came when the eldest son married. His wedding assumed the greatest importance, which confused the younger children in the family. "The notion of their son's marriage caught both my parents by surprise. They needed time to plan a wedding according to Korean custom befitting a first son. . . . The growing guest list, including adults and children, was nearing one thousand. Usually in Korea the whole village was invited when a yangban's son was married. 'Mama, why do you have to put on such a big, elaborate wedding? Why is tradition so important?' we asked." Clearly, this was one aspect of traditional culture that would not be perpetuated by the second generation.[43]

The privileged position of the eldest son was also reflected at mealtimes in some first-generation households, where age and gender determined how dinner was served. Older members of the family and guests were served with both hands, whereas a younger person was served with the right hand only. The order of service started with the head of the household, followed in descending order by the age of the other male members of the family. If there were male guests, the female members of the family would eat later or in another room. One eldest brother remembered his own experience: "I was allowed to sit at the table of the elders and partake in the special food prepared for them. . . . For my younger brothers, it was most tantalizing and aggravating at mealtimes. They had to sit and wait and watch the big helping of choice bits of food passed to me. Then they received their bowls, but not with too many choice bits. The status of my sisters was even one step lower compared to my brothers." While this scene mirrored that which would take place in Korea, not all Korean households in Hawai'i followed the practice at all meals, as one second-generation Korean observed: "[F]ormal Korean etiquette is less often used today than formerly, but at special dinners is often allowed."[44]

Being the eldest son, however, also carried with it duties and responsibilities. One was expected to help his younger brothers at all times and set a good example for them. In return, younger brothers were supposed to defer to and respect the older brother. Again, while the first generation in Hawai'i often adhered to this typical Confucian expectation, the eldest son was sometimes a less than willing participant: "My [first generation] mother insists I help my brother all the time," but this man replied that his younger brother "has two feet and two hands; we are in Hawai'i, not Korea." Another member of the second generation turned the issue of deference to elder brothers into a more egalitarian one of politeness to all, saying that younger brothers "have to learn respect regardless of age."[45]

Being the privileged eldest son also engendered resentment from their younger siblings.

> I had the misfortune to be the first-born son. Not only my parents and grandparents, but all the members of the clan regarded me as a new heir and lavished on me limitless indulgence. . . . I always received the first new suit of clothes and sandals. Only after that, new clothes for my younger brothers. On special holidays such as my uncle's birthday, I would be taken to the festivity by papa and Umma, but not the younger ones—they stayed at home. . . . There was distinction in the manner of speaking to the oldest son and to the rest of the children. . . . Papa always took me with him when he went to the public baths where hot water was abundant. The rest of the family first had to heat the water in a kerosene can over an open fire and bathe in a tub. . . . [T]he three other sisters had little recognition. . . . Enjoying to the full all the privileges of a number-one son, I was totally unaware of the anger and jealousy bordering on hatred of all my sisters and brothers.[46]

When the eldest brother left the family, his duties fell to the next-oldest sibling—sometimes a sister—and so on down the family hierarchy. One recalled, "During my high school career I missed one year of school because I was called home to take care of my mother who was very ill. Since I was the oldest one of the family, the responsibility laid on my shoulders." Another wrote, "I, being the oldest child in the family, had to take over the responsibilities and expectations left by the preceding brother and sisters. At first, I disliked the thought of it because I wanted to feel free and unrestrained in what I did without having the fear of setting bad examples for my two younger brothers. . . . Later, I realized that I should take heed of the expectations, especially for the benefit of my brothers, mother and father, if not for my own good."[47]

Korean tradition demanded deference not only to the elders within the immediate family, but also to more distant elderly relatives and in-laws. Thus in effect, aunts and uncles carried nearly the same authority over the children as the parents. Complicating matters was the fact that the first generation often considered themselves distantly related to those without any blood ties if they had the same surname (a frequent occurrence, since there are only about a dozen common Korean surnames). The second generation was not particularly happy with a system that made them responsible to all older members of their extended family—a feeling made all the more acute by the contrast with the practices of other households. As Bernice Kim noted, "[I]n contrast with the American family where the children are responsible almost entirely to the two parents, in the Korean system there are the parents, older brothers and sisters, and all the relatives who together bring pressure to bear upon the child." To eliminate this web of familial obligations, a successively more narrow definition of family and clan was created. The middle generation claimed as fellow clansmen only those with the same surname from their parents' home province in

Korea. And the second generation tended to regard only those related by marriage or blood ties as relatives.[48]

Many first-generation parents enforced deference to elders by insisting that the children address them formally by their titles rather than their actual names, with higher levels of respect reserved for those more elderly. Thus aunts and uncles who were older than one's parents were addressed as Big Mother *(k'un-ōmŏni)* and Big Father *(k'un-aboji)*; aunts and uncles younger than one's parents were addressed as Little Mother *(jak'un-ōmŏni)* and Little Father *(jak'un-aboji)*. Older male cousins were called Honorable Elder Brother, while older female cousins were addressed as Honorable Elder Sister. Naturally, the second generation objected to this practice. Bernice Kim was in essence speaking for her own second generation when she wrote that "the second generation finds it awkward to address older brother, sister and cousin in the customary honorifics in Korean. They prefer to follow the American manner of addressing an individual by his given name." Yet when they did that, "[t]o the elders, this lack of discrimination and respect is distasteful and crude." Despite this disapproval, the younger generation began to refer to their brothers and sisters by their given names, just as in American families. For older relatives, honorifics were dropped in favor of the generic terms *ajōssi* (uncle) and *ajumōni* (aunt), with the middle generation using the Korean version and the second generation using the English version.[49]

Since age conferred status in traditional Korean society, the first generation also expected their children to defer to nonfamily elders. "To our parents, anyone who is older is better: young ones should listen to older ones." And to be sure, some among the second generation did listen. One second-generation Korean said with some disappointment of his own children that "[a]ge means nothing to them." For others in the second generation, respect for elders included caring for indigent elderly Koreans without families. "One young girl who is a student at the University of Hawaii stated that, were she able to do so, she would provide upkeep for several old men who are intimate acquaintances of her family. She desired that her family care for an old man who is at the old men's home—to regard him as a grandparent and to afford him the essentials of comfort and security in his old age."[50]

But most in the second generation rejected the idea that age in and of itself should command respect. When presented with the statement "Age means wisdom and deserves respect," one second-generation Korean responded that that statement was "[m]ore true with old folk," while another said, "Age doesn't make any difference; equal understanding is more important." As for addressing older men and women, the second generation soon came to imitate other ethnic groups in Hawai'i and referred to them as "Uncle" or "Auntie" indiscriminantly, as noted earlier. Yet even with these modifications, there was the potential for confusion: "I never tell my children to call [the] first name of any elderly; rather, 'Uncle Charlie, Aunty Gloria.' Then they ask me, 'who is our *real* uncle?'"[51]

Age, of course, was not the only determinant of respect in traditional Korean Confucian thought. Many in the first generation believed that deference should also be accorded to those in positions of authority, such as employers or political figures like Syngman Rhee or Park Yong-man, in the belief that they were superior to ordinary people. Most of the second generation, on the other hand, split with their parents over granting automatic respect to those in authority. One who differed with his parents said, "They [the first generation] believed [this], but I don't," while another said, "It depends on the individual—what kind of person the ruler is." Finally, one second-generation Korean who disagreed said, "[Employers] don't deserve respect [just because they are the boss]. It depends on the employer. A job is only a job."[52]

Another determinant of respect was education. The first generation had distinct memories of the *yangban* elite in Korea, who had dominated education, culture, government and society because of their superior education. While the first and second generation disagreed about many things, they were in accord on the importance of education. Nonetheless, their reasons for believing this were different. The first generation tended to view education as a means to get a prestigious job to glorify the family, as the *yangban* had in Korea. On the other hand, the second generation saw education as a means to gain knowledge in whatever one is best fitted or inclined to do. For example, when Chung Nam Young chose to pursue a career in veterinary medicine, "Chung's father, a Korean immigrant, was furious . . . because Koreans who are associated with animals were considered low-class."[53]

Further, the second-generation Koreans rejected their parents' notion, brought from Korea and promoted by the Confucian scholar Mencius, that those who worked with their brains were superior to those who, like farmers, workers, or merchants, lacked education and worked with their hands. As one more egalitarian second-generation Korean commented, this artificial distinction was "[n]ot right for any generation; hand and brain go together." At the same time, the second generation was aware that education was needed ("Nowadays society needs more brains") and that, in keeping with the transformation of twentieth-century American society, the more education one received, the better off they would be. That is, they "want to be somebody and don't want to be laborers." The second generation's resulting high level of educational attainment testifies to their agreement with their parents about the importance of education.[54]

The desire of the first generation that their second-generation children get a good education can be easily documented by individual families' experiences. One second-generation Korean woman remarked about her mother that "[h]er last and only remaining wish is to see all her children finishing their education and settling down in life with more than what she and Papa began." Another woman recalled her own mother's goal: "The dream of a college education for herself was replaced by a vow to see that all four of her children earned college degrees; one had succeeded, the three others were on their way." Finally, there is the example of the young woman who recalled her parents' wishes:

> After graduation from Roosevelt High School, I was set upon a college education. . . . [But when my father got sick] I was worried and thought of giving up my education to go to work. . . . Mother wanted me to continue my schooling. . . . During father's last days, he encouraged me to return to school and become a nurse. He also encouraged my brother . . . to keep at his ambition of becoming a doctor. . . . [Mother] too wanted me to be a nurse, or whatever I desired, and she often stressed the importance of a college education. She and father have always reminded us of the splendid educational opportunities in Hawaii for the younger Korean generation of American citizenship as compared to their opportunities.[55]

For the Koreans, respect for higher education meant respect for teachers. As one second-generation remembered, "When we went to school, there were no PTAs; when teachers spanked us, our parents scolded us too because parents believed we didn't behave well in school." While the second generation certainly respected teachers, one lamenting that "[k]ids hardly ever listen to teachers," they were also growing up in a capitalist society in which status was increasingly measured by wealth, rather than one's education level or occupation per se, a notion that their more traditional parents would surely have rejected.[56]

This capitalist idea of wealth as the primary determinant of status was aptly captured by one observer/participant on the scene:

> The New World taught me another lesson. . . . The more important possession, it seemed, was the size of the wallet in one's pocket. I discovered it was the boys with lots of money who wore stylish clothes and kept company with the best looking girls. Money also seemed to carry other hidden powers: respect of others and all kinds of advantages. Such high regard for money was contrary to all my childhood upbringing. In Korea, I was taught to be disdainful, not only of money, but of all material possessions. By tradition, the most honored one in the Korean society was not the richest, but the "Teacher," and the lowliest was the tradesman who handled money. . . . I was becoming aware of my growing respect for money. In the beginning I found it seemed strange to hear everyone talking about money everywhere: How much? How cheap? How expensive! I was becoming conscious of what kind of clothes people wore, the kind of cars they drove, and the kind of houses they lived in. The variations and gradations were determined by money—by the amount of money a person or a family had. "What do you do?" was the

first question asked of people; it offered clues to their financial status. When I found myself feeling envious and covetous of material things, I felt alarmed. All through my childhood and adolescence, wasn't I taught to be disdainful of money and all material possessions? Wasn't I taught above all to respect and seek knowledge and wisdom?[57]

While the first and second generations generally agreed on the importance of education, this was not the case with the issue of church attendance.[58] Since Koreans of both generations were mostly Protestant Christians, there was no denominational rift; rather, the problem was that the churches were dominated by the first generation, leaving the second generation disaffected. On the one hand, the second generation admired the role of the church and those called to serve in it, especially if one's father was a preacher. One female recalled, "My father . . . was a Methodist minister. . . . I used to be spellbound by his sermon. I can see the flash in his eyes. I can see his handsome figure appealing so earnestly and sincerely to his friends, of the gospel." And the son of another minister spoke approvingly of the church's work on the island of Maui: "The church was organized in 1923. Its stated purpose was to further the teachings of the messiah and to bring about a cooperative spirit among the Koreans which was sadly lacking at that time. . . . [The church] is a means to bring the young as well as the old members of the church into closer harmony by the various activities put on."

On the other hand, many second-generation Koreans found the churches lacking. Since the first generation dominated the church, the service was conducted in Korean. Sunday school for the second-generation children was usually conducted in English. But when these youngsters became teenagers and began attending church, problems arose, even among those whose fathers were ministers. "The first Sunday in father's church in Honolulu was an eventful day. Children began arriving early in the morning for their Sunday school. They were all American-born Koreans. They looked Korean, but they could neither speak nor understand Korean. . . . Not only did father preach in Korean, but the congregation was mostly first generation Korean immigrants." Another minister's son complained: "It seems to me that the needs of the older people rather than we, the younger, are met. The sermon being conducted in Korean is way above the heads of the striplings and no satisfaction is derived from the sermon." Finally, another complained that "all church services were conducted entirely in Korean. The Korean language lost its significance to the second generation Koreans."

When the churches tried to remedy the situation, they were often unsuccessful. "All this time these two churches had ministers that only preached in Korean, but none that preached in English. There is a strong desire among the younger generation who was born and raised in Hawaii for an English speaking minister. This problem is very difficult because as yet there are many older people coming to church who do not understand English. The Christian church now has a Korean minister who speaks both English and Korean fluently but he is not preaching in English but in Korean to his congregation." This particular church then instituted a plan to alternate between English and Korean sermons, but "[t]his wasn't so successful since the older people not understanding English, did not care to come to church on the Sunday when there was to be an English sermon. Many methods were suggested and tried out but they all were not satisfactory since they satisfied just one party and not all."

Another church was similarly unsuccessful. "[T]he introduction of a bilingual minister had brought on a host of negative reactions. For the sake of their children, the parishioners had requested the Methodist Headquarters to provide a minister who could preach in English for the young, as well as in Korean for the older people. At first, the suggestion was hailed as intelligent and appropriate. For the youngsters were ignoring their parents' native language and favoring the language they learned and used in the public school. They refused to attend the Sunday services unless the preacher could communicate with them. There was the rub. Bilingual ministers came and went, some in a huff before their term was up, some with feelings of failure, others in near tears after receiving merciless criticism. When a preacher spoke fluent English his Korean suffered, and he was ridiculed by the older members; when one preached in eloquent Korean, his English was weak."

Language was not the only problem facing the second generation in the Korean churches. Equally vexing was the fact that the interests of the generations differed. One member of the second generation complained, "Activities are carried on more for and to the satisfaction of the older and the more reverent members [of the first generation]." The elders were "afraid to let us take a hand in teaching Sunday school the way we want to, so many of us quit or transferred to another church." Moreover, the elders railed against "intermarriage, discussion of sexual matters, poor church attendance, and family feuds. The mores or moral codes of the M[ethodist]. E[piscopal]. church are the mores of the old people. There is no 'keeping up with the times.'" These "upholders of the mores [use] [g]ossip, action, or shunning the violator . . . as means of enforcement and punishment. . . . Gossip is one of the most effective means of enforcing the moral codes of the church and the group." Because of the churches' close ties to the often feuding Korean nationalist organizations, one observer noted also that "Korean churches . . . are losing the younger members of their congregation. Only the older generation is drawn by the appeal to its nationalistic ties to the homeland. A boy who was a constant church goer remarked in disgust, 'All the minister does is preach how the Koreans were wronged, how wicked the Japs were, and how God would punish them.' . . . Korean churches, like the political factions, are jealously split into independent units."

As a result, the young people began deserting their parents' church. As one second-generation Korean noted, "The diminishing number of young people in attendance disturbed the old-time custom for the whole family to attend church and worship together." One report suggested that "church . . . plays a very small part in the social life of the young Korean set since many are employed in Defense jobs, are in the army, or seek school or other outside agencies for recreation." Another observed that "[m]ost of the young people have gone to churches with English speaking ministers or are too busy working to find time to go to church. . . . In spite of the fact that the first generation Koreans belong to a certain church their children have not remained in their parents' churches. The younger generation has broken from their family churches and have joined churches they liked. For example a Korean friend told me that recently many young people of Korean ancestry have become Baptists. The church is under the direction of a 'Haole' minister who just recently arrived from the mainland."

The final and perhaps widest gulf between the first and second generation concerned the Korean nationalist movement. For the first generation, this was perhaps the most important issue facing the Korean community outside of work and home. The vast majority of the first generation belonged to one or another nationalist organization, donating time and money to the cause. By contrast, the second generation did not share their parents' nationalist fervor for Korea's independence from Japan. Few Korean children had visited Korea or had the opportunity to attend Korean language schools, where they might have learned about the struggle. Moreover, the education that the second generation received emphasized American history and government. Most second-generation Koreans, as American citizens, viewed Korea as a foreign country and Korean nationalism as an alien concept. As one second-generation Korean said, "[A]ffiliation with the Korean nationalistic groups is most fervent among the older generation, of toleration among the middle generation, and the attitude of 'won't have a thing to do with it' among the second generation." Another said, "We don't know our parent's country; there is no kinship tie." Yet another said, "So far I have read very little about my parents' native land; I have never felt a sense of pride in knowing about my parents' native land, but I have pity and sympathy for them." Finally, one second-generation Korean said of his peers, "Many young people admit that . . . [they] possess . . . only a scant knowledge of the existing political set-up."[59]

In sum, there were a number of issues that divided the generations in Hawai'i's Korean community. We would expect the second generation of any immigrant group to be more Americanized than their parents. But the process was accelerated by the fact that—although the second generation would not admit it—their first-generation parents were themselves relatively more "liberal" than first-generation Chinese or Japanese and transferred these values to their American children. Moreover, the second-generation Koreans, like their parents, were a relatively small group in the Hawaiian mosaic, thus accelerating acculturation. As a result, they ended up being more "liberal" than second-generation Chinese and Japanese. One anthropologist who quantified the results of an extensive survey found that second-generation Koreans rejected traditional East Asian culture by a score of −.15, while second-generation Chinese and Japanese accepted traditional East Asian culture by scores of +.09 and +.07, respectively. Most second-generation Koreans saw their parents as painfully old-fashioned: "In some way, our parents' way of life hampered our attempt to adjust to this society. Parents try to keep old country ways so that they established a little Korea and lived in it. Offspring should go out of the town. I would say there was confusion."[60]

Although this chapter has examined many points of tension between first- and second-generation Koreans, there was one issue so explosive that it had the potential to override any of the other issues covered so far—interracial dating and marriage. Because this involved relations not only between generations but also across racial lines, it is treated separately in the following chapter.

10

Race Relations

Most younger Koreans viewed the larger society on the basis of equality, just as they had within the family. Second-generation Koreans who were asked generally agreed with the statement "All human beings are equal." Indeed, the life experiences of many second-generation Koreans in Hawai'i convinced them that this was true. One Korean female noted that "I have never encountered any incidents showing race prejudice. I believe the young people in these islands are working together harmoniously. . . . In school I mingle and enjoy the friendship and companionship of all my school mates. I feel there is no race differences and that everyone is a brother or sister to each other."[1]

Others acknowledged racial tension but saw reason for optimism in institutions like the church or military. One Korean female who had abandoned her parents' church for the Baptist Church in Wahiawa saw racial equality there: "One can fully recognize what democracy means when one sees persons of all races and diverse backgrounds gathering together for a common purpose. There were haoles, Japanese, Koreans, Chinese, Filipinos, civilians and soldiers alike who got up and thanked God for all that he had done for them. The Church always welcomes all people and is acting as a great influence in dissolving race prejudice." A nineteen-year-old Korean woman said, "Young boys from all families are now being drafted for the service; people of all nationalities are affected by this draft, and by their interest to do the best for their boys, people of all races are more and more united." Another Korean, this one a forty-four-year-old Korean man, agreed: "The different races are getting along better now because we are all fighting for one cause."[2]

But most second-generation Koreans realized that just as family relationships were not always equal, so also was society not always based upon equality and that racial stereotyping, segregation, and prejudice continued to be a problem. Reacting to the statement that all human beings are equal, one second-generation Korean said, "[T]his statement is only philosophizing, not reality." Another said, "In a democratic society, why do we have prejudice? I must be equal only in opportunity, not equal in discrimination." Others noted that the start of the war did not alter the situation. One thirty-five-year-old

Korean saleswoman, when asked, replied, "No, there seems to be no marked change in the relationship between the local racial groups."[3]

In fact, ethnic separatism seemed to be the rule, as one Korean woman observed: "In school especially during intermediate and high school days I noticed that the various races seemed to cling together. The various oriental groups banded themselves in various competing student alliances and the haoles in their sororities and fraternities. The army society kept strictly to themselves and only athletes were invited to their socials." Adding to this segregation were nicknames and stereotypes that enjoyed wide currency throughout Hawai'i. For example, Japanese had nicknames like "Jap" and "Buddhahead" and were stereotyped as humorless, unemotional, clannish, industrious, and courteous. Chinese were often referred to as "Pake," Filipinos as "Bayao," and Portuguese as "Cashicong."[4]

This separatism and stereotyping was indirectly augmented by the efforts of first-generation Korean parents to instill in their children a sense of Korean pride. Often, it had the desired effect. One girl whose father was Korean and whose mother was Spanish recalled, "Our family tried very hard to be accepted and accomplished this by adopting the Korean language, food habits and cultural thoughts. . . . When only a child I realized that . . . the Korean mode of living had influenced my thoughts and style of life. Even my [Spanish] mother succumbed to this eastern influence." Another female recalled: "It was the first week of school at the university [of Hawai'i]. I was interested in the names of my classmates and of their racial ancestries. I don't know if others feel the same way as I do but being a Korean, whenever I heard a Korean name in the roll call, I took special interest in those names. It's queer that way, but I have a tender spot in my heart for all Koreans. I feel proud when a Korean name appears on the honor roll or in any other manifestation of honor. I have always tried to do my best in school so that the Koreans especially would notice me and be proud of me. I like [Governor] Farrington because he has done much for Korean welfare. It makes me happy to hear [Sociology Professor] Dr. [Andrew] Lind mention the Koreans so often in class."[5]

But more often than not, and alone among all the ethnic groups in Hawai'i, Koreans described themselves more unfavorably, using terms such as hot-tempered, stubborn, independent, unpredictable, and temperamental. Moreover, non-Koreans, who gave Koreans nicknames like "yobo," "kimchi," and "chili pepper," not only agreed with these negative characterizations, but also added unfriendly, clannish, untidy, oily-tongued, cunning, talkative, and outspoken to the list. When Koreans were characterized favorably, along with the Japanese and Chinese, as quiet, traditional, neat, and polite, researchers explained away such favorable traits by noting that most people were not well acquainted with the Koreans because of their small number and the difficulty in distinguishing Koreans from other East Asians.[6]

To reinforce a sense of Korean unity, Korean parents wanted their children to befriend other Koreans. According to one survey, almost all first-generation Koreans themselves had only Koreans as close friends. One Korean girl remembered, "Before entering the Summer Session [at the University of Hawai'i], Mother was very careful and concerned as to who my friends were." And sometimes second-generation Koreans did make a special effort to befriend other Koreans. One female recalled, "Although we left Waialua Plantation after my eighth birthday, I have always tended to seek Korean girls as my chums."[7]

But the hope of Korean parents that their children would have mostly Korean friends was dashed because the number of Koreans in Hawai'i was simply too small and because their children were too Americanized. Moreover, the social institutions where they could meet other Koreans, such as the Korean churches, did not, as we have seen, meet the needs of the second generation. "Although at various times young peoples' clubs sponsored by churches and political organizations have been started, they have never wholly succeeded for the want of interest and co-operation." As a result, "[Korean] children are always ordered by parents not to play with certain bunches of boys but still they waste their time playing with them. The parents want their children to stay at home and play with children of their own race, but it can't be done."[8]

If it was impossible for Koreans not to mix with the other races in Hawai'i, then it behooves us to examine the interactions between them and the various other nationalities that populated the islands.

Caucasians

There is little evidence that Caucasians, or haoles as they were generally known in Hawai'i, distinguished Koreans from the more numerous Chinese and Japanese. For example, take the following comment on Koreans written by a white student at the University of Hawai'i: "The Koreans were the only group that was considered so closely related to the Japanese. Their language was somewhat similar to the Japanese language, and their foods did not vary too greatly. I can't recall of any deep difference, apparent or real, that marked these two groups. However, the Koreans have been commonly thought of as being in the same group with the Chinese, and the distinction is not made sometimes."[9] So if Koreans were virtually indistinguishable from other East Asians in Hawai'i, it meant they suffered from whatever anti-Asian sentiment existed among the white population, which dominated Hawai'i politically, economically, and socially.

Because of its multiethnic makeup, Hawai'i's racial climate had never been as hostile as on the mainland. And by the 1930s and 1940s, racism had become less prominent than it had been earlier in the century. Yet anti-Asian prejudice still existed in Hawai'i, often expressed in ways more subtle than on the mainland, and Koreans were affected by it. Some attributed this lingering prejudice to the legacy of the sugar plantations. One first-generation Korean who had worked on the plantations "never had too much respect for haoles . . . because he never had trust in them." And one second-generation Korean said, "We are brought up on plantations, where whites look down on all Orientals." Finally, one Korean who was convinced that the Pacific War had improved race relations did not include Caucasians. As he cynically observed, "I still think that the haoles think that they are better than any other race, especially with things concerning orientals; the oriental will never be given a chance to be on an equal basis with a haole." [10]

Anti-Asian prejudice affecting Koreans could be personal as well as institutional. Often, individual acts of prejudice cut more deeply than institutional prejudice. For example, a Korean woman who was a respected department head in a social welfare organization recalled with "high indignation" what happened to her one day: "On Saturday a friend and I (both Orientals) were waiting in line at the Waikiki [Theater]. A haole woman in front of us happened to drop a small coin and naturally, I bent over to pick it up for her. She looked like an intelligent person, well-dressed, and I expected some word or gesture of thanks. Well, I was never so infuriated! Do you know that she didn't even look at me or even nod? So I thought—maybe she is prejudiced toward the Japanese and took me for one of them, or perhaps any Oriental is just an Oriental to her and she expects them to respectfully pick up things for her! Well, I certainly gave her a good 'long' look because I'm not going to stand that kind of thing. You would expect an intelligent-looking haole to at least nod her thanks. I guess you have to expect some contacts with haoles like that." [11]

Sometimes Caucasians gave Koreans a hard time because they mistook them for Japanese, especially after the 1941 attack on Pearl Harbor. Consider the following experience of a twenty-year-old seaman aboard a ship plying the waters between Hawai'i and California: "When I first was assigned to this ship in September 1942, there was a feeling of hostility. I was the only Oriental on ship at a time when bitterness against the Japanese was very strong. At that time in the mainland all Orientals were viewed with suspicion. On board all eyes were cast on me. I was very much afraid of foul play. That night a bunch of haoles came to me while I was on my bunk and questioned me. In threatening tones they asked who I was, my nationality, name, and where I was and what I was doing on Dec. 7. They threatened to throw me overboard if I lied. I had no doubts of them carrying out their threat. My answers must have been satisfactory for they let me alone. My last name Kim really saved my life, for they were positive that it was not a Japanese name. They had never heard of a Korean, that got me a little angry." [12]

Adding to individual acts of discrimination was a more pervasive institutional racism—something with which Koreans were also familiar. One example of this was the mass media and its handling of race relations. One Korean man recalled, "I remember . . . around 1940 a Caucasian killed two Orientals and injured several while driving. Very little was said of it in the newspaper. If it had happened to an Oriental, how would it be?"[13]

Institutional racism was also manifest in the Hawai'i school system, where de facto segregation often existed. One Korean wrote about his own experience on Maui: "The experience with school segregation on the ocean side of the camp as contrasted with the Spreckelsville School on the eastern side, reveals the sharp social and economic distinctions between the laboring and the 'moneyed' class. The Kaunoa School is mostly attended by the sons and daughters of the rich. To keep out the children of the laboring class and also of different racial extractions, there is a rigid oral examination which practically excludes them due to their meager knowledge of English grammar. High expenses also is a factor in restraining the children of the poor."[14]

The only example of institutional racism in which whites specifically singled out Koreans occurred in the financial institutions of the islands. There was a tacit "understanding" that Koreans would not be bonded for employment in firms where valuables or large amounts of cash were routinely handled—effectively preventing them from being hired at many businesses. One result of this practice was that Koreans were channeled into independent family-owned and operated concerns as noted in Chapter 5.[15]

The armed forces also discriminated against Koreans. At the beginning of World War II, one Korean woman wrote: "My [Korean] brother-in-law volunteered as the other American students. His one life, just as dear to his mother as the life of an American boy to his American mother, was given willingly for the Great Cause. But partiality was shown in the training camps, for his classmates were commissioned to lieutenancy, and others to captaincy, while he was only made a corporal. In this instance it was not a matter of education or character but color. What tragedy to the young man who was willing to give up his life to the cause of his adopted country when she turned him down."[16]

Institutional racism occurred in the workplace as well. During the Depression, out of economic necessity, many second-generation Asians, including Koreans, applied for work on the sugar plantations where their parents had originally labored. Whites also applied for work on the plantations. One Korean recalled, "When I was a high school junior, I went to the plantation with a haole friend to work. My haole friend was called to the manager. He said 'We don't want to see white doing labor work.' Next day he became a 'supervisor.'"[17]

This employment discrimination against Koreans and other Asians also occurred in the highly skilled professions. Consider what happened to a well-educated second-generation Korean when he applied for such a job:

> One afternoon when I was on the verge of taking a nap, the doorbell rang and in walked T, a twenty-four year old Korean boy who had graduated from the University [of Hawai'i] with the class of 1944.
> "Hello," I said, "long time no see."

"Hi," he returned, "I've been busy."

"Doing what?" I inquired.

He replied, "Working. I work at Royal Brewery Company in the bottles department at a dollar an hour. I'm trying to scrape up . . . [illegible]."

"How are you going to be able to save enough by next year?"

"I dunno, but if I apply for better paying jobs I'm afraid of being frozen."

"Surely you can find something else?"

"Yeh, if I was a haole maybe. I majored in chem and physics and when it comes to anything in that line, I can hold my own."

He was [not] merely boasting either. T had acquired a reputation in school of being very intelligent and industrious.

"Well," he continued, "I heard about a position open at the chemistry lab at the police department. It paid well too, and the good thing was that I wouldn't be frozen. I went to apply. ———— is the head of the lab. He's a good 'guy,' married to a part-Negro, part-haole girl. He looked over my credentials and told me that I looked like a good prospect, but he had to have the approval of the chief of police. Well, he came back and told me that the chief had said I wouldn't do."

"Why?"

"The chief said I wouldn't be able to convince the jury as effectively as a haole could, especially if the defendant is a haole. If I did get the job, I would have to testify in court quite often as a chemist and the juries here seem more partial to the word of a haole than an Oriental. Tough luck that's all."

"Too bad," I agreed.[18]

The Korean response to discrimination varied. Some simply shrugged it off because they did not see it as a major factor in their lives. For example, the Korean crew member mistaken for a Japanese quoted earlier wrote, "After that the crew and I became pals. When we hit Frisco on our return trip, they really showed me the town." Other Koreans were more deeply affected. As for the young Korean above who failed to get the police position, "The fact that T didn't obtain this job on the basis of racial extraction shattered a great deal of his confidence. He realized that better opportunities would come his way if he were white and that in certain professions the line was drawn against the oriental. He secured tentative employment in a local brewery but he resented the fact that with his education and training, he had to accept that kind of a job." The man who complained about the media, quoted earlier, chose a unique way to protest: "I gave my boy a Korean name so that he should retain something Korean; it is a mark of rebelling to Caucasian society." And the woman quoted earlier who complained that her brother-in-law had been discriminated against by the military wrote that "[he] told me that he lost his vigor and enthusiasm for the fight and all he wanted was to die."[19]

Sometimes Koreans reacted with ambivalence toward the dominant white society because they identified with many of the values of the Caucasians while at the same time those Caucasians looked down on them. As more Caucasians—mostly soldiers and defense workers—flooded into Hawai'i in the late 1930s and early 1940s, the interaction between many Koreans and Caucasians was marked by a kind of approach-avoidance pattern. Consider the following example: "One day while watching two haole soldiers perform at the diving board, a Korean boy said, 'Aw, I got no use for those haoles.' 'What kind of haoles do you mean?' I asked. He replied, 'Any of those in the Army. They are a bunch of good-for-nothings always trying to show off.'" While at first glance it appears that he disliked white military men, his interlocutor then revealed something else about this Korean boy: "I have noticed that this boy gets around quite a lot with boys of the Navy. He swims and plays tennis quite often with them. However, at the time of the conversation, he did not bring out the Navy factor."[20]

Other Koreans expressed a feeling of slight discomfort in the presence of Caucasians. The following vignette, narrated by a Japanese, demonstrates this in a social setting.

> We, my wife and I, were at a cocktail party this evening (August 6, 1944) given by a haole couple of high standing socially and politically. It was a large party composed mostly of haoles, both civilian and military. . . . In making our rounds we stopped for a few minutes with the Oriental couples. I observed that they kept more or less together throughout the evening. We knew the Korean doctor and were introduced to his wife. . . . As we were standing with them, the Korean doctor said, "After the party, let's go down to my house. It is nice to have *haole* friends and to attend their parties. But there isn't anything like being with our own kind." Directing the next comment at me, he said, "You know what I mean. Among our own kind (evidently he included my wife and myself) we feel freer. We can take off our coats, our shoes, and even our pants, if we want to."[21]

Meanwhile, the relationship between Koreans and Caucasians on the mainland was markedly different. During the 1930s and early 1940s, when some second-generation Koreans from Hawai'i went off to college or work on the mainland, they were not always prepared for what they would encounter. Accustomed to Caucasians being exclusively in managerial positions, they found a completely different situation. One Korean who recalled his boat docking in Los Angeles said, "What did impress me were the workmen on the dock—there were so many *haoles*. No Hawaiians, Filipinos or Chinese. That was the first revelation that not every white man was rich and didn't have to do any menial labor." Another recounted, "During the War, when my friend went to Yale, she said she was very shocked to see haole shoeshiners. She couldn't imagine [a] menial job among Caucasians while she was in Hawaii."[22]

More shocking was the overt racism Koreans encountered on the mainland, unlike anything they had ever experienced in multiracial Hawai'i. One who attended college in Indiana wrote of "the feelings of frustration and resentment at being pointed at and stared at as an 'Oriental.' . . . I could feel the surreptitious stares of . . . hate." After graduating and moving to presumably more cosmopolitan New York City in 1930, this Korean found anti-Asian racism there as well:

> They would . . . sometimes even ignore me. I knew what the problem was: an "Oriental" giving them orders! Behind my back, they would say to each other (loudly for my benefit), "What's a Chinaman doing here?" Of course, it hurt me. . . . It wasn't only that I was a foreigner; I was an Oriental, a "Chinaman," an inferior. Not too infrequently some stranger loitering on the street would call out to me, "Hey, Chinaman!" . . . [E]ven some friends in school . . . would ask me if my family was in the laundry business. When I walked down the street with [my Caucasian girlfriend] May or we were seated together in the theatre, I had to ward off all the hostile glances and muffled whispers." . . . I was never allowed to feel completely at home in [mainland] America. Time and time again, I was reminded that I was not just a foreigner, but an Oriental. For me to rise from the accorded level of servitude, such as a "houseboy" or "laundryman" . . . was inconceivable and unacceptable to most Americans. . . . "Hey! Chink! Hey! Charlie!" These names were hurled at me at odd moments and at odd places.[23]

Word of such racism on the mainland eventually made its way back to Hawai'i, making some Koreans reluctant to travel there.

> On April 27, 1943 I visited Mrs. X, a Korean woman with six children, who live in a congested area of the town. Her husband is in California and wants to have the family join him if they are able to get funds to go to the Mainland. . . . When I asked Mrs. X if she wanted to evacuate to the Mainland as she previously had suggested, she said that she wasn't keen about going, although her children want to go badly, because she heard from some of her friends that Orientals were not treated kindly in California. When I asked her if she believed this statement, she said, "Yes, because Koreans, Chinese and Japanese look so much alike that the haoles don't like us Orientals." She feels that although the Japanese are in War Relocation centers, the haoles on the Mainland are also antagonistic toward the Koreans. Mrs. X states that her husband does not write what some of the happenings are in California, such as racial prejudice, because of censorship.[24]

Of course, Hawai'i's Koreans had to deal with other ethnic groups besides Caucasians. While the Caucasians usually did not distinguish between the three East Asian groups in Hawai'i and the three groups often saw themselves in many ways united when dealing with Caucasians, they nonetheless distinguished between themselves in many cases.

Chinese

The relationship between Koreans and Chinese groups appears largely unexceptionable, with positive patterns of interaction outweighing the negative. Both groups (or their parents) shared a resentment toward Japanese imperialism and aggression in their ancestral homelands. Note the following observation about Koreans by a Chinese American: "The Koreans are considered as the nicest and mildest group here. They are unassuming, simple and very hard working. We feel they don't cause anyone any trouble, but most Chinese tend to like the older Koreans more than the youths because the youths have picked up the ways of the Westerners. The Koreans aren't looked upon as inferiors—Chinese claim them to be fellow Chinese under the oppression of the Japanese."[25]

On the other hand, some Koreans of the first generation considered the Chinese "money-hungry" and lacking in patriotism toward China. Second-generation Koreans tended to stereotype Chinese as traditional and clannish. And there were occasional incidents like the following: "I think the interracial relationships are pretty bad in some cases. My mother (Korean woman) sometimes comes home angry after shopping. She is a regular customer of a Chinese store but she claims that they don't sell her all the commodities she asks for. Sometimes, she knows that the store has just received a shipment of meat, but when she asks for some, they claim they don't have any. Meat isn't the only commodity that the stores hoard. They also refuse to sell fruit when they are scarce. This fact makes my mother very angry because although she is a regular customer, they refuse to sell goods to her, but sells them to their good Chinese friends."[26]

While the relationship between Chinese and Koreans was relatively uncomplicated and largely favorable, such was not the case between the Koreans and the largest ethnic group in Hawai'i—the Japanese.

Japanese

The relationship between the Japanese and the Koreans in Hawai'i was a complex one. Issues such as the Japanese occupation of Korea since 1910 and the Japanese attack on Pearl Harbor complicated their interaction. While earlier chapters examined the relationship between first-generation Japanese and Koreans, the discussion here focuses on the second generation. Because the Japanese were more numerous than Koreans, there is more information on Japanese thoughts on Koreans than vice versa.

Some Koreans kept their distance from the Japanese. Part of the blame, of course, can be laid at the feet of the first-generation parents who attempted to indoctrinate their children, sometimes successfully. One second-generation Korean woman said that her "very temperamental" father "used to lecture us about what the Japanese people did to the people in Korea. He already had strong feeling against the Japanese, so naturally we as his children felt the same

way, too. He never did encourage us to associate with Japanese people. He
didn't want us to be associated with anything made in Japan. In school, you
couldn't help but talk with them (Japanese students), but we would never be
close friends. So I had two good friends—a Chinese girl and a Portuguese girl."
Because the parents often had deep feelings of hatred toward Japan, the children, even if they agreed, became uncomfortable: "I never liked to hear his
[my father's] political discussion at home at anytime because I knew he was
going to get riled up and upset the household. As soon as he walked into the
house, the boys were all quiet." [27]

Similarly, some first-generation Japanese *(issei)* imbued their *(nisei)* children with anti-Korean attitudes. Consider the following episode: "Even among
our generation there were fistfights between our family and some of the Japanese kids because they used to look down on us and remind us that Korea was
under the domination of Japan, just to show how strong their nationalism was.
I once attended a traveling theater-type movie which showed the Japanese at
war with China. Japanese people showed these movies. I remember very distinctly how they tried to build up the Japanese as heroes. I was maybe fourteen
or fifteen at the time. We had Japanese friends, but we know with the remarks
they made that they put the Koreans in a subservient role." [28]

Another reason Koreans sometimes did not get along with their Japanese
counterparts was that they harbored the same suspicions about Japanese
Americans early in the war that some white Americans did. Indeed, one second-generation Korean admitted that "[a]t the outbreak of the war, I felt that
all the Japs were disloyal," while another indirectly echoed similar sentiments:
"Although the antagonistic feeling against Japan is still prevalent among the
first generation, the second generation, if they feel strongly against the Japanese, have no deep nationalistic feeling toward Korea; therefore they have no
more reason to hate Japan than any Caucasian group." [29]

Some second-generation Koreans perceived the *nisei* to be clannish and
lacking in Americanism. One Korean female wrote that, unlike Koreans, "[t]he
Japanese group as a whole tenaciously clung to their parents' native tongue and
observed with much pomp and ceremony some of Japan's holidays." Still, this
woman tried to avoid a blanket condemnation: "I am very critical of the Japanese as a group but speaking of individuals within this group, there are many
who are fine citizens and are very good friends of mine. I have tried to curb my
anti-racial feeling and have succeeded very well I think." [30]

As we saw earlier in chapter 7, the *issei* were evenly divided in their attitude
toward Koreans and were therefore, in a sense, neutral. By contrast, the *nisei*
were less positive than their parents toward the Koreans, ranking them sixth in
racial preference (their parents had ranked them fourth) due to their lower
socioeconomic status, the lack of any nationalistic sentiment toward Koreans,
and the high Korean delinquency rate. [31]

Moreover, the stereotypes the *nisei* held of Koreans mirrored their negative attitude and included "boisterous, don't think before acting, carefree, slow in adopting American ways, selfish and suspicious." Of these stereotypes, "boisterous" is of some interest. The leading researcher of racial attitudes during the 1930s, Jitsuichi Masuoka, suggested that Koreans, like other members of a small ethnic group, attempted to compensate for their minority status by resorting to boisterousness. One *nisei* gave some credence to this notion in his own experience: "I met many Korean girls, too. My job was that of a foreman that these Korean girls kind of looked up to me, and because of it I did not have any difficulty in getting to know them. What I noticed particularly about them was their too big-mouthedness. They talk altogether too much. They were very free with their language, too. They can swear as well as boys can. They talk pretty bad about the Japanese boys in general. They were also too sarcastic about everything they said. I have no use for them, and I am prejudiced against them and if you ask me why I would say, 'I don't know.'"[32]

The *nisei* also objected to Koreans because of their "garlic smell." As one put it: "I must walk with a yard stick whenever I walk with a Korean so I can keep at least three feet of distance from him. Otherwise, I shall faint because of their garlic smell!" Another, a college student, said, "Once on my way back from the University, I picked up an old Korean man. He was so fully saturated with garlic smell that he could kill the whole people." And another college student said, "I am very sensitive to smell and I can notice the peculiar odor of every individual I meet. There was a nice-looking and neatly dressed Korean student in our dramatic class. One day he sat right next me and, oh! how I felt. His garlic smell was so strong and repugnant that I almost fell over. It was a very very unpleasant experience."[33]

According to some *nisei*, Koreans also appeared to be obsessed with money. One observed, "I have a definite prejudice against the Koreans of the younger generation. . . . My experiences with a few Koreans made me believe more firmly than ever that they are simply 'bums.' They steal and beg. They beg for money. No return of course." Another *nisei* made a similar observation: "For the last three summers I worked at one of the local pineapple canneries, where I met several Koreans of my age. I know a particularly good case of a man who begs like a professional beggar. He has never been in school long enough to know what is right and what is wrong. One day as I was walking in front of the Empire Theatre, he approached me and asked for a dime. He said, 'Loan me a dime so I can go to the show.' I gave him the dime and this is what came to my mind at the time. It was that he was doing this to all he knows so that he could make about fifty cents, just enough to pass into the show."[34]

Not all interactions were negative, however, making the relationship between second-generation Japanese and Koreans bimodal in nature. For example, just as white Americans came to admire the exploits of *nisei* army units such as the 100th Battalion and the 442nd Brigade, so did Korean Americans. When one forty-year-old Korean woman was asked whether she thought that race relations were improving in Hawai'i, she answered, "Definitely! We are sympathizing with every other race, especially the Japanese Americans, because they are doing a great job in proving their loyalty . . . after seeing all their wounded sons and friends." [35]

In addition, not all *nisei* held negative stereotypes of Koreans. For example, some positive statements included "kind, good, friendly, bright student, unselfish, polite, quite sociable, respectable, loyal, industrious, cooperative, helpful, nice, serious, cheerful and hard worker." Indeed, personal experience could work both ways—that is, just as *nisei* sometimes came away with a negative impression of Koreans, the opposite was also true. Such an experience was recounted by one *nisei* student who befriended a Korean at school. "I have a very good Korean friend. . . . The first night when he visited my room and asked me his homework, I did not feel at ease. I know that he was not a welcome guest in my room. I felt very hard to talk to even though he was an extrovert. I was afraid that he would take something away if I should be his friend. However, there were something which brought us together. My fear of insecurity of his presence—a fear that he would steal my property—passed away as he made several visits to my room and proved to me that he was a honest fellow and furthermore rather interesting. As we became rather liking to each other, he made several and frequently visit to my room. Later we too studied together in my room. We are still very good friends." [36]

In addition, while the first-generation's negative racial attitudes were sometimes passed on to the children, so, too, were their positive impressions. One *nisei* recounted his own childhood experience in his neighborhood: "Here again the attitude is different toward the Korean group as a whole and the Korean as an individual. We once had some Korean neighbors whom my mother regards with utmost respect and consideration. They liked us pretty much too. We were neighbors for three years and during these years we exchanged food and gossip and ideas. My mother especially liked the cleanliness of the Korean lady. However, the prejudice against the Korean population as a whole is not pronounced as it is for the Chinese. Perhaps this is because Korea was under Japan's rule for a long time. Moreover, Koreans are thought to be of high intellectual calibre." [37]

Some *nisei* acknowledged Japan's imperialism and Korea's resulting victimization and thus empathized with the Koreans. Such an attitude was reinforced after the bombing of Pearl Harbor, when Japan became the enemy of the United States. Thus when second-generation Koreans criticized Japan, the *nisei* agreed with them. One *nisei* named Mary recounted the following conversation just after the liberation of Korea from Japanese rule in 1945: "I have a Korean friend who is extremely frank with me. She airs her Korean views without much consideration for my feelings. Says she, 'Mary is a Japanese, but she's good. . . . We Koreans at last have our independence. . . . [W]e have had enough of Japan.' It seems that Koreans dislike Japanese—for a justifiable reason."[38]

A final—and perhaps the primary—reason for the lack of animosity between second-generation Japanese and Koreans was that they saw themselves as Americans and Japan and Korea as foreign countries. Such an attitude was illustrated by the following incident: "Elizabeth also possesses a very democratic attitude. Though her ancestors are being persecuted and oppressed in Korea by my ancestors, she has no ill feeling toward me or towards any other person of Japanese extraction. One day in English class in connection with a topic presented to the class by the instructor I mentioned to her the Japanese domination of Korea. But Elizabeth sweetly smiled and said, 'Why should we worry? It isn't our fault.' I admired her response. It is nice to know that we here in Hawaii—we Americans—are little concerned with the things that are happening in our parents' homeland."[39]

In sum, the relationship between second-generation Japanese and Koreans was both complex and bimodal, with positive and negative attributes. Unlike many of their first-generation parents, the second generation generally responded to each other as Americans, on an individual basis.

African Americans, Filipinos, Puerto Ricans, and Hawaiians

Just as Koreans shared many values with Caucasians, they also shared some of the same prejudices. This meant, ironically, that Koreans who were sometimes the victims of prejudice themselves discriminated against other racial groups. In many cases, Korean prejudice was based on the color of one's skin. Koreans acknowledged that they were not only victims, but also perpetrators of discrimination: "[There is] [s]till some racism among our generation. Koreans look down on Blacks and others to Koreans." And a second-generation Korean woman stated flatly, "Our generation has been prejudiced racially; we still look down on Blacks (Filipino, Puerto Ricans, and Negro)." Moreover, Koreans often looked down on the dark-skinned Hawaiians because of their lack of racial pride and orientation toward the future.[40]

Before the advent of the Pacific War, there was little opportunity for interaction between Koreans and African Americans. Some Koreans, like the second-generation female quoted below, observed how whites reacted to these newcomers and perhaps copied them: "I attended a skating party one day at the skating rink in Schofield. I had been to that rink a few times in the past but never had seen so many Negroes there. I was skating with one of the instructors there and we began talking of this sudden increase. He told me that the Negroes were the worst offenders of the skating rules; that they insisted on going fast and thus knocked down quite a few people. Because of the increase of Negroes, the manager of the rink wanted to set a special night a week for

Negroes only. I don't know whether this plan went into effect but it shows that the increasing number of Negroes is straining the relations between the black and the white race."[41]

But other Koreans were sympathetic to the plight of African Americans in American society, while acknowledging widespread sentiment against them. For example, a Korean woman wrote: "Booker T. Washington's story of his life touched me deeply, though I never really understood the position of a negro. Negroes were feared and spoken harshly of in Wahiawa and Schofield [Army Barracks] because during the first World War negro soldiers had been stationed there and many of them became unmanageable and were nuisances. However after the war practically all were sent back to the mainland so very few people living there (Wah & Sch) now had had direct contact with the negro soldiers."[42]

In contrast to African American soldiers, Koreans interacted more frequently with the large numbers of Filipinos. It is clear that many Koreans evinced prejudice toward this group, not only because of their darker complexion but also because, as later arrivals to Hawai'i (between 1907 and 1931), they were lower on the social and economic ladder. Most Filipinos still worked on the plantations, whence most Koreans had long since departed. Many first-generation Koreans considered Filipinos "barbarians," while the second generation stereotyped them as "ignorant, sporty, passionate, and sex crazy." And while Koreans were generally sympathetic toward the independence movement of the Filipinos, many considered it premature, given their alleged low morals and lower level of civilization. One second-generation Korean woman remembered, "When I reached the age of fourteen my parents thought it was best for me to come to Honolulu because the Filipinos were gradually invading our community."[43]

Yet, as often happens, prejudice can give way to friendly feelings once one gets to know someone from another culture personally. In the following vignette, a Korean family was identified as one who initially harbored negative feelings toward their new Filipino neighbors: "Only a few months ago [Mrs. X] had threatened to leave the neighborhood when she learned that Filipinos had purchased the house. The reactions of the neighboring families, Hawaiian, Chinese, Japanese, Haole and Korean were the same. . . . 'Filipinos! I'm afraid of them. They're always carrying knives. You know, they'll cut you up for nothing—and ugh! they're dirty.' Yesterday Mrs. X showed a genuine friendly interest in her neighbors. 'They're nice people, mind their own business.' This change of opinion occurred after Mrs. X and her immediate neighbors observed that the family complied with the same mode of living socially and economically as they and behaved according to convention."[44]

Up to this point, we have examined many of the interactions between Koreans and other races in Hawai'i. However, no interaction stirred more emotion than interracial dating and marriage, which involved not only race relations but also an important aspect of the tension between the first and second generation discussed in chapter 9. Interracial dating and marriage was a matter of utmost concern to first-generation parents, most of whom preferred that their sons and daughters marry within their own ethnic group. In this respect, Koreans were no different.

Second-generation Koreans in Hawai'i had a very high rate of outmarriage (or intermarriage)—that is, marriage to non-Koreans. During the 1930s, about one out of four Korean men married non-Koreans, and two out of five Korean women married non-Koreans. By 1940, the rate had increased to the point where fully half of all Korean males married non-Korean females, and two-thirds of all Korean females married non-Korean males. In fact, all three East Asian groups experienced increases in the rate of outmarriage. Nonetheless, the rate of Japanese outmarriage still remained relatively low, and the Chinese rate was not much higher, while the Korean rate increased "phenomenally," according to one contemporary sociologist.[45]

So prevalent was outmarriage among second-generation Koreans that not only were sociologists able to document it statistically, but it was also plainly obvious to Koreans themselves. One Korean female, under the heading "Disappearance of Koreans," recorded in her journal: "I do not know all the Koreans living in Honolulu but I do know there has been a tremendous increase in intermarriages. I shall mention a few: Barbara Pang married a haole sergeant; Lila Lee married a Chinese boy who was a fellow worker; Elsie Kim also married a Chinese fellow worker; Esther Hong married Walter Kau; Sandra Lee married a haole sergeant; Peggy Moon married a haole staff-sergeant; Alice Kong married a Japanese boy." The advent of the Pacific War further accelerated the incidence of outmarriage, as another Korean female recalled: "Spring in 1942 was marked by a profusion of flowering romances in the islands. In fact, it was a season for weddings everywhere in America as young men married their girls before going off to battle. The couples who found it difficult to meet in the evenings in areas where blackout was enforced decided it was easier to be together if they were married."[46]

The first-generation Koreans had also experienced a high rate of outmarriage, primarily because of the highly skewed ratio of men to women, a situation relieved to some extent by the arrival of picture brides between 1910 and 1924. But a skewed sex ratio does not really explain the high rate of outmarriage among the second generation, who began dating and marrying in the 1930s and 1940s. In 1930, the ratio of male to female Koreans aged fifteen to forty-five was 162 to 100; it dropped to 137 to 100 by 1940, due to the coming of age of the second generation. Indeed, by 1940, about two-thirds of the nearly seven thousand Koreans in Hawai'i were native (Hawaiian) born. And yet even as the ratio decreased, the rate of outmarriage increased rather than decreased. Since the gender ratio cannot explain the high and rising rate of outmarriage for second-generation Koreans, we must look elsewhere for answers.[47]

One explanation was the small size of the Korean population, both in absolute as well as relative terms. In an absolute sense, it meant that there were few Korean marriage partners from which to choose. In a relative sense, as one sociologist put it, "[B]y virtue of their limited numbers, [Koreans] were unable to impose their traditional definitions of marriage selection, which correspond in many essentials to those of the Japanese and Chinese, with anything like the same effectiveness, and hence individual choice operates much more extensively among both men and women." That is, it was difficult to insulate Korean children from competing social forces and interaction with other ethnic groups. Outmarriage for other small groups in Hawai'i, such as the Puerto Ricans, was also high.[48]

Geographic isolation was also a factor in the high incidence of outmarriage. By 1930, about two-thirds of all Koreans lived in Honolulu County, two-fifths in the city of Honolulu, and one-quarter in the rural part of Oahu—the suburbs of Honolulu. By contrast, only half the Japanese lived in Honolulu County. Thus for the relatively few Korean families still living on the outer islands, it was very difficult to find a Korean marriage partner. Consider the predicament of the Woos, who "were the only Koreans at Huleia Plantation. This plantation, located about twelve miles from Lihue [Kauai], was small—there were approximately forty or fifty laborers, mostly Filipinos and Japanese. . . . By 1941, however, the family had decided to move to Honolulu [because] the Woo girls were of marrying age, and there were no eligible Korean boys around." Indeed, outmarriage rates among Koreans were higher in rural areas of Hawai'i. From 1932 to 1934, for example, 37 percent of the Koreans brides and grooms outside of Honolulu outmarried, but in Honolulu the percentage was half that. Not only were there more Koreans in the city, but since Korean organizations were also largely confined to Honolulu and its vicinity, community sentiment against outmarriage was relatively weaker in the rural districts.[49]

Still another reason for the high rate of outmarriage was a generational transfer of values. A significant erosion of traditional values among first-generation Koreans has already been noted, especially when compared to first-generation Japanese and Chinese in Hawai'i. The evidence suggests first-generation Koreans had a slightly more lenient attitude toward their children's outmarriages than first-generation Chinese and Japanese parents. In one survey, all but sixteen of the eighty-four respondents indicated that at least one son or daughter had married a non-Korean. When asked their opinion on their children's mixed marriages, the most frequent response was "up to them," followed by "cannot help it." While these first-generation respondents were polled after the fact and their responses may indicate they had come to terms with their children's outmarriage, it does suggest some ambivalence among the first generation about the absolute desirability of their children marrying fellow Koreans.[50]

Such ambivalence was noticed by the second generation: "I interviewed a Korean girl who told me that although the Koreans talk about the old customs, very few adhere to the old customs. Consequently, marriage between two families with the same surname or intermarriage with another racial group is frowned upon but is prevalent and common. There is hardly any of the matchmaker marriages performed today in Hawaii. She believes that of the three Oriental groups, the Chinese, Japanese, and Koreans, the Korean group is the most Americanized group. She stated that in spite of their resentment the old generation gives way to the young and are becoming passive to the changes."[51]

In fact, often factors other than ethnicity carried greater weight in the minds of at least a few first-generation Korean parents, and this contributed to their ambivalence toward outmarriage. In one family, for example, "Father especially never tried to discriminate against any individual because of his race, creed or social status but he definitely advised us (his children) when seeking a mate to consider the problem carefully. He stressed equal status in education and our mates should have obtained emotional maturity." In another family, a daughter discovered that her mother "disapproved of [her Korean fiance] . . . primarily because he lacked a college degree. But it was common knowledge that most young men of Korean ancestry his age had dropped out of college during the Depression to help support the family. . . . To my surprise, I learned that to my mother nothing mattered more than a college degree held by the man or woman any of her children married." Finally, a young woman recalled what had happened to her in 1938: "The reason why I left home after working in [my father's] tailor shop was because there was a Korean guy interested in me, but my parents didn't feel he was good for me. That's why they sent me to business school in town."[52]

If first-generation Koreans were slightly more ambivalent than other first-generation Asians toward outmarriage, then, given the generational transfer of values, we can surmise that second-generation Koreans would be even more "liberal" than their Chinese and Japanese counterparts. In other words, they would feel less pressure to marry "their own" than would second-generation Chinese and Japanese. So when sociologists characterized outmarriage as "a definite movement on the part of the second generation away from the traditional familial controls" and stated that "the pressures of old-country values had declined," it is clear that more than just a lack of numbers was responsible for the high rate of Korean outmarriage.[53] In fact, the high rate of Korean outmarriage was partly a result of what one second-generation Korean called their "rapid Hawaiianization." He cited as proof "the reputation Korean girls have of jitter-bugging and dancing at an earlier age." Continuing, the writer noted "many conflicts," because parents, who "still clung to the oriental way of life . . . did not have great influence on [the second generation]." Moreover, because "ties between families are loose and gossip does not have the force it would have in a smaller area . . . the number of intermarriages is constantly increasing."[54]

As a result, most second-generation Koreans felt they had the right to marry whomever they chose and that their parents should have no say in the matter. One young Korean expressed it in this way: "Even intermarriages are quite frequent with the young Koreans, although the older people object very strongly to such action. . . . The young Koreans believe in following the dictates of their hearts and are in every way free from restraint which their parents have been obliged to undergo. They are imbued with the ideals of freedom and equality and are thoroughly 'human' in respect of modern conventions." Another second-generation Korean also stressed the primacy of individual choice over what parents or other Koreans might think: "At present intermarriage is more prevalent than ever. To me it depends on the individuals concerned and not on public sentiment." Finally, one Korean female summed up the feeling of the second generation in four words: "It's their own business."[55]

Contributing to the high rate of outmarriage were the different socialization and expectations of Korean young men and women. As one second-generation Korean wrote:

> The average Korean boys' and girls' interest and emphasis of education were geared toward opposite ends. The girls directed their interest in music, arts, and other refined activities. On the other hand the boys did not follow the same pattern. They resorted to participation in sports and more practical education. This made their social interests incompatible to each other. The girls were interested in the more refined arts and demanded refined manners from the boys. The boys, conditioned by their patriarchal parents at home, were inclined not to condescend to the egalitarian refined manners desired by the girls. Due to this conflict of interest situation as described above, the boys were not able to conform to the standards desired by the girls. This prompted the girls to look elsewhere for their prospective husbands. They readily found this in the Caucasian group and tended to marry them. This resulted in an extreme shortage of eligible women of their own race for the boys. Thus the boys had to seek mates of different races. Of course the Korean boys rationalize by saying the girls are not there.[56]

From the male perspective, Korean females were snobs. Consider the experience of a twenty-four-year-old Korean airplane mechanic: "The dames down the country are all spoiled. They expect too much from the boys (meaning in the way of manners, gifts, and entertainment). Now when you take them out you have to go over to their house and wait for them. Then they want you to open the car door and lift them in and close the door. When it's time to get out, they expect you to get out of the driver's seat and open the door for them. Then you can start closing up your car. When it rains you have to reach over and close the windows for them. After a show they want to go straight home and not park the car somewhere for a while. When they go out with Macs (soldiers) they're willing to walk and some of them lolo dames even pay for the tickets. The Macs treat them too much like babies. They are spoiling the dames."[57]

Consider also the following account, which points to the differing expectations between Korean young men and women: "Had a little chat with one of my Korean friends. He seemed to be in a grouchy mood. He was griping about this and that. Finally he got around to talking about his girlfriend who was of Japanese ancestry. I asked him, jokingly, why didn't he go with a member of his own race and help build up the Korean race as statistics show that it is dying out. At this he 'blew up' and said, 'Huh! Waste time!!' Among other things, he claimed that the Korean girls were too high toned; they spoke stilted 'good' English; and besides, they would rather marry haoles, and marines especially."[58]

The Korean women themselves provide a glimpse at why the ideal and the real differed so radically: "Another reason [that we Korean girls do not go out with Korean boys] is the fact that Korean girls have rapidly taken in American ways but the boys have been relatively slow. Certain Korean girls cannot stand these unmannerly and rather sissified boys. These girls would rather have a haole who has good manners and who does not make a too naive demonstration of superiority complex as most Korean boys do. Even at this university [of Hawai'i] boys are very scarce. Even at that the Korean boys are not too popular. Personally, I would rather go with a boy of another race than one of the Koreans. It is apparent that the boys have not become as assimilated as the Korean girls have." Another young woman observed, "The girls have a greater tendency to mix with the other racial groups. In doing so they have achieved an almost stereotyped conception of notoriety among service personnel and local men. I asked a popular Korean girl of the younger set what her brothers' friends were doing. She replied: 'They're going in their own cliques, stag, or dating girls of other nationalities because they know they haven't a chance with Korean girls.'"[59]

When polled by a sociologist, only 18 percent of Korean young men indicated that they wanted to marry a Korean woman, whereas about half of the Japanese and Chinese young men (47 percent and 59 percent, respectively) hoped to marry women of their own ethnic group. As for Korean females, while nearly two-thirds (65 percent) indicated that they hoped to marry a Korean young man (the comparable figures for Japanese and Chinese females were 63 percent and 75 percent, respectively), their actual outmarriage rate was considerably higher than this rather idealized figure.[60]

Thus a lack of numbers, liberal attitudes resulting from rapid acculturation, and differing expectations between Korean young men and women were three important factors that led to high rates of outmarriage. This occurred despite the fact that their parents generally (with some exceptions of course) did want them to marry Koreans, and some parents were willing to exert themselves to that end. In this respect, they were not much different from first-generation Chinese or Japanese parents. Had the first generation remained in Korea, their children naturally would have married other Koreans, as marriages there were arranged by the parents, with scant regard for the wishes of the children, who could do little but obey as filial piety dictated. In fact, there was a certain nostalgia for the old ways for some in the first generation. As one second generation Korean wrote: "[The first generation in] Hawaii today resent and object to girls 'going' with boys. This is due to the fact that the older generation is unable to mate boys and girls at an early age and can't conform to the match-maker marriage which is desired in old Korea." Another Korean wrote, "Although Philip and I knew that my mother favored ceremonies and formalities, we had no go-between to arrange a betrothal as was the custom in the old country."[61]

Some Korean parents tried to solve the problem of outmarriage by resorting to a modified method of arranged marriages. As the following vignette demonstrates, what made this particular match more important was the fact that it involved the eldest son, who bore the primary responsibility of carrying on the family name: "My older brother, who is about thirty years old, is still single. I know my mother has often wished he would get married so she could see him settled down and also because she wants some grandchildren. She has often brought up the subject with him and told him that a certain girl was good, another girl was nice, each time naming the girls. She would talk about all of his friends who were married and had two or three children. This talk sometimes ended with everyone laughing; other times with my brother angry. Some of my mother's friends also bring up this subject when they visit our house. My brother objects to this and tells my mother so after the guests are gone. He claims that they should let him live his own life and let him do his own worrying. . . . In these times my mother can't hire a go-between, as was the custom of Korea long ago, to bring the boy and girl together. She hopes my brother will find a good girl for himself before long and settle the marriage problem for himself." But in fact, most parents did not try to arrange their children's marriages, either because of resistance from the children or because they believed they had no right to interfere. One woman recalled that her parents "do not believe in forced marriages. . . . Many a time proposals came to my parents for my hand, but they refused every one, saying that it was not their business to thwart my ambition."[62]

While most Korean parents shied away from even informally trying to arrange marriages, there was still substantial opposition to the outmarriage of their children, not only because of what might be termed "ethnic nationalism" but also because of the fear of becoming the object of scorn in other Koreans' eyes. Given the need to maintain the prestige of the family in the wider Korean community, an outmarriage threatened to call into question the reputation of the family. Some second-generation children felt the pressure of filial piety and avoided outmarriage to spare their parents. As one female recalled: "I thought it was important to marry a Korean, not a Japanese or any other nationality, to avoid the wrath of the Korean community and escape bringing embarrassment to my family."[63] Other second-generation Koreans sought to marry within the Korean ethnic group because of their own deeply held convictions. One female wrote: "I don't think that intermarriage is a good thing because I believe that persons of the same racial group have a common understanding that is far above that of different races. Although there may be cases where intermarriage has been successful, I cannot say that it is all [illegible] bad nor good. I believe in the idea that peoples of same race are better suited than another."[64]

But the majority of the second generation felt free to marry whoever they wanted. And if they indicated a desire to marry someone other than a Korean, it often led to intergenerational conflict. The amount of turmoil could sometimes be predicted depending upon the ethnicity of the proposed partner. That is, Korean parents operated within a hierarchical ordering of ethnic groups as potential marriage partners for their children. Aside from Koreans, at the top of the list came the Chinese as the least objectionable to the first generation. As this was a relatively unexceptionable pairing, there is consequently not much evidence of conflict. We can hypothesize that the first generation had little objection to their children marrying a Chinese because, traditionally, the Koreans had looked up to China and had consciously borrowed Chinese culture, language and philosophy, particularly Confucianism, which informed much of the value system held by the first generation.[65]

Nonetheless, Chinese were different than Koreans, which posed problems for potential marriage partners: "Clara is an example of being between two worlds. She is of Korean ancestry and finds her associates among girls and boys of Chinese ancestry. Many people have mistaken her for a Chinese. But the other day I heard someone say to her, 'Clara, I've always thought that you were Korean.' Clara, being called on the spot amongst a group of Chinese girls, had to admit that she was Korean. However, at that moment she seemed rather insecure and unhappy. She has sought the companionship of Chinese young-folk because there are not many young people of Korean ancestry. Perhaps she isn't accepted by the Korean group. At any rate, Clara is at a disadvantage when Chinese habits or speech pop up. I've heard her attempting to say short phrases in Chinese and not be very successful in her attempt. This voluntary association is now superficial. The real trouble will come if, and most probably, she marries into the Chinese race."[66]

Also parental opposition was still a possibility, since the partner was not Korean. Consider the following example: "My eldest sister spoke of her boyfriend, a Chinese boy, and my parents immediately flared up. They knew that she liked this boy but they didn't know that those two were seriously thinking about marriage until this evening. Harsh words went on between my parents and my sister because my parents claim that marriages between racial groups are not successful and that they will never give her their consent to marry a boy who isn't a Korean. My sister was naturally angry and hurt because she knows that the boy's parents would object to their marriage also but nevertheless they intend to get married. I feel the same way she does."[67]

Later, however, her parents relented: "The attitude of my parents has changed and now they have accepted this Chinese boy. It was pretty hard for my parents to accept this boy because they were afraid of the ill reputation our household was to get from the Korean people but finally, they realized that they either had to accept the gossip or lose one of the daughters. My sister had planned on leaving the house immediately after the cold reception she received from my parents. She was hurt because she felt that all people of the younger generation should have broader ideas and my parents, who were old, seemed to turn to the more old-fashioned ideas. My parents finally realized that her happiness meant more than the community attitude and consented to her going with this boy. Now they have a courtship like any other couple without having to sneak to do the things they want to do."[68]

If marriages with Chinese caused relatively little conflict, the same cannot be said for proposed unions with Caucasians. Many Korean young women began dating and marrying Caucasian young men who had come to Hawai'i as servicemen starting in the late 1930s, as war approached. Given the more liberal attitudes of second generation Koreans as compared to Japanese and Chinese, it is not surprising that only about one in five women (19 percent) disapproved of the idea of dating servicemen, while nearly one-third of the second-generation Japanese and Chinese disapproved (31 percent and 29 percent, respectively). Sheer numbers also played a factor in unions between Korean women and Caucasian men because local young men, including Koreans, were drafted and sent to bases on the mainland while Caucasians continued to be stationed in Hawai'i. Wartime restrictions against Japanese also promoted interaction between Caucasian servicemen and Korean women. One contemporary Korean observer illustrated these trends: "There have been many other marriages between Korean girls and servicemen. One reason that more Korean girls have married these servicemen than the Japanese is the fact that there are very few Korean boys who are eligible bachelors. Another reason is the fact that Korean girls have had a better chance to meet haole boys in the service because they are eligible for a CIB pass and therefore have held jobs in naval air stations and army offices."[69]

One Korean female attributed the numerous liaisons between Korean women and Caucasian servicemen not only to numbers, but also to the social climate brought on by the war: "Some intermarriages are probably due to the girls' or boys' lack of boyfriends and girlfriends of their own race. Those are the ones that resort to friendships with members of other races. The war situation has a great influence in the social changes of the community. Marriages and divorces are exceptionally numerous due to the fact of an excess of the male population. Women are easily swayed by the 'lines' of the men, especially those in the service and the defense workers from the States. There seems to be an abundance of Oriental girls coupling up with white men. It may be that the girls are lonely because most of the local boys were drafted and sent to different posts in the war area. The moral standards of the community have been lowered noticeably, which may be due to the people's 'devil-may-care' attitudes. Having good times and paying no heed to the consequences are the chief faults. While working, I, too, thought of only enjoying myself by going to numerous social functions."[70]

While most of the outmarriages in the Korean community involving whites were between Korean females and Caucasian males, the gender roles were occasionally reversed. "Peter Kim, of Korean ancestry, married a haole girl in Idaho. She had hero-worshipped him in his amazing athletic career through an Idaho high school and an Idaho college. The daughter of a minister, she had not the courage to gain his acquaintance. Taller than he, extremely fair of skin, she is a decided contrast to his short, dark, and stocky form. She was beautiful and shapely, yet she was modest to the extreme. They finally met at a small town church social. For nine years they were together except when, as he thought, things just wouldn't work out and he returned to Hawaii. Finally five years ago *her* pleas brought them to marriage. They desired a family more than any other thing, but he withheld—he didn't want his children to fight for recognition as mixed ancestry kids. . . . [L]ater they tried for conception. This failed. She visited doctors, and he and she tried everything that might gain her pregnancy. Everything failed. A few days ago (July, 1944) they adopted a Korean-haole, two month old baby boy of illegitimate birth. Their happiness is almost to the extreme."[71]

Although first-generation opposition to Korean-Caucasian outmarriages never died, the outbreak of the Pacific War in 1941 led to an amelioration in the attitudes of both the first and second generation toward these marriages. One Korean female recorded the following observation: "Prior to the war, outmarriages were generally frowned upon and prohibited by parents. Long before the war, about five years ago, the mere going out with a serviceman was declared to be a sin. If one ever did go out with one, one's reputation was ruined. But just before the war, outmarriages were quite numerous and therefore, the people, even though they opposed such marriages, were not too shocked when some Korean girl did up and marry an 'outsider.' Since December 7, the servicemen have been and still are in the limelight. Everything is done with regard for them. Naturally, the Koreans, too, took up this attitude of hospitality toward the servicemen. I heard an elderly Korean man say, 'Soldiers are all right, are nice as long as they don't take away my daughters.' Marriages with men of the armed forces and defense workers are still not too warmly welcomed, but this feeling of opposition is not as strong as it was before the war. In almost every Wahiawa Korean family, there is a 'soldier-in-law.' Take my own family as an example. Before the war, my sister was seen going around with a soldier. My parents found out and tried to stop her but to no avail. A few months after December 7, she told my parents that she was going to marry him. My parents at first opposed, but later, consented to the marriage. Our in-law is now tolerated by my parents and is quite warmly welcomed by the rest of the family." [72]

Additional examples of changing attitudes toward servicemen can be found. "I was riding in Wahiawa one day when I saw a girl friend of mine (Korean girl) going to the movie with a soldier. This surprised me very much as she had always told me of her dislike for the white race. This girl is about twenty-three years old and always considered herself old compared to the rest of us. I had worked with her mother in Wheeler Field before I entered the university [of Hawai'i] and she used to tell me that she wanted to get married to a good, respectable Korean boy and would not lose her reputation by going around with a soldier. I know she had received many invitations for dates from servicemen but had always refused them. I had not seen her since I quit my job, so it was a great shock to me to see her with a serviceman. This incident shows the effect of the increasing influx of servicemen here plus the decreasing number of local boys due to the fact that a number of the local boys have been drafted and sent to the mainland for training." [73]

But not everyone in the family changed their attitude toward servicemen. A young Korean woman named Mary relates: "When I was in High School I had the same feeling as my parents against boys of different races. After I left school I obtained a job at Hickam Field. Here, I associated with men of the armed forces. Gradually my feelings toward them changed. There was one boy who attracted me. The feelings were mutual so we began dating each other. One day while out on a date with this soldier we came upon my little brother. Naturally he went straight home to 'spill the beans.' When I returned home I was met with angry looks from my parents. After dinner they called me to their side and began lecturing me. My father said, 'Don't you know that the Haole looks down upon us Orientals? Don't think for a moment that his heart is filled with love for you. Don't think he'll marry you, and if he does he'll never take you back to the mainland with him. His family couldn't class you as a human. If you do marry him and live here you'll just be a slave to him!' My mother nodded assent to every word he uttered. From that moment on life at home became unbearable. My parents seemed unhappy and ashamed. However I went against their wishes and married him. I'm not too happy. Till today my dad refused to acknowledge him as my husband . . . [and my] brother would yell at [me] and say, 'I suppose you think you're grand marrying him. He's just a white trash, you hear. If you ever bring him here I'll knock his block off.'" [74]

Aside from the argument that marrying within the Korean race upheld traditional Korean values, parents also attempted to prevent their daughters from dating and marrying servicemen by citing the "reputation" that servicemen brought with them. As one Korean women recorded in her journal: "I can't go out with this sailor because my parents think that I should stick to my own kind. My parents have heard so many things about these servicemen that they want me to keep away from them. My parents say, 'You no go out with the sailor because he haole—no good.'"[75]

Korean parents also feared the potential community opprobrium that might sully their family's reputation if their daughter dated or married a serviceman. Consider the following two incidents on a Honolulu city bus. "Whenever I take my little niece on the bus—she's four years old, part Irish and part Korean—people immediately look at my left hand to see whether I'm married. Not seeing any ring, they betray on their faces just what they're thinking—that the child is illegitimate and therefore I, as its mother, am an untouchable, a social outcast." In the second incident, "My girl friend and I boarded the Wahiawa bus at the terminal. . . . An Oriental man (very old) sat a few seats away from us and he was intoxicated. He started swearing, spitting and cussing at everyone and at first it seemed funny as everyone was laughing and making remarks about 'Grandpappy being drunk.' I was amused at first but my amusement turned to utter disgust and shame later. The old man yelled at all of the soldiers and girls in the bus in the most vile language. He then announced that he was a *Korean* and not a Japanese or a Chinese. My smile immediately vanished and I began to be ashamed of the way he was acting especially since I belonged to the same racial group."[76]

To avert the prospect of their daughters marrying servicemen, Korean parents actively discouraged them from dating them and signaled their disapproval in far from subtle ways. "Recently, a Korean boy, a good friend of mine, invited me to his house for a dinner . . . when a haole soldier showed up to visit one of the daughters. The father hardly acknowledged the arrival of the soldier and just civilly thanked him for the box of cigars he brought. He completely ignored the soldier throughout the evening and when time came for the soldier to leave, his departure almost went unnoticed. The mother had remained in the kitchen most, but not all, of the time. This conduct was not because of any natural rudeness or ignorance in the father. . . . He is well spoken of by all who know him and his acquaintance is wide-spread because of his former connection with the police department. Yet he registered such definite disapproval of the soldier that I would have been embarrassed for him." As for the rest of the family, "The attitude of the brothers is not as definitely crystallized as that of the father but they certainly register[ed] disapproval and the sister [was] left to her own devices to entertain her visitor."[77]

If a Korean girl actually married a white serviceman, there sometimes were dire consequences. In one case where a Korean woman defied her parents and married a serviceman, her friend wrote, "Her parents have refused to recognize her as a daughter. I wonder if Fanny will regret this decisive estrangement from family ties." Another Korean woman wrote, "I recall a case where a young Korean girl of sixteen became pregnant but could not marry her soldier because her mother objected. The mother was said to have gone around saying that she wanted to kill him because he had gotten her daughter into trouble." Perhaps the most tragic outcome of parental opposition was that recalled by a second-generation Korean female: "Then, one day I heard of a lover's suicide. A gunshot killed her. It was the first suicide in our community. She was a Korean girl whose parents refused her marriage to a white soldier. The soldier killed her and then himself. We all went to the church at the corner of Olive and Ohai Streets and asked for forgiveness amidst flowers and pain. I viewed the bodies of the two lovers as it was polite to do. I barely knew them but felt pained by their deaths as the Korean women and men wailed and mourned their dead."[78]

If most Korean parents opposed their daughters' associations with white soldiers, an even more complex situation arose when their sons and daughters began dating and marrying Japanese, because the political issue of Korean nationalism was injected, once again raising the specter of intergenerational conflict. This was especially so when a daughter married a Japanese. As one second-generation Korean female wrote: "The Koreans in Hawaii are as a whole opposed to intermarriage. A Korean male can marry a foreigner and bring her into his family and make her a Korean but a Korean girl must never marry a foreigner. Above all, no Korean must marry a Japanese. Koreans do not have faith in intermarriage. They feel that intermarriage cannot be a success. They believe that a Korean must or should marry a Korean. They believe in keeping the race pure. Intermarriage is not frequent among the more educated classes but it is common among the day laborers. But still the feeling is very strong against a Korean maid marrying an alien, especially a Japanese." In other words, if a son married a Japanese, she would take his Korean surname, and the children would still have the Korean surname to carry on. But, when a daughter marries, she would lose her Korean surname and adopt a Japanese surname and therefore no longer be Korean.[79]

To be sure, some second-generation Koreans who had grown up hearing about the evils of the Japanese from their parents and who practiced filial piety resolved never to date or marry Japanese. "Mother and father have always stressed to us the evils of inter-marriages. They were especially against the Japanese race because they were in Korea when Japan invaded and conquered Korea. They knew of the horrors inflicted upon some of their close friends and grew to hate the Japanese. We of the younger generation are not very prejudiced against the Japanese because of our associations with them in school and social activities. Although I associate with them, I can never think of marriage with one of them, nor with any other race, because of my parents' advice lingering like a haunting refrain in my mind." Another similar account notes also the weight of the Korean community: "My girlfriends and I were aware of the strong anti-Japanese feeling in the community, especially in regard to intermarriage. We agreed the prudent thing to do was to avoid dating Japanese boys. And even if we were invited to a dance or a movie by a Chinese or Caucasian, perhaps we should keep the relationship from turning serious."[80]

But more often than not, second-generation Koreans began dating Japanese even though they knew such actions would meet with disapproval from their parents and their first-generation friends. Consider the following conversation, which was transcribed verbatim in a student journal:

> The most talked about thing in our neighborhood is a Korean girl who goes steady with a Japanese boy. Both of them are American citizens. She is eighteen years old and is a student in one of our big high schools. She has been going with him for a year and her parents show their disapproval outwardly, but she doesn't care because she likes this boy very much. Her father objected most and when he died, the immigrant group of our neighborhood said that she had driven him to death. He died a horrible death, but it was not connected with this affair. He died when he was hit by an automobile. Here's an example of what I heard in a group where this particular topic was the center of gossip:
>
> Mrs. K: "She is a disgrace to our race."
>
> Mrs. S: "I should think she would be ashamed to show her face in this area."
>
> Mr. K: "If she were my own daughter, I would chase her out of my house. Imagine her going with a Japanese—our number one enemy."
>
> Mr. S: "Of course, if she wants to go with a foreigner, that's her business. I'd rather see her going with a haole—but a Japanese—never."
>
> Miss S (She is a friend of this girl and has many Japanese friends—both girls and boys): "I think you folks are being unjust and catty. In this land, which is America, we don't think of the Japanese, who are living in this community, or any other community for that matter, as our enemy. They are a group of people who came to Hawaii just as you and others did. Their sons and daughters are Americans just as we are. I would marry one if I fell in love with him."
>
> Mrs. S (very much disturbed): "If your grandparents were still living and if they heard you say that last sentence, they'll probably never think of you as their granddaughter."
>
> Miss S (She's the only daughter and is very spoilt; also she can voice her opinions in front of her parents freely which is not the case of many other boys and girls of alien Korean parents.): "Oh, the whole lot of you make me sick. Why don't all of you mind your own business. Maybe this whole world would be a better place to live in if people would only mind their own business." (She slams the door and goes out. The others leave, too.)

After everyone had gone, Miss S tried to tell her parents that there's proof that the second generation Japanese boys are loyal to America. They volunteered their services and they are risking their lives for the country who had given them opportunities of many sorts. But her parents insist that the Japanese boys are doing it because it is their duty and obligation. After arguing for a while, Miss S threw her hands up in disgust and just kept her mouth shut while her parents rattled off about this and that.

She left the room calmly; so I followed her. She says, "How can I ever argue with an alien Korean—for that matter, any kind of Korean."

I told her, laughingly, that she is one of them and that I was one also. She laughed and said, "I guess you're right, but I wish I could get my parents to give up the idea of judging every Japanese as being our enemy. As some people say, the militarist of Japan is our real enemy, not the people. But I guess it's impossible for me to have them see this viewpoint because they were brought up with that tradition and I can't change their mores." Here our little talk ended.

Now here's a conflict where an old prejudice still persists that has been carried away from the old country. The Korean immigrant group still has the feeling of sensitiveness toward the Japanese. The reason for this hatred goes back to many years. They hate and despise the Japanese because they are the conquerors of Korea and who had suppressed the people of Korea. So the immigrant group have always felt and still feels that all Japanese, alien or second generation, as their enemy. Of course, the second generation boys and girls don't ever think of this fact. And if their parents bring it up, they just listen thru one ear and let it go out through the other. Some of my good friends are of Japanese ancestry."[81]

Another second-generation Korean recorded a similar incident concerning marriage to a Japanese, which pitted first generation against second: "Last night mother was telling us of a family friend. She said that one of the girls in the family had married a Japanese. The mother (Korean) having definite views against the Japanese, opposed strongly to the marriage. Her daughter, nevertheless, against her wishes, married him. She was so wrought with shame over her daughter's action that she became ill. She said that she didn't want to see her daughter any more. My mother, as well as many of the Korean women, sympathized with her for they too are biased against the Japanese people. We others in the family—my sisters and I—have always tried our best to reason with mother that there is no justification in her and her friends' attitude toward the Japanese. But it seems well nigh impossible, for they always have in mind that it was the Japanese people who enslaved the Koreans, and that to them is reason enough for disliking those people."[82]

A similar situation where a Korean girl was dating a Japanese boy was resolved in an unusual way: "Some years ago two young people who were both attending the same school became rather intimately attached to each other. The boy was the son of a Japanese merchant and the girl was the daughter of a Korean minister. I used to see the boy escorting the Korean girl to work at the Cannery. I used to see him bring her to his home. The girl used to run away from her home and spend many evenings out riding. After the matter became very serious, a natural sequence of such a thing was a grave matter, the question of marriage was brought up before the boy's parents. The boy's father was very angry at first and strongly opposed seeing his son marrying a Korean but later he gave in. He consented his son to marry her. But the Korean man was terribly angry. He came over one evening to the boy's home, and showed his prejudice against the Japanese. This is what he shouted. 'I don't let my daughter marry a Japanese! I rather see her dead than to marry a Japanese!' So to make the boy and the girl forget each other, the boy was sent to Japan. There he remained for about three years."[83]

There were also problems when Korean boys started dating and marrying Japanese girls. "I found a 'girl friend' . . . Haruko (Daughter of Spring), Hawaiian-born Japanese-American. My [Korean] friends in Shanghai would not have forgiven me for consorting with a Japanese girl and would have branded me a traitor. But Haruko was slim and willowy with an impish face. And she was an excellent dancer." In such a relationship, Japanese as well as Korean parents might object: "I knew a Japanese American girl who fell in love with a Korean. When the two decided that they wanted to get married, her parents told her bluntly, 'You listen and you listen good. If you marry that Korean we will not only lose a daughter but you will lose a family.'"[84]

When a Korean son or daughter married a Japanese, the parents had to face the Korean community. Two incidents illustrate how difficult this could be. "Mrs. Chun spoke next. 'Hee Kyung, you don't know how happy I am for you because your daughter is marrying a Korean boy.' She sounded wistful. I knew she had been feeling ashamed because her only daughter recently had chosen a Japanese for a husband, who forced a pregnancy on her, besides. A hush fell over the group, as if Mrs. Chun were crying and the other ladies were in sympathy." In the second incident, the parents sanctioned their daughter's marriage to a Japanese in spite of community disapproval: "In the midst of this fever and furor against the [Japanese] enemy one of the parishioners announced his daughter was marrying a young man of Japanese ancestry. He said the couple had met at a mainland college and they were very much in love. This impending marriage provoked an uproar in the Korean community. The wedding, which was to be quiet and private, became a public issue. The handsome aunt of the bride, a staunch Christian and an influential leader in the church, was unable to dissuade the bride from 'the unforgivable act of bending to serve the enemy.' She refused to sanction the marriage. The church people disapproved the use of the church for the wedding ceremony. 'This is a traitorous union,' the vocal members in the community declared. The wedding took place in the bride's parents' home with only a few members from the bride's and groom's families present."[85]

This anti-Japanese antipathy on the part of the first-generation Koreans was not lost upon the *nisei* in Hawai'i. As one Japanese teenager recorded: "I have heard that [the] majority of the Korean parents will never consent their sons and daughters to marry Japanese—'any other racial group but the Japs.' To me this seems like a pathetic situation. Why should the Koreans vent their feeling toward those Japanese who have lived, not under Jap. Government, but under good old U.S.A.? After Dec. 7th, I, like many other AJAs [Americans of Japanese Ancestry], felt deeply the resentment and distrust of the other racial groups. I didn't mind the remarks that the haoles made half as much as I did the other racial groups such as the Chinese, Koreans, Portuguese—these people who lived among us."[87]

Thus it is clear that there was a generation gap with respect to suitable marriage partners. But the first-generation Koreans had other concerns to occupy them. When World War II came to Hawai'i in 1941, political forces were unleashed that threw the entire Korean community into turmoil and raised the level of discourse to the American government itself.

11

The Pacific War and
Wartime Restrictions

When Japan bombed Pearl Harbor, Koreans everywhere sensed that the liberation of their country was at hand. The United States had finally weighed in against Japanese imperialism, and there was little doubt as to who would emerge victorious. Koreans in Hawai'i welcomed the American entry into the war, and the Korean nationalist movement, which had been moribund since the 1920s, was immediately revived. Collectively, the Korean community made strenuous efforts to transcend their previous differences and present a united front to the American government. Despite these efforts, however, centrifugal forces internally and martial law restrictions externally tore at the Korean community in Hawai'i. Much of the material for this chapter relies on the pioneering research of Michael Macmillan and the confidential intelligence reports on the Korean community collected by U.S. intelligence agencies.

Individually and collectively, Koreans reacted to the Japanese attack much like everyone else in Hawai'i. Here is how one Korean family reacted: "I heard Omanee (mother) waking me up to get ready for church. Then she asked me to pick papaya for breakfast. I was standing on the roof of the garage to easily reach for the yellow ripe fruit when the planes swooped down towards me. Omanee had exited from the chicken coop with fresh eggs in her pocket. Bullets pierced the ground in her path as she raised her fist and yelled something. Her voice was drowned by the roaring of the airplanes. I saw smoke billow from the U.S. air base at Wheeler Field and pointed over the eucalyptus trees. The highway of the king, Kamehameha, was strafed as bullets crashed glass one street over from where I stood."[1]

In another Korean family on that day, "My eighteen-year-old brother, Young Mahn, who was enrolled in the Reserve Officers Training Corps (ROTC) class at the University of Hawaii, responded to a radio call for all ROTC men to report to the armory. . . . My younger brother, Young Chul, left home the day of the attack to join other fifteen-year-old Boy Scouts of Troop Eleven reporting to the Royal Hawaiian Hotel as 'trained litter bearers.' . . . My father joined volunteer truck drivers, taking his own company vehicle to the Civil Defense Headquarters set up at Iolani Palace and awaited orders from the military.

Dozens of [Korean] men brought their trucks and blankets, and waited night after night for some assignment of duty." Soon, Koreans in Hawai'i started selling pins with the words "Korea for Victory with U.S." emblazoned on them.[2]

The Japanese attack initiated military rule based mainly on fears of espionage and sabotage by members of Hawai'i's large population of Japanese ancestry. With the acquiescence of Governor Joseph B. Poindexter, Lt. Gen. Walter C. Short, commander of the army's Hawaiian Department, established martial law on the afternoon of December 7, 1941, and assumed full executive, legislative, and judicial authority over civilian affairs in the territory. Short and his successors took the title "military governor" and remained in control until the revocation of martial law in the fall of 1944. Martial law meant curfews and blackout regulations, rationing, censorship, and job freezes. Martial law also restricted enemy aliens, and Koreans immediately began inquiring about their status. The issue was referred to the judge advocate, who determined in consultation with the Immigration and Naturalization Service that alien Koreans (the first generation) in Hawai'i were legally subjects of Japan and were therefore to be classified as enemy aliens. This decision mobilized the now-revitalized Korean nationalist movement to work to remove the stigma of "enemy alien" from Koreans in Hawai'i.[3]

To be sure, Koreans in Hawai'i were not in the same bad position as the Japanese. Within the first few months after Pearl Harbor, more than two thousand Japanese residents whose loyalty was suspect were interned either in Hawai'i or on the mainland. While no Koreans were similarly rounded up, alien Koreans of the first generation, who were viewed as subjects of Japan, also felt the weight of the restrictions, some of which had been imposed even before war began. In the summer of 1941, the assets of Japanese nationals (which included first-generation Koreans) had been frozen by presidential order. After December 7, alien Japanese and Koreans were permitted to continue their commercial activities only under a licensing system that allowed "normal activities" but forbade activities such as the purchase, sale, or transfer of real property and securities; capital transactions; "unusual" accumulations of inventory; payment, transfer, or withdrawal from blocked bank accounts; and any transaction that might imperil the financial position of the business or organization involved. Other regulations restricted bank withdrawals to two hundred dollars per month for necessary living expenses, but no more than fifty dollars could be withdrawn in a single week. And any payment of wage or salary or commission to enemy aliens in excess of two hundred dollars per month had to be deposited in blocked accounts.[4]

Other restrictions had a greater impact on alien Japanese and Koreans. These restrictions prohibited possession or operation of binoculars, field glasses and telescopes, firearms or other weapons, ammunition, bombs, explosives, shortwave receivers, radio transmitters, signal devices, codes and ciphers, cameras, and papers, documents, or books containing invisible writing, photographs, or drawings of military or naval installations or equipment. Also prohibited were the writing, publishing, or printing of any attack or threat on the government, its agents, or its policies. Permission was required from the military before one could make an airline flight, change residence or working place, and undertake any travel. Enemy aliens were required to carry at all times the certificates issued to them at the time of their registration under the Alien Registration Act of 1940. Although allowed to go about their normal activities without special permission during the day, enemy aliens were more restricted than the general population in that they were required to be off the streets during blackout periods, which began earlier than the curfew for the general population.[5]

With their well-established reputation as outspoken enemies of Japan, few of the first-generation Koreans could foresee that they would become enmeshed in the security measures implemented in the wake of the Pearl Harbor attack. What was especially galling to them was that they were being treated like Japanese enemy aliens when in fact they were, and had been, more anti-Japanese than most Americans. One researcher who conducted interviews during the first year of the war noted that these older Koreans exhibited a "consistently antagonistic and suspicious attitude toward . . . alien and citizen Japanese alike."[6] While it is fair to say that Koreans were unanimous in their resentment of the restrictions placed upon them as "enemy aliens," a close examination of the Korean community during the war reveals that it was anything but united. Given the experiences of the earlier independence movement in Hawai'i, it is not surprising to find continuing dissension. This is not to say, however, that the Korean community did not try to resolve their differences.

As the Pacific War loomed, the Korean nationalist movement, which had been splintered and largely inactive since the 1920s, attempted to reunify. In April 1941, the Kungminhoe (Korean National Association, or KNA) and the Dongjihoe (Comrade Society) called a conference of all Korean groups in Honolulu to unify their political activities and pool their financial resources and personnel. Joining these two larger organizations were smaller groups such as the Korean Women's Patriotic Society, the Korean Revolutionary Party, the Korean National Emancipation Party, the Korean Independence League, the Korean Volunteer League, the National Emancipation Party, and the Sino-Korean People's League. The outcome of this conference was the establishment of the United Korean Committee (UKC), with a branch in Los Angeles. The UKC was formed to support the United States in the coming war effort, provide financial support for the Korean provisional government, now located in Chungking, maintain an office in Washington (occupied by Syngman Rhee) for propaganda, and aid Korean military activities in Asia.

One concrete manifestation of the desire to resolve differences in the Korean community was the merging of the KNA and Dongjihoe publications into a single newspaper named *Kungminbo-T'aep'yŏngyang chubo (Korean*

National Herald-Pacific Weekly). The cooperative newspaper made its first appearance on January 21, 1942, concentrating on war news, Korean contributions to the war effort, and the securing of better treatment of Koreans. Like other Hawai'i newspapers of the time, it was subject to censorship and was required to publish in English as well as Korean.[7]

After the bombing of Pearl Harbor, the UKC set about to create an executive committee consisting of ten representatives (one from each Korean organization), which would be authorized to deal directly with the martial law authorities. The Public Morale Section in the Liaison Division of the Territorial Office of Civilian Defense wanted such committees to enlist each ethnic group "in a common Territorial effort to give fullest expression of loyalty to the United States during the present emergency." On January 17, 1942, the Korean Executive Committee was organized, chaired by J. Kuang (Jacob) Dunn, with (Mrs.) Nodie Sohn as secretary, and members Won Soon Lee, Young Ki Kim, Reverends Doo Wha Lim and Chang Ho Ahn, David C. Youth, Father Noah Cho, C. D. Choy, and Miss Hasoo Whang.

The first meeting of the Korean Executive Committee took place twelve days later, on January 29, 1942. As requested, the committee submitted a report on Korean activities, such as service in kitchens for the Territorial Home Guard, sewing and collection of clothes and money for the Red Cross, and preparation of surgical dressings for the Red Cross. Also present at the meeting was a member of the martial law administration, Gordon T. Bowles, who filed an initially optimistic assessment: "My estimate of the Korean Executive Committee is that they have moderately well hurdled the difficulty of internal politics, now that they have something to get their teeth into [clarification of the status of alien Koreans], and I believe they will go on now on their own steam, with occasional prompting." In another memo written apparently in February, an anonymous writer noted that most of the Koreans "now work together relatively harmoniously. They have at least temporarily agreed to shelve their local dissensions in favor of a united program, which appears to be concerned largely with the national defense effort. At least the leaders of the different groups realize that now is not the appropriate time to agitate for Korean independence."[8]

Almost immediately, however, problems surfaced that threatened the fragile unity so recently achieved. Confidential intelligence memos placed much of the blame on one organization—the Sino-Korean People's League. It will be useful to examine this organization and its leadership as an indication of how the unity of the Korean community came apart at the seams.

One unsigned intelligence memo dated January 9, 1942, suggests that the Korean Executive Committee itself almost did not get off the ground because of the Sino-Korean People's League. The memo lays the blame at the feet of Hyŏn Sun, who was one of the league's leaders. "On Monday morning Rev.

Hyun came in for about a half hour and told me he had been at the . . . meeting held by the Koreans to try to choose an executive committee. Rev. Hyun wants to see such a committee formed, but he wants to see it independent of the United Korean Committee. Apparently it is a matter of jealousy for the control of the executive committee between himself and Mr. Lee [Won Soon]. Rev. Hyun . . . has worked himself into the position of leading man in the opposing faction to the United Korean Committee. I am told that Mr. Hyun, who is very strong willed, combines with this characteristic a changeable policy with regard to issues of importance."[9]

Yet another confidential memo the following month criticized the Sino-Korean League. "While this is a small group of only about thirty members, it is quite active, and probably the most radical. Without the consent of the other Korean organizations, this group has issued statements to the press of a somewhat unsatisfactory character, much to the consternation of the more level-headed leaders representing the bulk of the Korean population. Fortunately the following is not large and, if anything, is decreasing. The inference that Chinese are active in the League is largely misleading, since few Chinese are sympathetic." An addendum to the memo stated: "[T]he most violent member of this group is probably the Rev. Soon Hyun. This gentleman has been selected by the League to be their official spokesman. His record and activities are under scrutiny of the authorities."[10]

Another unsigned memo (probably written by Bowles) records the views of UKC member Won Soon Lee on Hyŏn's organization and offers an assessment: "Since the Sino-Korean People's League at one time was active in the forwarding of United Korean Committee they [Hyŏn's group] should now knuckle under [according to Lee] and reaffirm their desire to be associated with them again. This somewhat naive position [of Lee's] was stated rather simply as a desire to see the Korean Executive Committee function under the United Korean Committee. The controversy boils down to Hyun vs. Lee, with Appenzeller, Jacob Dunn, Miss Whang, Lim Doo Wha and myself as peace-makers."[11]

At about the same time, the Public Morale Section was called upon to make a recommendation when the league asked for permission to publish a separate periodical—The *Sino-Korean Weekly Journal.* The military government turned them down, citing a number of reasons. First, it noted that the league had only fifty regular members in contrast to the approximately one thousand members of the KNA and Dongjihoe combined. Second, it noted that the league and the two much larger organizations "are bitter rivals on political matters and the appearance of a publication by a stormy 10 percent of the active Koreans opposing the remaining 90 percent will merely increase the muddiness of what are already greatly discolored waters." Third, the appearance of a new publication would start another "mud slinging campaign." Fourth, since the league had not published a paper before the war, and since the two prewar papers had united, why change an already satisfactory arrangement? Fifth, the Filipino community was ten times the size of the Korean community but had only two newspapers. Sixth, the joint newspaper—the *Korean National Herald-Pacific Weekly*—had already demonstrated its willingness to accept articles about and on behalf of the league, and the number could be increased without difficulty. Seventh, the newspaper would no doubt be used for furthering the league rather than the best interests of all Koreans, since the league believed that their point of view was the only one worth consideration. Eighth, publication would disturb the majority of the Koreans and would be construed as bias in favor of a small minority.[12]

By April 1942, American intelligence concluded that the UKC alliance had disintegrated: "In May 1941 the SKPL agreed to unite with all others to form the UKC. The ties have not been officially renounced but personality differences grew increasingly difficult and the members gradually withdrew and largely revived their previous independent status. Technically the union still exists but in reality there is a distinct chasm. The league is anxious to cooperate with the US and feel they can best accomplish [this] by spying on the enemy and sleuthing." Since the military government still had to work with Hyŏn and his organization, a strategy was suggested: "For general consultation and cooperation with the Sino-Korean People's League and for any planning, Dunn and Y. K. Kim. Representing the Sino-Korean People's League, two key men to work with are Rev. Hyun, . . . who trusts me, and Rev. Hong. . . . These men are both very determined and adamant on their point of view but willing to compromise on a number of matters of importance."[13]

While Hyŏn was an important figure in the Sino-Korean People's League, an even more enigmatic figure was its reputed founder, Kilsoo K. Haan (Han Kilsu). Haan, who had grown up in Hawai'i, claimed that his organization had been founded in 1933 and controlled 1,500 volunteer Korean espionage agents. According to Haan, "In order to find out things, I obtained employment in the Japanese consulate in Honolulu and worked there from 1935 to 1937. I used the name of Kenneth Maida, and easily passed for a Japanese. . . . I saw with my own eyes, right in the consulate, blueprints and detailed technical information of the construction at Pearl Harbor."[14]

Another account of Haan's exploits against the Japanese, the source of which appears to be Haan himself, states:

> A Korean in his early thirties, Kilsoo K. Haan, one of the organizers of a secret anti-Japanese organization called the Sino-Korean People's League, had succeeded in deceiving attaches of the Japanese Consulate in Honolulu into believing that his sympathies lay with Japan. Haan was a young man who knew his way about the Orient. In addition to his native language, he spoke Chinese and Japanese fluently. Some time in 1935 Haan had sold attaches of

the Japanese Consulate in Honolulu on the idea that he could convert the Hawaiian Koreans into seeing things Japan's way, and the Japanese had arranged for him to take a job as a bellboy in a Honolulu hotel to act as a cover for his real activities on their behalf. The plan, as the Japanese had it figured out, was for Haan to present the picture of a poor bellboy rather than a person of affluence, and he was to circulate at Korean gathering places in Honolulu and begin a propaganda campaign of selling Japan to his own people. . . . Haan, during his "plant" in the Honolulu hotel, made it a point to listen in on every Japanese conversation within earshot. When, for example, he was summoned to a room occupied by Japanese to serve whiskey-and-soda, he would stall around on various subterfuges, or suddenly pop back into the room for something he had forgotten.[15]

Haan had first come to the attention of the American public and American politicians in October 1937, when he argued before Congress against statehood for Hawai'i because of the large number of Japanese living on the islands. Haan later testified before the House Immigration Committee in 1940 and again in 1941 alleging anti-American activities among Japanese Americans in Hawai'i. It was at about this time that Haan left Hawai'i for the mainland under somewhat of a cloud. J. Kuang Dunn of the UKC publicly accused Haan of having served the Japanese consulate solely for mercenary reasons, of having left Hawai'i because of involvement in fraud and embezzlement, and of having deluded his followers in Hawai'i in order to solicit money for himself.[16]

Despite such criticism, Haan, now on the mainland, continued to rail against Japanese Americans. In an interview in Seattle in early 1942, he suggested:

> There are far too many American leaders in Hawaii, the Pacific Coast and the national capital who are too anxious to defend the so-called rights of American citizens of Japanese ancestry, thousands of whom hold dual citizenship and who have returned to the United States after acquiring Japanese education. . . . Not until every Japanese, American-born or otherwise, is rounded up and 'put away' for the duration, will the Pacific Coast be properly protected against a planned campaign of sabotage timed to coincide with military attack. . . . Two-thirds of the Japanese-Americans are dual citizens. . . . Until these doubtful American citizens and all other Japanese are taken into protective custody the Pacific defense will not be complete. . . . The reason there has been no great outbreak of sabotage in the United States so far is that the Japanese government has ordered the Japs in this country to withhold such activity until the military attacks.[17]

Haan, Hyŏn, and the Sino-Korean People's League were, of course, not the only Koreans who accused Hawai'i's Japanese of supporting Japan. An undated memo from a prominent Korean Christian leader averred: "We know the fact that there were many subversive or 5th Columnists activities during the [Pearl

Harbor] attack by the Japanese invaders. Supposing there will be another major attack in the future, what guarantee do we have that these 160,000 Japanese in Hawaii would not concertedly cooperate with the invaders?"[18]

While Haan's claims and activities brought him a certain degree of notoriety, it also attracted the attention of the intelligence services of the United States. Initially they tolerated him: "Haan is a Hawaiian Korean with a gift for oratory, a facile tongue and a none too savory reputation when it comes to his past history and activities. These shortcomings are tolerated for the useful service he is now rendering the league." But a year later they reevaluated him and placed him under surveillance after a June 7, 1943, meeting of representatives of various intelligence agencies in Washington: "In discussing Kilsoo Haan there was general agreement that much of his propaganda and many of his actions were of the sort that the Japanese Government might desire, that an alien of shady character to be operating an intelligence organization which purports to be in contact with enemy sources and yet for the Government not to know the full details about it is an intolerable situation in wartime, and that Haan has been an important factor in sowing disunity and confusion among Koreans and in blocking the more effective alignment of the Korean movement behind the cause of the UN." At that meeting, an FBI representative characterized Haan as "an astute propagandist out to make as much money out of the situation as he could."[19]

Three weeks after that meeting, on June 28, 1943, Haan addressed a dissident CIO (Congress of Industrial Organizations) local in Detroit, and, naturally, the FBI was in attendance. The group wanted Haan to speak because they, like Haan, viewed Japanese Americans as disloyal and did not want the War Relocation Authority (WRA) to allow these "California Japanese" being held in concentration camps in the west to be relocated to Michigan. At one point the WRA toyed with the idea of having the CIO call the meeting off, but it was finally decided that the meeting would go ahead on the grounds that America believed in free speech, that the local was not influential, and that prevention of the meeting would give this local too much prominence.

The intelligence report on that meeting, which had one hundred people in attendance, began, in part, as follows: "The meeting was addressed by Kilsoo K. Haan, representative of the Sino-Korean People's League. Mr. Haan was once attached to the office of the Japanese Consul General in Hawaii. His presence in Detroit was viewed with some alarm by friends of the War Relocation Authority, whose program Haan had opposed.... According to Harry Whang, chairman of the Detroit Chapter of the Korean National Association, many Koreans in the United States were not satisfied with the way in which Mr. Haan conducted [his] affairs ... because he engaged in activities other than the sale of war bonds and the collection of funds for war relief. He has been expelled from office ... although he still remains ... influential ... by virtue of his leadership in the Sino-Korean People's League."

The report then summarized the substance of his remarks: "Finally Mr. Haan was introduced. He made four points: 1) One phase of the Japanese war plans is to undermine the internal security of the United States through infiltration into key strategic positions in Hawaii and America. 'Latest reports say the Japs are ready to attack Alaska and the West Coast this year.' 2) The Japanese Government understands America better than America understands the Japanese and Japan. 3) Too many Americans in America depend on the judgment of 'a few handfuls of former American friends of Japan and Japanese who are now considered experts on the Far Eastern affairs,' and who hold key positions which deal with Japanese problems. 4) Pro-Fascist Japanese aliens and Japanese-Americans control the majority of the Japanese in Hawaii and the United States mainland. The meeting did not discuss the question of an independent Korea after the war. The audience was weary and apparently bored by the time Mr. Haan spoke; there was no discussion afterwards. They were very quiet and orderly when they left the building."[20]

Haan by this time had set up an office in Washington, where he found himself in direct competition with Syngman Rhee, who had also taken up residence there as the official spokesperson for the UKC. In an editorial titled "Why We Oppose Dr. Rhee's Policy," Haan attacked Rhee: "Since the Jap attack on Pearl Harbor Dec. 7, 1941, many Americans have asked me, 'Why do you oppose Dr. Rhee?'" Haan gave several reasons. First, he took Rhee to task for telling the State Department that he would not encourage Koreans to fight Japan unless it granted diplomatic recognition to his [Rhee's] provisional government, a stance that led Cordell Hull to ask if Rhee's assistance was "for sale." Second, Haan accused Rhee of not taking a tough stance against Japanese Americans, because Rhee had made a distinction between the government of Japan and Japanese in America. Haan noted in this regard the absence of Japanese newspaper editorials against Rhee. Third, Haan noted Rhee's propensity for labeling his opponents communists, particularly those Koreans in China who were fighting with Chinese forces against the Japanese. Haan noted that the Japanese also called these Korean soldiers communists. Fourth, Haan harked back to events some twenty years earlier in Hawai'i, asking rhetorically why Rhee's men had smashed Park Yong-man's printing press and why a judge in Honolulu had ruled against Rhee when his followers had illegally occupied the property of the KNA. The reaction from Rhee's organization was predictable: the Chicago chapter of the Dongjihoe criticized Haan for the "sinister motive behind his irresponsible statements and falsehoods."[21]

This brief look at Haan Kilsoo, Hyŏn Sun, and the Sino-Korean People's League illustrates some of the problems the Korean nationalist movement in Hawai'i had in trying to unite in a common cause. And while Haan, Hyŏn, and their group were perhaps the most abrasive, raising the hackles of the American intelligence community as well as other Korean nationalists, other leading members of the nationalist community in Hawai'i had personalities and agendas that had the potential to engender discord. Confidential intelligence files offer a fascinating and candid glimpse at some of these key actors. They were evaluated twice, once anonymously in January 1942 and again three months later in April by Gordon Bowles.[22]

J. Kuang Dunn. **January:** "Jacob Dunn, who has spent most of his life on the mainland, has recently come here, and largely because of his non-partisan background appears to be a likely prospect as a reconciler. His position as Public Relations Chairman of the United Korean Committee makes it possible for him to be used as such in an official capacity. Dunn is not familiar with all the ins and outs of Koreanism here, and I am impressed by what appears to me to be his innocence and sincerity to act as go-between. He assured me that he is one hundred percent for the establishment of an executive committee, which would for the period of the duration supercede but not interfere with existing organizations." **April:** "Although he is aggressive, ambitious and is at present ingratiating himself with the authorities, he is the best man to work with since he is the only one who can work with all parties. The trouble with him is that while he does nothing contrary to what has been discussed with him, he does things on his own initiative which often cause trouble. Colonel Green is not going to solve the problem by giving him permission to do these things. The only way to solve the problem is to tell him point-blank to work through the Morale Section. Dunn thinks he has sold himself to me. Let him continue in this emotion and urge him to write me, if he shows any hesitation in playing ball. Dunn has certain personal matters of a private nature which somewhat becloud his relationships here but I do not believe they seriously affect his standing on community matters. He has had many discussions with Colonel Green, Colonel Fielder, G-2, especially with various naval intelligence men and the district attorney, not to mention the Governor and a host of local politicians."

Henry Cu Kim, editor of the *Korean National Herald,* the newspaper of the KNA, and secretary of the Defense Committee of the UKC. "Although a true Korean, Henry Kim is quiet, level-headed, alive to the realization that Koreans are residents of Hawaii and that this should be the principal guiding factor in their relationships here."

Won Soon Lee, chairman of the UKC, involved in real estate, prominent in Syngman Rhee's Korean Christian church, and whose wife is superintendent of the Korean Christian Institute. **January:** "Lee is probably the best balancing agent among the various factions. He can get along with business men and religious groups as well as with the quieter thinkers such as Kim [Young Ki]. Although he is not probably as keen a thinker as some of the others, he is able to evaluate fairly clearly and is disturbed that the radical factions [Haan, Hyŏn, and the Sino-Korean People's League] will not play ball. He is anxious to see more Koreans agree at the present time in getting a solid expression of their determination to work with the community here at least during the emergency." **April:** "W. W. [sic] Lee is not very broadminded. He is trying to get all Koreans to work under the United Korean Committee and hence is not too enthusiastic about our Morale Section executive committee, although he has been persuaded by Dunn that this is an advisable thing. He is concerned with the ins and outs of his own political faction, the Dong Gi Hoi and wants to hold his own place as the most important Korean but he hasn't the broad outlook necessary. He is a well-to-do business man and is at present in California at the national annual convention of the United Korean Committee."

Young Ki Kim, editor of the *Korean Civic Magazine,* who worked at Pearl Harbor and later Schofield Barracks. **January:** "He is very quiet and apparently not inclined to agitational tactics." **April:** "Y. K. Kim is broad-minded so far as comprehension is concerned. He is probably the most level-headed and one of the keenest Koreans and as editor of the paper has a controlling interest in the leadership of thought. He is a firebrand, however, for independence; a stickler for phraseology, with a Korean temper. He is not so much anti-other things as he is anti-Korean [sic]." (Bowles obviously means anti-Japanese here).

Reverend Lim Doo Wha, the minister of the Korean Methodist Church. **January:** "Wha [sic] is the most impartial of all the Koreans I have yet met. He is constantly insisting upon avoiding taking sides with any one of the several Korean factions. He uses the good psychological side-play of pointing out constantly the necessity during the present emergency for ironing out the internal ruffles. Although possibly not a very deep thinker, he is a very good balancing wheel and may be counted on always as oil on troubled waters." **April:** Rev. Lim, a Methodist minister, is well known among Koreans. On the whole, he is well liked but by some he is looked upon as being too pro this or pro that more than pro Korean because of his impartiality. He is the best man to consult on matters affecting the Korean community although I believe that Dunn is the one with whom negotiations and plans should be developed. In other words, Lim should be consulted often for quiet advice as should also Dr. Appenzeller, but Dunn is the one with whom plans should be drawn."

David Youth. **January:** "David appears to be on a trigger itch because he and other Koreans are classed as enemy aliens. I think it will be possible to get him to see a common sense point of view but I doubt if he will accept anything more than a rather sullen and griped acquiescence. He cites the injustice of Korean funds being frozen and is rather sympathetic with Korean counterespionage work. David suggests that a great deal of difficulty would be relieved if Korean accounts could be thawed. He insists upon a clarification of the status of Koreans, and suggests a strong committee to be appointed by the Military Governor to represent and apparently to push Korean interests." **April:** "Youth is a firebrand—a wealthy business man at Wahiawa—hyper Korean and practically nothing else. His words are pretty bitter in anti-Japanese expressions. He is known to be very suspicious of local Japanese citizens and aliens alike. David Youth is, however, important in the Korean community because of his radical but vigorous attitude, and thus far he has been a good consultant. He should not be relied upon too much in matters involving trusted confidence of local Japanese."

Nodie Sohn, a supporter of Syngman Rhee whose husband would soon become well known to martial law authorities. **January:** "Mrs. Sohn apparently will not be reconciled to any sort of cooperation with Japanese whether citizens or aliens. After giving a resume of how Koreans came here as Korean nationals and after describing the tragedies of her country, she asked how Koreans could be expected to be anything but 100 percent Koreans. She misunderstood the purpose of the meeting, misjudged the intentions of the committee and started off on the wrong foot altogether. At best her condition might be summarized as assuaged when she left. I believe, however, that her condition was due largely to lack of comprehension of the purpose of this initial meeting. She will certainly cooperate to the extent of getting a united Korean expression toward America. I do not believe, however, she will be very helpful in any sort of activities which might throw her into relationship with Japanese in any way, whether citizens or aliens." **April:** "Mrs. Nodi [sic] Sohn, on the other hand, is extremely anti-Japanese (both local and enemy) and her Korean patriotism takes the form of anti-Japanism. Her husband is wealthy (in Army concessions) and [she] gives her time to Korean women's relief societies and various Korean women's activities. She is the key woman but very narrow-minded."

Father Noah Cho. "Father N. Cho, an Episcopalian minister, is a very smiling and geneal [sic] soul, very quiet and relatively unbiased. His importance is primarily as a representative of Episcopalian Koreans. He is not an outstanding leader but he is very much interested in the work of the Committee and may be relied upon to take a sensible point of view. Cho is the only representative of the Sino-Korean People's League, but unfortunately, he is not very active in the league and therefore cannot serve the desired purpose by acting as a liaison. He is, however, relatively unbiased and serves as a consultant, [a] constant reminder to the two groups that their points of view are not incompatible. His usefulness is therefore internal and he should not be counted upon as being a consultant or an advisor."

Whang Hasoo. **January:** "Miss Whang is with the International work of the Y.W.C.A. She spends her time with Koreans in their homes, as one of them, but in a sense looking on from the outside. She appears to have a very impartial point of view, and is helping them to get a clear picture of the various personalities involved." **April:** "Miss Whang represents in a way Korean youth, although she has not the complete sympathy of all the leaders. She will also be a good person to consult privately about Korean matters."

Ahn Chang-ho, a Korean minister in Hawai'i (not to be confused with An Ch'ang-ho, the nationalist leader with the same name whose base had been in California until his death in 1938). "C. H. Ahn is quiet and rather unassuming and is of importance only as he represents a certain body of the community. He is likely to vote sensibly and is a powerful man."

Bowles concluded his April 1942 memo thus: "For private advice and how things are going in the Korean community and committee and an impartial point of view, Lim, Choy and Whang. The rest of the committee members are important because of their relationship to the community and the committee and are not to be considered as useful for matters of advice."

Such was the composition and attitudes of the leaders of the Korean community as seen through the eyes of the American intelligence community. But what of the bulk of the Korean population in Hawai'i? There was little question that the Koreans supported the United States against Japan. In a survey conducted during the war, Koreans were found to be more "patriotic" than part-Hawaiians, Japanese, or Chinese, with 88 percent approving of the way Roosevelt was handling the war, compared with 85 percent of the Chinese and 80 percent of the Japanese. And over half of the Koreans (54 percent—the highest rate) felt that Japan would attack again, versus the average of 23 percent.[23]

Contributing to such high rates of approval as well as the high level of suspicion toward Japan was that the noncitizen first generation was primarily oriented toward Korea and resented Japanese control, which had been in place there since 1910. Comparisons with the Chinese and Japanese in Hawai'i are instructive here. The *issei* tended to be polite and not speak of the war. First-generation Chinese opposed Japan because it had invaded China in 1931 and again in 1937, although the Chinese usually maintained a distinction between the warring nations abroad and their Japanese neighbors in Hawai'i. But not only were the first-generation Koreans hostile toward Japan, but sometimes, as we have seen, also toward Japanese Americans in Hawai'i. Hostility toward local Japanese may also have been due to local factors, with one account stating that Koreans "have met rebuffs, large and trivial, of the numerically superior and dominant Japanese population," while another account averred that "the Japanese in Hawaii kept the Koreans down in every way possible." Manifestations of this attitude appeared when Koreans wanted Japanese Americans dismissed from the Territorial Guard and disapproved of the formation of an all *nisei* battalion. In addition, people could not help but notice the efforts Koreans made to distance themselves from Japanese. One non-Korean stated:

"I am inclined to conceive of the Korean as an excessively proud individual, more indignant when mistaken for a Japanese than is the Chinese."[24]

In contrast to their parents, second-generation Koreans, as American citizens, were not subject to the restrictions imposed on "enemy aliens." Moreover, the second generation was not usually hostile toward local Japanese in Hawai'i and made a clear distinction between Japan and Japanese Americans. As one commentator noted, "Hawaiian-born [Koreans] don't care and don't take sides." One thing they shared with their parents, however, was their resentment over the suggestion that they might possess dual nationality or owe some allegiance to Japan because their mothers had come to Hawai'i as picture brides with Japanese passports.[25]

Although the *ilse* sometimes did not distinguish between Japanese in Japan and Japanese in Hawai'i, they were able to distinguish between Japanese and Koreans who served in the Japanese Imperial Army, a distinction that was sometimes lost on their children.

Recently a lot of Korean prisoners of war have been working on the gov't areas in Wahiawa. The old Korean people seem to have a sentimental feeling toward them rather than the hostile feeling that would ordinarily exist between the people of the enemy country and our country. They feel that they should provide these Korean prisoners with sweets and delicacies to cheer them up just because they were Koreans. I was pretty mad over this as I felt that they were still enemy prisoners even if they were Koreans. I guess that these old Koreans have a feeling of ethnocentrism towards these other unfortunate Koreans who are prisoners. I probably don't understand the reason for it as I've been brought up with American ideas and Korea is nothing to me except that it [is] the place where my ancestors came from. This is a rather difficult situation for the older Koreans as they are torn between loyalty to the United States and feeling for these PW Koreans who might be, perhaps, a close relative.[26]

As American citizens, second-generation Koreans also served in the war against Japan and thus indirectly proclaimed their patriotism. One young man who had been sent to Korea for his schooling put his language skills to good use: "When war broke out, Yee became a Korean-Japanese-English interpreter for the army. Since he was excellent in his Oriental languages, the army drilled English into him and got in return a person who could 'crack' the Japanese code on Guam." Another Korean family saw both brothers and husbands in the service of the American armed forces: "Our family was adjusting well to wartime living when suddenly a stark letter from my brother Young Mahn arrived one morning, notifying us he had been shipped out to 'somewhere in the Pacific' with the 298th Infantry. . . . My husband [in 1944] said he was ready to join the armed forces. . . . Our son was only two months old when my husband was called to combat duty. . . . No sooner did my brother Young Chul turn eighteen in February 1945, but he too was called to serve. Now we had three men from our family in the U.S. Armed Forces."[27]

Because of the anti-Japanese orientation of Koreans, some of the enemy alien regulations in Hawai'i were not rigidly enforced against them by the martial law authorities. Alien Koreans were allowed to work in some areas where alien Japanese were not. Liquor licenses were granted to Koreans but denied to Japanese. Koreans were able to ignore the ban on the possession of short-wave radios and cameras. Clearly there was a tacit understanding that in some areas alien Koreans were to be distinguished from alien Japanese, but these exceptions were not specifically stated in any of the published regulations, and many restrictions were in fact enforced. For example, Koreans could not change their place of residence or employment without permission. And Koreans received discriminatory treatment in the purchase of drugs and medical supplies until well into 1943. Nor were they permitted to travel by air—a Korean was denied permission to fly from Maui to Oahu because of his status as an enemy alien. In another example of restrictions, a prominent Korean physician, Y. C. Yang (later the Korean ambassador to the United States), volunteered for the army immediately after the attack on Pearl Harbor, was accepted and commissioned, and worked for a number of days without pay before being dismissed when it was realized he was an alien.[28]

One key restriction involved employment in defense projects or on military bases, where nearly eight hundred Koreans made their living. Here, too, there were contradictory policies. Some first-generation Koreans were dismissed, as the following account, written by a grandson, details: "In 1941 Mr. Lee [Man-kee] became a truck driver for Hickam [Air] Field Cleaners. War broke out in 1941 and Mr. Lee was refused work at Hickam Field, being an alien. He was rather furious about this decision, since he was a Korean and Koreans were noted enemies of the Japanese. The next day he went back to work [in] the Laundry Shop." Occasionally, and inexplicably, some second-generation Koreans found themselves out of a job as well: "[M]y Korean girl friend [r]ecently . . . wrote to me saying that she was discharged from her job. She held a governmental position. The reason she lost her job was that her parents were born in Korea."[29]

Other Koreans were able to keep their jobs in military areas but were forced to identify themselves as enemy aliens. Those so affected were required to exchange their white-bordered identification badges for black-bordered badges of the type issued to persons of Japanese ancestry and used to restrict the wearer's movements within defense areas. The protests of the workers won only a small concession: the words "I am Korean" were stamped across the bottom of their new badges. Yet even here exceptions were made. One second-generation Korean remembered that his father, who as a sheet metal worker fixed broken military aircraft, had a white badge, unlike most other alien Koreans.[30]

Exceptions notwithstanding, the *ilse* understandably remained upset that

they were treated as enemy aliens. The notion that they were sympathetic to
Japan rankled in the hearts and minds of Koreans who had been struggling for
independence from Japan since annexation in 1910. For many it was the classification itself rather than the inconvenience that bothered them. One Korean
recalled that they were hardly affected by martial law and the curfew, which for
enemy aliens was earlier than for others. For some the curfew simply meant
having dinner out earlier than usual: "My new husband and I hurried to the
dinner, for the guests would have to leave for their homes before the eight
o'clock curfew." Another said, "Of course, we Koreans do not worry much about
going to bed early or stay[ing] in the house after blackout time in the nights, as
we are all hard working people and need rest and good sleep, but what we are
greatly concerned about is that we are classified as ENEMY aliens. Japanese
say Koreans are Number One enemy to Japan, and our American friends put
us on the enemy side, while we are trying to show our loyalty. . . . It is really
hard to understand."[31]

This enemy classification of non-citizen first-generation Koreans also irritated their second-generation American children: "I am heartsick and sore. . . .
I act, speak and think like an American. . . . I never thought of myself as anything but an American. My parents have always taught my sister and I to be
good Americans. And for themselves they always thought of the United States
as their liberator. . . . Why should the alien Koreans be classified as enemies
and let them pass the taint to their children, when they hate the Japs and taught
their children to hate the Japs?"[32]

Spurred by these feeling, Koreans began what was to be a long-term effort
to remove the enemy alien stigma and the restrictions that accompanied the
label. Initially, they sought to have the restrictions against them lifted based on
the fact that Koreans had been permitted to register as Koreans rather than as
Japanese under the Alien Registration Act of 1940. Koreans on the mainland
who had registered as Koreans under that Act were for the most part free of
the kinds of restrictions visited upon alien Japanese, such as forced internment
during the war. Indeed, Justice Department regulations dealing with alien
Japanese specifically exempted Koreans. But once martial law was declared in
Hawai'i, the Justice Department had no authority in the islands, and the treatment of Koreans was determined by the military governor, regardless of how
Koreans may have registered in 1940.[33]

Koreans also attempted to change their enemy alien status with letters,
cables, petitions, and personal representations to public officials in Washington. After the Pearl Harbor attack, one of the first targets of this campaign was
the State Department, because Korean leaders linked their enemy status to the
United States' refusal to recognize Korean independence and a Korean government in exile. After all, the United States recognized the Chinese nationalist government of Chiang Kai-shek in Chungking. On December 16, 1941, the

UKC in Hawai'i cabled Secretary of State Cordell Hull, pointing out that most of the alien Koreans in Hawai'i had left Korea before annexation and had themselves never submitted to Japanese authority. It appealed for a designation as "friendly aliens" so that Koreans might be spared the "undeserved stigma of an enemy at war with the United States." Hawai'i's delegate to Congress, Samuel Wilder King, called for both reclassification of Korean aliens and formal recognition of a Korean government in exile. The State Department, however, was not in a position to change the status of Koreans in Hawai'i nor was it persuaded of the value of recognizing the Korean provisional government, so the appeals were turned away with noncommittal replies and references to the Justice Department. But the Justice Department could not overrule the martial law authorities in Hawai'i. Thus neither the State Department nor the Justice Department wielded much influence in Hawai'i.[34]

Koreans also pressed for reclassification through the Public Morale Section. The Korean Executive Committee was unanimous in reporting that the greatest need of the Koreans in Hawai'i was clarification of their legal status. The committee also reported that Koreans were deterred from contributing to the war effort by purchasing war bonds because any bonds they bought were classified as enemy alien property and impounded. On the other hand, the committee stressed Korean loyalty and the desire to participate in the war effort in every way possible, including military service, and it downplayed Korean hostility toward the Japanese in Hawai'i. It also pleaded for reclassification: "The Koreans in being enemies of Japan are determined to help this country and allied nations to bring about an immediate defeat of the Japanese Government, and to suffer the restrictions placed on them as enemy aliens is felt deeply and sensitively." Lifting the freeze on the funds of alien Koreans was suggested as a first step toward reclassification.[35]

Although the Public Morale Section did support the reclassification of Koreans, it was clearly troubled by the main focus of Korean activities: "[T]heir primary concern appears to be still foreign to our American problems. . . . [T]he most important immediate objective is to find their place in the concern of the large national problems of this country." Another memo elaborated: "The UKC supports an old scholar somewhat pompous and rather ineffective speaker, Dr. Syngman Rhee in Washington. The main purpose of the UKC is to agitate for [recognition] of immediate independence of the KPG by China and the US."[36]

Given the direction of the flow of Korean financial donations, this assessment of the focus of Korean activities would seem to be accurate. For example, in 1943, the UKC set its annual budget at $60,000 of which $40,000 was to be raised in Hawai'i. Of the total, $30,000 was to be sent to the Korean provisional government in Chungking and $15,000 to Rhee's Korean Commission in Washington. Quoting the Public Morale Section worker: "The adult Koreans

here are interested first of all in the liberation of their land. They are only sec-
ondarily interested in America. As long as helping America will help Korea,
they will do what they can." He went on to suggest that agitation for a change
in status and lifting of the financial freeze were valued more for the attention
they would bring to the Korean cause than for the improved conditions they
would create for alien Koreans.[37]

Despite this reservation, the Public Morale Section worker prepared a
memorandum recommending that alien Koreans be officially classified as
"friendly aliens." The memorandum pointed out that the Japanese government
itself distinguished between those of Korean and Japanese ancestry and delib-
erately discriminated against the former. It suggested that this distinction
would be a convenient basis for the proposed reclassification and noted that a
separate category for Koreans had been virtually established in the 1940 census and Alien Registration Act. And it predicted that the change would dispel
the feeling of injustice harbored by Koreans and would result in more enthusiastic support of the war effort. Moreover, it concluded, there seemed to be no
means by which Japan could benefit from the change. The memo was based in
part on a paper written by the UKC that emphasized the distinctions between
the Korean and Japanese people in cultural and political matters and said that
Koreans were not disgruntled by restrictions necessary for the territory's security and could be expected to participate even more in defense work if "the
revolting technicality" of being classed as Japanese subjects was changed. It
expressed appreciation for the extralegal privileges already granted, which constituted a kind of unofficial recognition, but declared that "to be continuously
placed in the ranks of the enemy aliens is frankly mentally damaging."[38]

Despite all this urging, including that of its own Public Morale Section, the
military still refused to change the status of Koreans from enemy aliens to
friendly aliens. Nonetheless, the Koreans got some relief when Governor Poindexter lifted financial controls on Koreans in March 1942 by designating them
"generally licensed nationals." This allowed Koreans to conduct business without special licenses and permitted withdrawal of any amount from their bank
accounts.[39]

The governor's measure, while welcome, still fell short of what Koreans
wanted—to be considered allies in the war against Japan. And so the campaign
continued. A petition to Lieutenant General Delos C. Emmons from the UKC
recounted the history of guerrilla attacks against Japanese in Korea since 1905,
the establishment of the Korean provisional government in Shanghai and its
declaration of war against Japan, and its participation with the Chinese in the
war against Japan since 1937. It also cited the privileges already granted to
Koreans without damage to the war effort or security: the easing of the financial freeze; exclusion from Justice Department enemy-alien restrictions on the
mainland; exclusion from the West Coast relocation program; permission for

Koreans in California to form their own unit of the State Guard; and the lenient treatment of Koreans in Hawai'i under military rule. What was desired now, the petition noted, was formal recognition of Koreans as "friendly aliens." All this was to no avail, however.[40]

While the Koreans primarily tried to persuade the military government in Hawai'i and the national government in Washington, they also attempted to make their case to the public at large. Koreans in Hawai'i did their best to maintain the distinction between themselves and the Japanese in the public eye. They did this by carrying special identification cards, buttons, and automobile stickers prepared by Korean nationalist organizations. And women began wearing their traditional Korean-style dresses more frequently to emphasize that they were not Japanese. Commenting on the behavior of Korean women during this period, one observer noted: "There were many cases of old Korean ladies dressed in their white, native costumes (to show the authorities that they were not Japanese women) who were caught on the street after black-out. In more than one case one of these women loudly asserted that she was a Korean in her native tongue and scolded the policeman for stopping them. As you would expect they were taken down to the police station in a police-wagon. . . . There is something strange in the 'night hawking' of these old ladies because prior to the war they never had any intense craving to go to the movies at nights; if they did go out it was just for a friendly visit."[41]

Other efforts were made through the printed word, primarily through the English-language section of the *Korean National Herald-Pacific Weekly*. Editorials argued that Koreans were not Japanese but a distinctly separate people, had never professed loyalty to Japan, had received no benefits from the Japanese government, had declared themselves enemies of Japan since the annexation of Korea in 1910, had come to Hawai'i on Korean passports, and had been loyal to the United States. In addition, they stated, the U.S. government had on numerous occasions recognized Koreans as distinct from Japanese, having listed Koreans separately in its censuses, had supported Korean workers in California in their rejection of a Japanese consul's attempt to represent them in a 1913 dispute, and had allowed Koreans to enter the country without passports between 1913 and 1916. Although barred from naturalization, the editorials argued that Koreans had been "loyal to the principles, practices and institutions of the US" and "by every reason and act of history an enemy of Japan."[42]

After more than a year without a change in status, the newspaper further editorialized: "In spite of all our strenuous efforts to get away from that hateful appellation, a Japanese subject or an enemy alien, that name is repeatedly tagged onto us by this and that authority, totally against our will. Is there in this world a worse Jap hater than a Korean? The most ready answer from all those who know anything about those two peoples would be an emphatic no! . . . The reason why some authorities insist on pushing a friend, of however meager means, away into the category of an enemy, is quite beyond the grasp of the unsophisticated mind of a Korean. . . . The Koreans are willing to do anything within their power to get rid of this hideous and tormenting tag. . . . Were not all American people or their forebears once fugitive from some form of tyranny themselves?"[43]

In the spring of 1943, the cause of the Koreans was taken up by Hawai'i's two major newspapers. Referring to the situation as "an injustice and a tragedy," the *Honolulu Star-Bulletin* observed that Koreans were being "stigmatized by inclusion with the people who have proved their worst enemies, their most ruthless exploiters, their most implacable oppressors. . . . [I]t is outrageous that Koreans should continue to be treated as enemy aliens." Two months later the same newspaper editorialized that the classification of Koreans was "a legalistic interpretation which needs to be knocked out, and knocked out quickly. If any country and its people deserve kindness and mercy and sympathy and under-standing and help from the United States it is Korea and the Korean people." The *Honolulu Advertiser* was also supportive, although in a more guarded fash-ion. It suggested that Congress take up the matter and counseled Koreans to "bear their cross with all possible patience, finding what comfort they can in the knowledge that American sympathy is with them." At the same time, the news-paper also suggested that part of the reason for the predicament of the Kore-ans was their own political infighting.[44]

Concurrently with these efforts, Koreans in Hawai'i attempted to build their image as cooperative allies through participation in defense-related activities, such as volunteer work and financial contributions to the war effort. Koreans raised over one thousand dollars for the American Red Cross in the spring of 1942, and a "Korean Victory Drive" in 1943 raised more than $26,000, which was sent to President Roosevelt for use in fighting Japan. One Korean remem-bered how this effort played itself out in her own family: "My father hired a young, capable seamstress, so my mother was relieved of her work at the fac-tory. She then found time to devote to community work. . . . A large number of Korean women volunteered daily at the Red Cross. With them my mother devoted hours and hours to rolling bandages. She also made contacts from house to house selling U.S. War Bonds. . . . In our family alone each of us chil-dren owned numerous twenty-five-dollar bonds; our parents bought them in larger denominations."[45]

Koreans also submitted recommendations on the defense of the territory— tinged, to be sure, with an anti-Japanese bias. They argued, for example, that Japanese residents should be kept under closer surveillance, since, in the event of a Japanese invasion of Hawai'i, Koreans could be the first attacked in any internal uprising by resident Japanese and Japanese Americans. They also gave reassurances, both privately and publicly, that despite the intensity of their hatred for the Japanese, they would cooperate in the maintenance of order and would refrain from inflammatory attacks on Japanese residents. Korean charity did not extend, however, to allowing Japanese residents to use the Korean Christian Church in Honolulu as an evacuation shelter in case of an emergency. All of these efforts failed to change their classification. When new enemy-alien regulations were issued in March 1943, there was still no exemption for Koreans.[46]

Soon afterward, the "enemy alien" issue received its greatest public exposure when a Korean civic leader, Sohn Syung Woon, was arrested for violation of the curfew. Sohn, fifty-nine years old, had come to Hawai'i in 1905 and owned a shoe repair business. He was also active in Korean independence activities as the president of Syngman Rhee's Dongjihoe. Sohn's wife, Nodie, had served as superintendent of Rhee's Korean Christian Institute, was an officer of the Dongjihoe, and was a close friend of Rhee's. On the evening of March 28, 1943, Sohn's car stalled, preventing him from reaching his home before the beginning of blackout at 7:45 P.M. He was arrested by two Honolulu policemen—one of them a Japanese American—at 8:15 P.M., charged with violating the regulations prohibiting enemy aliens from being out during blackout, and released on fifty dollars bail. The case received no publicity until April 30, when Sohn appeared to answer the charge in the provost court.

During the hearing, Sohn's attorney argued that Sohn deserved to be treated as a friendly alien because he had left Korea on a Korean passport before the Japanese annexation and had made himself known as an enemy of Japan through his participation in Korean patriotic organizations. He had remained an alien only because American law denied him the privilege of naturalization. The lawyer also cited the attorney general's ruling on the status of Koreans on the mainland as precedent for more lenient treatment, although he conceded that it was not binding on the War Department. The provost judge expressed sympathy for Sohn's predicament and that of other alien Koreans but maintained that he was bound by the general orders of the military governor and had no choice but to find Sohn guilty. He fined Sohn ten dollars, with payment suspended. While this was not the only instance of a Korean alien being arrested for a curfew violation, the Sohns were not willing to let the matter drop.[47]

Sohn petitioned General Emmons for a review of his conviction, but Emmons declined to reverse the findings of the provost court, declaring, in effect, that Koreans would continue to be treated as enemy aliens under the curfew regulations. Sohn's wife, Nodie, then sought the intervention of Syngman Rhee, who responded with a promise to take the issue to Congress: "US seems to be at war with Korea rather than Japan," Rhee wrote to her in late April. "Send Jap police to arrest a Korean patriotic leader is almost the awfulest thing I ever heard of. . . . We are determined to find out who is running this country, the Americans or the Japs." Rhee at that moment was facing a serious challenge to his domination of the independence movement in the United States. Months of friction over his position vis-à-vis the UKC had led to the suspension of that organization's monthly payments to support his Washington office and to a serious effort, especially among UKC leaders in Los Angeles, to force Rhee aside in favor of new leadership. Rhee counterattacked by making charges against the Los Angeles leaders and encouraging a separatist movement among his supporters in California. One observer, admittedly an opponent of Rhee, viewed Rhee's interest in the Sohn case cynically as an attempt to solidify his position in Hawai'i.[48]

Whatever Rhee's motive, he was quickly in touch with Hawai'i's congressional delegate, Joseph R. Farrington, officials in the War Department, Secretary of State Henry L. Stimson, and President Roosevelt. Farrington joined Rhee's appeals, writing to Assistant Secretary of War John J. McCloy to ask whether the Sohn conviction would be allowed to stand, and if so, how this could be reconciled with the treatment of Koreans as friendly aliens in so many other matters. An official at the War Department replied that the local military commander in Hawai'i had determined that "because of military necessity" alien Koreans should continue to be classified as enemy aliens. The official said that he was not at liberty to explain why this was insisted upon, but pointed out that virtually all the privileges of friendly aliens were being extended to Koreans despite their classification, and he suggested that Farrington "quiet the fears of Koreans by informing them that the Hawaiian Department does and will give careful consideration to all individual cases so that no injustice will be occasioned to any loyal Korean."[49]

Stimson's reply to Rhee on July 7, 1943, listed the various privileges already extended to Koreans in Hawai'i and gave assurances that the War Department valued the cooperation of Koreans and their opposition to Japan. Nevertheless, because of "military necessity" and in the interest of "internal security," it was considered essential that the few remaining restrictions be enforced. Rhee also received a reply from Assistant Secretary of State Adolf A. Berle, Jr. on behalf of Roosevelt on July 12, denying Rhee's claim that the authorities in Hawai'i had violated regulations in holding Sohn as an enemy alien and emphasizing the "special conditions prevailing in Honolulu and nearby areas" that made it essential to allow the local commander considerable discretion.[50]

Despite the flurry of activity that surrounded the Sohn case, then, there was no apparent movement toward a change of status. After General Emmon's refusal to reverse Sohn's conviction, the *Korean National Herald-Pacific Weekly* observed: "Koreans of Hawaii, disappointed and depressed at the thought of being classed as enemy aliens by military authorities here, are in a state of mental agony and suffering. . . . Korean national conscience is clear beyond doubt no matter what the technicality of law interpretation may class them. . . . No matter how much the Koreans bemoan the enemy alien status, let's prove ourselves worthy of being called the American ally. Let us work harder and sweat more to accelerate the war efforts. . . . The American sense of justice and fairness will eventually prevail." The two local papers also weighed in against the decision, with the result that "although very indignant, the Koreans were some-what calmed when editorials and articles appeared in local papers stating that the law was unjust to the Koreans."[51]

The enforcement of enemy-alien curfew regulations on Koreans—which had come to symbolize enemy-alien status itself—was finally dropped with lit-tle fanfare on December 4, 1943, when the military government promulgated General Order 45. This order amended earlier orders relating to curfew restrictions and enemy aliens, adding a specific exemption for Koreans. The change coincided with the publication on December 1 of the Cairo Declara-tion, in which the United States, Great Britain, and China declared their deter-mination "that in due course Korea shall become free and independent." The official army history states that it was in keeping with this declaration that the curfew restriction was lifted. However, in view of the oft-expressed concern about internal security, in all likelihood the Cairo Declaration was found to be a convenient pretext for dropping a policy that could no longer be rationally defended in a way that involved minimum embarrassment. Six months later, on May 6, 1944, General Order 59, issued by Lieutenant General Robert C. Rich-ardson, military governor of Hawaiʻi, formally removed the stigma of enemy aliens from Koreans. And five months later, in October 1944, martial law was revoked.[52]

So why was the policy toward Koreans put in place originally? The answer is provided by Michael Macmillan, the leading interpreter of the Korean war-time experience in Hawaiʻi. Clearly, the policy was based on considerations of national security. Reference to national security often appeared in governmen-tal replies to inquiries about the status of Koreans. For example, Stimson told Rhee that intensive surveillance would continue to be necessary because Axis sympathizers were thought to be operating in the guise of refugees and foreign nationals. And a War Department memorandum prepared for the Sohn case contended that although it had not seemed essential to hold alien Koreans to all of the original limitations placed on enemy aliens, "nevertheless, consider-ations of internal security . . . made it necessary to treat Koreans as enemy aliens for purposes of certain restrictions."

The War Department's policy was based on the assessment provided by three intelligence agencies: army intelligence (G-2), naval intelligence, and the FBI in Hawaiʻi, which worked together on all matters touching on internal security, espionage, and subversive activities. Of these three services, it was the naval intelligence office in Hawaiʻi that was "particularly insistent that alien Koreans in Hawaii should retain their present status as enemy aliens and should not be regarded as friendly aliens" when the matter was considered in early May 1943, shortly after Sohn's conviction. Army intelligence and the FBI did not challenge this assessment. At the War Department, the assessment was weighed against the fact that there had been few protests against the policy in

Hawaiʻi and the opinion that the protests to Washington were largely based on the desire of a few Korean political leaders to further their own ends. The result was a recommendation that the policy be affirmed.[53]

What, then, were the specific reasons these intelligence agencies gave for considering Koreans a threat to national security? First, many alien Koreans were believed to have ties to Japan through families or other relatives living in Korea or in Japan; many of them were said to have made trips to those countries. Second, many Koreans were said to "have connections which might allow them to sell their services to the highest bidder." In particular, Haan Kilsoo was "known to have a private pipeline of information from Tokyo which could be assumed to work in both directions." Haan was reported by naval intelligence to have worked as an informant for both the Japanese consulate in Honolulu and for the American military intelligence services, making him highly suspect. Third, Korean nationalist leaders were said to "appear to be opportunists who are more interested in personal aggrandizement than they are in organizing a movement representing sincere expression of a people who desire to maintain their own national integrity." Fourth, it was contended that language problems would make the work of counterintelligence officers and police more difficult if alien Koreans were classified as friendly aliens. "It is almost impossible to distinguish between Koreans and Japanese by sight alone, and Japanese who speak Korean might try to represent themselves as Koreans," it was argued. Fifth, a change of status for Koreans "might provide an opening wedge for the Formosans, Okinawans, and other colonists not of pure Japanese blood." And finally, existing restrictions were not severe and affected only about 2,500 people, but to exempt these people would unduly strain intelligence agencies by making it necessary to process them through alien hearing boards, as had been done with many Japanese, and this, in turn, would only "invite further unrest and give their leaders a stronger platform for protest."[54]

These concerns hardly give an impression of a compelling threat to the security of the islands and, indeed, seem as weighted with political considerations as with genuine fears of national security. The only person actually named as a possible threat, Haan Kilsoo, was not even in Hawaiʻi during the war, although he did have a small following among the members of the Sino-Korean People's League, which he represented in Washington. He was, it should be noted, as widely distrusted among Koreans as he was among American officials. Although investigated by the FBI, no charges were brought against him, nor was it ever proved that he actually had the network of secret agents he claimed to command. Office of Strategic Services (OSS) reports to Washington likewise reflect an absence of firm evidence of Korean disloyalty or espionage. These reports indicated that prior to December 7, 1941, the Japanese consulate had had on its payroll three Koreans, only one of whom denied it. Besides these three, there was the case of a Korean Buddhist priest who was said to be a "good Japanese scholar" and "a likely tool." The FBI had investigated him but had "found nothing definite." These were the most specific allegations the OSS could report. In sum, there was ample suspicion but not a single case in which investigation had warranted the arrest of a Korean.[55]

In the development of a policy toward alien Koreans, these suspicions, nebulous as they were, and the cynical views of the aims of Korean nationalist leaders must have been combined with an awareness that the Koreans in Hawai'i were a small minority with neither significant influence nor the power to challenge successfully any policy adopted. Moreover, the military was well aware that this minority was splintered by political differences, making it unlikely that there could arise the kind of united action that might force revision of the policy before the military was itself ready to make changes.[56]

In general, the policy toward Koreans was characterized by the same better-safe-than-sorry thinking that marked many wartime activities. But if the evidence supporting the decision to restrict alien Koreans in Hawai'i was no more substantial than that discussed above, then one may fairly conclude that the Korean community as a whole was treated unjustly. Of course, the magnitude of the injustice does not approach that of the injury done to the hundreds of thousands of Japanese, alien and citizen alike, who were incarcerated in concentration camps during the war. Nor does it compare to what Stalin in the Soviet Union did in 1937, when he forcibly transported by boxcar nearly two hundred thousand Koreans from the area near Vladivostok to the Central Asian republics of Uzbekistan and Kazakhstan. Michael Macmillan's concluding thoughts on this episode deserve to be quoted here without abridgment: "In contrast to the approach adopted on the mainland by the Department of Justice, the policy invoked by the military governor of Hawaii, with its deceptive claim of treating Koreans on an individual, case-by-case basis, was a perversion of the American ideals of individual responsibility and presumption of innocence. Those ideals would have been better honored by a policy that presumed the loyalty of all except those against whom some specific allegation could be brought."[57]

Once martial law and the enemy-alien restriction against Koreans were lifted, the unity of the Korean community, which had been tenuous at best, once again dissolved. For example, in 1944 Syngman Rhee's Dongjihoe withdrew from the UKC alliance and reestablished the separate publication of its official organ, the *T'aep'yŏngyang chubo (Korean Pacific Weekly)*, to rally support for the Korean provisional government in China and for Rhee's Korean Commission in Washington. Rhee was now aiming to assume the leadership of a liberated Korea after the defeat of Japan. And a non-Korean who attended a Korean meeting in Honolulu in 1944 noted: "My personal observation at a recent group discussion of the Korean problem was that the Korean groups here in Hawaii . . . differ so greatly in their opinions that the problem seems not to be consolidating the Korean homeland after independence is won but rather attempting to transcend their party lines and regional or local differences so that they will be able to work together in harmony and in the most efficient way possible."[58]

Despite the disputes amongst their leaders, the reaction among the first-generation Koreans in Hawai'i when Japan surrendered on August 15, 1945, was predictable: "My parents and their compatriots in Hawaii were jubilant beyond words when they learned of Japan's capitulation to the Allies. They rejoiced! They believed Korea would be freed at last of Japan's imperialist rule." And the local newspapers reported that "Koreans will take off their white kimonos, national badge of mourning, which was adopted after 1910."[59]

While a few now turned their focus to the politics of a postwar independent Korea, the vast majority of the first-generation Koreans, now nearing retirement, with children and grandchildren who were American citizens, turned their attention once again to leading a normal life in the Territory of Hawai'i.

12

Epilogue—The Postwar Years

With the liberation of Korea from Japanese rule in 1945, Korea was once again an independent nation. When they had first arrived, some of the immigrants had entertained hopes of someday returning to Korea, with the wherewithal to live out the rest of their lives in relative comfort from savings accumulated from years of hard work in Hawai'i. But in 1945, their advanced age and the fact that many had American-citizen children and even grandchildren with established homes and jobs made the prospect of returning to Korea unlikely.

Consider the dilemma of one first-generation Korean when presented with an opportunity to return, as told from a second-generation viewpoint:

> I've heard many of the older Koreans (Koreans of the first generation) say they want to go back to Korea after the war. They want to see their country, their parents and all the people they know. They also believe that Korea will offer many promising opportunities for businessmen after the war is over and Korea is free again. A Korean man came to see my father one day for just that reason. He believed that my father would want to return to Korea too and he wanted my father to be a partner to him in starting a business there. He had great plans for a future in Korea, his native land. I know some parents who wanted to return to Korea a long time ago but were held back because of their children. The children, born in Hawaii, are reluctant to go to Korea which they consider a foreign country. Some believe that Korea is a very backward country and are surprised to know that there are buses, large department stores, and even universities there. The children are also held back because of their inability to converse in the native language. They believe this is a great handicap to them . . . [as] . . . they have a slight foundation of the language.[1]

Others were reluctant to return to Korea after the war because they had visited Korea prior to it and found the gap between life in Hawai'i and life in Korea too wide to bridge. For example, one picture bride who had originally come to Hawai'i in 1922 returned to Korea in 1932 to visit her sick mother for three months. Reflecting on the experience, she said: "Now, I cannot live in

Korea, very difficult. Only visits I enjoy because I've been living in America too long. After ten years living the American way, I went back to Korea. Very difficult, very hard, very hard to use the bathroom. I cannot stay there because everything is difficult. . . . Everything primitive, very, very difficult, you know. . . . Before I visited Korea, I like going back to Korea to live. . . . Then I went to Korea after ten years and I change my mind. . . . I made up my mind to make my life here. In May, 1955 I became an American citizen." Another picture bride had a similar experience, as her daughter relates: "In my third year of high school it became necessary that I took up the household duties at home for mother had gone to visit relatives in Korea. . . . When mother returned she brought back poor reports of relatives and the conditions in general. She expressed that she would never want to leave Hawaii again. Both mother and father have so changed that it would be unendurable for them to go back to our native land to live and for us children it would be impossible."[2]

As a result, few first-generation Koreans returned to Korea permanently after the war. If they did go at all, it was likely for brief visits as tourists. Others—both the first and second generation—went to Korea as part of the American military government either as servicemen or civilian advisers, but these trips were also temporary. Yet while most of the first generation did not return to Korea, they remained keenly attuned to Korean domestic politics.[3]

In fact, the only first-generation Koreans who seriously entertained notions of a permanent return to Korea were a few of those younger figures who had come to Hawai'i during 1910–1920 and who had been active in the independence movement. This small group returned to engage in Korean domestic politics, based on their nationalist record abroad. Syngman Rhee was the most prominent of these, but he was not the only one. For example, nine members of the United Korean Committee (UKC) went to Seoul after a meeting in October 1945 in Honolulu to assist the newly independent country. Predictably, the fractiousness that had characterized Korean nationalist politics in Hawai'i was now transferred to Korea. As one—an anti-Rhee figure—recalled: "When Syngman Rhee plunged into Korean politics . . . he repeated what he had been doing to the Korean community in America during all the years of his stay in the United States, stirring up and creating opposition between parties. . . . In spite of his history of having created constant dissension between political groups, Rhee was still popular among a considerable number of people in Korea who did not know him well, but knew by hearsay of his popularity abroad. Therefore, the warnings of the [UKC] delegation from America, based upon their bitter experience, went unheeded. Frustrated and disillusioned, the delegation decided to return home after nine months' stay in Korea."[4]

The arrival of Rhee in Korea did not end the factional struggles in Hawai'i; rather, it meant that these struggles took on a transnational character. One such struggle took place within the confines of the Korean Christian Church, which supported Rhee and his Dongjihoe. In 1943, a new minister, Reverend Kingsley K. Lyu, ordained and trained in Methodism, arrived from the U.S. mainland to take up the position as pastor at the invitation of Rhee. But Lyu soon ran afoul of Rhee and his supporters. The story that follows is told from Lyu's perspective.[5]

Upon assuming his position as pastor, Lyu was disturbed to find that some in the congregation would talk about Korean politics, sometimes loudly, during prayers and the sermon. At times, fistfights occurred on the church grounds. In response, the new minister attempted to separate politics from religion by prohibiting political meetings at the church—a policy that was approved by the church board. When a woman's political group attempted to meet at the church and was informed of the new policy, some agreed to comply with the new regulations, but others decided to defy Lyu and the church board, verbally attacking those who abided by the rules. Many of those who opposed the new regulations were staunch supporters of Rhee.

At this time, the church treasurer was discovered embezzling church funds and was dismissed from his post. The ex-treasurer allied himself with the faction that opposed the new regulations and began to accuse Lyu of being anti-Rhee for not repeating Rhee's name in prayers. This faction demanded the resignation of Lyu, and when the church board refused they stormed the pulpit on September 29, 1946, beating the minister and then dragging out and beating many of his elderly supporters. Rhee, by now in Korea, supported this faction, disappointing those who supported both the minister and Rhee. That Rhee opposed Lyu became evident in a fall 1947 radiogram from Rhee in Seoul to the president of the Dongjihoe that read: "All Koreans in and out of Korea except Reds are working for national cause. Liliha Dongjihoi *Chibangbo* [a newspaper] subversive attitude intollerable [sic]. Dismiss at once Reverend Lyu and keep him and all those supporting him out of church and Dongjihoi. All loyal members get together and agree to accept Reverend Kim Taimuk as pastor and wire me about his salary."[6]

Soon thereafter, when Rhee was elected president of South Korea in 1948, not everybody in Hawai'i was pleased: "The news of Syngman Rhee's election as President of the Republic of Korea met with mixed approval among the immigrant Koreans in Hawaii. There still remained a number of loyal supporters of Yongman Park, the man who originally opposed Rhee and who had planned to recapture his homeland from Japan by militaristic means. Park had been assassinated twenty years earlier, yet a vestige of his followers would have preferred to see a man other than Rhee heading their country. My mother and father and other Methodists greeted Rhee's ascension as head of their country with only mild enthusiasm."[7]

Factionalism and corruption, which had often gone hand-in-hand in some of the more bizarre episodes of internecine strife in the 1920s, continued to plague the Korean community and provided more ammunition for those in Hawai'i who saw Rhee as corrupt, no matter whether he was in Hawai'i or

Korea. One incident involved the Korean Women's Relief Society in Hawai'i, which raised seven thousand dollars to aid North Korean refugees in the south. The money was sent in February 1948 to Louise Yim, the only female cabinet member in Rhee's new government. When it became clear by August of that year that the money was not being used for the intended purpose, some members of the society went to Seoul requesting that the money be returned. After four such visits, Yim finally admitted that the money had been spent instead to celebrate Rhee's birthday.[8]

The continuing factional divisions among Hawai'i's first-generation Koreans involved not only churches and organizations, but also newspapers. As the foremost expert on Hawai'i's Korean press noted: "The end of the war removed Japanese colonialism as the principal target of Korean editorialists, but the division of the country, its occupation by the US and the USSR, the communization of the north, and the political turmoil in the south provided many columns of material in the immediate postwar years, as did the Korean war after its outbreak in 1950. Rhee, though now removed from Hawaii, was no less a controversial figure in the Hawaii Korean press. In 1949, for example, the editors of the *Kungminbo* criticized Rhee's South Korean government as 'the filthiest and most wicked dictatorship one can find today throughout the world.'"[9]

When the Korean War broke out in 1950, Koreans in Hawai'i generally supported South Korea and the cause of the United Nations, led by the United States. Most in the first generation (and the second generation) tended to blame the communists for the division of the country and for the outbreak of the war. But not all Koreans in Hawai'i supported the American war effort, due to continued factional struggle. One was a long-time opponent of Rhee in Hawai'i, Henry Cu Kim (Kim Hyŏn-gu), who was the editor of the Kungminhoe's (Korean National Association) newspaper:

> I once again became the *Kungminbo* [*Korean National Herald*] editor in 1949. Soon after that, the Korean War broke out. In what was purported to be the police action of that war, the United States committed the wanton massacre of noncombatants, even of women and children. I scathingly denounced this, and as a means of arousing concern among U.S. political circles, I expressed my support for communism, the archenemy of the American government and people. Thus for a time, I attracted the attention of compatriots and foreigners alike. . . . I made myself appear as if I supported communism, merely as a temporary tactic, and this caused no small criticism. Busybodies employed subterfuge to cause discord within the Kungminhoe. In 1951, I was elected president of the Kungminhoe, and two years later, I was reelected. But in order to avoid internal strife in the Kungminhoe, I resigned as president at the end of the year, and the vice president, Yim Song-gu, took over.[10]

With the Cold War at its height and with Rhee in Seoul proclaiming all Koreans who opposed him communists—even those Koreans who lived in

Hawai'i—factional struggle in the Korean community attracted the attention of the American government. When Henry Cu Kim additionally suggested that war relief funds be sent to both North Korean and South Korean victims, he was accused of being a communist and a federal investigation ensued. The Senate Judiciary Committee found that the KNA's anti-Rhee policy was "so strongly influenced by communist thinking as to be regarded as a willing tool of the communist propaganda apparatus." This conclusion was based on an earlier investigation that found "In Hawaii's Korean community there are two leading political factions, the pro-Syngman Rhee group and the anti-Rhee group. There are appearances of pro-communist activities within the anti-Rhee group. The Korean National Herald with a circulation of about 450 copies, has criticized U.S. policy in Korea in its editorials and has opposed U.N. 'intervention' in Korea."[11]

Another Korean from Hawai'i also ran afoul of the American government for his pro-communist leanings. The son of Hyŏn Sun, Peter Hyun, was one of those second-generation Koreans stationed in Korea as part of the American armed forces during the occupation. While there, he became disillusioned with the policies of the U.S. government: "I felt ashamed while listening to [my cousin's] accounts of what the American Military Government (AMG) had done to squelch all new-born activities of the people since liberation from the slavery of Japanese rule." As he turned against American policy, he made contact with the Korean Communist Party in Seoul. Soon he found himself being followed by the American military police and was later picked up and finally sent back to the United States and mustered out of the army, having been accused of being a communist.[12]

When the Korean War broke out, Hyun and some other members of the family continued to find themselves on the wrong side of the American government. Hyun's sister, Alice, defected to North Korea. As for Hyun: "I wanted to do something to help stop this senseless war. I joined the editorial staff of the Korean Independence News, a Korean-English bilingual weekly newspaper. Diamond Kim was the editor-publisher . . . and I was the editor of the English section. With little financial support, the three of us managed to bring out the newspaper and send it everywhere the Koreans lived: to all the major cities in the U.S., to Hawaii, and of course to Korea. Our editorial policy was clear: stop the war in Korea, oust Syngman Rhee, and all powers outside Korea —hands off. We exposed Rhee's sordid background. . . . [T]he supporters of Syngman Rhee in Los Angeles were outraged, and with threats of physical harm, staged a drive to shut down our press. They branded the Korean Independence News and its staff as 'Reds.'" As a result, Hyun was called to testify in front of the House Un-American Activities Committee.[13]

The year 1953 was important to the Korean community in three ways. First, it marked the end of the fratricidal Korean War. Several hundred Korean Americans from Hawai'i had seen action as part of the U.S. armed forces in

Korea. And many relatives of Koreans in Hawai'i had been killed in Korea during the course of the war. Second, 1953 was the fiftieth anniversary of the arrival of the first immigrants in 1903 and was cause for celebration in the Korean community. Nearly one thousand Koreans attended a "Golden Jubilee" gathering, a commemorative booklet was issued, and the two daily English-language newspapers took special note with a series of articles on the immigration and the Korean community in general. Third, 1953 was the first full year that first-generation Koreans could become naturalized citizens of the United States.[14]

During World War II, an effort had begun to end the restrictions that prevented alien Koreans from becoming citizens and to end the immigration restrictions that had been levied on the Koreans as a result of the Gentlemen's Agreement of 1908 and the Immigration Act of 1924. In 1944, Hawai'i's delegate to Congress, Joseph Farrington, introduced a bill that would give citizenship to Koreans and allow immigration based on a quota system of one hundred per year, just as such privileges had been extended to the Chinese when the Chinese Exclusion Act had been abolished the previous year. Supporting Farrington's efforts was the Korean Civic Association, which had been organized in 1932, reorganized in 1943, and which was made up largely of second-generation Koreans. In 1947, Farrington again introduced such legislation. It finally came to fruition five years later, when the Omnibus Immigration Bill, known as the McCarran-Walter Act, was passed. It became effective on December 24, 1952, and aliens over the age of fifty were exempted from the English examination.[15]

With the passage of this Act, first-generation Koreans, long denied the privilege of American citizenship, began exercising their new rights to become citizens, with nearly one hundred becoming naturalized within a year of its passage. Such a rite of passage was significant enough for younger generations to record the event: "[B]eing 72 years old and having lived in Hawaii for 52 years, [my grandfather] applied for his citizenship. He had been retired for five years before this. . . . His wife was naturalized in 1955." Another second-generation Korean recorded, "Some of the old men at the Methodist church persuaded my father to forget his problems and study with them to become U. S. citizens. His cronies spoke enthusiastically about their naturalization classes and how they enjoyed helping each other with the lessons. After months of diligent studying, each of them succeeded and was formally granted U.S. citizenship. How proud and happy they were to become American citizens!"[16]

With the end of the Korean War, a number of first generation Koreans sought to visit their homeland. In 1955, for example, four Koreans from Hawai'i ranging in age from fifty-eight to eighty-six years old returned to Korea for a seventeen-day visit sponsored by one of the Korean dailies, the *P'yŏngwha sinmun*. In another instance, in 1959, Lee Man-kee, who had retired in 1950 at the age of seventy, visited Korea with his wife. It was their first visit to Korea since 1918, and they "were treated with great respect because they were the

oldest tourists that came with the group." Numerous other Koreans from
Hawai'i also visited their homeland during the 1950s and experienced no obstacles. But that was not true for all would-be Korean visitors from Hawai'i.[17]

Even after the end of the Korean War in 1953, the residue of factional struggle, the corruption that plagued the Rhee regime, and the continued linkage
between Korea and Hawai'i continued to haunt Hawai'i's Korean community.
These factors manifested themselves most obviously when Koreans who had
not been affiliated with Rhee's faction attempted to obtain visas to Korea. One
such elderly man, who had applied for a visa in Tokyo, was told by Korean officials that because "[y]our party opposed President Syngman Rhee and the
Dong Ji Hoi," his visa would not be forthcoming. The man asked, "You're telling
me you won't let me in Korea because of my former political ties?" The officials
replied that the only way he could get a visa was "if you give us . . . money."
With "[a] feeling of indignation and helplessness," he refused to pay the bribe
and returned to Hawai'i without the visa.[18]

Similar problems arose when Koreans tried to obtain visas in Honolulu. It
was noted, for example, that it took at least two weeks to obtain a visa at the
Korean consulate, but only one day at the Japanese and Philippine consulates.
Moreover, Consul Oh Choong Chung, a Rhee supporter, had reportedly circulated a paper requiring signatures of Rhee supporters. Some residents believed
that they were refused visas if their names were not on the list, if they had been
a member of the KNA, or if they had not been a member of the Dongjihoe.
For example, one person whose father had held a high position in the KNA and
who had been affiliated with the Methodist Church stated in an interview that
her family had been refused visas because they "belonged to the wrong organization." Another KNA member, a Mrs. Kim, had twice applied for a visa and
twice been turned down, once after waiting two months, with no reason given
for the refusal. "Everyone knows that if you do not belong to Dr. Rhee's party,
you cannot go to Korea," she commented. A Mrs. Shon, who belonged to no
organization and was not a Rhee supporter, was also denied a visa with no reason given. These complaints, coming from some prominent members of the
Korean community, came to the attention of a Honolulu daily, who asked Consul Oh about the charges. He replied that he had issued visas to thirty members of the KNA and that only five had been turned down, and that those were
done by officials in Seoul rather than himself. Nonetheless, demands were
made for Consul Oh's recall, as it was clear that factional politics continued to
plague the Korean community even in the latter part of the 1950s.[19]

Events in Korea in the early 1960s provided the occasion for what were perhaps the final salvos in the factional politics of Hawai'i's Korean community.
When Rhee was overthrown in April 1960, Consul Oh changed his first name
to George and began working as a salesman for Sears, while his wife began
working at McInerny's Department Store in Ala Moana Shopping Center in
Honolulu. Commenting on Rhee's overthrow, the *Korean Pacific Weekly,* the

Dongjihoe's organ, argued that "we should remember his works in the past and recognize him as a great leader against communism." In the following year (1961), when Park Chung-hee seized power, the KNA averred that his military coup was good for Korea and took the opportunity to criticize Rhee and his regime, which had dominated South Korea from 1948 to 1960. Subsequently, the factionalism that had rent the Korean community in Hawai'i for over half a century began to dissipate. For one thing, many of the first generation were now quite elderly, and, as we have noted, the second generation was generally devoid of factional affiliation. Moreover, the institutions that had helped sustain factionalism were losing their relevance.[20]

Korean churches, for instance, which had helped sustain factionalism, in addition to promoting social, religious, and economic activities, had lost much of their importance. As one second-generation Korean noted: "Most of the immigrants were no longer poor; some affluent people seemed to find the church superfluous in their lives." Another second-generation woman whose parents had been associated with the Korean Methodist Church admitted that she did not associate with members of the Korean Christian Church, but she did so because they were like "strangers," not enemies. She added that there were no longer any bitter feelings but simply a "lack of communication."[21]

The Korean newspapers, which had also helped fuel factional struggles, began to struggle also. By the 1960s, the readership and financial support necessary to maintain the two papers had diminished to the point that neither the *Kungminbo* nor the *T'aep'yŏngyang chubo* could be sustained. The latter, which had claimed a circulation of 500 copies per week in 1941, was reduced by 1960 to a circulation of 180. The *Kungminbo* in 1960 had a circulation of only 200. Eight years later, the *Kungminbo* ceased publication, and the *T'aep'yŏngyang Chubo* ceased publication two years after that, in 1970. Thus by the 1970s, Hawai'i no longer had a Korean-language publication that could accurately be called a newspaper. Instead, news of Korea and local events in the Korean language were provided by American editions of Korean newspapers printed on the West Coast and served by correspondents in Honolulu.[22]

As for the rival political organizations, by the early 1970s, the Dongjihoe and the KNA each had fewer than one hundred members, with meetings held irregularly and few in attendance. They were now concerned with social and cultural affairs in the local Korean community rather than political issues. And the focus of the second generation was primarily oriented toward Hawaiian and American politics. Because of the small size of the Korean group, Koreans were not elected to political office until the 1950s, when the first person of Korean ancestry, Philip P. Minn, was elected to Hawai'i's legislature in 1954. By contrast, the first Chinese in Hawai'i had been elected to governmental offices in the 1920s and the first Japanese in the 1930s.[23]

Although factional struggle was the stuff of gossip and news among the first generation, perhaps more important in the life of the Korean community after the war was continued improvement in economic and social status. While delighted that their homeland was once again free, their day-to-day concerns revolved more around the well-being of their families in Hawai'i, since they would not be returning to Korea. The Depression had worked many hardships on the Korean community, but with the advent of the Pacific War, many Koreans were able to take advantage of the increased opportunities presented by the influx of servicemen, expanding defense industries, and the relatively high wages that prevailed despite the restrictions imposed on them as enemy aliens. These factors enabled the Korean community to occupy a relatively favorable economic position, especially when compared to their more modest circumstances of the prewar period. As one observer noted in the immediate aftermath of the war: "During the war the Koreans found abundant opportunities for earning good positions, so that they now constitute an increasingly strong and sound economic element in Hawaii."[24] How did this come about?

Many were driven by the knowledge that wartime prosperity was only temporary. As one laundryman said, "I make a lot of money washing clothes for the army, but when the war ends, my earnings will be just enough to support the family and nothing more." As a result, some of the first generation sought ways to turn short-term opportunity into long-term gain. Many were prescient enough to use whatever extra money they earned during the war to invest in real estate and rental properties. One second-generation Korean woman observed: "Naturally, the economic status of most of the Koreans is much higher now than before Dec. 7. Most of the money are being invested in war bonds or real estate. People are buying homes and renting them out to defense workers. New furniture and household articles, which formerly couldn't be afforded, are now being bought. Many of the Koreans are playing safe and are preparing for the predicted postwar depression." Indeed, a few had successfully dabbled in real estate even before the war. One third-generation Korean woman noted that "in our case, we had lots of money even before the war. My family was engaged in [the] rooming house business for over seventeen years and the mansion we have now is perhaps the result or end product of all the hard work of my parents and grandparents."[25]

Here is how one second-generation woman recalled her father's actions: "But then, . . . in December, 1941, I snatched the first opportunity and went to work. The family got along well with mother's and my earnings. With the help of my married brother and sisters, and father's reserve money from the bank, we purchased three houses. Buying the three houses was father's idea as some security for the family, for he knew, although he did not tell us, that he would not live very long. . . . Father's foresight in buying real estate property relieved me of one responsibility." Another example, this time told from the vantage point of the third generation, is also instructive: "[In 1938, my grandfather] hit a goldmine in a laundering and tailor business at the Army-Navy YMCA in downtown Honolulu. He made so much money from his military clientele that

he was able to move into his present house . . . in Palolo. Now he collects the
rent from his eight rental units and lives a comfortable life of retirement. . . .
He is now enjoying his remaining years quietly and is financially independent
from his children. He has brought over from Korea a woman relative and her
daughter to help take care of grandmother."²⁶ While these two cases illustrate
the *ilse* father's initiative, more frequently the *ilse* mother provided the initiative.

Many Korean women of the picture-bride generation invested in real estate
partly out of a shrewd business sense and partly out of the need to provide for
large families, since their much older husbands were often either enfeebled or
had passed away, leaving them as the sole family provider. Because many of
them had run boardinghouses for single Korean men on the plantations, their
entry into real estate was a natural outcome of their earlier experiences. The
following account, related by a second-generation girl about her widowed
mother, is not atypical: "The family I belong to consists of two boys, four girls
(including me), and Mother. My father died when I was nine years old. . . . My
mother is forty-eight years old and she is a landlady. . . . [S]he bought several
houses and a hotel. All these houses except one have been leased; my mother
takes care of this house now. She merely collects rent from the other houses
and checks on them now and then. We live in a home away from these houses.
This home in which we live was bought, more or less, with the money acquired
from the other houses."²⁷

Another account, this time by a third-generation woman, tells of her grandmother's venture into real estate: "She was not satisfied having only a rented
space but wanted a place of her own. They bought land in Kapahulu and built
a grocery store (which still operates today but owned by a relative). The store
prospered and they built another building right next to it. This was a department store. This took place during the war. She says that during this time that
money was so plentiful that they were able to pay off their twenty year building loan within one year! Boy, was Bank of Hawaii surprised! They then rented
out the grocery store so that they could concentrate on the department store.
Their savings grew and they purchased an acre of land in Manoa. On it they
built a huge two-story house. Her dream was that their children would build
their homes on the land also. After seven years the profits from the department
store began to decrease, so they closed it out and sold the grocery store to their
son-in-law. Their savings and investments enabled them to retire comfortably
without having money worries."²⁸

A similar tale is repeated by another third-generation Korean about his
grandmother. "After arriving in Honolulu in January of 1941 [from another
island], the family found lodging for $19 a month in Liliha. . . . Capitalistic
ingenuity blossomed as usual in my grandmother's mind after my grandfather
died in November of 1941. She, as did many other Koreans of the time, became
interested in real estate. With the $1,000 she received in insurance benefits

from my grandfather's death, she put a down payment on a house in Kaimuki. However, 'that house too small—no income come out,' she said. 'I want income come out.' In her search for larger dwellings, she found a nice, spacious home . . . in the Punchbowl-Makiki area. She borrowed $7,000 from a relative, sold her Kaimuki house for an $8,000 profit, and bought the house in which she still resides today. There are twenty rental units on her property and a tidy sum in rent helps to pay the mortgage. It was the Pearl Harbor attack that drove many Island Caucasians to sell their homes quickly and cheaply, and for this reason real estate was a profitable business even then. For my grandmother, this situation proved fortunate, for it had made her remaining years immensely easier and secure."[29]

One second-generation woman recalled her mother coming home with six hundred dollars in cash in early 1944. When she asked her mother why she was carrying so much cash around, she replied: "I might need that much some day. I might find a piece of property I like. I'll have the deposit ready. I want to buy for investment. I have friends who have bought rooming houses and are managing them. They're collecting rent. Making a good profit." The daughter replied, "You mean, like the rooming house Mrs. Kim bought on Hotel and Maunakea Street?" Her mother answered, "Not only rooming houses. I could buy a big, old-fashioned house and cut it up into small apartments. Mrs. Shon did that. She's just sitting down and getting rich." After her mother's final acquisition, the daughter noted that "[c]ombined with the rentals collected from the dwellings behind the family's Colonial house, the latest property purchase provided a good income for my parents."[30]

One woman who got involved in the real estate business explained how she was able to raise the necessary capital: "One day one of my friends came and told me there is a rooming house somebody wanted to sell. I went downtown to Hotel Street. Then, I go see the rooming house, 32 rooms. That time it cost only $1,400. I cry in front of my friend. That time I was in Honolulu four years already. Four years of work day and night and I only earned $400, how can I afford to buy? . . . So, I joined a tanomoshi meeting. The first tanomoshi, we made $50 a month. Then, I joined two. . . . From the two tanomoshi I draw $1,600. . . . That's how we first started business—by helping each other. We have a women's society lending each other money. It was also a fellowship society. Once a month we went to each other's house, for meeting and for lunch. We liked business that time, even a small amount. We call the meeting kye in Korean, hui in Chinese."[31]

While mostly a first-generation phenomenon, some second-generation Koreans also cashed in on the wartime prosperity and used it to acquire rental properties: "[M]y father . . . studied photography. . . . After he [at the age of 23] and mom married [in 1943], he invested their wedding money in photography equipment and opened up a concession on Hotel Street. 'I eventually joined up with a man in the store who ran another concession,' dad recalls.

. . . After getting together, they created a colorful backdrop of a grass shack, complete with lauhala mats and spears. The other man would be the barker, and would encourage servicemen to come in with their buddies and take a Hawaiian picture for back home. Lucrative as business with servicemen was in those days (for this was during World War Two), my parents had to moon-light. . . . Yet, with little overhead, they were making as much as $2,000 per month at times. Times were too good. . . . The family income is supplemented by six rental units which pull in an average of $1,200 monthly."[32]

This newly acquired wealth did not come without cost, however. Sometimes unforeseen consequences ensued. For example, raising money via the *kye* to purchase property could lead to legal problems with the government: "When my mother died, I think she had the greatest amount of property among the Koreans. Throughout her life she'd have one kye and buy one property, and get rent. Then she'd make another kye and did the same thing over and over again. Later, she had so many mortgages I think that's how she knew all the bankers in town. I remember going downtown with her to interpret her business deal-ings for her. We were still a Territory of the United States, but someone from Washington, from the IRS, had come to investigate her because here she was with property worth five hundred thousand dollars. She had never paid taxes and kept on going on a shoestring paying interest. The man from Washington kept asking my mother questions and she kept on talking about kye. But the man from Washington didn't know what kye was. Finally he gave up. He said to not get into problems again because nobody would be able to solve them. He left and my mother never had another audit from the IRS."[33]

Another unforeseen consequence of sudden wealth was that younger mem-bers of the family sometimes did not learn the value of a dollar. Consider the following account by an intermediate school teacher: "I have a Korean boy in my class who is always influencing the other boys to 'shoot crap' with him. My explanation was of no avail so I paid a home visit to his parents and through the sympathetic understanding of the mother, learned that they now have lots of money and that it was a new experience to her youngsters. Prior to the war, they didn't even have enough to pay all the monthly bills. The war has imprinted a good and a bad effect on the family. I looked around the house . . . there was a new refrigerator, a grand piano and modern, comfortable furniture. Before the war, they had none of this, so the mother said."[34]

Another consequence of acquiring rental properties was that some Korean landlords became slumlords in declining neighborhoods. A sociologist who was doing fieldwork in one such neighborhood (Aala) noted the following: "Socio-logically the most interesting group are the Koreans. With the exception of one who operates a bar, all of them are owners of tenements in which the Hawai-ians, Puerto Ricans, and others are roomers. When questioned as to her atti-tude towards the prostitutes living in her building, the reply of one of the Korean landladies was, 'Me, I no care. Me only sell room. 'Nother men make business; me no boss. Me, I get money 'nough.' At another tenement, the writer approached a young Korean girl of high school age, who, with her mother was the proprietor of the building. After learning of the occupation of the tenants, the question was put to her: 'What are these Portuguese and Haole women doing? Aren't they married?' 'Oh, they're prostitutes,' she replied unhesitantly." The researcher concluded that "[t]hese attitudes [indicate that they do not care what they do] in a business as long as [they make] money."[35]

A final, unforeseen consequence of newly acquired wealth awaited Koreans when they used their money to relocate. Most of those who relocated simply moved to a better neighborhood in Honolulu or its vicinity. Often these new neighborhoods were dominated by Caucasians, who sometimes looked askance at the diversification of their previously sacrosanct domains: "The [Korean] family moved in. They discovered many of the neighbors were old-time residents, *kamaaina,* with names like Judd, Lowrey, Martin, Oakley, Halford, and Greenwell. . . . [T]hese *kamaaina* families were not particularly receptive of newcomers in their neighborhood." Such neighborhoods often also had customs that were unfamiliar to Koreans. In one instance, confusion reigned when, on Halloween, a newly arrived older Korean woman did not understand the meaning of the words "trick or treat," which the neighborhood children shouted when she opened her door.[36]

A much smaller number of Koreans relocated to the mainland after the war, a move made easier by the advent of regularly scheduled airline service. For many the experience was a shock, accustomed as they were to a subtropical climate, a relatively short distance from home to work, a slower pace, a relatively small "big city," a population that was overwhelmingly Asian, and, by now, a lack of overt discrimination. Consider, for example, the experience of one family: "By late July, 1948, my husband . . . and I were packed and ready to make the move to the West Coast with our children. We were starting a new life in new surroundings. We trembled at the thought of not knowing what to expect. Unbelievably cool weather greeted us the evening we arrived in San Francisco. We had never before experienced chilling winds, biting and assaulting, in the middle of summer. . . . Before school started in September I shopped for warm clothes for the children. Like other shoppers in town, I walked fast; the crisp air made everyone appear full of resolute purpose. I saw crowds on the wide sidewalk fronting the stores. Inside, every store was bursting with customers. So this was a big city! I had never seen so many shoppers packed in shops. . . . [It was] our first experience in driving long distances to homes outside of San Francisco, where most of our future business lay."[37]

Few were prepared for overt discrimination. "All of a sudden I was aware of the sea of *white* faces all around me. I could pick out only one or two women with yellow skin. And for the first time in my life I experienced prejudice. A sharp pain accompanied this strange feeling. With my Oriental face I found it difficult to flag a salesgirl. I was passed over time and time again. When there were three or four of us at a counter with articles to purchase, it was as if I were invisible. When I did finally get the attention of one salesperson, her voice seemed needlessly curt. . . . I watched the would-be customers who braved their way into our shop. I noted that as soon as they opened the door and saw *me* they seemed apologetic and wanted to back out and leave. Once inside, they quickly viewed the displays, asked a few questions, then left. I said to my husband, 'I believe we need a *haole* front. Anyone who responds to our ad just seems to freeze and lose interest when they see an Oriental in this showroom.' So we hired an attractive young girl with golden hair framing her face, a peaches-and-cream complexion, and a pretty smile. It was amazing how quickly the drop-in trade improved. . . . My husband and I remained in the background. When he drove out to clients' homes to verify orders, he was taken as a factory hand skilled in his craft, not as the boss. I was merely the book-keeper operating in the background."[38] It was clear that the racial climate on the mainland was not as liberal as Hawai'i's.

Of course, economic advancement for many Korean families rested not only on real estate, but also on the results of decades of hard work in small shops after leaving the plantations. One view has the Koreans holding their own in an improving socioeconomic climate. According to this view, Koreans by the mid-1930s had achieved a position in the middle of the socioeconomic ladder in Hawai'i. Twenty years later, by the mid-1950s, Koreans had maintained their standing in the middle. At the top were the Caucasians and Chinese, who had arrived in Hawai'i much earlier than the Koreans. In the middle with Koreans were the Japanese, most of whom had also arrived before the Koreans. In this middle group, the Koreans ranked first in management and ownership of busi-nesses such as tailoring, laundry, furniture, music, shoe repair, groceries, and rooming houses. Below the middle group were the Puerto Ricans, who had arrived at the same time as Koreans, and the Filipinos, who had arrived after the Koreans.[39]

But other indicators suggest that Koreans were actually moving upward socially and economically, especially if one considers the career paths of the second-generation Koreans. Such upward mobility can be inferred by compar-ing occupational statistics for 1930, which reflected primarily the first genera-tion, with similar statistics for 1950, which reflected primarily the second gen-eration. As the second generation graduated from high school and college, married, and started their careers, they began to occupy positions commensu-rate with their educational achievements, as racial discrimination continued to retreat into the background.

During that period (1930–1950), the number of professionals in the Korean community quadrupled, with one out of every eleven Korean adults classified as professional. Also quadrupling was the number of managers and officials, with one out of every six Korean adults falling in this category. The number of clerical workers had risen to one out of every ten adult Koreans. The number of salesworkers doubled during this period, to 6 percent of all Koreans. Skilled craftsmen tripled, with one out of every four males found in this category. Categories in which Koreans were either "surprisingly high," according to one sociologist, or were represented at least twice as frequently as other racial groups were architecture, chemistry, dentistry, social work, real estate, airplane mechanics, church ministry, law, pharmacy, insurance, tailoring, design, civil engineering, drafting, medicine, and policework. Korean females were usually employed as actresses, entertainers, teachers, and nurses. Only about one out of eight Koreans were laborers. The most notable statistic, however, was the precipitous decline in the number of agricultural workers: by 1950, only about 4 percent of all Koreans were so employed. The Japanese, by contrast, had twice as many agricultural workers.[40]

As the second generation entered the economic life of the islands, with many holding prestigious positions and commanding comfortable salaries, the non-Koreans' perception of Koreans rose as a result. For example, the largest racial group in Hawai'i—the Japanese—who had ranked Koreans eighth in the 1930s, now, in the postwar period, ranked them fifth, behind Caucasians, Chinese, Japanese, and part-Hawaiians. One researcher characterized it as "the most striking rise" of any of the ethnic groups and attributed it to increased contact and the general diminishing of social distance as a result of assimilation, the recognition of Korean achievements in economic endeavors, and to the "Orientals okay" attitude of Japanese. As potential marriage partners, Koreans, along with Chinese and Japanese, received the highest rating from the Japanese.[41]

Paralleling the postwar rise in their socioeconomic fortunes was the continued rise in the number of outmarriages—a trend that had started during the prewar period. In this Koreans were not alone, as interracial marriages increased for all ethnic groups in Hawai'i. In fact, in 1963, about three out of every eight marriages in Hawai'i were interracial. Still, Koreans ranked near the top, whereas the Japanese had the lowest rate. Korean men had the second highest rate of outmarriage at 71 percent, second only to the Hawaiians at 85 percent. By contrast, only 15 percent of Japanese men married non-Japanese women. As for Korean women, 77 percent married non-Koreans, second only to Hawaiians at 84 percent. By contrast, only 25 percent of Japanese women married non-Japanese men. The high rate for Koreans, just as in the immediate prewar period, cannot be attributed to an unbalanced sex ratio. In 1950, for instance, there were 121 Korean males for every 100 Korean females. By 1960, this had almost completely evened out to 106 males for every 100 females. According to one sociologist, the high rate was instead the result of Korean "participation in the life of a common community and culture." In other words, Koreans had become completely assimilated. A second reason for the high rate was that both Korean men and women tended to marry younger spouses (sometimes much younger)—in other words, spouses who were not their Korean contemporaries—hence they naturally turned to other races.[42]

With the high rate of outmarriage among Koreans, it became clear that the third generation would not contain many "pure" Koreans. Indeed, of all Korean births between 1956 and 1960, only about one-quarter (27 percent) involved Korean mothers and fathers—the lowest rate of any ethnic group in the islands. By contrast, Caucasians had the highest rate at 98 percent, and the island average was 71 percent. Moreover, Korean attitudes had now changed. As the second generation married and had children of their own, eventually they—the third generation—would begin dating and marrying. On the subject of outmarriage, would the attitudes of the second-generation Korean parents be similar to those of their first-generation parents? The answer clearly was no: "The idea that we should 'marry our own kind' is no longer forced upon us. Very few of my third generation cousins have married Koreans. My older brother married a Caucasian and presently I have a Chinese fiancee. My parents are open-minded on these matters, although it wouldn't break their hearts to have one of their sons marry a Korean girl. 'Eric,' my dad jokingly tells my younger brother, 'you are our last hope.'"[43]

There was other evidence of social disorganization in the Korean community, however, in the form of high divorce rates. Given the high outmarriage rates of Koreans, one would perhaps expect high divorce rates, since outmarriages more often end in divorce than inmarriages. Indeed, for mixed marriages of all of Hawai'i's ethnic groups, only Hawaiians had a worse marital record than Koreans for both men and women. But even many Korean inmarriages were unsuccessful. In fact, unions between Koreans had the highest rate of divorce of any ethnic group in Hawai'i, with two-thirds of those marriages failing. Hawaiians were a close second, at 62 percent. By contrast, Japanese inmarriages recorded the highest rate of stability. Combining the figures for both inmarriages and outmarriages of Koreans, Korean men ranked next to last, better only than Hawaiian men, in the risk of divorce, while Korean women ranked last.

What explains the continued poor record of Korean marriages? One researcher pointed to assumptions concerning the Korean character: "Impressionistically, we might speculate that Koreans are popularly regarded as hot tempered, and hence likely to have marriages full of tumult and friction." This same researcher also warned of the inherent risks involved with marriages in which one partner was much older than the other—a trend that had been established in the years before the war. Others blamed it on the lack of ethnic solidarity among Koreans, with divorce rates inversely proportional to "degrees of ethnic and cultural ties." Some saw the increasing divorce rate of Koreans as a product of Americanization and length of residence in Hawai'i. Finally, others suggested that members of smaller groups such as Koreans and Puerto

Ricans tend to be more disorganized and hence more likely to divorce. In other words, divorce rates tend to be inversely proportional to the size of the group.[44]

As the second generation matured and the third generation began to reach adulthood in the early 1970s, Koreans in Hawaiʻi were confronted with a new wave of immigrants from Korea, a result of changes in the immigration laws in 1965 and 1968. Although a discussion of these new immigrants is beyond the scope of this book, it is interesting to take a brief glimpse at the initial encounter. The newly arrived Koreans were surprised to find that there were Koreans already in Hawaiʻi, that they had been there for nearly seventy years, and that over 90 percent had been born in America. There was not much interaction between the fully Americanized second and third generation and the new first-generation arrivals from Korea. When it was learned that Koreans were already in Hawaiʻi, reporters were sent from Korea, only to discover that Hawaiʻi's Koreans were more American than Korean. As one Korean newspaper article put it, "It is a shameful truth that Koreans [in Hawaiʻi] of the second and third generation almost do not know their native tongue."[45]

By the early 1970s, the work of the first generation had come to an end. Many had died, and the remainder, mostly the picture brides, had retired. The center of gravity had shifted to the second generation and their families, a predominantly urban community of nearly eight thousand, two-thirds of whom lived in Honolulu. As the second generation reached the peak of their careers and earning power—but before the new wave of Korean immigrants had begun to make their mark—Koreans boasted the highest per capita income and the lowest unemployment rate of any ethnic group in Hawaiʻi, including Caucasians.[46]

In 1973, the seventieth anniversary of the first Korean immigration was celebrated. Only nine survivors from the first boat, the *Gaelic,* which had docked in Honolulu on January 13, 1903, remained. Had the *ilse* been successful? Their children thought so: "With hard work, great sacrifice, and ultimate joy, my parents attained the dreams for the good life in their adopted land as well as a college education for each of their children."[47]

It is difficult to summarize the experiences of more than seven thousand people over a seventy-year period. The information in this book defies easy conclusions. Still, at the risk of oversimplification, the following conclusions are offered in the realms of economics, politics, and society.

Economically, Korean immigrants began like all the other immigrants from Asia, working in harsh conditions on the plantations for meager wages. But their urban origins in Korea quickly led them to abandon the plantations for self-employment opportunities in the city, primarily Honolulu. There, hard work and an entrepreneurial spirit paid off in the form of rising income levels. This trend, put on hold temporarily by the Depression, resumed with the coming of the Pacific War and investment in real estate by picture brides, and continued to rise when the well-educated second generation began to occupy well-paying professional jobs at a time when the racial climate was much more favorable than the one into which their parents had entered.

Politically, the Koreans were united in their opposition to the Japanese take-over of their homeland after 1905, and this sometimes spilled over into anti-Japanese sentiment directed at the Japanese in Hawaiʻi. But the Korean community was also divided from the beginning on the plantations. Later, when the Japanese placed the Koreans under surveillance, they found the Koreans still divided. And when the U.S. government tried to ascertain the loyalty of the Koreans during the Pacific War, it too found the Koreans divided. Koreans also found themselves embroiled politically with an American government that declared them enemy aliens during wartime. While this study has not attempted a complete history of the Korean nationalist movement in Hawaiʻi, those aspects that have been explored are suggestive for future research on this topic.

Socially, the first-generation Korean immigrants were able to adapt to their new environment rather quickly, partly because of their atypical backgrounds in Korea and partly because of the small size of their group. As a group, they were more "liberal" than first-generation Japanese and Chinese and quickly responded to missionary efforts to introduce them to Christianity. At the same time, they had to deal with anti-Asian racism, which, although it receded over time, operated to retard their advancement. These mostly male immigrants arranged the importation of picture brides to assure a stable family life and to perpetuate a Korean community in the new country. Their second-generation children excelled academically while at the same time exhibiting signs of social disorganization. They were also more "liberal" than their second-generation Chinese and Japanese counterparts, as well as their parents. This intergenerational gap over many issues created pockets of tension, with perhaps the most contentious being interracial marriage.

A final word is necessary on the impact of Koreans on Hawaiian and American societies in the twentieth century. It would be false to assert that the Korean community was a major influence in either society. The Chinese and Japanese experience will continue to overshadow the Korean experience based on numbers alone, and rightly so. Still, the story recounted here is important because it helps to complete our knowledge of the East Asian immigrant experience in the United States. In some ways the Korean situation was unique; in others it was similar to that of other East Asian immigrants. Knowing about the Korean experience ensures that in the future, the complete story can be told and that the Korean portion will no longer be omitted from our histories and our consciousness.

NOTES

1. Prologue—The Arrival of the First Immigrants

1. Honolulu: University of Hawai'i Press, 1988 (paperbound ed., 1994).

2. Patterson, "The First Attempt to Obtain Korean Laborers for Hawaii."

3. For additional details on the role of Horace Allen in the establishment of Korean immigration to Hawai'i, see my "Sugar-Coated Diplomacy."

4. The material of the following several pages is taken from Patterson, "Japanese Imperialism in Korea," and Patterson, "The Early Years of Korean Immigration to Mexico," 87–103.

5. The remainder of this chapter is excerpted from chapter 10 in my *The Korean Frontier in America,* and from my "Upward Social Mobility of the Koreans in Hawaii," 81–92.

2. Laboring on the Plantations

1. U.S. Department of Commerce and Labor, Bureau of Labor, *Fourth Report,* 23. The exact number was 4,946 or 4,893, depending on what time of the year the statistics were gathered. See also Adams, et al., *The Peoples of Hawaii,* table 15, and Territory of Hawai'i, Board of Immigration, *First Report.*

2. Lila K. Lee, "The History of My Life," UHSPJ; see also Charr, *The Golden Mountain,* 120, for the camp layout at Ewa where the Korean camp was located on the east side of the plantation. Later, as more Koreans came to Ewa, there were two Korean camps, an "up camp" and a "down camp." See Bernice Kim, Master's thesis, 102.

3. Charr, *The Golden Mountain,* 125–126.

4. Ibid.; Bernice Kim, Master's thesis, 116.

5. Bernice Kim, Master's thesis, 106.

6. Bernice Kim, Master's thesis, 105–106; Kim Hei-Won interview in Sunoo, *Korean Kaleidoscope,* 157. It should not be assumed that cultural interaction was unidirectional, however. When Yun Ch'i-ho visited Koloa Plantation, he was greeted by the Portuguese in obscene Korean. See Lyu, "Korean Nationalist Activities," 43.

7. Hyun Soon, "My Autobiography," 62; Bernice Kim, Master's thesis, 113–115; Jones, "Koreans in Hawaii"; see also Jones, "Koreans Abroad," 446–451; Territory of Hawai'i, Bureau of Labor, *Third Report,* 121; Yang Chu-en taped interview of February 27, 1974.

8. Yun Ch'i-ho *Ilgi,* September 11, 1905 (Waialua), September 25, 1905 (Hakalau),

and October 1, 1905 (Puunene); see also Jones, "Koreans Abroad"; Moore, "One Night with the Koreans in Hawaii," 529–532. Yang Chu-en interview in Choy, *Koreans in America*, 294–295; Kim Hyung-sun interview in Choy, *Koreans in America*, 304.

9. Bernice Kim, Master's thesis, 86, 102; Yang Chu-en interview in Choy, *Koreans in America*, 295–296, and taped interview of February 27, 1974.

10. Hawaiian Agricultural Company manager to Brewer, March 31, 1903. Hawaiian Agricultural Company, *Letterbook, 1903–1906;* Bishop to McStocker, April 13, 1903, PSC 17/11. HSPAPA; Bishop to McStocker, April 13, 1903, PSC 17/11. HSPAPA; Moore, "One Night with the Koreans in Hawaii"; Yi Chŏng-gŭn, *Insaeng palsipe ch'ŏnbyŏn manhwa,* 3; Mary Paik Lee, *Quiet Odyssey,* 9.

11. Peter Hyun, *In the New World,* 11.

12. Yang Chu-en interview in Choy, *Koreans in America,* 294; also Jones, "Koreans in Hawaii." Jones mentions that bread and butter were part of the meal, but it seems rather unlikely that Koreans would be using butter; Territory of Hawai'i, Bureau of Labor, *Third Report,* 117, 122. The report noted that while the Koreans at first tended to stint themselves in the matter of provisions, after a short time in Hawai'i they tended to resemble the Chinese in that they consumed more meat than the Japanese.

13. "I used to buy them [Hawaiian bananas] from the Bak-kay, or the Chinese, who also sold vegetables to our cook." Charr, *The Golden Mountain,* 126; Kown [Kwon?] Yong-ho interview in Sunoo, *Korean Kaleidoscope,* 114; Yang Chu-en interview in Choy, *Koreans in America,* 295. While there is no reason to doubt this account, the reader should be aware that similar "egg" stories have surfaced in the experiences of other non-English speaking immigrants.

14. Bernice Kim, Master's thesis, 105–106; Yi Chŏng-gŭn, *Insaeng palsipe ch'ŏnbyŏn manhwa,* 3; Territory of Hawai'i, Bureau of Labor, *Third Report,* 122.

15. Charr, *The Golden Mountain,* 129; Yun Ch'i-ho *Ilgi,* September 18, 1905.

16. Jones, "Koreans in Hawaii; Yun Ch'i-ho *Ilgi,* September 10, 1905; Yang Chu-en interview in Choy, *Koreans in America,* 294.

17. Bishop to McStocker, April 13, 1903, PSC 17/11. HSPAPA; Charr, *The Golden Mountain,* 125.

18. Watt to Bishop, March 30, 1905, PSC 3/2. HSPAPA.

19. McStocker to Dillingham Co., September 24, 1903, PSC 2/5. HSPAPA; Bernice Kim, Master's thesis, 118–119.

20. Paxton to McStocker, October 20, 1903. McStocker to Dillingham Co., October 22, 1903, PSC 2/5. HSPAPA.

21. McStocker to Dillingham Co., October 22, 1903, PSC 2/5. HSPAPA. Still, the manager was left to wonder, "What are we going to do with a man of this kind?"; *Honolulu Star-Bulletin,* October 10, 1921; Yang Chu-en interview in Choy, *Koreans in America,* 295.

22. McStocker to Dillingham Co., October 22, 1903, PSC 2/5. HSPAPA.

23. Bishop to McStocker, April 13, 1903, PSC 17/11. HSPAPA.

24. Cooke to Welch, January 6, 1903. Cooke, *Papers;* Bernice Kim, Master's thesis, 107–108.

25. Yun Ch'i-ho *Ilgi,* September 15 and 25, 1905.

26. Ibid., September 24 and October 1, 1905. The second plantation was Puunene, on the island of Maui; Moore, "One Night with the Koreans in Hawaii"; Yoon, *The Passage of a Picture Bride,* 69; Bernice Kim, Master's thesis, 107.

27. Sunoo and Sunoo, "The Heritage of the First Korean Women Immigrants," 156; Charr, *The Golden Mountain*, 127; *Honolulu Star-Bulletin*, October 10, 1921; Yang Chu-en interview in Choy, *Koreans in America*, 295; Kim Hyung-Soon interview in Choy, *Koreans in America*, 303.

28. Bishop to McStocker, April 13 and 17, 1903, PSC 17/11. HSPAPA; Hackfeld and Co. to Ahrens, August 1 and 2, 1904, OSC 1/16. HSPAPA; Yun Ch'i-ho *Ilgi*, September 16, 1905; Hyun Soon, "My Autobiography," 63.

29. Bishop to McStocker, April 27, 1903, PSC 17/11. HSPAPA.

30. Coman, "The History of Contract Labor in the Hawaiian Islands," 59.

31. *Maui News*, March 7, 1903; Wolters to Irwin and Co, LTD, December 16 and 29, 1903, April 6 and 11, 1904. Hutchinson Sugar Plantation Co., *Letterbook, 1903–1904;* McStocker to Dillingham Co., September 3, 1903, and Paxton to McStocker, September 8, 1903, PSC 2/5. HSPAPA; *Planters Monthly*, December 1903, 525.

32. *Pacific Commercial Advertiser*, December 9–12, 1904; Reineke, *Labor Disturbances in Hawaii*, 11; No, *ChaeMi Hanin saryak*, 13; Territory of Hawai'i, Bureau of Labor, *Third Report*, 136–137; Wakukawa, *History of the Japanese People*, 130. For a complete description of this strike, see Beechert, *Working in Hawaii*, 163–167; Cooke to Rithet, May 17, 1905. Cooke, *Papers; Pacific Commercial Advertiser*, October 6, 1905; Yun Ch'i-ho *Ilgi*, October 2, 1905; Saitō to Komura, April 24, 1905. Gaimushō Reports.

33. Wolters to Irwin and Co., LTD, March 1 and April 11, 1905. Hutchinson Sugar Plantation Co., *Letterbook to William G. Irwin and Co., LTD, 1905;* Saitō to Komura, April 24, 1905; HSPA Labor Committee, *Territory of Hawaii Report, 1905.*

34. U.S. Department of Commerce and Labor, Bureau of Labor, *Fourth Report*, 75; Bishop to Cooke, November 11, 1902. Cooke, *Papers.*

35. Mary Paik Lee, *Quiet Odyssey*, 9; McStocker to Dillingham Co., October 8, 1903, PSC 2/5. HSPAPA.

36. Lila K. Lee, "The History of My Life," UHSPJ; Sunoo and Sunoo, "The Heritage of the First Korean Women Immigrants," 154; Hei-Won Sarah Kim interview in Sunoo, *Korean Kaleidoscope*, 156; Yang Chu-en and Kim Hyung-Soon interviews in Choy, *Koreans in America*, 295, 303.

37. Bernice Kim, Master's thesis, 104; Hyun Soon, "My Autobiography," 63; Pai, *The Dreams of Two Yi-Min*, 5–6.

38. Sunoo and Sunoo, "The Heritage of the First Korean Women Immigrants,"154; Chang-sook Kim, "Migrations in My Family," UHSPJ; Charr, *The Golden Mountain*, 124.

39. Cooke to Wells, April 3, 1905; Cooke to [illegible], April 11, 1905; Cooke to [illegible], April 23, 1904. Cooke, *Papers;* Territory of Hawai'i, Bureau of Labor, *Third Report*, 144; No, *ChaeMi Hanin saryak*, 15; Territory of Hawai'i, Board of Immigration, *First Report, 1905–1907*, 24, table (statistics of immigration-arrivals and departures of immigrants at Honolulu).

40. Mary Paik Lee, *Quiet Odyssey*, 10–11.

41. Interviews with Yun Ung-ho in Los Angeles, September 25, 1974, and with Yang Chu-en in San Francisco, January 7, 1975, as cited in Moon, "The Korean Immigrants in America," 78–79. Many of those who went to the mainland stole away secretly in the middle of the night, apparently believing that they were obligated to remain on the plantations for the duration of their three-year work agreement; Bernice Kim, Master's thesis, 167; Lila K. Lee, "The History of My Life," UHSPJ.

42. Cooke to [illegible], September 23, 1904. Cooke, *Papers;* Territory of Hawai'i, Board of Immigration, *First Report, 1905–1907,* 24; see also *Pacific Commercial Advertiser,* March 21, 1906; Territory of Hawai'i, Board of Immigration, *Second Report,* 18, 61; see also U.S. Department of Labor, Bureau of Labor Statistics, *Labor Conditions in Hawaii,* 45; For a list of the ships and the number of Koreans aboard, see No, *ChaeMi Hanin saryak,* 21–37 passim.

43. Territory of Hawai'i, Board of Immigration, *First Report, 1905–1907,* 24–26, and *Second Report,* 18, 24, 38–39; also, U.S. Department of Labor, Bureau of Labor Statistics, *Labor Conditions in Hawaii,* 45.

44. As Bernice Kim recounts, "[D]iscouraged and disappointed, their first reaction was to save enough within three years and either return to Korea or get away to mainland America." Bernice Kim, Master's thesis, 104; Samuel S. O. Lee, "An Early Returnee to Korea," 57. Lee cites an interview with his son, Reverend Haeng-up Chung. Upon his return, he married, fathered eight children, was ordained a minister, and started church activities in various places in Korea. Hawai'i had definitely changed some of his ways of thinking. For example, he insisted that his family's meals would be different every day, as they had been in Hawai'i; *Kyŏnghyang sinmun,* November 13, 1906, and interviews with Kim Wŏn-yong [Warren Kim] on September 25, 1974, in Los Angeles and Kim Yu-taek in Honolulu on July 17, 1974, in Moon, "The Korean Immigrants in America," 83–84.

45. McStocker to Dillingham Co., October 22, 1903, PSC 2/5. HSPAPA; Yun Ch'i-ho *Ilgi,* October 3, 1905; Japanese consulate-general in Honolulu, *Hawai Chōsenjin jijō,* 38.

46. Ogg to Bishop and Co., Bankers, November 14, 1903. Hawaiian Agricultural Company, *Letterbook, 1903–1906;* Yun Ch'i-ho *Ilgi,* October 1, 1905.

47. Moore, "One Night with the Koreans in Hawaii," 529–532; Jones, "Koreans Abroad," 446–451; *Korea Review* 4, no. 2 (February 1904), 79; Moon, "The Korean Immigrants in America," 110, quoting *Sinhan minbo,* April 6, 1916.

48. Territory of Hawai'i, Bureau of Labor, *Third Report,* 122; Sunoo and Sunoo, "The Heritage of the First Korean Women Immigrants," 156–157.

49. Jones, "Koreans Abroad."

50. Adams, *Interracial Marriage in Hawaii,* 31–32.

51. Ibid.; Bishop to Cooke, November 11, 1902. Cooke, *Papers.*

52. See Patterson, "Upward Social Mobility of the Koreans in Hawaii," 81–92. Moreover, one can argue that the Koreans were merely trading one set of problems for another. That is, instead of poverty and oppression, they were made to suffer from racism and discrimination. While it will become apparent that Hawai'i was not immune from racism and anti-Asian discrimination, they were able to cope with these. Simply put, they felt better off in Hawai'i and realized it early on, even while they were still on the plantations, the lowest rung of the socioeconomic ladder.

53. Jones, "Koreans in Hawaii," 404; Hulbert, "Koreans in Hawaii," 411–413. Hulbert had stopped in Hawai'i in late 1905 en route to Washington, D.C., to deliver a message from the Korean emperor; Territory of Hawai'i, Bureau of Labor, *Third Report,* 118. This report is interesting because it notes that already the Koreans were spending more money, as settlers would, rather than hoarding it, as sojourners might for an eventual return to the homeland with a great deal of accumulated wealth; Chun, "Older Koreans Planning to Note Arrival Anniversary." The speaker was Jared Smith, who

owned a tobacco farm in Kona; Allen to Underwood, December 6, 1905. Allen, *MSS;* Reineke, "Language and Dialect in Hawaii," 202.

54. Quoted in Grajdanzev, *Modern Korea,* 34–35.

55. Bishop, "Koreans in Russian Manchuria," 41–44.

56. Jones, "Koreans Abroad," 446–451; Hulbert, "Koreans in Hawaii"; Allen to Underwood, December 6, 1905. Allen, *MSS.*

57. Jones, "Koreans Abroad," 448. Since the earlier-arriving men—who had come from all over the Korean peninsula speaking different dialects—were concentrated on the plantations, they gradually came to speak the standard dialect as well as their own local dialect, using the former in formal occasions and the latter in informal occasions. See Dong Jae Lee, "Sociolinguistic Implications of Korean in Hawaii," 418.

58. Lind, *An Island Community,* 254, 262; Lind, *Hawaii's People,* 50; Livesay, *A Study of Public Education in Hawaii,* 71, 81; Shin-pyo Kang, "The East Asian Culture," *passim; Honolulu Star-Bulletin,* September 10, 1973.

59. The most prominent sociologists using this type of analysis were Romanzo Adams and Andrew W. Lind. Their causal model, linking small size with rapid acculturation, can be found in Adams, et al., *The Peoples of Hawaii,* 41, and Lind, *An Island Community,* 252–265; Madorah D. Smith, "A Comparison of the Neurotic Tendencies," 395–417; Wedge and Abe, "Racial Incidence of Mental Disease in Hawaii," 337–338; Kalish, "Suicide: An Ethnic Comparison in Hawaii"; Lind, "Some Ecological Patterns of Community Disorganization in Honolulu," 206–220; Schmitt, "Age, Race and Marital Failure in Hawaii"; Lind, *An Island Community,* 292; Adams, et al., *The Peoples of Hawaii,* 36, 38.

60. The remainder of this chapter is excerpted from Patterson, "Upward Social Mobility of the Koreans in Hawaii."

3. Organization and Disorganization

1. HSPA, Trustees, *Minutes,* November 16, 1903; Giffard to Irwin, December 29, 1903, and Irwin's response to Giffard, January 8, 1904. Giffard/Irwin *Papers; Pacific Commercial Advertiser,* July 30 and August 1, 1904, June 6, 1905; see also Reinecke, "Labor Disturbances," 11–12; Watt to Bishop and Co., August 26, 1904, and August 31, 1904, PSC 3/2. HSPAPA. The correspondence read as follows: "Since Saturday last we have had the Korean gang at Mountain View on the strike and they seem to have some imaginary trouble as far as we can find out, and there is no reason for them striking. They complain that the luna is not good but as far as we can find out everything is alright. This is the second time these men have gone on a strike inside of the last two months and this time we were in a fortunate position and have given these men the alternative of going to work immediately or leaving the camp. A number have left again, yesterday afternoon, the overseer for that section notified them to leave the camp as the houses were needed for the laborers and I think that a number of them will go to work this morning but at this writing we have no means of finding out whether they are at work or not." And, "Since last Friday the Koreans whom we mentioned have returned to work, only a few having left the plantation. Their troubles were only imaginary and we gave them the option of returning to work or leaving the plantation at once. At first they said they were all going to leave but when they found we would not relent at all most of them turned to"; Territory of Hawai'i, Bureau of Labor, *Third Report,* 144.

2. Yang Chu-en interview in Choy, *Koreans in America,* 295.

3. See Bernice Kim, Master's thesis, 101–102; when asked the reason for moving, the two most frequent responses were: "better working conditions," followed closely by "higher wages," for a total of 40 percent of the respondents. Oh, et al., Interview Data; Kang and Kang interview in Sunoo, *Korean Kaleidoscope*, 142–43; Yun Ch'i-ho *Ilgi*, September 9, 1905; Renton to Ahrens, June 18, 1904, OSC 1/15. HSPAPA.

4. Hyun Soon, "My Autobiography," 66.

5. Yun Ch'i-ho *Ilgi*, September 14, 15, and 22, and October 3, 1905; Kim Hyung-soon interview in Choy, *Koreans in America*, 303.

6. Yun Ch'i-ho *Ilgi*, October 1 and 3, 1905; HSPA Trustees, *Minutes*, October 3, 1905.

7. Yun Ch'i-ho *Ilgi*, October 3, 1905.

8. Ibid., September 10, 18, and October 2, 1905; Lyu, "Korean Nationalist Activities," 44.

9. Hongki Lee and Kyungsur Lee interviews in Lyu, "Korean Nationalist Activities," 43; Lyu, "Korean Nationalist Activities," 44; Kim Wŏn-Yong, *ChaeMi Hanin osimnyŏnsa*, 87; Yun Ch'i-ho *Ilgi*, September 13, 1905, at McBryde Plantation.

10. Kim Hyŏng-sun interview with Choy, March 26, 1976; Territory of Hawai'i, Bureau of Labor, *Third Report*, 118; Bernice Kim, Master's thesis, 104, 115, 138; Hyŏn Sun, *P'owa yuram-ki*, 7.

11. Lyu, "Korean Nationalist Activities," 42 and 74, from interviews with Kyungsur Lee and Hongki Lee.

12. Lyu, "Korean Nationalist Activities," 30–31; Kim Hyŏng-sun interview with Choy, March 26, 1976; Sunoo and Sunoo, "The Heritage of the First Korean Women Immigrants," 153.

13. Yun Ch'i-ho *Ilgi*, September 15 and 20, 1905.

14. *Honolulu Star-Bulletin*, October 10, 1921; Yun Ch'i-ho *Ilgi*, September 18, 24, 28, and 29, and October 3, 1905. Kim would also be involved in political infighting.

15. Wadman, *Annual Report*.

16. Yun Ch'i-ho *Ilgi*, September 11, 13, and 20, 1905; Yun's pro-Christian bias leaves unanswered the question of whether in fact non-Christians predominated among the discontented and the lawbreakers.

17. Hulbert, "Koreans in Hawaii," 411–413.

18. Yang Chu-en interview in Choy, *Koreans in America*, 294; Bernice Kim, Master's thesis, 104; "The Kim Family," UHSPJ.

19. Yun Ch'i-ho *Ilgi*, September 14, 20, 21, 24, and 25, 1905.

20. Bernice Kim, who interviewed respondents in the 1930s, Kingsley Lyu, who interviewed respondents in the 1940s (and who did not see or refer to Bernice Kim's study), Kim Wŏn-yong, writing in the 1950s, and Hyŏn Sun, who was a founder of one of these organizations, all provide primary source material describing the structure and function of the organizations. See Bernice Kim, Master's thesis, 108–112; Kim Wŏn-yong, *ChaeMi Hanin osimnyŏnsa*, 85; Hyŏn Sun, *P'owa yuram-ki*, 7, and Hyun Soon, "My Autobiography," 62–63; and Lyu, "Korean Nationalist Activities," 30–33. Lyu cites interviews with Lee Kyungshik, Cho Pyung-yo, Nahm Chancho, and Lee Hong-ki, the first of whom was the *sachal*, or Sergeant-at-Arms, at Camp Four, Makaweli, Kauai, in 1906.

21. Lyu, "Korean Nationalist Activities," 31; Hyŏn Sun, *P'owa yuram-ki*, 7; Hyun Soon, "My Autobiography," 63–64.

22. Hyŏn Sun, *P'owa yuram-ki*, 7.

23. Ibid.

24. Bernice Kim, Master's thesis, 108n, 110–111; Lyu, "Korean Nationalist Activities," 29–30 (interview with Kwon Pong-sun).

25. *Pacific Commercial Advertiser,* August 12, 1903.

26. Moon, "The Korean Immigrants in America," 133, quoting Kim Yu-taek interview in Honolulu, July 17, 1974; Yang Chu-en interview in Choy, *Koreans in America,* 296.

27. Bernice Kim, Master's thesis, 110–111.

28. Lyu, "Korean Nationalist Activities," 29–30; Bernice Kim, Master's thesis, 119–120. Kim contends that this regionalism "was not strong enough to split the group into factions."

29. Hyŏn Sun, *P'owa yuram-ki,* 12; Yun Ch'i-ho *Ilgi,* September 18, 1905.

30. Kim Wŏn-yong, *ChaeMi Hanin osimnyŏnsa,* 85–86; Hyŏn Sun, *P'owa yuram-ki,* 7, 12; Lyu, "Korean Nationalist Activities," 37–38; Hyun Soon, "My Autobiography," 64. Other founding members were Yun Pyong-gu, Mun Hong-sik, Pak Yun-sop, Im Ch'i-song, Im Hyong-ju, Kim Chong-guk, An Chong-su, Yi Kyo-dam, Chung Chai-kwan, Kim Kyu-sop, and An Kyong-su. Lyu cites an interview with Yi (Lee) Hong-gi stating that these men were better educated than the other Korean immigrants.

31. Hyŏn Sun, *P'owa yuram-ki,* 14. The newspaper contained editorial comment, news of Korea and foreign countries, plantation news, and Methodist Church news. Reverend Wadman, who succeeded Reverend Pearson, and Min Chan-ho continued the publication after Hyŏn and Hong returned to Korea, purchasing Korean printing types. It became a monthly with six hundred subscribers. That there was also a regional cast to this split is indicated by a reference to this group as the "Kyŏngju faction"; see also Kim Wŏn-yong, *ChaeMi Hanin osimnyŏnsa,* 87.

32. Yun Ch'i-ho *Ilgi,* September 18, 1905. The editors of *Sinjo sinmun* were Kim Ik-song and Ch'oe Yun-baek; see also Macmillan, "The Korean Press in Hawaii"; Kim Wŏn-yong (87) says that this opposition "began to dissent and stir up troubles for no reason at all."

33. See the discussion on pages 100–102 in Patterson, *The Korean Frontier in America;* Kim Wŏn-yong, *ChaeMi Hanin osimnyŏnsa,* 86–87, and No, *ChaeMi Hanin saryak,* 12. Among those in opposition were Yi Kyo-dam, Im Hyŏng-ju and Mun Kyŏng-ho.

34. Hyŏn Sun, *P'owa yuram-ki,* 12; Yun Ch'i-ho *Ilgi,* September 18, 1905.

35. Kim Wŏn-yong, *ChaeMi Hanin osimnyŏnsa,* 87. The word *"sinmin,"* or "subject," should not be confused with the *sinmin* in Sinminhoe, since they refer to two completely separate Chinese characters.

36. Lyu, "Korean Nationalist Activities," 37–38, and Yun Ch'i-ho *Ilgi,* September 18, 1905. Yun mistakenly labels the Sinminhoe as the Sikminhoe (Migrants Society).

37. Lyu, "Korean Nationalist Activities," 40–41, and Kim Wŏn-yong, *ChaeMi Hanin osimnyŏnsa,* 87.

38. Yun Ch'i-ho *Ilgi,* September 8 and 18, 1905.

39. Ibid., September 18, 1905.

40. Kim Wŏn-yong (*ChaeMi Hanin osimnyŏnsa,* 87), states that the Sinminhoe was disbanded on April 20, 1904; Hyŏn Sun, *P'owa yuram-ki,* 14; Hyun Soon, "My Autobiography," 65.

41. Hyun Soon, "My Autobiography," 65–69.

42. Lyu, "Korean Nationalist Activities," 38–39; Kim Wŏn-yong, *ChaeMi Hanin osimnyŏnsa,* 91, 94; Hyŏn Sun, *P'owa yuram-ki,* 14; *75th Anniversary of Korean Immi-*

gration to Hawaii, 1903–1978, 28. All four of these sources differ slightly. For example, one source says the Ch'inmokhoe was founded by Pak Sang-ha, another states that the leader was one Chŏn Wŏn-myŏng, and a third states that Kim Ik-sŏng was the leader. I have used Kim Ik-sŏng, since his name has previously appeared as a leading member of the opposition faction within the Sinminhoe. Its purpose, according to one source, was anti-Japanese activities, boycott of Japanese goods, and fraternal love. Another source states that it sought to restore the Korean empire and promote education.

43. Kim Wŏn-yong, *ChaeMi Hanin osimnyŏnsa*, 91–95; Lyu, "Korean Nationalist Activities," 38–39; Hyŏn Sun, *P'owa yuram-ki*, 7, 12, 14.

44. Hyŏn Sun, *P'owa yuram-ki*, 12, 14; Lyu, "Korean Nationalist Activities," 39; Kim Wŏn-yong, 86, *ChaeMi Hanin osimnyŏnsa*, 97–98.

45. Kim Wŏn-yong, *ChaeMi Hanin osimnyŏnsa*, 104; *75th Anniversary of Korean Immigration to Hawaii, 1903–1978*, 17; Bernice Kim, Master's thesis, 119–120.

46. Bernice Kim, Master's thesis, 108.

4. Methodist Mission Work

1. Jones, "The Koreans in Hawaii."

2. Watt to Bishop and Co., October 12, 1909, PSC 4/3. HSPAPA.

3. Makee Sugar Plantation, Labor Statement; Lihue Plantation Company, V. 128, 1910–1925; Wolters to Watt, March 23, 1912; Watt to Wolters, March 27, 1912, KAU 31/4. HSPAPA.

4. Adams, et al., *The Peoples of Hawaii*, table 15 (laborers employed on sugar plantations). The numbers vary somewhat depending on what time of the year the census was taken. Jones, for example, found 4,683 Koreans on the plantations in late 1905. And the *First Report* of the Board of Immigration of the Territory of Hawai'i, January 31, 1907, which took the census on July 31, 1906, came up with 3,675 Koreans on the plantations for that year.

5. Sarah Lee Yang, "75 Years of Progress for the Koreans of Hawaii," 17; Hyun Soon, "My Autobiography," 63; Bernice Kim, Master's thesis, 137–138.

6. Hyŏn Sun, *P'owa Yuram Ki*, 9; Stevens to the author, May 7, 1976. The Ewa record books are not open for perusal; Sarah Lee Yang, "75 Years of Progress for the Koreans of Hawaii," 17.

7. Hyun Soon, "My Autobiography," 64.

8. Wadman, "Educational Work among the Koreans," 146–150; Hulbert, "Koreans in Hawaii."

9. Hyun Soon, "My Autobiography," 64–65. Hyŏn names the following as the core founding members of this church: Ahn Chung Su, Woo Byung Gil, Kim Ri Je, Dora Kim (later Dora Moon), Lim Chi Chung, Lee Kio Dam, Lim Hyung Choo, Yun Pyung Koo, Hong Sung Ha, and Park Yun Sup (the interpreter at the immigration station) and his wife; Sarah Lee Yang, "75 Years of Progress for the Koreans of Hawaii," 32–33; for a complete history of the church, see Ryu Tongshik (Yu Tong-sik), *Hawai ŭi Hanin kwa kyohoe.*

10. Myong-sun "Jim" Paek was interviewed on January 2, 1976, by Sunoo; Hyun Soon, "My Autobiography," 65; Hyŏn Sun, *P'owa yuram ki*, 9. Some of the other pastors recruited by Wadman and sent to various places for religious work among the Koreans were: Moon Pyung Ho, who remained in Honolulu; Kim Young Sik for Ewa Plantation; Hong Chi Pum for Puunene, Maui; Lee Kyung Jik for Eleele, Kauai; and Lim Chung Soo for Hawai'i.

11. Hyun Soon, "My Autobiography," 65–66.

12. Ibid., 66.

13. "History of St. Luke's," 28–29; Restarick, *Hawaii, 1778–1920*, 322; Dutton, *The Episcopal Church in Hawaii*, 22.

14. Restarick, *Hawaii, 1778–1920*, 322; "History of St. Luke's."

15. "History of St. Luke's"; Restarick, *Hawaii, 1778–1920*, 319; *Hawaiian Church Chronicle*, September 1908.

16. Restarick, *Hawaii, 1778–1920*, 324–325, 376, 378; Gulick, *Mixing the Races in Hawaii*, 144, table 21.

17. Hyun Soon, "My Autobiography," 67. Hyŏn's responsibility included the plantations of Koloa, Lawai, Eleele, Makawili, Kikaho, and Mana. The west side of the island was entrusted to Lee Kyung Gik; Hulbert, "Koreans in Hawaii," 412.

18. Hyun Soon, "My Autobiography," 66–67.

19. Ibid., 63; Bernice Kim, Master's thesis, 183.

20. Hyun Soon, "My Autobiography," 67–68.

21. Ibid., 68–69; see also Peter Hyun, *Mansei!*, 27–28.

22. HSPA Trustees, *Minutes*, August 10 and 17, 1905; *Yamato shinbun*, September 11, 1905.

23. HSPA Trustees, *Minutes*, August 14 and 27, 1908, November 30, 1910, and July 10 and 24, 1912.

24. Wadman to Bull, December 9, 1904; Wadman to Watt, October 6, 1905, OSC 5/12. HSPAPA; Hulbert, "Koreans in Hawaii."

25. Wadman to Watt, October 17, 1905. HSPAPA. Emphasis in the original.

26. Watt to Wadman, October 12, 1905; Wadman to Watt, October 17, 1905, OSC 6/15. HSPAPA.

27. Wadman to Bull, May 11, 1906, OSC 5/18; Wadman to Watt, May 7, 1911. Emphasis in the original; Watt to Wadman, May 19 and 25, 1911; Wadman to Watt, May 22, 1911. PSC 19/12. HSPAPA.

28. Morisson to F. A. Schaefer & Co., Ltd., June 1, 1911; F. A. Schaefer & Co., Ltd., to Morisson, June 18, 1911; Morisson to F. A. Schaefer & Co., Ltd., June 22, 1911; F. A. Schaefer & Co., Ltd., to Morisson, December 18, 1911. HSC 2/10 and HSC 5/1. HSPAPA.

29. HSPA Trustees, *Minutes*, November 17, 1915, March 28, 1917, May 1, 1918, April 2, 1919, and June 23, 1920.

30. Fry to Eckart, January 19, 1915, PSCV.160; Fry to Naquin, March 27, 1916, HSC 22/4. HSPAPA.

31. Eckart to Fry, January 25, 1915, PSCV.160. HSPAPA.

32. Fry to Jamieson, November 2, 1915, and January 7, 1916; Fry to Naquin, March 27, 1916. HSC 22/4. HSPAPA.

33. Fry to Campsie, March 28, 1918, and April 19, 1918; Campsie to Fry, April 3, 1918. HSC 22/4; Manager to HSPA, Bureau of Labor and Statistics, February 26, 1921. KAU 25/2. HSPAPA.

34. Hyun Soon, "My Autobiography," 102–103.

35. Sung-hi Lim, "Ecological Study of the Community of Spreckelsville (Camp One) Maui," UHSPJ.

36. Hyun Soon, "My Autobiography," 104.

37. These statistics come from two sources. The first is dated December 23, 1941, and is Memo Number Four, Territorial Office of Civilian Defense, Liaison Division,

Public Morale Section. The second is dated April 1, 1942, from the same office in a memo entitled "Recommendation Concerning the Republication of the Hawaiian Korean Christian Advocate." Intelligence Files; "History of St. Luke's," 28–29, 32–33. 38. Bernice Kim, Master's thesis, 137–138.

5. Exodus to the City

1. U.S. Department of Commerce and Labor, Bureau of Labor, *Fourth Report,* 23, 87; Reinecke, *Labor Disturbances in Hawaii, 1890–1925.*

2. U.S. Department of Labor, Bureau of Immigration and Naturalization, *Industrial Conditions in the Hawaiian Islands,* 8, 12; Beechert, *Working in Hawaii,* 170.

3. U.S. Department of Labor, Bureau of Immigration and Naturalization, *Industrial Conditions in the Hawaiian Islands,* 6; also, U. S. Department of Labor, Bureau of Labor Statistics, *Fifth Report,* 18; also Adams, et al., *The Peoples of Hawaii,* table 15 (laborers employed on sugar plantations); Liebes, "Labor Organization in Hawaii," 57. This had also been evident on a lesser scale two years earlier (summer 1918), when a Japanese strike to protest the Oahu Railway Company's firing of seventy-nine fellow countrymen was broken by fifty Korean strikebreakers who filled their places.

4. Liebes, "Labor Organization in Hawaii," 35; Reinecke, "The Big Lie of 1920."

5. HSPA Trustees, *Minutes,* March 9, 1920; Beechert, *Working in Hawaii,* 204–205, 208; see also Takaki, *Pau Hana,* 170.

6. Hutchinson Plantation, KAU 23/1.

7. Beechert, *Working in Hawaii,* 216; HSPA Trustees, *Minutes,* February 27, 1920; Gulick, *Mixing the Races in Hawaii,* 81, table 11; and U.S. Department of Labor, Bureau of Labor Statistics, *Labor in the Territory of Hawaii, 1939,* 35; Lind, *An Island Community,* 129n.

8. List of contractors in Puna. Olaa, Hawaii, June 23, 1916, PSC 31/11. USPAPA.

9. U.S. Department of Labor, Bureau of Labor Statistics, *Fifth Report,* 26, 32–33; Weatherbee to Zimmerman, June 6, 1911, PSC 19/12; Kim Choong Han to Morisson, October 28, 1914, HSC 22/10; Honokaa Sugar Company to F. A. Schaefer & Co., Ltd., January 5, 1911, HSC 2/9. HSPAPA.

10. Fry to Eckart, January 19, 1915, PSCV.160. HSPAPA; Jared G. Smith, "Do You Remember?"; Bernice Kim, Master's thesis, 158.

11. Kim Sung-jin interviews on January 17, 1976, and February 1, 1977, in Sunoo, *Korean Kaleidoscope,* 191–208; Japanese consulate-general in Honolulu, *Hawai Chōsenjin jijō,* 27.

12. U.S. Department of Labor, Bureau of Labor Statistics, *Fifth Report,* 45; Beechert, *Working in Hawaii,* 183, 243. No female Koreans were reported in the pineapple fields in 1915. There were also a few Koreans on the island of Lanai, which was given over entirely to the cultivation of pineapple.

13. Bernice Kim, Master's thesis, 158; U.S. Department of Labor, Bureau of Labor Statistics, *Labor in the Territory of Hawaii, 1939,* 102. The exact figures were male: $18.92, female: $12.68.

14. U.S. Department of Labor, Bureau of Labor Statistics, *Fifth Report,* 45; U.S. Department of Labor, Bureau of Labor Statistics, *Labor in the Territory of Hawaii, 1939,* 102.

15. Bernice Kim, "The Koreans in Hawaii," 409–413; see also Lind, *An Island Community,* 58.

16. Hyŏn Sun, *P'owa yuram ki,* 13.

17. Lind, *An Island Community,* 41, 272; Bernice Kim, Master's thesis, 160; Chun, "Older Koreans Planning to Note Arrival Anniversary." In this respect, the Koreans who came to the cities in the 1970s and 1980s to open independent businesses were little different from those Koreans who went to Honolulu in the 1910s and 1920s; the source of this statement prefers to remain anonymous.

18. Lind, *An Island Community,* 273; Lind, "Economic Succession and Racial Invasion in Hawaii," 330; Lind, "Occupational Attitudes of Orientals in Hawaii," 248.

19. Kim Hei-won (Sarah) interviews on December 8, 1975, and February 23, 1977, in Sunoo, *Korean Kaleidoscope,* 155–168; Hyŏn Sun, *P'owa yuram ki,* 13; Japanese consulate-general in Honolulu, *Hawai Chōsenjin jijō,* 24–26; Lind, "Economic Succession and Racial Invasion in Hawaii," 352–353.

20. Bernice Kim, Master's thesis, 159–168; Lind, "Economic Succession and Racial Invasion in Hawaii," 354; *Honolulu Star-Bulletin and Advertiser,* January 7, 1973; Pai, *The Dreams of Two Yi-Min,* 6–7; for another example of a Korean who worked on a plantation and then left to run a furniture company, see the story of Kim Chang-su in the *Honolulu Star-Bulletin,* June 1, 1953.

21. Ahn Young-ho interview on January 6, 1976, in Sunoo, *Korean Kaleidoscope,* 123–132; Lind, "Economic Succession and Racial Invasion in Hawaii," 372–373; see also Chun, "Older Koreans Planning to Note Arrival Anniversary."

22. Kang Won-shin interview on December 10, 1975, in Sunoo, *Korean Kaleidoscope,* 139–154.

23. Kim Hei-won (Sarah) interviews on December 8, 1975, and February 23, 1977, in Sunoo, *Korean Kaleidoscope,* 155–168; Lind, "Economic Succession and Racial Invasion in Hawaii," 372–373; see also Chun, "Older Koreans Planning to Note Arrival Anniversary."

24. Hyŏn Sun, *P'owa yuram ki,* 13.

25. Bernice Kim, Master's thesis, 164–165. Later generations of Koreans generally used banks rather than *kye* to raise capital.

26. Pai, *The Dreams of Two Yi-Min,* 6.

27. Rhee Pyong-uk interview on January 5, 1976, and Yoon Yong-ho interview on November 26, 1975, in Sunoo, *Korean Kaleidoscope,* 1–6 and 53–72.

28. Lind, "Occupational Attitudes of Orientals in Hawaii," 249; Japanese consulate-general in Honolulu, *Hawai Chōsenjin jijō,* 24–26 and 37–38.

29. Lind, *Hawaii's People,* 78; Lind, "Occupational Attitudes of Orientals in Hawaii," 262.

30. Lind, "Hawaii's People"; Japanese consulate-general in Honolulu, *Hawai Chōsenjin jijō,* 26–27 and 37–38; Lind, "Hawaii's Koreans—Some Basic Considerations," 78, lists the various lines of work entered into by Koreans; see also Japanese consulate-general in Honolulu, *Hawai Chōsenjin jijō,* 20–27; Lind, "Occupation and Race on Certain Frontiers," 66, table (percentage distribution of gainfully employed males of Hawaii, 1930).

31. Lind, *Hawaii's People,* 51–52; Schmitt, "Hawaii's Koreans, 1960"; Adams, *Interracial Marriage in Hawaii,* 40; in 1940, over half (54 percent) of the Koreans lived in Honolulu, and by 1950 more than two-thirds (68 percent) lived there. By that time, the proportion of the Korean population in Honolulu was the same as the Chinese, who had arrived much earlier. Much of the same difference existed in 1950, when the propor-

tion of the Puerto Ricans living in Honolulu was 41 percent, compared to 68 percent of the Koreans.

32. Lind, *Hawaii's People*, 57–58; also Lind, *An Island Community*, 310, 311n.

33. Student Journal, Sociology 151, 1944, UHSPJ. (The writer is a Japanese.)

34. Lind, *Hawaii's People*, 81; Lind, *An Island Community*, 258–260, 265.

6. The Picture-Bride System

1. Warren Kim, *Koreans in America*, 22–23, gives the number as 951, with an additional 115 going directly to the mainland; see also Kim Wŏn-yong, *ChaeMi Hanin osimnyŏnsa*, 27–29; Lyu, "Korean Nationalist Activities," 9, gives a low number of 300.

2. *Sinhan Minbo*, November 24, 1909, as cited in Moon, "The Korean Immigrants in America," 122; Lyu, "Korean Nationalist Activities," 8; Sŏ Kwang-un, Miju ŭi Hanin ch'ilsimnyŏn"; Warren Kim, *Koreans in America*, 22–23.

3. Bernice Kim, Master's thesis, 121; Shin Sung-il and Lyu Sungsoo were the names of the initiators, according to Lyu, "Korean Nationalist Activities," 8–9; Anna Choi [pseud.] remembered: "[M]y uncle's family in Korea knew of a man there [in Hawai'i] looking for a wife. . . . So, when I was fifteen, equipped with an introduction and a photograph . . ." Anna Choi interview in Choy, *Koreans in America*, 320–324; Weiner, *The Origins of the Korean Community*, 49–56.

4. Bernice Kim, Kim Wŏn-yong, Lyu, and Moon, citing *Sinhan minbo*, December 14, 1910. Moreover, Houchins and Houchins ("The Korean Experience in America, 1903–1924") assert that the Japanese government was willing to give exit permits to Korean picture brides as a means of calming political passions among the Koreans in America, but there is little evidence for this and no reference to support this assertion.

5. HSPA Trustees, *Minutes*, January 10, 1912.

6. Yoon, *The Passage of a Picture Bride*, 36.

7. Oh, et al., Interview Data; Moon, "The Korean Immigrants in America," 126; Lyu, "Korean Nationalist Activities," 9–10; Kyung Lee, "Settlement Patterns of Los Angeles Koreans," 13n.

8. Chai, "A Picture Bride from Korea," 2; Yoon, *The Passage of a Picture Bride*, 22; Douglas Woo, "The Story of the First Two Generations of My Family in Hawaii," UHSPJ.

9. Chai, "A Picture Bride from Korea," 2; Anna Choi interview in Choy, *Koreans in America*, 320–322.

10. Yoon, *The Passage of a Picture Bride*, 21, 24; Pai, *The Dreams of Two Yi-Min*, 5.

11. Yoon, *The Passage of a Picture Bride*, 22; Yim, *My Forty Year Fight for Korea*, 158; Chai, "A Picture Bride from Korea," 2

12. Chai, "Contributions of the Early Korean Immigrant Women in Hawaii"; Douglas Woo, "The Story of the First Two Generations of My Family in Hawaii," UHSPJ; interview with Hong Soon Yong in Rhodes, "How Oral History of the First Koreans to America Advances Archival Research," 5; see also Chai, "A Picture Bride from Korea," and Arinaga, "Contributions of Korean Immigrant Women."

13. Sŏ Kwang-un, "Miju ŭi Hanin ch'ilsimnyŏn"; Yoon, *The Passage of a Picture Bride*, 27, 37.

14. Pai, *The Dreams of Two Yi-Min*, 1; Sunoo, "Korean Women Pioneers," 54–56.

15. Chai, "A Picture Bride from Korea," 2; Pai, *The Dreams of Two Yi-Min*, 5; Yoon, *The Passage of a Picture Bride*, 21.

16. Pai, *The Dreams of Two Yi-Min*, 5; Anna Choi interview in Choy, *Koreans in America;* Yoon, *The Passage of a Picture Bride*, 23; Chai, "A Picture Bride from Korea," 2–3; Sŏ Kwang-un, Miju ŭi Hanin ch'ilsimnyŏn."

17. Yoon, *The Passage of a Picture Bride*, 29–30; Anna Choi interview in Choy, *Koreans in America.*

18. Yoon, *The Passage of a Picture Bride*, 40.

19. Ibid., 31; Chai, "A Picture Bride from Korea," 2; Sunoo, "Korean Women Pioneers," 53.

20. Yim, *My Forty Year Fight for Korea*, 78.

21. Yoon, *The Passage of a Picture Bride*, 19–21.

22. Pai, *The Dreams of Two Yi-Min*, 1.

23. Yoon, *The Passage of a Picture Bride*, 22, 86.

24. Pai, *The Dreams of Two Yi-Min*, 6; Rhodes, "How Oral History of the First Koreans to America Advances Archival Research," 2. Interview with Margaret Ok Hee Lee Nam about her parents Lee Suk Chun and Hannah Park

25. Kyung Lee, "Settlement Patterns of Los Angeles Koreans," 13n; Yoon, *The Passage of a Picture Bride*, 26.

26. According to Warren Kim, *Koreans in America*, 22–23, the women did the choosing. And Houchins and Houchins, "The Korean Experience in America, 1903–1924," 560n, also imply that women had the first choice in that sometimes only the groom supplied a photograph. This does not seem borne out by the evidence.

27. Yoon, *The Passage of a Picture Bride*, 22–25, 27. It may be that Mr. Chung bribed the marriage broker. Young Oak was the second of six children and the oldest of three girls.

28. Pai, *The Dreams of Two Yi-Min*, 1–2, 6; Yim, *My Forty Year Fight for Korea*, 79.

29. Sŏ Kwang-un, "Miju ŭi Hanin ch'ilsimnyŏn"; Yoon, *The Passage of a Picture Bride*, 25, 28; Lyu, "Korean Nationalist Activities," 9; Bernice Kim, Master's thesis, 122.

30. Lyu, "Korean Nationalist Activities," 9; Yoon, *The Passage of a Picture Bride*, 31; Kyung Lee, "Settlement Patterns of Los Angeles Koreans," 13n.

31. The following sequence of events transpired in the life of Miss Kim Soon-yon, who married Eum Shi-Mun: her name was entered into the Eum family register by marriage on July 10, 1917. She received a Japanese passport (number 108622) on June 28, 1918, with the handwritten note (in English), "Laborer's Emigrant Relative," signed by Baron Goto Shimpei. The passport gave her age as sixteen years, one month, and described her as follows: height: 4 feet, 11 inches; face: short; complexion: dark; eyes: large; eyebrows: thick; mouth: large. The Japanese family register was issued on July 5, 1918. The register listed Eum's name, the names of his father and mother, and his birth date. Then it listed Kim's name; she was identified as the eldest daughter of Kim Chi-son (father) and Kim Kyong-im (mother) and was born on June 11 in the thirty-fifth year of Meiji (1902). Since he had been born in 1884, this meant he was eighteen years older than she was. Her family address was listed as Kyongsang Namdo, Pusanfu, Chun Dong, No. 185. Three weeks later, on July 26, 1918, she was issued a visa (number 6551) to the United States at the office of the American consulate-general in Yokohama, signed by the vice consul. Eum died in 1963. Eum Shi-Mun *Papers.*

32. Yoon, *The Passage of a Picture Bride*, 31; Sunoo, "Korean Women Pioneers"; failing the physical examination in Honolulu was even more traumatic than failing it in Japan. It was also much more costly, as another picture bride soon learned: "When she

arrived in Honolulu, she was immediately deported to Japan by the immigration authorities because of an eye condition [trachoma] that needed medical correction. She
returned and was deported a second time, then detained for another three months at
the immigration station until her eye disease was cleared. All the expenses incurred
were being borne by her husband-to-be."

33. Yoon, *The Passage of a Picture Bride*, 46–47; Bernice Kim, Master's thesis, 207;
Anna Choi interview in Choy, *Koreans in America*. Some of the picture brides were
refused admission to Hawai'i by the immigration authorities if they were not claimed by
their intended husband. This situation sometimes occurred when the husband was
delayed in arriving from one of the outer islands. To be left alone on the dock after traveling such a long distance was a traumatic experience: "We were kept in the immigration quarantine quarters until we were cleared. The other five girls were cleared after
three days and left with their grooms-to-be. Feeling awfully cheated and left behind, I
spent most of my time crying. Finally, after five days, I was cleared of immigration with
the help of not my fiance but my uncle. My uncle advised me not to marry this man I
had not even met, since I was only fifteen and had a long life ahead of me. He advised
me to get an education."

34. Pai, *The Dreams of Two Yi-Min*, 5; Gima, "Marriage to a Cobbler Really Lasts";
Chai, "A Picture Bride from Korea," 3; Anna Choi interview in Choy, *Koreans in Amer-
ica;* Helen Young interview on July 25, 1992, in Hilo; Douglas Woo, "The Story of the
First Two Generations of My Family in Hawaii," UHSPJ; interview with Eunice Hak
Bong Whang Kealoha (born 1917) in Rhodes, "How Oral History of the First Koreans
to America Advances Archival Research," 3; Yoon, *The Passage of a Picture Bride*, 41.

35. Pai, *The Dreams of Two Yi-Min*, 2; Yoon, *The Passage of a Picture Bride*, 48,
51–59, 86; Anna Choi interview in Choy, *Koreans in America*.

36. Yoon, *The Passage of a Picture Bride*, 41, 49, 55; Chai, "A Picture Bride from
Korea," 3.

37. Gima, "Marriage to a Cobbler Really Lasts"; Chai, "A Picture Bride from Korea,"
3; Anna Choe interview in Choy, *Koreans in America;* Sunoo, "Korean Women Pioneers"; Yoon, *The Passage of a Picture Bride*, 86; Pai, *The Dreams of Two Yi-Min*,
131–132.

38. Bernice Kim, Master's thesis, 122; Yoon, *The Passage of a Picture Bride*, 48, 55;
Pai, *The Dreams of Two Yi-Min*, 3; Rhodes, "How Oral History of the First Koreans to
America Advances Archival Research," 5; Sunoo, "Korean Women Pioneers," 55–56.

39. Yoon, *The Passage of a Picture Bride*, 59; Sunoo, "Korean Women Pioneers,"
55–56; Pai, *The Dreams of Two Yi-Min*, 2–3.

40. Pai, *The Dreams of Two Yi-Min*, 5; Gima, "Marriage to a Cobbler Really Lasts"
(This couple returned to Puunene plantation on Maui and remained there for eleven
more years before moving to Oahu in 1930 to do laundry work for the military and, later,
shoe repair.); Hyok Sonwu interview, Honolulu, July 20, 1974, cited in Moon, "The
Korean Immigrants in America," 127; Yoon, *The Passage of a Picture Bride*, 66; Anna
Choi interview in Choy, *Koreans in America;* Douglas Woo, "The Story of the First Two
Generations of My Family in Hawaii," UHSPJ.

41. Yoon, *The Passage of a Picture Bride*, 111. Her name was Lee Sunhee; Anna
Choi interview in Choy, *Koreans in America*, 322; Oh, et al., Interview Data. 34 percent
responded that they had not changed plantations at all, which may have meant that their
husbands had already left. Most (but not all) of the people surveyed were surviving pic-

ture brides. The most frequent response, cited by one-third of the respondents, was that they had left the plantation searching for a better job and better earnings, with 85 percent indicating that their first residence after leaving the plantation was an urban one.

42. Chang-Sook Kim, "Migrations in My Family," UHSPJ; Shular, "Halmunee with a Korean Accent," 22–24.

43. Bernice Kim, Master's thesis, 122, 171; see also Anderson, "From Laborer to Leader in Seventy Years in Hawaii": "The Korean women largely had no desire to live on the plantations. And most of the men, who had spent most of their hard-earned money bringing their new mates to Hawaii, had no desire to remain on the plantations." See also Ch'oe Kap-sin, "Imin Ilse," about Ms. Kim T'ae-yun (in English in *Honolulu Star-Bulletin*, January 7, 1973, entitled "Korean Woman Toiled in Camps.")

44. Pai, *The Dreams of Two Yi-Min*, 3.

45. Yoon, *The Passage of a Picture Bride*, 61, 93.

46. Anna Choi interview in Choy, *Koreans in America*; Yoon, *The Passage of a Picture Bride*, 66.

47. Yoon, *The Passage of a Picture Bride*, 62, 104.

48. Dong Jae Lee, "Sociolinguistic Implications of Korean in Hawaii," 57–58.

49. Yoon, *The Passage of a Picture Bride*, 65. This is to be distinguished from the traditional Korean appellation of "father of my children"; Choy, *Koreans in America*, 322; Anna Ch'oe, "Hawai Imin Ch'ilsimnyŏn-sa," in *Sin Tong-A*, April 1974, 288, as cited in Moon, "The Korean Immigrants in America," 123.

50. Chai, "A Picture Bride from Korea," 3; Bernice Kim, Master's thesis, 207. An opposing view is presented by Louise Yim, who wrote: "I wondered how many of these marriages turned out and I learned that many of them were extremely successful." Yim, *My Forty Year Fight for Korea*, 158. Here she is probably referring to those picture brides who went directly to California.

51. Presentation at the University of Hawai'i by Kenneth P. H. Nam, former deputy attorney general of Hawai'i, January 7–9, 1979; Yoon, *The Passage of a Picture Bride*, 86; Adams, *Interracial Marriage in Hawaii*, 214, 222; Sunoo, "Korean Women Pioneers"; Bernice Kim, Master's thesis, 207–208. According to Kim, the fact that there were few picture brides who were educationally better than their husbands accounts for the fact that there were not even more divorces—the 1913–1916 period saw 5.0 for the Japanese and 2.4 for the Chinese. Compared to the Korean divorce rate, the Japanese and Chinese maintained a relatively steady rate. While divorce was rare among the small number of married couples who had come during the original immigration wave in 1903–1905, they were not uncommon in the picture-bride group. Two cohorts were particularly prone to divorce: those picture brides who came later rather than earlier and those who had been widowed or divorced in Korea and for whom this was their second marriage. The divorce rate of Koreans per 1,000 married population in Hawai'i during the years 1913–1916 was 3.7. The rate doubled to 7.6 during 1917–1920, and went up again, to 8.5, during 1921–1924. The rate was highest during the years 1925–1927, at 10.7, after which it declined.

52. Yoon, *The Passage of a Picture Bride*, 115; Shular, "Halmunee with a Korean Accent."

53. Il Ki (pseud.), "Hawai esōnŭn yukch'ŏn tongp'o ŭi sirhwang," 32–36; Sin Hŭng-u, "Miju ŭi p'alch'ŏn tongp'o kŭnhwang."

54. Bernice Kim, Master's thesis, 208; Anna Choi interview in Choy, *Koreans in America*, 322–324.

55. Youngsook Kim Harvey presentation at University of Hawai'i conference, "Korean Migrants Abroad," January 7–9, 1979; Yoon, *The Passage of a Picture Bride*, 112.

56. The results of the Oh, et al. Interview Data confirm this impression. Six (children) was the number most frequently given, followed closely by eight or more. The mean number of children was around five. Data from U.S. Census of 1930, cited in table 5 in Reineke, "Language and Dialect in Hawaii," 102. Also in Reinecke *Language and Dialect in Hawaii*, 59; Lind, *Hawaii's People*, 86, table 13.

57. Kenneth P. H. Nam presentation at University of Hawai'i conference, "Korean Migrants Abroad," January 7–9, 1979; Anna Choi interview in Choy, *Koreans in America;* one might also argue that the arrival of the picture brides helped the nationalist movement in Hawai'i indirectly by eroding the regionalism that at times rent the Korean community. This occurred because the picture brides from southeastern Korea married men from the north and all other parts of Korea.

58. Yŏngnam is an alternate way of designating the southeastern region of Korea from which most of the picture brides came. Pai, *The Dreams of Two Yi-Min*, 7, 20–31, 120–121.

7. *Futei Senjin:* Japan and "Rebellious Koreans"

1. *Ku Han'guk oegyo munsŏ: Ilan*, 161–162 (June 25, 1904) and 278–279 (August 2, 1904); *Hwangsŏng sinmun*, January 25, 1905; see also *Korea Review*, January 1905, 35; *Hansŏng sinbo*, May 5, 1905; also *Ku Han'guk oegyo munsŏ: Ilan*, 540–541; *Hwangsŏng sinmun*, May 17, 1905; see also *Korea Review*, May 1905, 194.

2. *Hwangsŏng sinmun*, August 10 and 15, 1905; *Korea Review*, August 1905, 318; translation by Yun Yŏ-jun in Kim Hyung-chan, ed., *The Korean Diaspora*, 38.

3. *Yamato shinbun*, September 11, 1905; HSPA Trustees, *Minutes*, August 10 and 17, 1905; see chapter 4 for a discussion of this association from the point of view of Wadman and the planters; No, *ChaeMi Hanin saryak*, 19–20; Lyu, "Korean Nationalist Activities," 80.

4. Chung, *The Oriental Policy of the United States*, 241–245; No, *ChaeMi Hanin saryak*, 18; *Yamato shinbun*, July 17, 1905.

5. Government-general of Chosen, *Annual Report;* Japanese consulate-general in Honolulu, *Hawai Chōsenjin jijō*, 96, 105, 111. However, the report continued, those who have visited Korea do know Korea's actual condition and talk about it quite accurately.

6. Japanese consulate-general in Honolulu, *Hawai Chōsenjin jijō*, 114.

7. Williams, Chief of the Division of Far Eastern Affairs, to Lansing, Secretary of State, June 26, 1915. Territory of Hawai'i, *Governor's Files*. This memorandum was sent to A. A. Jones, acting secretary of the interior, on July 6, 1915, labeled "Confidential" and numbered 14243. Jones sent the memo on to Pinkham on July 12, 1915. Wadman to Pinkham, July 26, 1915, and Fry to Pinkham, July 27, 1915. Territory of Hawai'i, *Governor's Files*.

8. Pinkham to Jones, July 27, 1915. Territory of Hawai'i, *Governor's Files*. The incident to which Pinkham refers occurred in May, when an embezzlement case gave Syng-

man Rhee an opportunity to dislodge the president of the KNA, Kim Chong-hak, and the treasurer.

9. Lyu, "Korean Nationalist Activities," 54. Lyu mistakenly says the ship arrived in 1915; Suh, ed. and trans., *The Writings of Henry Cu Kim*, 17, 253–276.

10. The first of these reports was "The state of recalcitrant Koreans in the United States and Hawaii." Government-general of Korea, Bureau of Police Affairs, *Beikoku*. A second report containing information on Koreans in Hawai'i appeared six months later, titled, "The recent state of recalcitrant Koreans abroad." Government-general of Korea, Bureau of Police Affairs, *Zaigai*. In the following year came another report containing information on Koreans in Hawaii: "The state of public peace and order in Korea in 1922 abroad" and "Supplement: Abroad." Government-general of Korea, Bureau of Police Affairs, *Taishō* and *Taishō tsuika;* the final study, which was issued by the consulate-general in Honolulu, was titled, "The state of Koreans in Hawaii." Japanese consulate-general in Honolulu, *Hawai Chōsenjin jijō*. This source is the most valuable, since it is the only one devoted solely to Koreans in Hawai'i. This was the last of the reports and was seemingly issued twice, once in December 1925 and again in October 1926. The December 1925 version appears in Kim Chŏng-ju, ed., *Chōsen tōchi shiryō*, 927–1008.

11. Government-general of Korea, Bureau of Police Affairs, *Beikoku*, 3.

12. Ibid., 6, 13; Government-general of Korea, Bureau of Police Affairs, *Zaigai*, 33–38.

13. Government-general of Korea, Bureau of Police Affairs, *Beikoku*, 3–6; government-general of Korea, Bureau of Police Affairs, *Zaigai*, 38; Japanese consulate-general in Honolulu, *Hawai Chōsenjin jijō*, 104; Government-general of Chosen, *Annual Report*.

14. Government-general of Korea, Bureau of Police Affairs, *Beikoku*, 14, 26–27; government-general of Korea, Bureau of Police Affairs, *Zaigai*, 37.

15. Laupahoehoe Sugar Company, LSC 22C/1. HSPAPA.

16. Ibid.

17. Appenzeller, "A Generation of Koreans in Hawaii," 81–82; Evans, "Se Won Kim," 17–19; that this might be construed as spying or exercising control was apparently on the minds of the Japanese government as recently as 1985. In that year, as part of the celebrations surrounding the 100th Anniversary of Japanese Immigration to Hawaii (Kanyaku Imin), the Japanese consulate in Honolulu lent to the Bishop Museum ten volumes of registry that had been bound in the late 1970s. Included in those volumes were two devoted to Koreans. Realizing their mistake, the consulate took back those two volumes. When I visited the consulate that year armed with the consulate's own filing number for the volumes (TL 1977.114) and the invoice (number 5752) from the Bishop Museum and asked to see the two volumes, no one seemed to know anything about them; Suh, ed. and trans., *The Writings of Henry Cu Kim*, 135.

18. Japanese consulate-general in Honolulu, *Hawai Chōsenjin jijō*, 34; "Koreans in Hawaii Angered by Japan," *Los Angeles Times*, May 18, 1925. This appeared the following day in Rising to Lockhart, Chief, Division of Far Eastern Affairs, U.S. Department of State, May 19, 1925, in *Records of the Department of State;* one unfortunate Korean named Choy Yong Jo was murdered in 1910 for being a spy for the Japanese, *Pacific Commercial Advertiser,* September 2, 1910.

19. An ad hoc organization called the Kongdonghoe was organized, and fifty of its

members penned the protest, which was printed in the *Kungminbo* on May 23, 1925; Japanese consulate-general in Honolulu, *Hawai Chōsenjin jijō*, 114–115; six weeks later, on July 7, Yang's car was attacked and the driver was severely injured, causing Yang to leave Hawai'i. Warren Kim, *Koreans in America*, 90.

20. Japanese consulate-general in Honolulu, *Hawai Chōsenjin jijō*, 113.

21. Ibid., 114.

22. Government-general of Korea, Bureau of Police Affairs, *Taishō*, 118; Chai, "A Picture Bride from Korea," 9; Harry Kim, Civil Defense director, interview by author, July 25, 1992, Hilo; "I recall an incident of some years ago when some Korean children were sent to a language school by their parents to learn Japanese." Student Journal, June 18, 1943, UHSPJ.

23. See U.S. Department of State, Division of Far Eastern Affairs, *Records of the Department of State*, for the U.S. attitude toward the Korean independence movement; Chong-Sik Lee, *The Politics of Korean Nationalism;* Robinson, *Cultural Nationalism in Colonial Korea, 1920–1925.*

24. Blackey, "Cultural Aspects of Case Work in Hawaii," 30–45; Eubank, "The Effects of the First Six Months of World War Two," 38.

25. Japanese consulate-general in Honolulu, *Hawai Chōsenjin jijō*, 113; Masuoka, "Race Attitudes of the Japanese People in Hawaii," 141–142.

26. Student Journals, October 7, 1944, and Summer 1943, UHSPJ.

27. Student Journal, Sociology 151, 1944, UHSPJ. (The writer is a Japanese.)

28. Quoted in Masuoka, "Race Attitudes of the Japanese People in Hawaii," 140.

29. Spanish-Korean female, Student Journal, Summer 1943, UHSPJ.

30. Masuoka, "Race Attitudes of the Japanese People in Hawaii," 186. The standard deviations, moreover, were large, indicating a wide range of opinions about the Koreans.

31. Ibid., 61–62, chart 1 and table 4, 139–140, 142, 230–231; the Japanese *overall* ranked Koreans fourth out of all the various racial groups in Hawai'i in 1931. When he surveyed *all* Japanese five years later, the Koreans had slipped from fourth to fifth place. Chinese ranked Koreans eighth, and Caucasians ranked them one notch lower at ninth. Masuoka, "Race Preferences in Hawaii," 635; Student Journal, November 19, 1943, UHSPJ.

32. Masuoka, "Race Preference in Hawaii," 639; Masuoka, "Race Attitudes of the Japanese People in Hawaii," 138–139, 187–188, table 9.

8. Educational Achievement and Social Disorganization

1. Wadman to Pinkham, July 26, 1915. Territory of Hawai'i, *Governor's Files;* also, Wadman, "Educational Work among the Koreans."

2. "Life History," University of Oregon Library.

3. Adams, "The Functions of the Language Schools in Hawaii," 178–179. That the *ilse* parents wanted their children to gain facility in the Korean language was confirmed in the Oh, et al. Interview Data, in which only 10 percent said that it was not necessary to teach Korean language to the children. Item 42.

4. Livesay, *A Study of Public Education in Hawaii*, 30; Gulick, *Mixing the Races in Hawaii*, 54, table 7. In 1910, there were 362 native (Hawaiian)-born Korean children, representing just 8 percent of the Korean population in Hawai'i; Crawford, "Characteristics of the Public and Alien Schools of Hawaii," 112–120; there may have been unli-

censed Korean language schools in addition. A survey taken in 1920 estimated that about 800 Korean children attended language schools, although only 729 Koreans were enrolled in the public schools. Reineke, "Language and Dialect in Hawaii," 202, citing *A Survey of Education in Hawaii,* 112; Gulick cites a smaller figure of 535 registered in the public schools in 1920. See Gulick, *Mixing the Races in Hawaii,* 54, table 7; Territory of Hawai'i, Department of Public Instruction, *Biennial Report,* tables 1 and 6. Another source from the same period, Territory of Hawai'i, Department of Public Instruction, *Biennial Report,* says there were eight Korean language schools with 13 teachers and an enrollment of 224.

5. Livesay, *A Study of Public Education in Hawaii,* 30; Gulick, *Mixing the Races in Hawaii,* 54, table 7; Midkiff, "The Economic Determinants of Education in Hawaii," 48, 60, table 12, quoting the 1930 U.S. Census; Crawford, "Characteristics of the Public and Alien Schools of Hawaii"; Reineke, "Language and Dialect in Hawaii," 202, quoting *Report of 1932.*

6. Reineke, "Language and Dialect in Hawaii," 202; Crawford, "Characteristics of the Public and Alien Schools of Hawaii"; William C. Smith, *The Second Generation Oriental in America,* 7.

7. Crawford, "Characteristics of the Public and Alien Schools of Hawaii"; Midkiff, "The Economic Determinants of Education in Hawaii," 213.

8. Reineke, "Language and Dialect in Hawaii," 202–203, citing the 1930 census; also Reineke, *Language and Dialect in Hawaii* (1969), 104; Adams, *Interracial Marriage in Hawaii,* 187–188; Hormann, "Speech, Prejudice, and the School in Hawaii," 74–80, 79; Schmitt, "Hawaii's Koreans, 1960."

9. Adams, et al., *The Peoples of Hawaii,* 46; Student Journal, Summer 1943, UHSPJ. (The writer was a Korean female.)

10. Jones, "Koreans Abroad," 446–451.

11. Kenneth Nam recalled that his picture-bride mother always reminded him to get an education or he would remain on the plantation. Five of her six children completed college. Kenneth Nam presentation at University of Hawai'i, January 7–9, 1979.

12. Lind, *Hawaii's People,* 89.

13. Gulick, *Mixing the Races in Hawaii,* 48, table 6; Midkiff, "The Economic Determinants of Education in Hawaii," 203–205; Livesay, *A Study of Public Education in Hawaii,* 71, 78, 81, 92–93, 95–97; Adams, *Interracial Marriage in Hawaii,* 268; Adams, "Immigration and Enterprise," 6; Jarrett, "Mathematical Achievement," table 23; to supplement the macroview presented here with a microview, it is instructive to look at a group of thirteen second-generation Korean students (eight boys and five girls) at Maui High School and their parents in 1930. Their families were large, averaging about seven persons. Eighty-two percent of the parents wanted their children to enter professional fields, about the same percentage as the children. Only four students had been out of school for any length of time, due only to sickness. Seven out of the thirteen read during their leisure time. Stratford, "Cross-Section of a High School Student's Life," 16 (table 6), 50, 53 (table 22), 54 (table 23), 57 (table 24), and 90 (table 40).

14. Midkiff, "The Economic Determinants of Education in Hawaii," 213; Adams, "Functions of the Language Schools in Hawaii," 197–198.

15. Adams, et al., *The Peoples of Hawaii,* 49–50; Adams, *Interracial Marriage in Hawaii,* 163–164, 210, 283, 289–290, 315–316.

16. Adams, et al., *The Peoples of Hawaii*, 2; Schmitt, "Hawaii's Koreans, 1960."

17. Hormann, "Racial Complexion of Hawaii's Future Population," 68–72; Adams, *Interracial Marriage in Hawaii*, 314.

18. Student Journal, Summer 1943, UHSPJ.

19. Lind, *Hawaii: The Last of the Magic Isles*, 114, table 7; Adams, *Interracial Marriage in Hawaii*, 323; while the city receives most of the blame for aiding and abetting tendencies for social disorganization, in the case of outmarriage, it appears that among the *ilse*, one was more likely to outmarry if in a rural setting rather than already in the city. As one scholar suggests, there was relatively more Korean social control over this one issue in the cities where there were, after all, many Koreans, than there was on isolated plantations. Adams, *Interracial Marriage in Hawaii*, 20, 23.

20. Lind, *Hawaii's People*, 108. While sociologists who studied this phenomenon in the 1930s declared outmarriage a negative indicator, readers of this work viewing it from the perspective of many decades later may well wish to question whether outmarriage, per se, is a valid indicator of social disorganization.

21. Schmitt, "Age, Race and Marital Failure in Hawaii," 9; Lind, "Divorce Trends in Hawaii, 1940–1950"; Adams, *Interracial Marriage in Hawaii*, 214, 225 and 250. The divorce rates for Koreans per one thousand were 3.66 for the years 1913–1916, 7.57 for 1917–1920, 8.50 for 1921–1924, 10.67 for 1925–1927, 7.57 for 1928–1929, 6.55 for 1930–1931, and 5.19 for 1932–1933.

22. Adams, *Interracial Marriage in Hawaii*, 288. The statistics reflect the number of persons employed by the Federal Emergency Relief Administration in November 1934; Lind, "The Ghetto and the Slum," 214–215; in 1930 there were 165 Koreans over the age of sixty-five. Midkiff, "The Economic Determinants of Education in Hawaii," 60, table 12, taken from the 1930 U.S. Census.

23. June Lee and Hisoon Chung, "Changing Attitudes of Koreans in Hawaii toward Old Age Dependency," UHSPJ; while it was the *ilse* who generated these high rates of dependency, there were predictions that the same fate could befall some in the second generation. In contrast to many Koreans who were excelling academically, there were those who had little education because their poorly educated parents saw no need to educate them. These parents "believed that since they did not have any education and got along fine, why, their children could do the same." Some older Koreans worried: "What will become of the children of these parents?" Student paper, no date, no author, no title. UHSPJ.

24. Madorah D. Smith, "A Comparison of the Neurotic Tendencies," 395–417. Koreans were tied for first with the part-Hawaiians as most neurotic; Wedge and Abe, "Racial Incidence of Mental Disease in Hawaii," 337–338, table 2; Lind, "Some Ecological Patterns of Community Disorganization in Honolulu," 206–220.

25. Midkiff, "The Economic Determinants of Education in Hawaii," 96; Adams, *Interracial Marriage in Hawaii*, 287. The number of cases for Caucasians during this period was 1,250, slightly less than the Koreans; Yamamura and Sakumoto, "Residential Segregation in Honolulu," 45–61; Lind, "The Ghetto and the Slum," 206–215. One can speculate that one reason for high rates of juvenile delinquency was that many young Koreans were deprived of a father figure early on.

26. Emma Shin, "Korean Family in Hawaii," University of Oregon Library. (The writer was born in 1907; the article was written in 1927.)

27. Lind and Weaver, comp., *Data Bearing on Delinquency and Crime in Hawaii*,

10, 33; Territory of Hawai'i, Board of Prison Directors, *Report of the Board of Prison Directors.* The figures for inmates are: 1932, 4.27 percent; 1933, 4.61 percent; 1934, 4.61 percent; 1935, 3.81 percent; 1936, 4.24 percent. The figures for Japanese (in percent) were, respectively, 9.48, 10.89, 11.33, 11.82, and 11.52. The figures for Japanese parolees rose from 8.03 percent in 1933 to 9.85 percent in 1936; Adams, et al., *The Peoples of Hawaii,* 35.
    28. Coulter and Bernice Kim, "The Koreans in Hawaii," 9–10.

9. Intergenerational Conflict

    1. Peter Hyun, *In the New World,* 136.
    2. Japanese consulate-general in Honolulu, *Hawai Chōsenjin jijō,* 41; see also student paper, no date, no title, no author. UHSPJ.
    3. Peter Hyun, *In the New World,* 25; Pai, *The Dreams of Two Yi-Min,* 150–151.
    4. Oh, et al., Interview Data; Pearl Yim, "Cultural Practices of the Koreans in Hawaii," UHSPJ; Pai, *The Dreams of Two Yi-Min,* 160–161.
    5. Rhodes, "Shirley Temple Feet," 127; student paper, no date, no title, no author (by a second-generation Korean). UHSPJ; see also Japanese consulate-general in Honolulu, *Hawai Chōsenjin jijō,* 41; Pai, *The Dreams of Two Yi-Min,* 101; Emma Shin, "Korean Family in Hawaii," University of Oregon Library.
    6. Pearl Yim, "Cultural Practices of the Koreans in Hawaii," UHSPJ .
    7. Ibid.
    8. Ibid.
    9. Bernice Kim, Master's thesis, 115–118.
    10. Choy and Sutton, "Ha Soo Whang"; also, Sutton, "Korean Music in Hawaii," 99–120; Warren Kim, *Koreans in America,* 45–46. In 1940, the Hyung Jay group evolved into the Muyongdan, but this dissolved during the Pacific War. Whang would be with the YWCA for seventeen years.
    11. Oh, et al., Interview Data, items 31, 40, 41, and 42; Pearl Yim, "Cultural Practices of the Koreans in Hawaii," UHSPJ; student paper, no date, no title, no author, but written by a second-generation Korean; second anonymous paper, UHSPJ.
    12. "Meet My Family" (Korean female), UHSPJ.
    13. Peter Hyun, *In the New World,* 16.
    14. Ibid., 27, 31. Ironically, for that writer, he found proper English to be a liability in another way: "Just when I thought I was speaking correct English, I would be ridiculed for doing just that outside the classroom. Correct English was for the classroom only; once outside, everyone spoke Hawaiian pidgin."
    15. Shin-pyo Kang, "The East Asian Culture." Kang interviewed twenty second-generation Korean Americans, mostly between the ages of forty and sixty. Shin-pyo Kang, Statement (hereafter abbreviated as S) 9, 249.
    16. Kang, S21, 240; Pearl Yim, "Cultural Practices of the Koreans in Hawaii," UHSPJ.
    17. Kang, S17, S18, S20, S21, and S23, 237–240, 251.
    18. Pai, *The Dreams of Two Yi-Min,* 157.
    19. Ibid., 156, 160. Their mother died in 1947 at the age of fifty-three.
    20. "The Kim Family, UHSPJ"; "Life History," UHSPJ.
    21. Pai, *The Dreams of Two Yi-Min,* 56; Kang, S10, 232.
    22. Kang, S20, 238–239; Handley, "Our Standards Are Different," 52–53.

23. Grace K. Lee "My Family," UHSPJ.

24. For how this concept operates in contemporary American society, see Kwang Chung Kim, et al., "Filial Piety and Intergenerational Relationship," 233–245.

25. Pearl Yim, "Cultural Practices of the Koreans in Hawaii," UHSPJ; Kang, S11, 233; June Lee and Hisoon Chung, "Changing Attitudes of Koreans in Hawaii toward Old Age Dependency," UHSPJ, 11–12.

26. Oh, et al., Interview Data, items 30, 44, and 45; June Lee and Hisoon Chung, "Changing Attitudes of Koreans in Hawaii toward Old Age Dependency," UHSPJ, 10–11, 13.

27. Kang, S11, 233; June Lee and Hisoon Chung, "Changing Attitudes of Koreans in Hawaii toward Old Age Dependency," UHSPJ, 12–13.

28. "Life History of E. S." University of Oregon Library; "Meet My Family" (Korean female), UHSPJ.

29. Peter Hyun, *In the New World,* 133–134.

30. Kang, S13, S24, S25, S32, and S33, 234, 244–245, 251–252; "Life History," UHSPJ.

31. Oh, et al., Interview Data, item 52.

32. Kang, S10, S13, S30, S33, and S45, 232, 234, 242, 245, and 251–252; student paper, no date, no title, no author (2). UHSPJ.

33. Pai, *The Dreams of Two Yi-Min,* 171–172, 196.

34. Oh, et al., Interview Data, items 23, 25, and 27; Lind, *Hawaii's People,* 101.

35. Pai, *The Dreams of Two Yi-Min,* 142; Kang, S14 and S16, 235, 236; circumstantial evidence indicating a preference for sons can be adduced from the Oh, et al. Interview Data, which reported "four" as the most frequent response to the number of sons and "three" for the number of daughters. In other words, it appears that many *ilse* couples stopped procreating after having a boy as their last born. Oh, et al., Interview Data, items 23, 25, and 27.

36. Lila K. Lee, "The History of My Life," UHSPJ.

37. Ibid.; Pearl Yim, "Cultural Practices of the Koreans in Hawaii," UHSPJ.

38. Peter Hyun, *In the New World,* 29.

39. Emma Shin, "Korean Family in Hawaii," University of Oregon Library; Kang, S2 and S3, 228–229.

40. Douglas Woo, "The Story of the First Two Generations of My Family in Hawaii," UHSPJ. (The speaker here is Douglas Woo's mother.); Pearl Yim, "Cultural Practices of the Koreans in Hawaii," UHSPJ.

41. "A Life History," University of Oregon Library; Peter Hyun, *In the New World,* 26–28.

42. Oh, et al., Interview Data, items 50 and 51.

43. Pai, *The Dreams of Two Yi-Min,* 151.

44. Peter Hyun, *In the New World,* 276; student paper, no date, no title, and no author, but written by a second-generation Korean. UHSPJ.

45. Kang, S5 and S6, 230–231.

46. Peter Hyun, *In the New World,* 276.

47. "The Story of Life," University of Oregon Library; Grace K. Lee, "My Family," UHSPJ.

48. Bernice Kim, Master's thesis, 124–125.

49. Ibid., 123–124.

50. Kang, S1, 246; June Lee and Hisoon Chung, "Changing Attitudes of Koreans in Hawaii toward Old Age Dependency," UHSPJ, 12.

51. Pearl Yim, "Cultural Practices of the Koreans in Hawaii," UHSPJ; Bernice Kim, Master's thesis, 125; Kang, S1, 246.

52. Kang, S8 and S22, 248, 250.

53. Pearl Yim, "Cultural Practices of the Koreans in Hawaii," UHSPJ; *Honolulu Advertiser,* July 18, 1993.

54. Kang, S7, 247.

55. "Meet My Family" (Korean female), UHSPJ; Grace K. Lee, "My Family," UHSPJ; Pai, *The Dreams of Two Yi-Min,* 150.

56. Kang, S1 and S22, 246, 252.

57. Peter Hyun, *In the New World,* 16, 29.

58. This paragraph and the five paragraphs that follow are based upon the following sources: "Life History of E. S." University of Oregon Library; Tai Hi Lim, "The Personal and Cultural Approach to the Study of a Community," UHSPJ (The community is Spreckelsville, Maui.); student paper, no date, no title, no author; "The Korean Group and Discrimination" (apparently written around 1945 by a Korean), UHSPJ; "The Korean Church and Religion in Hawaii," UHSPJ; Peter Hyun, *In the New World,* 8–9; Pai, *The Dreams of Two Yi-Min,* 140–141.

59. Kang, S22, 190, 252; William C. Smith, *The Second Generation of Orientals in America,* 7; Pearl Yim, "Cultural Practices of the Koreans in Hawaii," UHSPJ; "The Korean Group and Discrimination," UHSPJ.

60. Kang Shin-pyo, "The East Asian Culture," 109, 190.

10. Race Relations

1. Kang, S28, 241; Lila K. Lee, "The History of My Life," UHSPJ.

2. "Church—Melting Pot," UHSPJ; Student Journal, Sociology 151, Fall 1944, UHSPJ; "Report on Racial Group Feeling," UHSPJ.

3. Kang S28, 241; Student Journal, Sociology 151, Fall 1944, UHSPJ; "Report on Racial Group Feeling," UHSPJ; Student Journal, December 29, 1944, UHSPJ.

4. Spanish-Korean female, Student Journal, Summer 1943, UHSPJ; "Different Races and What We Say About Them," UHSPJ; "Groups in Hawaii: Their Nicknames and Characterization," UHSPJ; "List of Nicknames as I Have Heard Them Used on Kauai," UHSPJ; "Characterizations Given to the Various Groups," UHSPJ; Peter Hyun, *In the New World,* 31.

5. Spanish-Korean female, Student Journal, Summer 1943, UHSPJ; "Categorizing People and Group Feeling," UHSPJ.

6. Vinacke, "Stereotyping among National-Racial Groups in Hawaii," 272 (table 2), 275, 278.

7. The figure was 86 percent, according to the Oh, et al. Interview Data; Grace K. Lee, "My Family," UHSPJ.

8. "The Korean Group and Discrimination," UHSPJ; student paper (2), no date, no title, and no author, but written by a Korean. UHSPJ.

9. "Race Stereotypes—'Koreans,'" UHSPJ.

10. Douglas Woo, "The Story of the First Two Generations of My Family in Hawaii," UHSPJ; "Report on Racial Group Feeling," UHSPJ; Kang, S28, 241.

11. Student Journal, November 12, 1943, UHSPJ.

12. Student Journal, December 27, 1944, UHSPJ.

13. Kang Shin-pyo, "The East Asian Culture," 190.

14. Sung-hi Lim, "Ecological Study of the Community of Spreckelsville (Camp One), Maui," UHSPJ.

15. An informant who wished to remain anonymous made this observation to me.

16. "Life History," UHSPJ .

17. Kang Shin-pyo, "The East Asian Culture," 190.

18. Student Journal, Sociology 151, 1944, UHSPJ (The writer is a Japanese.); also, "Chi Pum Hong's brother-in-law held three degrees from various universities but could not find a job. The situation was to remain fairly unchanged until World War Two." Clifford Hong, "A Korean Grandfather," UHSPJ.

19. Kang Shin-pyo, "The East Asian Culture," 190; Student Journal, December 27, 1944, UHSPJ; Student Journal, Sociology 151, 1944, UHSPJ (The writer is a Japanese.); "Life History," UHSPJ.

20. Student Journal, Sociology 200, Fall 1942, UHSPJ.

21. "Oriental-Haole Relations," UHSPJ.

22. Peter Hyun, *In the New World*, 50–51; Kang Shin-pyo, "The East Asian Culture," 190.

23. Peter Hyun, *In the New World*, 78, 99–100, 132, 290.

24. Student Journal, Spring 1943, UHSPJ.

25. Verbatim Reports, Student Journal, Fall 1944, UHSPJ.

26. Japanese consulate-general in Honolulu, *Hawai Chōsenjin jijō*, 118; Vinacke, "Stereotyping among National-Racial Groups in Hawaii," 270 (table 2), 282; Verbatim Reports, Student Journal, Fall 1944, UHSPJ.

27. Douglas Woo, "The Story of the First Two Generations of My Family in Hawaii," UHSPJ.

28. Ibid. The speaker is the writer's father.

29. "Report on Racial Group Feeling," UHSPJ; "The Problem of a Minority Group during War Time," UHSPJ.

30. Spanish-Korean female, Student Journal, Summer 1943, UHSPJ.

31. Masuoka, "Race Preference in Hawaii," 339–340, table 1; Masuoka, "Race Attitudes of the Japanese People in Hawaii," 92–93 (chart 2, table 5), 143; from the other perspective, Japanese were viewed favorably by all groups except Korean females. Koreans specifically characterized Japanese, as they had the Chinese, as traditional and clannish. Vinacke, "Stereotyping among National-Racial Groups in Hawaii," 270 (table 2), 282.

32. Masuoka, "Race Attitudes of the Japanese People in Hawaii," 144–146.

33. Ibid. The last speaker also added, somewhat cryptically, "What I do not like about them is their thick faces—that mysterious looking faces."

34. Ibid.

35. "Report on Racial Group Feeling," UHSPJ.

36. Masuoka, "Race Attitudes of the Japanese People in Hawaii," 144–146

37. "Race Stereotypes—'Koreans,'" UHSPJ.

38. Ibid.

39. Student Journal, Spring 1943, UHSPJ.

40. Kang, S28, 241; Japanese consulate-general in Honolulu, *Hawai Chōsenjin jijō*, 118.

41. Verbatim Reports, Student Journal, Fall 1944, UHSPJ.

42. Spanish-Korean female, Student Journal, Summer 1943, UHSPJ.

43. Japanese consulate-general in Honolulu, *Hawai Chōsenjin jijō*, 118; "Groups in Hawaii: Their Nicknames and Characterization," UHSPJ; Lila K. Lee, "The Way Migrations Have Played a Role in My Family," UHSPJ.

44. "Prejudice and the Primary In-Group," UHSPJ.

45. Looking at one early year, 1932, for example: out of 37 Korean grooms, 30 had Korean brides. In absolute numbers, between 1930 and 1934, 195 men outmarried and 223 women outmarried. Adams, *Interracial Marriage in Hawaii*, 81, 323. Of all children born between 1940 and 1960 with at least one Korean parent, 60 percent had a non-Korean other parent, and by 1960, this had increased to 86 percent. Lind, *Hawaii's People*, 109, 115. What this suggests is that the later a Korean was born, the less likely he or she would marry another Korean.

46. "Disappearance of Koreans," UHSPJ; Pai, *The Dreams of Two Yi-Min*, 128.

47. Schmitt, "Hawaii's Koreans, 1960"; Hormann, "Racial Complexion of Hawaii's Future Population"; the exact outmarriage figures are: 1930–1940: grooms 24 percent, brides 39 percent; 1940: grooms 49 percent, brides 67 percent. Lind, *Hawaii: The Last of the Magic Isles*, 114, table 7.

48. Lind, *Hawaii's People*, 111; Adams, *Interracial Marriage in Hawaii*, 210.

49. Douglas Woo, "The Story of the First Two Generations of My Family in Hawaii," UHSPJ; Adams, *Interracial Marriage in Hawaii*, 187–188.

50. Oh, et al., Interview Data, items 28 and 29. Only one objected outright, while eighteen (21 percent) said they wished they would keep away from it.

51. Student Journal, n.d., UHSPJ.

52. Pai, *The Dreams of Two Yi-Min*, 129; Spanish-Korean Female, Student Journal, Summer 1943, UHSPJ; Douglas Woo, "The Story of the First Two Generations of My Family in Hawaii," UHSPJ.

53. Lind, *Hawaii's People*, 109; Lind, *An Island Community*, 306.

54. "The Problem of a Minority Group during War Time," UHSPJ.

55. Student paper, no date, no author, no title (but written by a Korean), UHSPJ; Pearl Yim, "Cultural Practices of the Koreans in Hawaii," UHSPJ; "A Life History," University of Oregon Library.

56. Stanley Kim, "Factors Contributing Towards High Amalgamation of Koreans in Hawaii," UHSPJ.

57. "Our Girls Are Being Spoiled," UHSPJ.

58. "Korean Conception of Themselves," UHSPJ.

59. "Disappearance of Koreans," UHSPJ; "The Korean Group and Discrimination," UHSPJ.

60. Hormann, "A Study of Civilian Morale, 1944," 17–24.

61. Student Journal, n.d., UHSPJ; Pai, *The Dreams of Two Yi-Min*, 129.

62. "Role of Family in Marriage Selection Disappearing," UHSPJ; Lila K. Lee, "The History of My Life," UHSPJ.

63. Pai, *The Dreams of Two Yi-Min*, 129.

64. "The Story of Life," University of Oregon Library; "Life History of E. S." University of Oregon Library. It should be noted that both of these excerpts came from Koreans of the small middle generation, who would be more likely to hold more conservative views than the second generation.

65. Pearl Yim, "Cultural Practices of the Koreans in Hawaii," UHSPJ. Tied for second place, according to Yim, were Japanese and Caucasians, while the Filipinos came in last. The order of preference among the small middle generation was Chinese, Japanese, and Caucasians. Hawaiians do not generate much comment, but one source indicates that Hawaiians did not like Japanese because of their exclusiveness, but Hawaiian girls seemed to like the Koreans very much. Beaglehold, *Some Modern Hawaiians*, 130, chart 2.

66. Student Journal, January 16, 1944, UHSPJ.

67. "Mores—Marriage between People of Different Racial Extractions Contrary to Mores of Oriental Marriages," Student Journal, December 10, 1944, UHSPJ.

68. Ibid.

69. Hormann, "A Study of Civilian Morale, 1944"; "Disappearance of Koreans," UHSPJ.

70. Grace K. Lee, "My Family," UHSPJ.

71. "Peter Kim and Wife," UHSPJ.

72. Violet Kim, "Changes in Controls Exercised by the Koreans in Wahiawa Since the War," UHSPJ.

73. "Effect of War—Lack of Local Boys," UHSPJ.

74. Student Journal, Spring 1943, UHSPJ.

75. Student Journal, January 6, 1943, UHSPJ.

76. "Prejudice and the Mores," UHSPJ; "Group Feeling—Consciousness Felt Through Embarrassing Situation," UHSPJ.

77. Student Journal, Sociology 151, November 8, 1944, UHSPJ. (The writer is a haole).

78. Student Journal, Fall 1944, UHSPJ; Violet Kim, "Changes in Controls Exercised by the Koreans in Wahiawa Since the War," UHSPJ; Rhodes, "Wahiawa Red Dirt," 9.

79. Emma Shin, "Korean Family in Hawaii," University of Oregon Library; Eubank, "The Effects of the First Six Months of World War Two," 53.

80. Student Journal, Spring 1943, UHSPJ; Pai, *The Dreams of Two Yi-Min*, 122.

81. "Topic of Gossip—Dating of Other Nationality," UHSPJ.

82. "Conflict in Primary Group," UHSPJ.

83. Masuoka, "Race Attitudes of the Japanese People in Hawaii," 140–141.

84. Peter Hyun, *In the New World*, 31–32; Ogawa, *Jan Ken Po,* 39.

85. Pai, *The Dreams of Two Yi-Min*, 121, 132.

86. Student Journal, Summer 1943, UHSPJ.

11. The Pacific War and Wartime Restrictions

1. Rhodes, "Wahiawa Red Dirt," 7–8.

2. Pai, *The Dreams of Two Yi-Min*, 123–124; Violet Kim, "Change in Controls Exercised by the Koreans in Wahiawa Since the War," UHSPJ.

3. Macmillan, "Koreans under Martial Law," 5–6. Although this unpublished paper was revised for publication later as "Unwanted Allies: Koreans as Enemy Aliens in World War II" (*The Hawaiian Journal of History* 19 [1985]), I have found the earlier and more lengthy unpublished paper to be of greater utility. Much of the information that follows relies on this pioneering research, and I am grateful for his permission to cite it extensively in this chapter.

4. Macmillan, "Koreans under Martial Law," 7–8.

5. Ibid., 8–9.
6. Ibid., 4.
7. Ibid., 7.
8. J. Kuang (Jacob) Dunn to Gordon T. Bowles, January 20, 1942; undated memo apparently written by Bowles; "Summarization of Korean Political Organizations," no date, but probably written in February. These and other letters and memos to follow are contained in a file maintained by Andrew W. Lind, a sociology professor at the University of Hawai'i who served as a consultant on race relations during the war and who was privy to confidential information collected by various government intelligence agencies. I found these materials among the papers of Lind at the offices of the former location of the sociology department at the University of Hawai'i. Some of these memos are unsigned and/or undated. They will be cited hereafter as *Intelligence Files.*
9. Unsigned memo dated January 9, 1942. *Intelligence Files.*
10. "Summarization of Korean Political Organizations." *Intelligence Files.*
11. Memo with no date and no signature; soon after this memo was produced, the UKC announced in a memo dated March 14, 1942, that the Sino-Korean People's League had withdrawn from the UKC. *Intelligence Files.*
12. "Recommendation Concerning Publication of a Periodical by the Sino-Korean Peoples' League," March 14, 1942. *Intelligence Files.*
13. Memo from Bowles dated April 4, 1942, and titled "Korean Committee." *Intelligence Files.*
14. *Seattle Post-Intelligencer,* February 19, 1942. Haan's claim also appears in Sweethaven, *Gentlemen of Japan,* 16–18, in which the source is, once again, Haan himself.
15. Hynd, *Betrayal from the East,* 108–109.
16. Macmillan, "Koreans under Martial Law," 5, also note 102.
17. *Seattle Post-Intelligencer,* February 19, 1942.
18. The undated memo titled "Fear or Suspicion in Korean Community" identified Tai Sung Lee as the source of this opinion. *Intelligence Files.*
19. Bowles, "Korean Committee," *Intelligence Files;* Macmillan, "Koreans under Martial Law," note 102.
20. Office of Strategic Services (OSS), *Foreign Nationalities Branch Files, 1942–1945,* 175.
21. Haan's editorial appeared on October 14, 1942, but it is not clear in which newspaper it appeared. The editorial is contained in *Intelligence Files.* Haan cites as his sources an editorial in Rhee's Dongjihoe publication, *T'aep'yŏngyang chubo (Pacific Weekly),* of January 18, 1941, and an article in the May 27, 1942, issue of the *Honolulu Star-Bulletin* titled "Koreans Outline Their Fairness to the Japanese"; Macmillan, "Koreans under Martial Law," note 102. While on the mainland, Haan attempted to affiliate himself with a left-wing organization called the Korean National Revolutionary Party (Chosŏn minjok hyŏngmyŏngdan), which was based in China and was associated with Kim Yak-san, a communist who headed the Korean Volunteer Army in China. But even this group did not take Haan seriously. Anonymous, "Korean Revolutionary Nationalism in America," 18.
22. The memo dated January 8, 1942, was titled "Discussion with Korean Leaders." The memo of April 4, 1942, by Gordon T. Bowles was titled "Korean Committee." *Intelligence Files.*
23. Hormann, "A Study of Civilian Morale, 1944," 17–24.

24. *Honolulu Star-Bulletin,* May 27 and July 27, 1942; Eubank, "The Effects of the First Six Months of World War Two," 44, 80; Burrows, *Chinese and Japanese in Hawaii,* 18; Student Journal, Sociology 151, 1944, UHSPJ.

25. Macmillan, "Koreans under Martial Law," 5, citing Eubank, "The Effects of the First Six Months of World War Two," 12, 53–54, 182. See also *Honolulu Advertiser,* August 29, 1940, and January 9, 1942. While any *ilse* who returned to Korea for a visit had to apply for a Japanese passport, American-born Koreans could be claimed as dual citizens of the United States and Japan only if they had been registered with the Japanese census by his or her parents before their fourteenth birthday.

26. "Patriotism—Ethnocentricity among the Wahiawa Koreans and the Prisoners of War," UHSPJ; Clifford Hong, "A Korean Grandfather," wrote that there were three thousand Korean POWs held on Sand Island and that his grandfather, Chi Pum Hong, served as interpreter. UHSPJ.

27. "Meet My Family" (Korean female), UHSPJ; Pai, *The Dreams of Two Yi-Min,* 127, 143.

28. Macmillan, "Koreans under Martial Law," 9–10.

29. Duke Moon, Jr., "A Korean Pioneer;" UHSPJ.

30. Eubank, "The Effects of the First Six Months of World War Two," 85–86, cited in Macmillan, "Koreans under Martial Law," 10; Harold Kim presentation at University of Hawai'i conference, "Korean Migrants Abroad," January 7–9, 1979.

31. Kenneth Nam presentation at University of Hawai'i conference, "Korean Migrants Abroad," January 7–9, 1979; Pai, *The Dreams of Two Yi-Min,* 133; *Honolulu Star-Bulletin,* May 18, 1943, quoted in Macmillan, "Koreans under Martial Law," 11.

32. *Honolulu Star-Bulletin,* July 27, 1943, quoted in Macmillan, "Koreans under Martial Law," 11.

33. Macmillan, "Koreans under Martial Law," 5, 9.

34. Ibid., 12–13.

35. Ibid., 15–16, citing *Korean National Herald-Pacific Weekly,* February 4, 1942.

36. Bowles memos of March 1942 and April 4, 1942. *Intelligence Files.*

37. Ahn, "Korean National Association," 35; Macmillan, "Koreans under Martial Law," 16.

38. Macmillan, "Koreans under Martial Law," 16–17, quoting United Korean Committee, "The Korean Status in the Territory of Hawaii," undated.

39. *Honolulu Star-Bulletin,* March 21, 1942, in Macmillan, "Koreans under Martial Law," 18.

40. "A Petition for Clarification of Korean Status," undated, signed by J. K. Dunn, Secretary of Public Relations, UKC, and addressed to Gen. Delos C. Emmons, in Macmillan, "Koreans under Martial Law," 18.

41. Eubank, "The Effects of the First Six Months of World War Two," 84–85; Warren Kim, *Koreans in America,* 139; Hormann, "Race Relations in Hawaii," 131; Macmillan, "Koreans under Martial Law," 11; "The Problem of a Minority Group during War Time," UHSPJ.

42. Macmillan, "Koreans under Martial Law," 19.

43. Ibid., 20, citing *Korean National Herald-Pacific Weekly,* May 12, 1943.

44. *Honolulu Star-Bulletin,* May 6 and July 15, 1943, and *Honolulu Advertiser,* May 17, June 5, and July 21, 1943, as quoted in Macmillan, "Koreans under Martial Law," 20.

45. Pai, *The Dreams of Two Yi-Min,* 124–125.

46. United Korean Committee, "Korean Observations and Recommendations on American National Defense," March 7, 1942, cited in Macmillan, "Koreans under Martial Law," 21–22, and note 70, citing Eubank, "The Effects of the First Six Months of World War Two," 90–91.

47. *Honolulu Star-Bulletin,* April 30, May 15, July 14, and July 15, 1943, and *Honolulu Advertiser,* July 15, July 19, and July 21, 1943, cited in Macmillan, "Koreans under Martial Law," 22–23 and note 79.

48. *Honolulu Star-Bulletin,* May 5 and June 2, 1943; Macmillan, "Koreans under Martial Law," 24; Warren Kim, *Koreans in America,* 142–145.

49. Macmillan, "Koreans under Martial Law," 25.

50. Ibid., 26–27. Rhee was not alone in trying to capitalize on the Sohn incident. His main rival in Washington, Kilsoo Haan, and—at Haan's behest—Senator Guy M. Gillette of Iowa, were also writing letters.

51. It appeared in the June 9, 1943, issue, as cited in Macmillan, "Koreans under Martial Law," 27; "The Problem of a Minority Group during War Time," UHSPJ.

52. Macmillan, "Koreans under Martial Law," 28; *Honolulu Advertiser,* May 25, 1944.

53. Macmillan, "Koreans under Martial Law," 29–31.

54. Ibid., 31–32.

55. Ibid., 32–33, and note 102.

56. Ibid., 33.

57. Ibid., 33–34.

58. Ibid., 7; Lorne W. Bell, "A Brief Description of Certain Korean Institutions Active in Honolulu in January 1945," UHSPJ; Bernice Yamagata, "Korean Political Parties in Hawaii," UHSPJ.

59. Pai, *The Dreams of Two Yi-Min,* 144; *Honolulu Advertiser,* September 13, 1945.

12. Epilogue—The Postwar Years

1. "Possible Immigration Back to Korea after the War," UHSPJ.

2. Chai, "A Picture Bride from Korea." This particular woman had visited Korea nine times between the end of the war and the time of the interview; "A Life History," University of Oregon Library.

3. Dunn, "Progress of Koreans in Hawaii," 90–91; *Honolulu Star-Bulletin,* June 23, 1947. A few from the middle generation who had come to Hawai'i as young children in 1903–1905 or who had been born soon thereafter and were in their forties went to Korea after the war. For example, Esther Park, a graduate of the University of Hawai'i who had been with the Honolulu YMCA for eighteen years, accepted a similar post in Seoul.

4. Warren Kim, *Koreans in America,* 148–150.

5. Rhee to Lyu, July 1, 1943, in Lyu, "Korean Nationalist Activities," appendix, 139.

6. Radiogram of Syngman Rhee to Chungyil Sur, president of Dongjihoe, November 10, 1947, in Lyu, "Korean Nationalist Activities," appendix, 149 (punctuation added). For over two years this faction claimed to be the true congregation, until court action in October 1948 reunited them. Lyu, "Korean Nationalist Activities," 73–76. This account should be viewed with some caution, since the source is Lyu himself. See also "Dr. Rhee Asks Korean Church To Oust Lyu," *Honolulu Advertiser,* November 14, 1947.

7. Pai, *The Dreams of Two Yi-Min,* 145.

8. Lyu, "Korean Nationalist Activities," 81.

9. Macmillan, "The Korean Press in Hawaii," 8. The editor was Henry Cu Kim.

10. Pai, *The Dreams of Two Yi-Min*, 145, 196; Suh, ed. and trans., *The Writings of Henry Cu Kim*, 147–148.

11. "Rift Over Korean Benefit," *Honolulu Star-Bulletin*, September 7, 1950; U.S. Congress, Senate Committee on the Judiciary, "Report of the Committee on Subversive Activity," 2691, and appendix I, 2956.

12. Peter Hyun, *In the New World*, 216, 246–251.

13. Ibid., 264, 273. Alice was later executed in a purge in North Korea.

14. One source lists 166 second-generation Koreans from Hawai'i who fought in the Korean War. *Honolulu Advertiser*, December 26, 1952, and January 9, 1953; using one individual's experience as typical, Harry Kim's brother served in the Korean War, and several of his relatives in Korea were killed in the war. Harry Kim, Civil Defense director, interview by author, July 25, 1992, Hilo; Chun, "Older Koreans Planning to Note Arrival Anniversary"; *Honolulu Star-Bulletin*, February 3, 1953; "850 Attend Korean Golden Jubilee," *Honolulu Advertiser*, November 21, 1953; Chun, "Korean Golden Jubilee"; Jared G. Smith, "Do You Remember?", *Honolulu Star-Bulletin*, June 1, 1953; Meyers, "First Korean Immigrants Will Be Honored at Jubilee"; Meyers, "Korean Immigrant's Story of Advancement Is Told."

15. *Honolulu Star-Bulletin*, June 5, 1944; *Hilo Tribune*, June 7, 1944; Lorne W. Bell, "A Brief Description of Certain Korean Institutions Active in Honolulu in January 1945," UHSPJ; "The Korean Civic Association," *Honolulu Star-Bulletin*, January 22, 1945; *Honolulu Advertiser*, January 23, 1945; *Honolulu Star-Bulletin*, May 15, 1947; *Honolulu Star-Bulletin*, April 25, 1952.

16. Francis Kang, "Korean Milestone"; Duke Moon, Jr., "A Korean Pioneer," UHSPJ; Pai, *The Dreams of Two Yi-Min*, 188.

17. *Honolulu Advertiser*, October 17, 1955; Duke Moon, Jr., "A Korean Pioneer," UHSPJ.

18. Pai, *The Dreams of Two Yi-Min*, 163–164.

19. Roberta Chang interview in Patricia Hong, "The Myth of Korean Factionalism," UHSPJ; "Visas to Korea Refused, Many Say," *Honolulu Advertiser*, May 16, 1960.

20. *T'aep'yŏngyang chubo (Korean Pacific Weekly)*, April 27, 1960, and *Kungminbo*, November 22, 1961, trans. Hong Jong Sook in Patricia Hong, "The Myth of Korean Factionalism," UHSPJ.

21. Pai, *The Dreams of Two Yi-Min*, 148; Chun, "Older Koreans Planning to Note Arrival Anniversary," which noted that "[f]actionalism hampered the progress of the Koreans, but there is no factionalism among the second generation"; Roberta Chang interview in Patricia Hong, "The Myth of Korean Factionalism," UHSPJ.

22. Macmillan, "The Korean Press in Hawaii," 8.

23. Patricia Hong, "The Myth of Korean Factionalism," UHSPJ; *Honolulu Advertiser*, November 4, 1954; Yamamoto, "Political Participation among Orientals in Hawaii," 359–364. Yamamoto argues that political participation is a measure of assimilation and that, on this measure, the Koreans ranked low.

24. Dunn, "Progress of Koreans in Hawaii," 90–91.

25. "Korean Economics," UHSPJ; Violet Kim, "Changes in Controls Exercised by the Koreans in Wahiawa Since the War," UHSPJ.

26. Grace K. Lee, "My Family," UHSPJ; Douglas Woo, "The Story of the First Two Generations of My Family in Hawaii," UHSPJ.

27. "The Family," UHSPJ.

28. Lorinda Hong, "Halmoni," UHSPJ.

29. Douglas Woo, "The Story of the First Two Generations of My Family in Hawaii," UHSPJ.

30. Pai, *The Dreams of Two Yi-Min*, 138–140.

31. Chai, "A Picture Bride from Korea."

32. Douglas Woo, "The Story of the First Two Generations of My Family in Hawaii," UHSPJ.

33. Eunice Hak Bong Whang Kealoha interview about her mother, Cho Kyung Ai, in Rhodes, "How Oral History of the First Koreans to America Advances Archival Research," 4.

34. Student Journal, n.d., UHSPJ.

35. Kaneshiro, "Assimilation in a Slum Area of Honolulu," 19.

36. Pai, *The Dreams of Two Yi-Min*, 142.

37. Ibid., 173–178.

38. Ibid., 175, 178.

39. Lind, "Mounting the Occupational Ladder in Hawaii," 4–8; see also Chun, "Older Koreans Planning to Note Arrival Anniversary."

40. Lind, "Occupation and Race on Certain Frontiers," 49–70. The table on 66–68 compares percentage distribution of gainfully employed males of Hawai'i from 1930 and 1950. The exact figures comparing 1930 with 1950 are: professionals from 1.9 percent to 8.7 percent; managers and officials, 4.1 percent to 16.2 percent; clerical workers, 8.0 percent to 9.8 percent; salesworkers, 3.4 percent to 6.1 percent; craftsmen, 9.9 percent to 24.3 percent; operatives, 8.3 percent to 12.6 percent; farm labor, 47.3 percent to 4.2 percent, with Japanese at 8.1 percent in 1950 in this latter category. Moreover, in 1950, only 11.5 percent of Koreans were laborers of any kind. Schmitt, "Hawaii's Koreans, 1960"; Lind, "Mounting the Occupational Ladder in Hawaii," 6, 10.

41. Samuels, "The Effect of Social Mobility on Social Distance," 26, 28, 33, 72, 92, 93; Vinacke, "Stereotyping among National-Racial Groups in Hawaii," 265–291. If the Koreans were faulted at all by the Japanese, it was for being temperamental and clannish. While the alleged temperamental nature of the Koreans remained similar to prewar perceptions, the clannish label was perhaps a misperception. Japanese attributed clannishness to other groups as well, notably the Chinese. But the clannishness ascribed to Koreans was more a function of the relatively small number of Koreans (there were about 7,300 Koreans in Hawai'i in 1952). That is, not coming into contact with many Koreans might have led Japanese to assume exclusiveness on the part of Koreans.

42. Schmitt, *Demographic Correlates of Interracial Marriage in Hawaii*, 465. Outmarriage rates for Koreans were: 1912–1916: grooms 26.4 percent, brides 0.0 percent; 1920–1930: grooms 17.6 percent, brides 4.9 percent; 1930–1940: grooms 23.5 percent, brides 39.0 percent; 1940–1950: grooms 49.0 percent, brides 66.7 percent; 1950–1960: grooms 70.3 percent, brides 74.5 percent; 1960–1964: grooms 77.7 percent, brides 80.1 percent; Lind, *Hawaii: The Last of the Magic Isles*, 114, table 7; since some second-generation Korean men served in the armed forces and participated in the postwar occupation of Japan, a few married Japanese women and brought them back to Hawai'i,

where the new bride had to make some adjustments: "Since he was a Korean and kim chee is part of the customary diet of the Koreans she naturally followed suit. At first she didn't like the taste of kim chee but as time went by she ate kim chee regularly and seemed to like it. Now even her two year old son eats kim chee." "Adjustment of War Brides in Hawaii," 13; Schmitt, "Hawaii's Koreans, 1960"; Hormann, "Racial Complexion of Hawaii's Future Population," 68–72; Schmitt, "Age Differences in Marriage in Hawaii," 57–61, which includes a table on age difference by ethnic group of groom and bride. It is interesting that sociologists no longer considered outmarriage a form of social disorganization.

43. Taeuber, "Hawaii," 97–125, especially table 9 on 114; Douglas Woo, "The Story of the First Two Generations of My Family in Hawaii," UHSPJ; in another example, none of the third-generation Yangs, whose grandparents came on the *Mongolia,* married other Koreans. Alan In-Su Yang, interview by author, July 25, 1992, Hilo.

44. Lind, "Divorce Trends in Hawaii, 1940–1950"; Schmitt, "Age, Race and Marital Failure in Hawaii"; Cheng and Yamamura, 77–84.

45. It was two-thirds in 1940, three-quarters in 1950, and six-sevenths (86 percent) American-born by 1960. The age distribution in 1960 was: 38 percent under 15, 41 percent 15–44, and 21 percent over 45, Schmitt, "Hawaii's Koreans, 1960"; Kang Sung-jae, "Hawai ŭi Han'guk kyop'o dŭl."

46. In the mid-1950s, a Korean Old Men's Home was established. Within a few years it would have a famous resident—Syngman Rhee—who returned to Hawai'i after being overthrown in 1960 and who died at the home in 1965. Other Koreans made their own burial arrangements by joining a "burial society" run by both political organizations. Upon the death of any of the members, every other member contributed a fixed amount —originally one dollar, then two dollars—with the total amount going to the family of the deceased; "Tenants Wait Patiently for Korean Old Men's Home," *Honolulu Star-Bulletin,* June 27, 1956; Lorne W. Bell, "A Brief Description of Certain Korean Institutions Active in Honolulu in January 1945," UHSPJ; Violet Kim, "Changes in Controls Exercised by the Koreans in Wahiawa Since the War," UHSPJ; *Honolulu Star-Bulletin,* September 10, 1973. Caucasians may be ranked below Koreans because the statistics included the military Caucasians stationed in Hawai'i.

47. *Honolulu Star-Bulletin,* November 7, 1973; Francis Kang, "Daughter to Represent Park at Isle Korean Fete"; Anderson, "From Laborer to Leader in 70 Years in Hawaii"; Pai, *The Dreams of Two Yi-Min,* 196.

BIBLIOGRAPHY

Adams, Romanzo C. "Functions of the Language Schools in Hawaii." *The Friend* XCV, no. 8 (August 1925): 178–179.

———. "Functions of the Language Schools in Hawaii." *The Friend* XCV, no. 9 (September 1925): 197–198.

———. "Immigration and Enterprise." *Korean Students Annual, 1936–1937*. Honolulu: Korean Students' Alliance of Hawaii, 1937.

———. *Interracial Marriage in Hawaii: A Study of the Mutually Conditioned Processes of Acculturation and Amalgamation*. New York: Macmillan, 1937.

———, with T. M. Livesay and E. H. Van Winkle. *The Peoples of Hawaii: A Statistical Study*. Honolulu: Institute of Pacific Relations, 1925.

"Adjustment of War Brides in Hawaii." *What People in Hawaii Are Saying and Doing* 17 (August 28, 1950). Hawaii Social Science Laboratory.

Ahn, Chung Song. "Korean National Association." In *75th Anniversary of Korean Immigration to Hawaii, 1903–1978*. Honolulu: 75th Anniversary of Korean Immigration to Hawaii Committee, 1978.

Allen, Horace N. *MSS*. New York Public Library.

Anderson, John G. "From Laborer to Leader in Seventy Years in Hawaii." *Honolulu Advertiser*, January 11, 1973.

Anonymous. "Korean Revolutionary Nationalism in America: Kim Kang and the Student Circle, 1938–1956." Typescript, n.d.

Appenzeller, Alice R. "A Generation of Koreans in Hawaii." *Paradise of the Pacific* 56, no. 12 (December 1944): 81–82.

Arinaga, Esther Kwon. "Contributions of Korean Immigrant Women." In *Montage: An Ethnic History of Women in Hawaii*, ed. Nancy Foon Young and J. K. Parrish. Honolulu: University of Hawai'i, General Assistance Center, 1977.

Beaglehold, Ernest. *Some Modern Hawaiians*. Honolulu: University of Hawai'i Press, Research Publication no. 19, 1939.

Beechert, Edward D. *Working in Hawaii: A Labor History*. Honolulu: University of Hawai'i Press, 1985.

Bishop, Isabella Bird. "Koreans in Russian Manchuria." *The Korea Repository* 4 (February 1897): 41–44.

Blackey, Eileen. "Cultural Aspects of Case Work in Hawaii." *Social Process in Hawaii* 5 (June 1939): 30–45.

Bonacich, Edna, and Ivan Light. *Immigrant Entrepreneurs: Koreans in Los Angeles, 1965–1982*. Berkeley: University of California Press, 1988.

Burrows, Edwin Grant. *Chinese and Japanese in Hawaii during the Sino-Japanese Conflict.* Honolulu: Institute of Pacific Relations, 1938.

Chai, Alice. "A Picture Bride from Korea: The Life History of a Korean-American Woman in Hawaii." Typescript, n.d. University of Hawai'i Center for Korean Studies Library.

⸻. "Contributions of the Early Korean Immigrant Women in Hawaii." Typescript, n.d. University of Hawai'i Center for Korean Studies Library.

Chan, Sucheng. *Asian Americans: An Interpretive History.* Boston: Twayne, 1991.

Charr, Easurk Emsen. *The Golden Mountain: The Autobiography of a Korean Immigrant, 1895–1960,* ed. Wayne Patterson. Chicago and Urbana: University of Illinois Press, 1996.

Cheng, Ch'eng-K'un, and Douglas Yamamura. "Interracial Marriage and Divorce in Hawaii." Social Forces XXXVI, no. 1 (October 1957): 77–84.

Cheng, Lucie, and Edna Bonacich, eds. *Labor Immigration under Capitalism: Asian Workers in the United States before World War II.* Berkeley: University of California Press, 1984.

Ch'oe Kap-sin. "Imin ilse." *Han'guk ilbo,* 10 January 1973.

Chōsen sōtokufu (Government-general of Korea). *Chōsen no hogo oyobi gappō* [The situation concerning the annexation of Korea], 1917.

Chōsen sōtokufu keimukyoku (Government-general of Korea, Bureau of Police Affairs). *Beikoku oyobi Hawai chihō ni okeru futei Senjin no jōkyō* [The state of recalcitrant Koreans in the United States and the Territory of Hawai'i]. SP (Special Studies) 143, Reel SP 45, March 1921.

⸻. *Taishō II-nen Chōsen chian jōkyō.* [The state of public peace and order in Korea in 1922].

Sono ni: Kokugai [Abroad]. SP 150, Reel SP 46. LC.

Sono ni: Kokugai tsuika [Supplement: abroad]. SP 151, Reel SP 46. LC.

⸻. *Zaigai futei Senjin no kinkyō* [The recent state of recalcitrant Koreans abroad]. SP 141, Reel SP 45, September 1921.

Choy, Bong-Youn. *Koreans in America.* Chicago: Nelson-Hall, 1979.

Choy, Peggy, and Andy Sutton. "Ha Soo Whang: Woman Pioneer of Hawaii (1892–1984)." *Korea Times,* October 16, 1991.

Chun, Ella. "Korean Golden Jubilee." *Honolulu Advertiser,* November 8, 1953.

⸻. "Older Koreans Planning to Note Arrival Anniversary." *Honolulu Advertiser,* January 4, 1953.

Chung, Henry. *The Oriental Policy of the United States.* New York: Fleming H. Revell, Co., 1919.

Coman, Katherine. "The History of Contract Labor in the Hawaiian Islands." *Publications of the American Economic Association* 4, no. 3 (August 1903): 59.

Cooke, Charles M. *Papers.* Honolulu: Hawaiian Mission Children's Society.

Coulter, John Wesley, and Bernice B. H. Kim. "The Koreans in Hawaii." *Proceedings of the Hawaiian Academy of Science.* Honolulu: Bernice P. Bishop Museum Special Publication no. 21, 1933: 9–10.

Crawford, Will C. "Characteristics of the Public and Alien Schools of Hawaii." In *Administration of Hawaii,* U.S. Congress, Committee on Territories and Insular Affairs. Washington, D.C.: Government Printing Office, 1933.

Daniels, Roger. *Asian America: Chinese and Japanese in the United States Since 1850.* Seattle and London: University of Washington Press, 1988.

"Dr. Rhee Asks Korean Church to Oust Lyu." *Honolulu Advertiser,* November 14, 1947.

Dunn, J. Kuang. "Progress of Koreans in Hawaii." *Paradise of the Pacific* LVIII, no. 12 (December 1946): 90–91.

Dutton, Meiric Keeler. *The Episcopal Church in Hawaii: Ninety Years of Service, 1862–1952.* Honolulu: The Missionary District of Honolulu, Protestant Episcopal Church, 1952.

"850 Attend Korean Golden Jubilee." *Honolulu Advertiser,* November 21, 1953.

Eubank, Lauriel E. "The Effects of the First Six Months of World War Two on the Attitudes of Koreans and Filipinos toward the Japanese in Hawaii: A Study in Social Distance." Master's thesis, University of Hawai'i, 1943.

Eum Shi-Mun *Papers.* Bernice P. Bishop Museum. Honolulu.

Evans, Elizabeth H. C. "Se Won Kim." *Paradise of the Pacific* LXXIV, no. 11 (December 1962): 17–19.

Gaimushō (Japanese Foreign Ministry) Reports. Located in the Gaimushō gaikō shiryō-kan, Tokyo, and/or the Library of Congress, Washington, D.C.

Government-general of Chosen. *Annual Report on Reforms and Progress in Chosen [Korea], 1921–1922.* Keijō (Seoul), December 1922.

———. *Annual Report on the Administration of Chosen.* Keijō (Seoul), 1924.

Japanese Consulate-general in Honolulu. *Hawai Chōsenjin jijō* [General conditions of Koreans in Hawai'i]. SP 158, Reel SP 47. LC. December 1925. This also appears in *Chōsen tōchi shiryō* [Political studies of Korea], ed. Kim Chŏng-ju. Tokyo: Kankoku shiryō kenkyūjo, 1971, with the date of October 1926.

Giffard, Walter M./William G. Irwin *Papers.* Honolulu: University of Hawai'i Archives.

Gima, Dick. "Marriage to a Cobbler Really Lasts." *Honolulu Star-Bulletin,* June 17, 1964.

Grajdanzev, Andrew J. *Modern Korea.* New York: Institute of Public Relations, 1944.

Gulick, Sidney L. *Mixing the Races in Hawaii: A Study of the Growing Neo-Hawaiian American Race.* Honolulu: Hawaii Board Book Room, 1937.

Handley, Katherine N. "Our Standards Are Different." *Four Case Studies in Hawaii: Intercultural Problems and the Practice of Social Work.* Honolulu: University of Hawai'i Press, 1961.

Hansŏng sinbo, May 5, 1905.

Harvey, Youngsook Kim. Presentation at the conference, "Korean Migrants Abroad," University of Hawai'i at Manoa, January 7–9, 1979.

Hawaiian Agricultural Company. *Letterbook, 1903–1906.* In the possession of Edward Beechert.

Hawaiian Church Chronicle (Successor to the *Anglican Church Chronicle*), September 1908.

Hawaiian Sugar Planters' Association (HSPA). Labor Committee. *Territory of Hawaii Report, 1905.* Hawai'i State Archives.

———. *Planters' Monthly.*
     December 1903

———. *HSPA Trustees Minutes.*
     November 16, 1903.
     August 10, 1905.
     August 17, 1905.
     October 3, 1905.
     August 14, 1908.

August 27, 1908.
November 30, 1910.
January 10, 1912.
July 10, 1912.
July 24, 1912.
November 17, 1915.
March 28, 1917.
May 1, 1918.
April 2, 1919.
February 27, 1920.
March 9, 1920.
June 23, 1920.
Hawaiian Sugar Planters' Association Plantation Archives (HSPAPA). Aiea, Hawaiʻi.
Honokaa Sugar Company.
HSC 2/9.
HSC 2/10.
HSC 5/1.
HSC 22/4.
HSC 22/10.
Hutchinson Plantation.
KAU 25/2. HAW, C, HSPA Labor and Statistics, OUT, 1920–1921.
KAU 23/1.
KAU 31/4.
Laupahoehoe Sugar Company.
LSC 22C/1.
Lihue Plantation Company.
V. 128, 1910–1925.
Makee Sugar Plantation.
Labor statement.
Oahu Sugar Company.
OSC 1/15. Correspondence from Hackfeld: January–June 1904.
OSC 1/16. Correspondence from Hackfeld: July–September 1904.
OSC 5/12.
OSC 5/18.
OSC 6/15.
Olaa Sugar Company.
PSC 17/11. Sundry Letters, 1903.
PSC 2/5. B. F. Dillingham, Co., Letters—1903.
PSC 3/2. Bishop and Co. Letters, 1904–1905.
PSC 4/3. Bishop and Co. Letters, 1909–1910.
PSC 19/12.
PSC 31/11.
PSCV. 160.
Hawaiʻi, Territory. Board of Immigration. *First Report of the Board of Immigration of the Territory of Hawaii to the Governor of the Territory of Hawaii (Under Act of April 24, 1905) for the Period April 27, 1905 to January 31, 1907.* Honolulu: Hawaiʻi State Archives, 1907.

———. *Second Report of the Board of Immigration of the Territory of Hawaii.* Honolulu: Hawai'i State Archives, February 28, 1909.

Hawai'i, Territory. Bureau of Labor. *Third Report of the Commissioner of Labor in Hawaii, 1905.* Washington, D.C.: Government Printing Office, 1906. Hawai'i State Archives.

Hawai'i, Territory. Department of Public Instruction. *Report of the Supervisor of Public Instruction to the Governor of the Territory of Hawaii, 31 December 1910 to 31 December 1912.* Honolulu: Hawaiian Gazette Co., 1913.

———. *Biennial Report of the Supervisor of Foreign Language Schools, 1923–1925.* Mimeo. Honolulu, 1925. Hawai'i State Archives.

Hawai'i, Territory. *Governor's Files.* Pinkham-U.S. Departments. Interior. July–September 1915. Hawai'i State Archives.

Hawai'i, Territory. Office of Civilian Defense, Liaison Division, Public Morale Section. Cited as *Intelligence Files.*

Memo Number Four, December 23, 1941, "Discussions with Korean Leaders," January 8, 1942.

J. Kuang (Jacob) Dunn to Gordon T. Bowles, January 20, 1942.

"Fear or Suspicion in Korean Community," n.d.

Gordon T. Bowles, "Korean Committee," April 4, 1942.

Gordon T. Bowles, memo, March 1942.

"Recommendation Concerning Publication of a Periodical by the Sino-Korean Peoples' League," March 14, 1942.

"Recommendation Concerning the Republication of the Hawaiian Korean Christian Advocate," April 1, 1942.

"Summarization of Korean Political Organizations," February(?) 1942.

United Korean Committee, "The Korean Status in the Territory of Hawaii," n.d.

Unsigned memo, January 9, 1942.

Unsigned memo, n.d.

Hawai'i, Territory. *Report of the Board of Prison Directors, 1931/1932–1938/1939.* Mimeo. Honolulu, 1932–1939.

Hilo Tribune, June 7, 1944.

"History of St. Luke's." In *75th Anniversary of Korean Immigration to Hawaii, 1903–1978.* Honolulu: 75th Anniversary of Korean Immigration to Hawaii Committee, 1978.

Honolulu Advertiser.

August 29, 1940.
January 9, 1942.
May 25, 1944.
January 23, 1945.
September 13, 1945.
December 26, 1952.
January 9, 1953.
November 4, 1954.
October 17, 1955.
July 18, 1993.

Honolulu Star-Bulletin.
  October 10, 1921.
  March 21, 1942.
  May 27, 1942.
  July 27, 1942.
  May 5, 1943.
  June 2, 1943.
  June 5, 1944.
  May 15, 1947.
  June 23, 1947.
  April 25, 1952.
  February 3, 1953.
  June 1, 1953.
  September 10, 1973.
Hormann, Bernhard. "Race Relations in Hawaii." Pamphlet, n.d.
———. "Racial Complexion of Hawaii's Future Population." *Social Forces* 27, no. 1 (October 1948): 68–72.
———. "Speech, Prejudice, and the School in Hawaii." *Social Process in Hawaii* 11 (May 1947): 187–188.
———. "A Study of Civilian Morale, 1944." *Social Process in Hawaii* IX–X (July 1945): 17–24.
Houchins, Lee, and Chang-Su Houchins. "The Korean Experience in America, 1903–1924." *Pacific Historical Review* (November 1974): 548–575.
Hulbert, Homer. "The Koreans in Hawaii." *Korean Review* 5, no. 11 (November 1905): 411–413.
Hutchinson Sugar Plantation Company. *Letterbook to William G. Irwin and Co., LTD, 1905.* In the possession of Edward Beechert.
———. *Letterbook, 1903–1904.* In the possession of Edward Beechert.
Hwangsŏng sinmun.
  December 22, 1900.
  December 22, 1902.
  December 29, 1902.
  January 25, 1905.
  August 10, 1905.
  August 15, 1905.
Hynd, Alan. *Betrayal from the East: The Inside Story of Japanese Spies in America.* New York: Robert M. McBride and Co., 1943.
Hyŏn Sun [Hyun Soon]. *P'owa yuram ki* [A record of a sightseeing trip to Hawai'i]. Seoul: Hyŏn Kong-yŏm, 1909.
Hyun, Peter. *Mansei! The Making of a Korean American.* Honolulu: University of Hawai'i Press, 1986.
———. *In the New World: The Making of a Korean American.* Honolulu: University of Hawai'i Press, 1995.
Hyun Soon [Hyŏn Sun]. "My Autobiography." Typescript. Honolulu: University of Hawai'i, Center for Korean Studies, n.d.
Il Ki [pseud]. "Hawai esōnŭn yukch'ŏn tongp'o ŭi sirhwang" [The real condition of our six thousand compatriots living in Hawai'i] *Kaebyŏk* 36 (June 1923): 32–36.

Jarrett, Charles B. "The Mathematical Achievement of Eighth Grade Pupils from the Standpoint of Racial Ancestry." Master's thesis, University of Hawai'i, 1939.

Jones, George Heber. "The Koreans in Hawaii." Korea Review 6, no. 11 (November 1906): 401–406.

———. "Koreans Abroad." Korea Review 6, no. 12 (December 1906): 446–451.

Kalish, Richard. "Suicide: An Ethnic Comparison in Hawaii." Bulletin of Suicidology 36, no. 2 (December 1968): 37–43.

Kaneshiro, Kiyoshi. "Assimilation in a Slum Area of Honolulu." Social Process in Hawaii (May 1938): 19.

Kang, Francis. "Daughter to Represent Park at Isle Korean Fete." Honolulu Star-Bulletin, January 6, 1973.

———. "Korean Milestone." Honolulu Advertiser, November 7, 1953.

Kang, Shin-pyo. "The East Asian Culture and Its Transformation in the West: A Cognitive Approach to Changing World View among East Asian Americans in Hawaii." Ph.D. dissertation, University of Hawai'i, 1973.

Kang Sung-jae. "Hawai ŭi Han'guk kyop'o dŭl" [Hawai'i's overseas Koreans]. Dong-A ilbo (September 28, 1971).

Kim, Bernice Bong-hee. "The Koreans in Hawaii." Social Science 9, no. 4 (October 1934): 409–413.

———. "The Koreans in Hawaii." Master's thesis, University of Hawai'i, 1937.

Kim Chŏng-ju, ed. Chōsen tōchi shiryō [Political studies of Korea]. Tokyo: Kankoku shiryō kenkyūjo, 1971. Vol. 7, Dokuritsu undō [The independence movement].

Kim, Harold. Presentation at conference, "Korean Migrants Abroad," University of Hawai'i at Manoa, January 7–9, 1979.

Kim, Harry. Director of Civil Defense, State of Hawaii. Interview with author. Hilo, Hawai'i, July 25, 1992.

Kim Hyŏng-sun. Interview with Bong-Youn Choy, March 26, 1974. In the possession of the author.

Kim, Hyung-chan, ed. The Korean Diaspora: Historical and Sociological Studies of Korean Immigration and Assimilation in North America. Santa Barbara, Calif.: ABC Clio Press, 1977.

Kim, Kwang Chung, Shin Kim, and Won Moo Hurh. "Filial Piety and Intergenerational Relationship in Korean Immigrant Families." International Journal of Aging and Human Development 33, no. 3 (1991): 233–245.

Kim, Warren [Kim Wŏn-yong]. Koreans in America. Seoul: Po Chin Chai Printing Co., Ltd., 1971.

Kim Wŏn-yong [Warren Kim]. ChaeMi Hanin osimnyŏnsa [A fifty-year history of Koreans in America]. Reedley, Calif.: Charles Ho Kim, 1959.

Koh Seung-jae. Han'guk iminsa yŏn'gu [A study of the history of Korean immigration]. Seoul: Changmungak, 1973.

Korea Review.
  February 1904.
  January 1905.
  May 1905.
  August 1905.

"The Korean Civic Association." Honolulu Star-Bulletin, January 22, 1945.

"Korean Woman Toiled in Camps." Honolulu Star-Bulletin, January 7, 1973.

"Koreans are the Best Workers." *Pacific Commercial Advertiser,* July 28, 1906.

"Koreans in Hawaii Angered by Japan." *Los Angeles Times,* May 18, 1925.

"Koreans Outline Their Fairness to the Japanese." *Honolulu Star-Bulletin,* May 27, 1942.

Ku Han'guk oegyo munsŏ: Ilan [Diplomatic documents of the late Chosŏn dynasty: Japanese archives]. Vol. 7. Seoul: Koryŏ taehakkyo, Asea munje yŏn'guso, 1970.

Lee, Chong-Sik. *The Politics of Korean Nationalism.* Berkeley and Los Angeles: University of California Press, 1965.

Lee, Dong Jae. "Sociolinguistic Implications of Korean in Hawaii." *Korean Studies* 9 (1985): 57–63.

Lee, Kyung. "Settlement Patterns of Los Angeles Koreans." Master's thesis, University of California at Los Angeles, 1969.

Lee, Mary Paik. *Quiet Odyssey: A Pioneer Korean Woman in America,* ed. Sucheng Chan. Seattle: University of Washington Press, 1990.

Lee, Samuel S. O. "An Early Returnee to Korea." In *75th Anniversary of Korean Immigration to Hawaii, 1903–1978.* Honolulu: 75th Anniversary of Korean Immigration to Hawaii Committee, 1978.

Lee, Tai Sung. "The Story of Korean Immigration." *Korean Student Association Annual.* Honolulu, 1932.

Liebes, Richard Alan. "Labor Organization in Hawaii: A Study of the Efforts of Labor to Obtain Security through Organization." Master's thesis, University of Hawai'i, 1938.

Lind, Andrew W. "Divorce Trends in Hawaii, 1940–1950." University of Hawai'i, Romanzo Adams Social Research Laboratory Report no. 18, May 1, 1951.

———. "Economic Succession and Racial Invasion in Hawaii." Ph.D. dissertation, University of Chicago, 1931.

———. "The Ghetto and the Slum." *Social Forces* 9, no. 2 (December 1930): 206–215.

———. *Hawaii: The Last of the Magic Isles.* London: Oxford University Press, 1969.

———. "Hawaii's Koreans—Some Basic Considerations." *Bohk Dong* 1, no. 4 (April 29, 1956): 3–4.

———. *Hawaii's People.* 3d ed. Honolulu: University Press of Hawai'i, 1967.

———. *An Island Community: Ecological Succession in Hawaii.* Chicago: University of Chicago Free Press, 1938.

———. "Mounting the Occupational Ladder in Hawaii." University of Hawai'i, Romanzo Adams Social Research Laboratory Report no. 24, January 1957.

———. "Occupation and Race on Certain Frontiers." In *Race Relations in World Perspective: Papers Read at the Conference on Race Relations in World Perspective,* ed. Andrew W. Lind. Honolulu: University of Hawai'i Press, 1955.

———. "Occupational Attitudes of Orientals in Hawaii." *Sociology and Social Research* 12, no. 3 (January–February 1929): 249.

———. "Some Ecological Patterns of Community Disorganization in Honolulu." *American Journal of Sociology* 36, no.2 (September 1930): 206–220.

———, and G. R. Weaver, comps. *Data Bearing on Delinquency and Crime in Hawaii.* Honolulu: Territorial Conference of Social Work, 1929.

Livesay, Thayne M. *A Study of Public Education in Hawaii with Special Reference to the Pupil Population.* Honolulu: University of Hawai'i Research Publication no. 7, 1932.

Lyu, Kingsley K. "Korean Nationalist Activities in Hawaii and America, 1901–1945." Typescript. University of Hawai'i, Hamilton Library, 1950.

Maui News. March 7, 1903.

Macmillan, Michael. "The Korean Press in Hawaii." Unpublished paper, n.d.

———. "Koreans under Martial Law in Hawaii, 1941–1943." Paper presented at conference, "Korean Migrants Abroad," University of Hawai'i at Manoa, January 7–9, 1979.

———. "Unwanted Allies: Koreans as Enemy Aliens in World War II." *The Hawaiian Journal of History* 19 (1985): 179–203.

Masuoka, Jitsuichi. "Race Attitudes of the Japanese People in Hawaii: A Study in Social Distance." Master's thesis, University of Hawai'i, 1931.

———. "Race Preferences in Hawaii." *American Journal of Sociology* XLI, no. 5 (March 1936): 639.

Meyers, Margaret. "First Korean Immigrants Will Be Honored at Jubilee." *Honolulu Star-Bulletin,* November 7, 1953.

———. "Korean Immigrant's Story of Advancement Is Told." *Honolulu Star-Bulletin,* November 20, 1953.

Midkiff, Frank E. "The Economic Determinants of Education in Hawaii." Ph.D. dissertation, Yale University, 1935.

Moon, Hyung June. "The Korean Immigrants in America: The Quest for Identity in the Formative Years, 1903–1918." Ph.D. dissertation, University of Nevada-Reno, 1976.

Moore, S. F. "One Night with the Koreans in Hawaii. *Korea Review* 3, no. 12 (December 1903): 529–532.

Nam, Kenneth P. H. (former deputy attorney general of Hawai'i). Presentation at the conference, "Korean Migrants Abroad," University of Hawai'i at Manoa, January 7–9, 1979.

No Chae-yŏn. *ChaeMi Hanin saryak* [A short history of Koreans in America], vol. 1. Los Angeles: Amerika Printing Company, 1951.

Office of Strategic Services (OSS). *Foreign Nationalities Branch Files, 1942–1945.* Reel 260 (INT-33Z-29). Bethesda, Md.: Congressional Information Service, 1988.

Ogawa, Dennis M. *Jan Ken Po: The World of Hawaii's Japanese Americans.* Honolulu: University of Hawai'i Press, 1973.

Oh, In-hwan, Pyoung Wha Kim Park, and Seun-ung Kim. Interviews of eighty-four Korean immigrants in Hawai'i. University of Hawai'i, 1970. Cited as Interview Data. In the possession of Herbert Barringer.

Okihiro, Gary. "Migrant Labor and the 'Poverty' of Asian American Studies." *Amerasia Journal* 14, no. 1 (1988): 129–136.

Pacific Commercial Advertiser.
    August 12, 1903.
    July 30, 1904.
    August 1, 1904.
    December 9–12, 1904.
    June 6, 1905.
    October 6, 1905.
    March 21, 1906.

Pai, Margaret K. *The Dreams of Two Yi-Min.* Honolulu: University of Hawai'i Press, 1989.

Paik, L. George. *The History of Protestant Missions in Korea, 1832–1910.* P'yŏngyang: Union Christian College Press, 1929; Seoul: Yŏnsei University Press, 1970.

Patterson, Wayne. "The Early Years of Korean Immigration to Mexico: A View from Japanese and Korean Sources." *Seoul Journal of Korean Studies* 6 (1993): 87–103.

———. "The First Attempt to Obtain Korean Laborers for Hawaii, 1896–1897." In *The Korean Diaspora: Historical and Sociological Studies of Korean Immigration and Assimilation in North America,* ed. Hyung-chan Kim. Santa Barbara, Calif.: ABC Clio Press, 1977.

———. "Japanese Imperialism in Korea: A Study of Immigration and Foreign Policy." In *Japan in Transition: Thought and Action in the Meiji Era, 1868–1912,* ed. Hilary Conroy, Sandra T. W. Davis, and Wayne Patterson. London and Toronto: Fairleigh Dickinson University Press, 1984.

———. "The Korean Frontier in America: Immigration to Hawaii, 1896–1910." PhD. dissertation, University of Pennsylvania, 1977; Ann Arbor, Mich.: UMI, 1977. DA 77-30, 238.

———. *The Korean Frontier in America: Immigration to Hawaii, 1896–1910.* Honolulu: University of Hawai'i Press, 1988.

———. "Sugar Coated Diplomacy: Horace Allen and Korean Immigration to Hawaii, 1902–1905." *Diplomatic History* 3, no. 1 (Winter 1979): 19–38.

———. "Upward Social Mobility of the Koreans in Hawaii." *Korean Studies* 3 (1979): 81–92.

Presbyterian Church in the U.S.A., Board of Foreign Missions. *Korean Letters.* Philadelphia: Presbyterian Historical Society.

Reineke, John E. "The Big Lie of 1920: How Planters and Press Used the Big Lie of 'Japanese Conspiracy' in Breaking the Oahu Sugar Strike." Typescript. Honolulu, 1958.

———. *Labor Disturbances in Hawaii, 1890–1925: A Summary.* Typescript. Honolulu, 1966.

———. "Language and Dialect in Hawaii." Master's thesis, University of Hawai'i, 1935.

———. *Language and Dialect in Hawaii: A Sociolinguistic History to 1935,* ed. Stanley M. Tsuzaki. Honolulu: University Press of Hawai'i, 1969.

Restarick, Rt. Rev. Henry B. *Hawaii, 1778–1920 from the Viewpoint of a Bishop.* Honolulu: Paradise of the Pacific, 1924.

Rhodes, Daisy Young-Sil Chun. "How Oral History of the First Koreans to America Advances Archival Research." Paper presented at the Annual Meeting of the Association for Asian Studies, Honolulu, April 11–14, 1996.

———. "Shirley Temple Feet." *Hawaii Review* (April 1993): 127.

———. "Wahiawa Red Dirt." *Red Dirt* (Spring 1991): 7–9.

"Rift over Korean Benefit." *Honolulu Star-Bulletin,* September 7, 1950.

Robinson, Michael Edson. *Cultural Nationalism in Colonial Korea, 1920–1925.* Seattle and London: University of Washington Press, 1988.

Ryu Tongshik. *Hawai ŭi Hanin kwa kyohoe: Kurisuto yŏnhap kamri kyohoe 85 nyŏn sa* [A history of Christ United Methodist Church, 1903–1988]. Seoul: Christ United Methodist Church, 1988.

Samuels, Fred. "The Effect of Social Mobility on Social Distance: Some Changes in the Race Attitudes of Honolulu's Japanese." Master's thesis, University of Hawai'i, 1963.

Schmitt, Robert C. "Age Differences in Marriage in Hawaii." *Journal of Marriage and the Family* XXVIII, no. 1 (February 1966): 57–61.

———. "Age, Race and Marital Failure in Hawaii." Honolulu: University of Hawai'i, Romanzo Adams Social Research Laboratory Report no. 34, 1962.

———. *Demographic Correlates of Interracial Marriage in Hawaii.* Honolulu, 1964.

———. "Hawaii's Koreans, 1960: A Preview of Census Statistics." *Korean Bulletin of Hawaii.* Honolulu, 1960, 20–21.

Seattle Post-Intelligencer, February 19, 1942.

Shular, Helen. "Halmunee with a Korean Accent." *Paradise of the Pacific* LXIX, no. 3 (March 1957): 22–24.

Sin Hŭng-u. "Miju ŭi p'alch'ŏn tongp'o kŭnhwang" [The present situation of our eight thousand compatriots in the United States]. In *P'yŏnghwa wa chayu* [Peace and freedom], ed. Kim Tong-hwan. Seoul, 1931, 287–290.

Smith, Jared G. "Do You Remember?" *Honolulu Advertiser,* January 11, 1953.

Smith, Madorah D. "A Comparison of the Neurotic Tendencies of Students of Different Racial Ancestry in Hawaii." *Journal of Social Psychology* 9, no.4 (November 1938): 395–417.

Smith, William C. *The Second Generation Oriental in America.* Honolulu: Institute of Pacific Relations, 1927.

Sŏ Kwang-un. "Miju ŭi Hanin ch'ilsimnyŏn" [Seventy years of America's Koreans]. *Han'guk ilbo* (April 21–September 1, 1971). Twenty-six installments.

Stevens, E. Leigh, assistant secretary, Castle and Cooke, Inc., to the author, May 7, 1976.

Stratford, Jane. "Cross-Section of a High School Student's Life." Master's thesis, University of Hawai'i, 1930.

Suh, Dae-Sook, ed. and trans. *The Writings of Henry Cu Kim: Autobiography with Commentaries on Syngman Rhee, Pak Yong-man, and Chong Sun-man.* Honolulu: University of Hawai'i Press, 1987.

Sunoo, Harold Hakwon, and Sonia Shinn Sunoo. "The Heritage of the First Korean Women Immigrants in the United States: 1903–1924." *Korean Christian Scholars Journal* 2 (Spring 1977): 142–171.

Sunoo, Sonia Shinn. *Korean Kaleidoscope: Oral Histories. Vol. 1, Early Korean Pioneers in USA: 1903–1905.* Davis, Calif.: Korean Oral History Project, 1982.

———. "Korean Women Pioneers of the Pacific Northwest." *Oregon Historical Quarterly* (Spring 1978): 54–56.

Sutton, R. Anderson. "Korean Music in Hawaii." *Asian Music* 19, no. 1 (Fall/Winter 1987): 99–120.

Swallen, Mrs. William L. (Sallie). *Letters, 1901–1903.* In Samuel H. Moffett, *Documents,* no. 6 (1890–1903). In the possession of his son, Reverend Samuel A. Moffett, Seoul.

Sweethaven, Violet. *Gentlemen of Japan: A Study in Rapist Diplomacy.* Chicago and New York: Ziff-Davis Publishing Company, 1944.

Taeuber, Irene B. "Hawaii." *Population Index* 28, no. 2 (April 1962): 97–125.

Takaki, Ronald. *Pau Hana: Plantation Life and Labor in Hawaii, 1835–1920.* Honolulu: University of Hawai'i Press, 1983.

"Tenants Wait Patiently for Korean Old Men's Home." *Honolulu Star-Bulletin,* June 27, 1956.

United States Commissioner-General of Immigration. *Annual Report of the Commissioner-General of Immigration to the Secretary of Commerce and Labor for the Fiscal Year Ended June 30, 1906.* Washington, D.C.: Government Printing Office, 1906.

United States Congress, Committee on Territories and Insular Affairs. *Administration of Hawaii.* Washington, D.C.: Government Printing Office, 1933.

United States Congress, Senate Committee on the Judiciary. "Report of the Committee on Subversive Activity in the Territory of Hawaii." *Scope of Soviet Activity in the United States.* 84th Cong., 2d Sess., Part 41-A, Appendix II, 1953. Washington: Government Printing Office, 1957.

United States Department of Commerce and Labor, Bureau of Labor. *Fourth Report of the Commissioner of Labor in Hawaii, 1910.* Washington, D.C.: Government Printing Office, 1911.

United States Department of Labor, Bureau of Immigration and Naturalization. *Industrial Conditions in the Hawaiian Islands.* 63rd Cong., 1st Sess. House Doc. 53. Washington, D.C.: Government Printing Office, 1913.

United States Department of Labor, Bureau of Labor Statistics. *Labor Conditions in Hawaii: Fifth Report on Labor Conditions in Hawaii.* 64th Cong., 1st Sess. Senate Doc. 432. Washington, D.C.: Government Printing Office, 1916.

———. *Report of Commissioner of Labor Statistics in Hawaii, 1915.* Washington, D.C.: Government Printing Office, 1916.

———. *Labor in the Territory of Hawaii, 1939.* 76th Cong., 2d Sess. House Doc. 848. Washington, D.C.: Government Printing Office, 1939.

United States Department of State, Division of Far Eastern Affairs. *Records of the Department of State Relating to the Internal Affairs of Korea, 1910–1929.* Roll 4, National Archives.

University of Hawai'i Student Papers and Journals (UHSPJ).

    Bell, Lorne W. "A Brief Description of Certain Korean Institutions Active in Honolulu in January 1945." January 15, 1945.

    "Categorizing People and Group Feeling." Student Journal, 1944.

    "Characterizations Given to the Various Groups." Student Journal, Summer 1943.

    "Church-Melting Pot." Student Journal, January 1, 1945.

    "Conflict in Primary Group." Student Journal, December 12, 1944.

    "Cultural Practices of the Koreans in Hawaii." Sociology 250.

    "Disappearance of Koreans." Student Journal, December 31, 1944.

    "Different Races and What We Say about Them." Student Journal, Summer 1943.

    "Effect of War—Lack of Local Boys." Student Journal, January 3, 1945.

    "The Family." 1947.

    "Group Feelings—Consciousness Felt through Embarrassing Situation." Student Journal, October 14, 1944.

"Groups in Hawaii: Their Nicknames and Characterization." Student Journal, Summer 1943.

Hong, Clifford. "A Korean Grandfather." History 424.

Hong, Lorinda. "Halmoni." History 424, April 30, 1973.

Hong, Patricia. "The Myth of Korean Factionalism." History 424, June 12, 1972.

Kim, Chang-Sook. "Migrations in My Family." November 2, 1943.

"The Kim Family."

Kim, Stanley. "Factors Contributing towards High Amalgamation of Koreans in Hawaii." April 1949.

Kim, Violet. "Changes in Controls Exercised by the Koreans in Wahiawa Since the War." Sociology 151, Fall 1943.

"The Korean Church and Religion in Hawaii."

"Korean Conception of Themselves." Student Journal, October 21, 1944.

"Korean Economics."

"The Korean Group and Discrimination." Student Journal, January 14, 1945.

Korean student paper. Untitled, n.d.

Lee, Grace K. "My Family." Sociology 151, August 29, 1943.

Lee, Lila K. "The History of My Life."

———. "The Way Migrations Have Played a Role in My Family."

Lee, June, and Hisoon Chung. "Changing Attitudes of Koreans in Hawaii toward Old Age Dependency." February 6, 1941.

"Life History."

Lim, Sung-hi. "Ecological Study of the Community of Spreckelsville (Camp One), Maui." June 2, 1937.

Lim, Tai Hi. "The Personal and Cultural Approach to the Study of a Community." June 1, 1937.

"List of Nicknames as I Have Heard Them Used on Kauai." Student Journal, Summer 1943.

"Meet My Family."

Moon, Jr., Duke. "A Korean Pioneer." History 424, Summer 1972.

"Mores—Marriage between People of Different Racial Extractions Contrary to Mores of Oriental Marriages."

"Oriental-Haole Relations." Student Journal, 1944.

"Our Girls Are Being Spoiled." Student Journal, Fall 1944.

"Patriotism—Ethnocentricity among the Wahiawa Koreans and the Prisoners of War." Student Journal, October 20, 1944.

"Peter Kim and Wife." Student Journal, 1944.

"Possible Immigration Back to Korea after the War." January 12, 1945.

"Prejudice and the Mores." Student Journal, November 16, 1944.

"Prejudice and the Primary In-Group." Student Journal, October 12, 1944.

"The Problem of a Minority Group during War Time." Student Journal, Spring 1943.

"Race Stereotypes—'Koreans'." Student Journal, Fall 1945.

"Report on Racial Group Feeling." Student Journal, December 21, 1944.

"Role of Family in Marriage Selection Disappearing." Student Journal, December 11, 1944.

Spanish-Korean Female. Student Journal, Summer 1943.

Student Journal, Sociology 200, Fall 1942.

Student Journal, January 6, 1943.

Student Journal, Spring 1943. Various entries.

Student Journal, Summer 1943. Various entries.

Student Journal, June 18, 1943.

Student Journal, November 12, 1943.

Student Journal, November 19, 1943.

Student Journal, January 16, 1944.

Student Journal, October 7, 1944.

Student Journal, October 9, 1944.

Student Journal, December 10, 1944.

Student Journal, December 21, 1944.

Student Journal, December 27, 1944.

Student Journal, December 29, 1944.

Student Journal, Fall 1944. Various entries.

Student Journal, n.d. Various entries.

Student Journal, Sociology 151, 1944.

Student Journal, Sociology 151, Fall 1944.

Student Journal, Sociology 151, November 8, 1944.

Term Paper, Sociology 151, August 29, 1943.

"Topic of Gossip—Dating of Other Nationality." Student Journal, Sociology 251, Spring 1943.

Verbatim Reports. Student Journal, Fall 1944.

Woo, Douglas. "The Story of the First Two Generations of My Family in Hawaii." History 424, Summer 1972.

Yamagata, Bernice. "Korean Political Parties in Hawaii." Sociology 250.

Yim, Pearl. "Cultural Practices of the Koreans in Hawaii." Sociology 250.

University of Oregon Library, Special Collections. William C. Smith Documents Collection.

"The History of My Life."

"A Life History."

"Life History."

"Life History of E. S."

Shin, Emma. "Korean Family in Hawaii." Sociology 256, 1927.

"The Story of Life."

Vinacke, W. Edgar. "Stereotyping among National-Racial Groups in Hawaii: A Study of Ethnocentrism." *Journal of Social Psychology* 30 (1949): 265–291.

"Visas to Korea Refused, Many Say." *Honolulu Advertiser,* May 16, 1960.

Wadman, Rev. John W. *Annual Report of the Superintendent of the Hawaiian Mission of the Methodist Episcopal Church, 1904–1905,* December 29, 1905. Appears as "Methodists in Hawaii are Making Progress." *Pacific Commercial Advertiser,* January 1, 1906.

———. "Educational Work among the Koreans." Department of Public Instruction, *Report of the Supervisor of Public Instruction to the Governor of the Territory of Hawaii, 31 December 1910 to 31 December 1912.* Honolulu: Hawaiian Gazette Co., 1913.

Wakukawa, Ernest K. *A History of the Japanese People in Hawaii.* Honolulu: Toyo shoin, 1938.

Wedge, Bryant, and Shizu Abe. "Racial Incidence of Mental Disease in Hawaii." *Hawaii Medical Journal* 13, no. 5 (May/June 1949): 337–338.

Weiner, Michael. *The Origins of the Korean Community in Japan, 1910–1923.* Atlantic Highlands, N.J.: Humanities Press International, 1989.

Yamamoto, George Y. "Political Participation among Orientals in Hawaii." *Sociology and Social Research* 43, no. 5 (May/June 1959): 359–364.

Yamamura, Douglas S., and Raymond Sakumoto. "Residential Segregation in Honolulu." *Social Process in Hawaii* 18 (1954): 45–61.

Yamato shinbun.
    July 17, 1905.
    September 11, 1905.

Yang, Alan In-Su. Interview with the author, July 25, 1992, Hilo.

Yang Chu-en. Interview with Bong-youn Choy, February 27, 1974. In the possession of the author.

Yang, Sarah Lee. "75 Years of Progress for the Koreans of Hawaii." In *75th Anniversary of Korean Immigration to Hawaii, 1903–1978.* Honolulu: 75th Anniversary of Korean Immigration to Hawaii Committee, 1978.

Yi Chŏng-gŭn. *Insaeng palsipe ch'ŏnbyŏn manhwa* [Great changes in the eighty [years] of my life]. Unpublished manuscript. University of Hawai'i, Center for Korean Studies, n.d. (Appears to have been written in the 1950s.)

Yim, Louise. *My Forty Year Fight for Korea.* New York: A. A. Wyn, Inc., 1951.

Yoon, Won Kil. *The Passage of a Picture Bride.* Loma Linda/ Riverside, Calif.: Loma Linda University Press, 1989.

Young, Helen. Interview with the author, July 25, 1992, Hilo.

Yu Hong-yŏl. "Mi'guk e innŭn Hanindŭl" [Koreans in America]. *Sasang-gye* 6, no. 4 (April 1958).

Yun Ch'i-ho. *Ilgi* [Diary], ed. Kuksa p'yŏnch'an wiwŏnhoe. Seoul: T'amgudang, 1973–1976.

INDEX